Food Matters

Food Matters

SECOND EDITION

A BEDFORD SPOTLIGHT READER

Holly Bauer
University of California San Diego

bedford/st.martin's
Macmillan Learning

Boston | New York

For Bedford/St. Martin's

Vice President, Editorial, Macmillan Learning Humanities: Edwin Hill
Editorial Director, English: Karen S. Henry
Senior Publisher for Composition, Business and Technical Writing,
   Developmental Writing: Leasa Burton
Executive Editor: John E. Sullivan III
Developmental Editor: Leah Rang
Publishing Services Manager: Andrea Cava
Production Supervisor: Carolyn Quimby
Executive Marketing Manager: Joy Fisher Williams
Project Management: Jouve
Senior Photo Editor: Martha Friedman
Permissions Editor: Angela Boehler
Permissions Researcher: Mark Schaefer/Lumina
Senior Art Director: Anna Palchik
Text Design: Castle Design; Janis Owens, Books By Design, Inc.
Cover Design: John Callahan
Cover Photo: Bhaskar Dutta/Getty Images
Composition: Jouve
Printing and Binding: LSC Communications

Manufactured in the United States of America.

1   0   9   8   7   6
f   e   d   c   b   a

For information, write: Bedford/St. Martin's, 75 Arlington Street, Boston,
   MA 02116   (617-399-4000)

ISBN 978-1-319-04527-2

Acknowledgments

Text acknowledgments and copyrights appear at the back of the book on pages 313–314, which constitute an extension of the copyright page. Art acknowledgments and copyrights appear on the same page as the art selections they cover.

About The Bedford Spotlight Reader Series

The Bedford Spotlight Reader Series is a line of single-theme readers, each featuring Bedford's trademark care and quality. The readers in the series collect thoughtfully chosen readings sufficient for an entire writing course — about 35 selections — to allow instructors to provide carefully developed, high-quality instruction at an affordable price. Bedford Spotlight Readers are designed to help students make inquiries from multiple perspectives, opening up topics such as money, food, sustainability, gender, happiness, borders, monsters, American subcultures, language diversity and academic writing, and humor to critical analysis. An editorial board of a dozen compositionists whose programs focus on specific themes has assisted in the development of the series.

Bedford Spotlight Readers offer plenty of material for a composition course while keeping the price low. Each volume in the series includes multiple perspectives on the topic and its effects on individuals and society. Chapters are built around central questions such as "What Does It Mean to Eat Ethically?" and "What Rituals Shape Our Gender?" and so offer numerous entry points for inquiry and discussion. High-interest readings, chosen for their suitability in the classroom, represent a mix of genres and disciplines as well as a choice of accessible and challenging selections to allow instructors to tailor their approach. Each chapter thus brings to light related — even surprising — questions and ideas.

A rich editorial apparatus provides a sound pedagogical foundation. A general introduction, chapter introductions, and headnotes supply context. Following each selection, writing prompts provide avenues of inquiry tuned to different levels of engagement, from reading comprehension ("Understanding the Text"), to critical analysis ("Reflection and Response"), to the kind of integrative analysis appropriate to the research paper ("Making Connections"). A Web site for the series offers support for teaching, with sample syllabi, additional assignments, Web links, and more; visit **macmillanlearning.com/spotlight**.

Food matters to everyone. What we eat, where it comes from, and how we share it are important and increasingly visible issues in our public life. The ongoing debates about food that surround us present a real opportunity for writers; the complexities, nuances, and difficulties around the issues make food a compelling writing subject. This is surely a large part of the reason why so many professional writers focus on food—and why a writing course should center on food issues. Food offers real and engaging opportunities for students to weigh in on the issues and to learn about academic writing while doing so.

The idea for this book came from my own food-focused writing course. And many of the ideas for this second edition came from teaching *Food Matters* and from ideas shared with me by reviewers and instructors who use the book in their courses. My food-themed writing courses have been popular with students because they could see many ways to connect their own experiences and lives to the larger academic questions posed by the reading selections. A course that centers on a theme like food provides a real writing opportunity: Everyone has a lot of experiences with food and something at stake in the present and future food supply. There are many ways to join the conversation. Students can examine food from a variety of angles and write about it from a variety of perspectives — personal, academic, journalistic, historical, cultural, and scientific. Students can analyze, explain, argue, and advocate. While it goes without saying that everyone eats food, many people do not think much about the broader implications of their food choices or the political and socioeconomic structures that help determine what they eat. Because there are no easy answers or obviously right ways to think about food, the topic offers legitimate — and interesting — contested terrain for students to explore. Thinking and writing about food helps students learn to care about ideas; ideally, they will link their own experiences with food to larger academic questions that they can explore in writing.

After all, the course in which you will use this reader is not primarily about food; food is simply the occasion for engaging in the many practices that will help make your students successful college students: careful reading, critical thinking, textual analysis, argumentation, working with sources, synthesis, and academic writing. *Food Matters* offers meaningful ways to practice inquiry and engage with ideas through different genres: academic essays, journalistic accounts, personal narratives, interviews, blogs, memoirs, and arguments of various sorts. The book also includes photographs and diagrams that support and clarify arguments about food as well as images of the federal nutrition guidelines. A range of disciplinary viewpoints are represented — science, history, social sciences, philosophy. The texts come from a variety of sources — newspapers, magazines, academic journals, government recommendations, online forums and blogs, and chapters from books. This second edition includes a new section on identity, new readings on more current topics that raise questions about sustainability and the future of food, and updated questions that broaden the kinds of tasks and challenges students are asked to undertake.

In selecting texts, I have taken care to represent a range of viewpoints, many of which are in conversation with each other. I hope that this variety of tenable and legitimate perspectives, grouped carefully to respond to the questions that frame each chapter, will help your students to weigh the evidence, consider their values and beliefs, and think through what really matters to them when they write their narratives, analyze the various authors' positions, and construct their own arguments. The inquiry-based nature of the questions that introduce each chapter, along with the headnotes that introduce the readings and the questions that follow them, will spark productive discussion, critical engagement, and engaging assignments.

Food is a pertinent contemporary topic. We all eat to stay alive, and the way food is and will be produced matters to us all — whether we care to think about it or not. This reader provides real opportunities for students to engage with and write about the multidimensional controversies and debates surrounding food. My writing courses on food have been successful in engaging students in meaningful writing activities. I hope you and your students find this material as engaging as I do.

New to the Second Edition

Current and Diverse Reading Selections

Of this edition's 36 reading selections, 13 are new, providing more perspectives, topics, and disciplines to choose from and giving instructors more flexibility for using the topic of food in their writing courses. Notable new readings include **Richard Marosi**'s "Hardship on Mexico's Farms, a Bounty for U.S. Tables"; **Rachel Laudan**'s "The Birth of the Modern Diet"; **David Freedman**'s "How Junk Food Can End Obesity"; **Yuval Noah Harari**'s "Industrial Farming Is One of the Worst Crimes in History"; **Robert Kunzig**'s "Test-Tube Meat: Have Your Pig and Eat It Too"; and more.

A New Chapter, "If You Are What You Eat, Who Are You?"

This chapter asks how our food choices define us or uncover our personal and cultural values. Key readings from the first edition are enhanced by new readings from popular authors such as **Dan Jurafsky**, **Mary Roach**, and **Questlove**.

Greater Variety of Topics

Based on feedback from instructors, the second edition features more topics to engage your students, including social justice for food workers, global food issues, and economic disparities in eating habits.

New Visuals

To enhance readings with data and imagery, thirteen of this edition's fifteen images are new; the new images include photographs, the USDA's proposed nutrition facts label, diagrams illustrating the sounds of food names, and a government propaganda poster. Updated instructor resources also include suggestions for new films and suggested videos.

Acknowledgments

Many people helped and supported me in the creation of this book. First, I'd like to acknowledge the students in the courses I have taught that have focused on food; these students have offered insights and ideas that have helped me understand why our food choices matter in new ways. These students have also helped me think through how best to select materials and teach a writing course that focuses on food. I also would like to thank the Warren College Writing Program instructors at the University of California, San Diego, with whom I first taught a course on food: Amanda Brovold, Ben Chapin, Vidit Desai, and Veronica Pear. We developed our course through negotiation, making careful and deliberate choices about what to include. Our lively discussions were often on my mind as I selected texts for this book. More recent discussions I had with Cory Davia and Kathryn Joyce contributed to choices I made in the second edition. Also important to me were the conversations about teaching writing that I have had with my UC San Diego colleagues Madeleine Picciotto and Karen Gocsik.

I also would like to thank these friends with whom I chat (and learn) about food: Sam Przywitowski, Melissa Leasure, Therese Clark, Brian Keyser, and Eugene Ahn. In their own ways, each has nourished me with thoughts, suggestions, images, recipes, ideas, and arguments that have helped me to better understand the subject of food and to select texts for this book.

I am also grateful to all the reviewers who provided thoughtful and detailed feedback during the development process for this edition: Julie

Amberg, York College of Pennsylvania; Jessica Beaman, Cardinal Stritch University; Monica Ferguson Belus, University of North Carolina–Charlotte; Jayne Braman, California State University–San Marcos; Joseph H. Cooper, Gateway Community College; Ginny Crisco, California State University–Fresno; Nina J. Davidson, Middlesex Community College; Cecilia Kennedy, Clark State Community College; Ian D. MacKinnon, The University of Akron; Claudia Monpere McIsaac, Santa Clara University; Shannon Lyn Mondor, College of the Redwoods; Andrea Sanelli, City College of San Francisco; Julie A. Sparks, San Jose State University; Michael W. Stamps, Delaware Valley University; Davonna Thomas, Coastal Carolina University; Kristen Weinzapfel, North Central Texas College; and Elyse Zucker, Hostos Community College.

I also must acknowledge all of the wonderful people I have met at Bedford/St. Martin's. Amy Shefferd, sales representative, and Lauren Arrant, humanities specialist, have provided immeasurable support. I also would like to thank Leasa Burton, publisher for composition, business and technical writing, and developmental writing; and John Sullivan, executive editor, for encouraging me to take on this project (even when I hesitated) and for seeing me through the process. This project would not have been possible without Edwin Hill, vice president of editorial humanities at Macmillan Learning; Angela Boehler and Mark Schaefer, permissions researchers; Andrea Cava, publishing services manager; and Dmitry Rapoport, editorial assistant. My biggest shout-outs go to Sophia Snyder, editor of the first edition, and Leah Rang, editor of this second edition. I talked food and shared articles and links about food for more than a year with each of them. Sophia helped shape the project in important ways, and Leah helped re-envision the project. I appreciate their careful attention to the text and the many valuable suggestions they made. I am a better writer for having worked with each of them.

Last, my family deserves special recognition — especially my mother, Gayle Bauer, who taught me to value cooking, shopping for produce, and healthy eating; my late father, Walter Bauer, who used to squeeze orange juice for us every single morning and who made certain dishes (beef Wellington!) over and over again until he perfected them; and my children, Kai and Stella, who might not always be ready to help me grow and harvest the kale but who always drink it down in a breakfast smoothie. I am thankful for our rich food life and our ability to reflect on that life in conversation and in writing. I also thank them for the patience they offered when I spent large chunks of time on this project instead of with them (and our sometimes neglected fruit trees and vegetable garden).

Holly Bauer

With Bedford/St. Martin's, You Get More

At Bedford, providing support to teachers and their students who choose our books and digital tools is our top priority. The Bedford/St. Martin's English Community is now our home for professional resources, including Bedford *Bits*, our popular blog site, which offers new ideas for the composition classroom and composition teachers. In addition, you'll find an expanding collection of resources that support your teaching. Download titles from our professional resource series to support your teaching, review projects in the pipeline, sign up for professional development webinars, start a discussion, ask a question, and follow your favorite members. Join us to connect with our authors and your colleagues at **community.macmillan.com**. To learn more about or to order any of the following products, contact your Bedford/St. Martin's sales representative or visit the Web site at **macmillanlearning.com**.

Choose from Alternative Formats of *Food Matters*

Bedford/St. Martin's offers affordable formats — a paperback version and an electronic version — allowing students to choose the one that works best for them. For details about popular e-book formats from our e-book partners, visit **macmillanlearning.com/ebooks**.

Select Value Packages

Add value to your text by packaging one of the following resources with *Food Matters*. To learn more about package options for any of the following products, contact your Bedford/St. Martin's sales representative or visit **macmillanlearning.com/spotlight**.

Writer's Help 2.0 is a powerful online writing resource that helps students find answers whether they are searching for writing advice on their own or as part of an assignment.

- **Smart search**
  Built on research with more than 1,600 student writers, the smart search in Writer's Help 2.0 provides reliable results even when students use novice terms, such as *flow* and *unstuck*.

- **Trusted content from our best-selling handbooks**
  Choose *Writer's Help 2.0, Hacker Version,* or *Writer's Help 2.0,
  Lunsford Version,* and ensure that students have clear advice and
  examples for all of their writing questions.

- **Adaptive exercises that engage students**
  Writer's Help 2.0 includes LearningCurve, game-like online quizzing
  that adapts to what students already know and helps them focus on
  what they need to learn.

Student access is packaged with *Food Matters* at a significant discount.
Order ISBN 978-1-319-10781-9 for *Writer's Help 2.0, Hacker Version,* or
ISBN 978-1-319-10754-3 for *Writer's Help 2.0, Lunsford Version,* to ensure
your students have easy access to online writing support. Students who
rent a book or buy a used book can purchase access to Writer's Help 2.0
at **macmillanlearning.com/writershelp2**.

Instructors may request free access by registering as an instructor at
macmillanlearning.com/writershelp2.

LaunchPad Solo for Readers and Writers allows students to work on
whatever they need help with the most. At home or in class, students
learn at their own pace, with instruction tailored to each student's
unique needs. *LaunchPad Solo for Readers and Writers* features:

- **Prebuilt units that support a learning arc**
  Each easy-to-assign unit is comprised of a pre-test check; multimedia
  instruction and assessment; a post-test that assesses what students
  have learned about critical reading, writing process, using sources,
  grammar, style, and mechanics; and help for multilingual writers.

- **A video introduction to many topics**
  Introductions offer an overview of the unit's topic, and many
  include a brief, accessible video to illustrate the concepts at hand.

- **Adaptive quizzing for targeted learning**
  Most units include LearningCurve, game-like adaptive quizzing that
  focuses on the areas in which each student needs the most help.

- **The ability to monitor student progress**
  Use our Gradebook to see which students are on track and which
  need additional help with specific topics.

LaunchPad Solo for Readers and Writers can be **packaged at a significant discount**. Order ISBN 978-1-319-10764-2 to ensure your students
can take full advantage. Visit **macmillanlearning.com/readwrite** for
more information.

Critical Reading and Writing: A Bedford Spotlight Rhetoric, by **Jeff Ousborne**, is a brief supplement that provides coverage of critical reading, thinking, writing, and research. It is designed to work with any of the books in The Bedford Spotlight Reader Series. *Critical Reading and Writing: A Bedford Spotlight Rhetoric* (a $10 value!) can be packaged for **free** with your book. Contact your sales representative for a package ISBN.

Macmillan Learning Curriculum Solutions

Curriculum Solutions brings together the quality of Bedford/St. Martin's content with Hayden-McNeil's expertise in publishing original custom print and digital products. Developed especially for writing courses, our ForeWords for English program contains a library of the most popular, requested content in easy to use modules to help you build the best possible text. Whether you are considering creating a custom version of *Food Matters* or incorporating our content with your own, we can adapt and combine the resources that work best for your course or program. Some enrollment minimums apply. Contact your sales representative for more information.

Instructor Resources

macmillanlearning.com/spotlight

You have a lot to do in your course. Bedford/St. Martin's wants to make it easy for you to find the support you need — and to get it quickly.

The additional instructor's resources for *Food Matters*, Second Edition, are available as downloadable files from the Bedford/St. Martin's online catalog at the URL above. In addition to sample syllabi, the instructor's resources include a list of additional readings and films to assign with the book.

Contents

Introduction for Students   1

Chapter 1   What Is the Purpose of Food?   7

"Only when we participate in a short food chain are we reminded every week that we are indeed part of a food chain and dependent for our health on its peoples and soils and integrity — on its health."

"The distinction between artificial and natural flavors can be somewhat arbitrary and absurd, based more on how the flavor has been made than on what it actually contains."

"There's something about unnatural food colors that has always attracted me. What tastes or looks better than the frosting on grocery-store-bakery birthday cakes?"

"If nutrition science seems puzzling, it is because researchers typically examine single nutrients detached from food itself, foods separate from diets, and risk factors apart from other behaviors."

"Eaters . . . must understand that eating takes place inescapably in the world, that it is inescapably an agricultural act, and how we eat determines, to a considerable extent, how the world is used."

"Eating healthy food was extremely important to people of earlier eras, perhaps even more so than it is today. Activity in the kitchen mattered so much because physicians had so few other options."

Chapter 2   If You Are What You Eat, Who Are You?   65

Chapter 3   What Forces Affect Our Food Choices?   129

Chapter 4   What Does It Mean to Eat Ethically?   197

Chapter 5 What Is the Future of Food? 259

Contents by Discipline

Economics

History

Journalism

Public Policy

Contents by Theme

Environment

Food Justice

Food Movements

Foodie Culture

Globalization

Government and Food Policy

Junk Food

Race and Food

Food Matters

A BEDFORD SPOTLIGHT READER

Introduction for Students

When we sit down to write, we need something to write about, something that will stimulate our thinking and will interest others, too. All writers need a topic — journalists, historians, professional writers, poets, humorists, textbook authors like myself, and students like you. This book, *Food Matters,* aims to provide you with a topic: the subject of food. It offers reading and writing assignments that ask you to consider a range of questions about what you eat, how you make food choices, what those choices say about you and your culture, and why they matter. The book invites you to explore what others have written about food, and it provides a variety of writing opportunities for students with varied interests and backgrounds.

While the subject is food, the real purpose of this book is to provide you with a set of texts that provoke critical inquiry and lead to productive writing opportunities. To write well at the college level, you need to practice critical reading and critical thinking; you need to learn to analyze and evaluate the ideas you are asked to write about. Food is a great topic for engaging in a range of interesting, complex, thought-provoking issues — and thus for practicing critical reading, thinking, and writing. This book asks you to consider a range of issues, debates, problems, and questions about food. These are matters about which I hope you will care deeply — and thus about which you will have something to say, and, more important, *something to write.*

Why Food?

Do you eat breakfast? Is it from a box, your garden, or the corner coffee shop? Do you sit down with your family to eat? Or do you eat in your car, on the bus, or walking to work or school? Have you ever thought about where your food comes from? When you buy food, do you select what is cheapest, healthiest, or most ethically produced? Do you care if it is organic or conventionally grown? Does it matter if it was produced near where you live or on the other side of the globe? Do you think about whether it was picked or packaged or processed by workers who were compensated fairly? What is food anyway? Is it a product of nature? Is it a product of food science? Does it matter? What does it mean to *eat food*? Do you eat for health, for sustenance, for pleasure, or for something else? Where does your food come from? Do you know? Do you care? Is eating supposed to be pleasurable? social? for survival? How should we decide what to eat? On what should our decisions be based — on our sense of what is healthy, what is fast and easy, the organic food movement, the slow food movement, federal health guidelines, or on concern for the environment, animal rights, labor rights, or other ethical considerations?

These questions probably would not have been posed this way until recently. But an increasing number of authors and movements have propelled the topic of food to the forefront. News headlines, blogs, TV shows, documentaries, books, and advertisements bombard us with talk about food. What we eat, where it comes from, and why our food choices are important are issues that are increasingly visible in U.S. political, social, and cultural life. We are surrounded by writing about food, and the more we read about food and think through the lists of considerations, the more complex and confusing it gets.

You might start to wonder, as some prominent writers have, if much of what we eat can even be called food anymore. Or you might think that certain critics are too particular and their critiques are overblown. These complexities and difficulties are what make *food* such a viable writing subject. The confusion and controversy I describe — and the ongoing debates about food that accompany it — are a real opportunity for writers. I imagine that this is why so many professional writers focus on food, and I am certain that this is why writing about food is such a great opportunity for students like you to practice critical reading, thinking, and writing. In fact, it is because there are no easy answers and obviously right ways to think about food that the topic offers legitimate — and interesting — contested terrain for you to explore. There are many ways for you to join the conversation, and providing ways for you to consider, analyze, and write about real issues and controversies is the purpose of this book.

Reading, Thinking, Writing

While this book focuses on food and asks you to contemplate difficult questions, it does not advocate a particular ethical stance or political point of view. Instead, the book offers a range of tenable and legitimate positions and invites you to weigh the evidence, consider your values and beliefs, and think through what really matters to you as you construct narratives and arguments about food. After all, the course in which you will use this reader is not primarily a course about food. This is a writing course; food is simply the occasion for writing.

When you sit down to write, how do you decide what to do? The authors in this book demonstrate the importance of considering the purpose and audience for which they are writing, the idea or emotion or position that they are trying to put forward or communicate, and the argument they want to make. How they write about their ideas — the form and structure their writings take — is at least partially determined by what they want to say. I encourage you to compare the genres included here and how the writers use rhetorical strategies that help them say what they want to say. I have chosen pieces that take a range of forms — essays, blogs, humor, magazine articles, academic arguments, book excerpts, and images. Not only do the pieces offer a variety of viewpoints on food, they also offer a range of models for writing and taking a stand on a particular issue or problem.

One unique quality of this reader is that by focusing on a theme, it allows you to delve into the topic of food on various levels — personal, political, social, moral, academic, and scientific. As you develop a base of knowledge about the topic, a sense of the key issues, and an understanding of the values and beliefs that motivate and inform various perspectives, you will become a kind of expert; this will allow you an opportunity to write about the issues in meaningful and legitimate ways. I hope your engagement with these texts will lead you to feel that it is worth your while to figure out where you stand in relation to the narratives, arguments, and materials offered here. This book invites you to join the scholarly conversation and to position yourself in relation to real issues, ongoing problems, and contested positions.

Organization of the Book

Food Matters provides a sense of the contemporary conversations and debates about the purpose of food, the relationship between food and identity, the social and political forces that affect food choices, the ethics of eating, and the future of food. Each chapter poses a question and includes a set of carefully chosen selections that speak to the question by defining key terms, providing context, or taking a position. While each chapter includes selections you can use to explore the chapter's guiding question, you might find that these are artificial divisions, as many of the selections could be responses to the lead questions of other chapters, too. I encourage you to make connections between and among them as you go.

Each chapter begins with an introduction that summarizes the themes and issues that are central to that chapter, and poses some questions to think about as you read. Headnotes for each piece introduce the author and contextualize the selection. Following the readings, three sets of questions ask you to demonstrate your understanding of the text, to reflect on and respond to it, and to make connections between the readings and to conduct research. Effective responses to these questions will also take into account how your own values, beliefs, and experiences contribute to your understanding of the issues and the positions you take on them.

The book is organized around five questions for you to explore. These questions are intended as starting points for inquiry, though they are certainly not exhaustive in scope or topic. The first chapter, "What Is the Purpose of Food?," explores how we define food, the reasons we eat, and the varied purposes food serves in our lives — purposes that extend beyond nutrition to culture, politics, environment, and pleasure. The selections explore the complex ways food nourishes us, and in so doing they tie the definition and purpose of food to historical, cultural, linguistic, spiritual, and political matters.

The second chapter, "If You Are What You Eat, Who Are You?," encourages us to think about what our relationships with food and eating say about our culture, values, and identities. Selections by a gastronome, linguist, economist, food writer, musician, food justice advocate, science writer, and farmer-turned-philosopher encourage us to think about what our food choices and preferences say about who we are.

The third chapter, "What Forces Affect Our Food Choices?," examines the complex mix of laws, social realities, health guidelines, patents, and trade agreements that help determine what we eat. While in one sense *we* determine what we eat, the selections in this chapter ask us to look at the many larger forces at work that direct what food choices are available, where, and for whom.

The fourth chapter, "What Does It Mean to Eat Ethically?," turns to an exploration of the role of ethics in determining what we eat and why our food choices matter. While acknowledging the larger political, social, cultural, and economic forces that affect food choices, the selections in this chapter ask us to consider what it means to declare that eating is necessarily a moral act.

The fifth and last chapter, "What Is the Future of Food?," identifies problems and possibilities that will influence the future of food. The readings indicate that this future will be no less complex than the present and that food production and consumption will continue to evolve as other aspects of society, culture, science, business, politics, and environment change. The chapter returns to themes of previous chapters and asks us to think critically about the scope and variety of influences that will impact our food choices in the future.

While each chapter focuses on a specific aspect of food, the chapters also include a range of genres and approaches to the topic. Academic essays, journalistic accounts, personal narratives, blogs, memoirs, images, and arguments are included. A range of disciplinary viewpoints are represented — science, history, social sciences, philosophy. The texts come from a variety of sources — newspapers, magazines, academic journals, government recommendations, online forums, blogs, and chapters of books. The selections represent a range of viewpoints, which are in conversation with one another. While the questions are meant to be starting points for thinking, discussing, and writing, they are certainly not exhaustive. Thus, you might choose to pursue other fruitful questions, connections, and potential occasions for writing that this collection suggests.

Writing That Matters

A course that centers on a theme provides real writing opportunities for you. You can examine a topic from a variety of angles and write about it from a variety of perspectives — personal, cultural, political, academic, journalistic, and ethical. Working with this book, you will read and write personal narratives, political pieces, and academic arguments. One benefit of spending a significant amount of time studying one topic is that doing so yields more substantial writing opportunities. Writing about food is a great way to stimulate your thinking about how your own experiences, values, and positions are related to larger scientific, cultural, academic, and ethical questions. While it goes without saying that everyone eats food, many people do not think much about the broader implications of their food choices. We wake up and eat breakfast, or we order a sandwich in a deli. But we do not always think or know much about where our food comes from, how it was produced, how it affects the environment, or who harvested our vegetables or raised the livestock. Food matters to all of us, and we make food choices that affect the world around us whether we are aware of this or not.

We all need to eat to stay alive (or live to eat), and we all have a stake in the present and future food supply. This book gives you opportunities to examine, analyze, and write about the major arguments in the myriad controversies and debates surrounding food. This is good practice for the other kinds of writing you will be doing in college, work, and life. I hope you will find this to be an engaging and productive way to practice and develop your writing skills.

Bhaskar Dutta/Getty Images

1

What Is the Purpose of Food?

Strictly speaking, food is defined as edible and nutritious substances that we consume in order to live and grow. But food can be much more than this. The many ways we define food — and the varied purposes it serves in our lives — say something important about our health, values, culture, identities, even our psychology. Is food a product of nature? Is it a product of science? We eat and drink many things that we categorize as food even though they are produced in labs and no longer resemble their plant and animal sources. Why do we eat them? What purposes do they serve for us — sustenance, cultural reinforcement, comfort, status? Where does our food come from? Do we know, and do we care? What makes food "real"? What makes food "good"? And are those the same things?

The readings in this chapter ask us to consider these questions and more. Taken together, these readings complicate the definition of what food "really" is and suggest various purposes of food. Michael Pollan provides a set of rules on how to define food, which he differentiates from "foodish products." Eric Schlosser looks at the flavoring industry and how it affects the "authenticity" of our dining experiences. The very manufactured flavors and artificially produced "foodish products" that Pollan and Schlosser criticize are what Jill McCorkle loves most about food. Her vivid memories of her life as a junk-food junkie indicate that there might be more to authentic eating than the freshness, quality, and origin of what we eat.

Most people would agree that one purpose of food, at least, is nutrition. But how do we know what foods will keep us healthy? Marion Nestle focuses on the effects that food has on our bodies and reminds us that nutrition science can sometimes lead us astray. While Wendell Berry shares with Nestle a belief in healthy eating, he emphasizes that one important purpose of food is pleasure and that truly grasping the pleasure of eating requires an understanding of one's role in its production. Rachel Laudan tells us that some of our ideas about food and nutrition arose

photo: Bhaskar Dutta/Getty Images

hundreds of years ago, offering a history that might help us better understand the purposes for which we use food today.

To explore the purpose of food, then, it seems that an understanding of its nutritional components is not enough. Taken together, the readings in this chapter suggest that we need a broader set of considerations to understand the purpose of food in our lives. What roles does food play? Do we eat for nutrition? pleasure? cultural connection? spiritual health? status? What purposes might food be said to serve beyond being something we consume? Is the purpose of food largely cultural, linked to our historical, political, ethnic, and socioeconomic origins? Does the purpose of food complicate what counts as "food"? How does food nourish us — through certain chemical properties, or through something larger and more difficult to define? What are the different "pleasures" of food? This chapter encourages you to reflect on these questions.

Eat Food:
Food Defined

Michael Pollan

Best known for his engaging writing about food and his ability to tell complex stories that weave together politics, culture, nutrition, ethics, and history, Michael Pollan is an award-winning author, *New York Times Magazine* writer, and professor of journalism at the University of California, Berkeley. He has written numerous articles and books, including four *New York Times* best sellers: *Food Rules: An Eater's Manual* (2010); *In Defense of Food: An Eater's Manifesto* (2008); *The Omnivore's Dilemma: A Natural History of Four Meals* (2006); and *The Botany of Desire: A Plant's-Eye View of the World* (2001). This selection comes from *In Defense of Food: An Eater's Manifesto*, a book in which Pollan works to define just what should count as food. He argues that "food" must be differentiated from "foodish products" and makes a case for how to define the difference.

The first time I heard the advice to "just eat food" it was in a speech by Joan Gussow, and it completely baffled me. Of course you should eat food — what else is there to eat? But Gussow, who grows much of her own food on a flood-prone finger of land jutting into the Hudson River, refuses to dignify most of the products for sale in the supermarket with that title. "In the thirty-four years I've been in the field of nutrition," she said in the same speech, "I have watched real food disappear from large areas of the supermarket and from much of the rest of the eating world." Taking food's place on the shelves has been an unending stream of food-like substitutes, some seventeen thousand new ones every year — "products constructed largely around commerce and hope, supported by frighteningly little actual knowledge." Ordinary food is still out there, however, still being grown and even occasionally sold in the supermarket, and this ordinary food is what we should eat.

But given our current state of confusion and given the thousands of products calling themselves food, this is more easily said than done. So consider these related rules of thumb. Each proposes a different sort of map to the contemporary food landscape, but all should take you to more or less the same place.

• **DON'T EAT ANYTHING YOUR GREAT GRANDMOTHER WOULDN'T RECOGNIZE AS FOOD.** Why your great grandmother? Because at this point your mother and possibly even your grandmother is as confused as the rest of us; to be safe we need to go back at least a couple generations, to a time before the advent of most modern foods. So depending on your age (and your grandmother), you may need to go back to your great- or even great-great grandmother. Some nutritionists recommend going back even further. John Yudkin, a British nutritionist whose early alarms about the dangers of refined carbohydrates were overlooked in the 1960s and 1970s, once advised, "Just don't eat anything your Neolithic° ancestors wouldn't have recognized and you'll be ok."

What would shopping this way mean in the supermarket? Well, imagine your great grandmother at your side as you roll down the aisles. You're standing together in front of the dairy case. She picks up a package of Go-Gurt Portable Yogurt tubes — and has no idea what this could possibly be. Is it a food or a toothpaste? And how, exactly, do you introduce it into your body? You could tell her it's just yogurt in a squirtable form, yet if she read the ingredients label she would have every reason to doubt that that was in fact the case. Sure, there's some yogurt in there, but there are also a dozen other things that aren't remotely yogurtlike, ingredients she would probably fail to recognize as foods of any kind, including high-fructose corn syrup, modified corn starch, kosher gelatin, carrageenan, tri-calcium phosphate, natural and artificial flavors, vitamins, and so forth. (And there's a whole other list of ingredients for the "berry bubblegum bash" flavoring, containing everything but berries or bubblegum.) How did yogurt, which in your great grandmother's day consisted simply of milk inoculated with a bacterial culture, ever get to be so complicated? Is a product like Go-Gurt Portable Yogurt still a whole food? A food of any kind? Or is it just a food product?

There are in fact hundreds of foodish products in the supermarket 5 that your ancestors simply wouldn't recognize as food: breakfast cereal bars transected by bright white veins representing, but in reality having nothing to do with, milk; "protein waters" and "nondairy creamer"; cheeselike foodstuffs equally innocent of any bovine° contribution; cakelike cylinders (with creamlike fillings) called Twinkies that never grow stale. Don't eat anything incapable of rotting is another personal policy you might consider adopting.

There are many reasons to avoid eating such complicated food products beyond the various chemical additives and corn and soy derivatives they contain. One of the problems with the products of food science is that, as Joan Gussow has pointed out, they lie to your body; their artificial colors and flavors and synthetic sweeteners and novel fats confound the senses we rely on to assess new foods and prepare our bodies to deal

---

Neolithic: of or relating to the period of human history about 10,000 years ago, when humans began to develop agriculture and polished stone tools.
bovine: relating to cows.

with them. Foods that lie leave us with little choice but to eat by the numbers, consulting labels rather than our senses.

It's true that foods have long been processed in order to preserve them, as when we pickle or ferment or smoke, but industrial processing aims to do much more than extend shelf life. Today foods are processed in ways specifically designed to sell us more food by pushing our evolutionary buttons — our inborn preferences for sweetness and fat and salt. These qualities are difficult to find in nature but cheap and easy for the food scientist to deploy, with the result that processing induces us to consume much more of these ecological rarities than is good for us. "Tastes great, less filling!" could be the motto for most processed foods, which are far more energy dense than most whole foods: They contain much less water, fiber, and micronutrients, and generally much more sugar and fat, making them at the same time, to coin a marketing slogan, "More fattening, less nutritious!"

The great grandma rule will help keep many of these products out of your cart. But not all of them. Because thanks to the FDA's° willingness, post-1973, to let food makers freely alter the identity of "traditional foods that everyone knows" without having to call them imitations, your great grandmother could easily be fooled into thinking that that loaf of bread or wedge of cheese is in fact a loaf of bread or a wedge of cheese. This is why we need a slightly more detailed personal policy to capture these imitation foods; to wit:

＊ **AVOID FOOD PRODUCTS CONTAINING INGREDIENTS THAT ARE A) UNFAMILIAR, B) UNPRONOUNCEABLE, C) MORE THAN FIVE IN NUMBER, OR THAT INCLUDE D) HIGH-FRUCTOSE CORN SYRUP.** None of these characteristics, not even the last one, is necessarily harmful in and of itself, but all of them are reliable markers for foods that have been highly processed to the point where they may no longer be what they purport to be. They have crossed over from foods to food products.

Consider a loaf of bread, one of the "traditional foods that everyone 10 knows" specifically singled out for protection in the 1938 imitation rule. As your grandmother could tell you, bread is traditionally made using a remarkably small number of familiar ingredients: flour, yeast, water, and a pinch of salt will do it. But industrial bread — even industrial whole-grain bread — has become a far more complicated product of modern food science (not to mention commerce and hope). Here's the complete ingredients list for Sara Lee's Soft & Smooth Whole Grain White Bread.

FDA: United States Food and Drug Administration, the federal agency that is responsible for regulating and supervising food safety.

(Wait a minute — isn't "Whole Grain White Bread" a contradiction in terms? Evidently not anymore.)

Enriched bleached flour [wheat flour, malted barley flour, niacin, iron, thiamin mononitrate (vitamin B₁), riboflavin (vitamin B₂), folic acid], water, whole grains [whole wheat flour, brown rice flour (rice flour, rice bran)], high fructose corn syrup [hello!], whey, wheat gluten, yeast, cellulose. Contains 2% or less of each of the following: honey, calcium sulfate, vegetable oil (soybean and/or cottonseed oils), salt, butter (cream, salt), dough conditioners (may contain one or more of the following: mono- and diglycerides, ethoxylated mono- and diglycerides, ascorbic acid, enzymes, azodicarbonamide), guar gum, calcium propionate (preservative), distilled vinegar, yeast nutrients (monocalcium phosphate, calcium sulfate, ammonium sulfate), corn starch, natural flavor, beta-carotene (color), vitamin D₃, soy lecithin, soy flour.

There are many things you could say about this intricate loaf of "bread," but note first that even if it managed to slip by your great grandmother (because it is a loaf of bread, or at least is called one and strongly resembles one), the product fails every test proposed under rule number two: It's got unfamiliar ingredients (monoglycerides I've heard of before, but ethoxylated monoglycerides?); unpronounceable ingredients (try "azodicarbonamide"); it exceeds the maximum of five ingredients (by roughly thirty-six); and it contains high-fructose corn syrup. Sorry, Sara Lee, but your Soft & Smooth Whole Grain White Bread is not food and if not for the indulgence of the FDA could not even be labeled "bread."

Sara Lee's Soft & Smooth Whole Grain White Bread could serve as a monument to the age of nutritionism. It embodies the latest nutritional wisdom from science and government (which in its most recent food pyramid recommends that at least half our consumption of grain come from whole grains) but leavens that wisdom with the commercial recognition that American eaters (and American children in particular) have come to prefer their wheat highly refined — which is to say, cottony soft, snowy white, and exceptionally sweet on the tongue. In its marketing materials, Sara Lee treats this clash of interests as some sort of Gordian knot° — it speaks in terms of an ambitious quest to build a "no compromise" loaf — which only the most sophisticated food science could possibly cut.

And so it has, with the invention of whole-grain white bread. Because the small percentage of whole grains in the bread would render it that

---

Gordian knot: in legend, a knot impossible to untangle. Alexander the Great "untied" the knot by cutting it with his sword.

much less sweet than, say, all-white Wonder Bread — which scarcely waits to be chewed before transforming itself into glucose — the food scientists have added high-fructose corn syrup and honey to make up the difference; to overcome the problematic heft and toothsomeness of a real whole-grain bread, they've deployed "dough conditioners," including guar gum and the aforementioned azodicarbonamide, to simulate the texture of supermarket white bread. By incorporating certain varieties of albino wheat, they've managed to maintain that deathly but apparently appealing Wonder Bread pallor.

Who would have thought Wonder Bread would ever become an ideal of aesthetic and gustatory perfection to which bakers would actually aspire — Sara Lee's Mona Lisa?

Very often food science's efforts to make traditional foods more nutritious make them much more complicated, but not necessarily any better for you. To make dairy products low fat, it's not enough to remove the fat. You then have to go to great lengths to preserve the body or creamy texture by working in all kinds of food additives. In the case of low-fat or skim milk, that usually means adding powdered milk. But powdered milk contains oxidized cholesterol, which scientists believe is much worse for your arteries than ordinary cholesterol, so food makers sometimes compensate by adding antioxidants, further complicating what had been a simple one-ingredient whole food. Also, removing the fat makes it that much harder for your body to absorb the fat-soluble vitamins that are one of the reasons to drink milk in the first place.

All this heroic and occasionally counterproductive food science has been undertaken in the name of our health — so that Sara Lee can add to its plastic wrapper the magic words "good source of whole grain" or a food company can ballyhoo the even more magic words "low fat." Which brings us to a related food policy that may at first sound counterintuitive to a health-conscious eater:

• **AVOID FOOD PRODUCTS THAT MAKE HEALTH CLAIMS.** For a food product to make health claims on its package it must first *have* a package, so right off the bat it's more likely to be a processed than a whole food. Generally speaking, it is only the big food companies that have the wherewithal to secure FDA-approved health claims for their products and then trumpet them to the world. Recently, however, some of the tonier fruits and nuts have begun boasting about their health-enhancing properties, and there will surely be more as each crop council scrounges together the money to commission its own scientific study. Because all plants contain antioxidants, all these studies are guaranteed to find *some*thing on which to base a health oriented marketing campaign.

But for the most part it is the products of food science that make the boldest health claims, and these are often founded on incomplete and often erroneous science — the dubious fruits of nutritionism. Don't forget that trans-fat-rich margarine, one of the first industrial foods to claim it was healthier than the traditional food it replaced, turned out to give people heart attacks. Since that debacle, the FDA, under tremendous pressure from industry, has made it only easier for food companies to make increasingly doubtful health claims, such as the one Frito-Lay now puts on some of its chips — that eating them is somehow good for your heart. If you bother to read the health claims closely (as food marketers make sure consumers seldom do), you will find that there is often considerably less to them than meets the eye.

Consider a recent "qualified" health claim approved by the FDA for (don't laugh) corn oil. ("Qualified" is a whole new category of health claim, introduced in 2002 at the behest of industry.) Corn oil, you may recall, is particularly high in the omega-6 fatty acids we're already consuming far too many of.

Very limited and preliminary scientific evidence suggests that eating about one tablespoon (16 grams) of corn oil daily may reduce the risk of heart disease due to the unsaturated fat content in corn oil.

The tablespoon is a particularly rich touch, conjuring images of moms administering medicine, or perhaps cod-liver oil, to their children. But what the FDA gives with one hand, it takes away with the other. Here's the small-print "qualification" of this already notably diffident health claim:

[The] FDA concludes that there is little scientific evidence supporting this claim.

And then to make matters still more perplexing:

To achieve this possible benefit, corn oil is to replace a similar amount of saturated fat and not increase the total number of calories you eat in a day.

This little masterpiece of pseudoscientific bureaucratese was extracted from the FDA by the manufacturer of Mazola corn oil. It would appear that "qualified" is an official FDA euphemism for "all but meaningless." Though someone might have let the consumer in on this game: The FDA's own research indicates that consumers have no idea what to make of qualified health claims (how would they?), and its rules allow companies to promote the claims pretty much any way they want — they can use really big type for the claim, for example, and then print the disclaimers in teeny-tiny type. No doubt we can look forward to a qualified health claim for high-fructose corn syrup, a tablespoon of which probably does contribute to your health — as long as it replaces a comparable amount of, say, poison in your diet and doesn't increase the total number of calories you eat in a day.

When corn oil and chips and sugary breakfast cereals can all boast being good for your heart, health claims have become hopelessly corrupt. The American Heart Association currently bestows (for a fee) its heart-healthy seal of approval on Lucky Charms, Cocoa Puffs, and Trix cereals, Yoo-hoo lite chocolate drink, and Healthy Choice's Premium Caramel Swirl Ice Cream Sandwich — this at a time when scientists are coming to recognize that dietary sugar probably plays a more important role in heart disease than dietary fat. Meanwhile, the genuinely heart-healthy whole foods in the produce section, lacking the financial and political clout of the packaged goods a few aisles over, are mute. But don't take the silence of the yams as a sign that they have nothing valuable to say about health.

Bogus health claims and food science have made supermarkets particularly treacherous places to shop for real food, which suggests two further rules:

• **SHOP THE PERIPHERIES OF THE SUPERMARKET AND STAY OUT OF THE MIDDLE.** Most 25 supermarkets are laid out the same way: Processed food products dominate the center aisles of the store while the cases of ostensibly fresh food — dairy, produce, meat, and fish — line the walls. If you keep to the edges of the store you'll be that much more likely to wind up with real food in your shopping cart. The strategy is not foolproof, however, because things like high-fructose corn syrup have slipped into the dairy case under cover of Go-Gurt and such. So consider a more radical strategy:

• **GET OUT OF THE SUPERMARKET WHENEVER POSSIBLE.** You won't find any high-fructose corn syrup at the farmers' market. You also won't find any elaborately processed food products, any packages with long lists of unpronounceable ingredients or dubious health claims, nothing microwavable, and, perhaps best of all, no old food from far away. What you will find are fresh whole foods picked at the peak of their taste and nutritional quality — precisely the kind your great grandmother, or even your Neolithic ancestors, would easily have recognized as food.

Indeed, the surest way to escape the Western diet is simply to depart the realms it rules: the supermarket, the convenience store, and the fast-food outlet. It is hard to eat badly from the farmers' market, from a CSA box (community-supported agriculture, an increasingly popular scheme in which you subscribe to a farm and receive a weekly box of produce), or from your garden. The number of farmers' markets has more than doubled in the last ten years, to more than four thousand, making it one of the fastest-growing segments of the food marketplace. It is true that most farmers' markets operate only seasonally, and you won't find everything you need there. But buying as much as you can from the farmers' market, or directly from the farm when that's an option, is a simple act with a host of profound consequences for your health as well as for the health of the food chain you've now joined.

When you eat from the farmers' market, you automatically eat food that is in season, which is usually when it is most nutritious. Eating in season also tends to diversify your diet — because you can't buy strawberries or broccoli or potatoes twelve months of the year, you'll find yourself experimenting with other foods when they come into the market. The CSA box does an even better job of forcing you out of your dietary rut because you'll find things in your weekly allotment that you would never buy on your own. Whether it's a rutabaga or an unfamiliar winter squash, the CSA box's contents invariably send you to your cookbooks to figure out what in the world to do with them. Cooking is one of the most important health consequences of buying food from local farmers; for one thing, when you cook at home you seldom find yourself reaching for the ethoxylated diglycerides or high-fructose corn syrup. . . .

To shop at a farmers' market or sign up with a CSA is to join a short food chain, and that has several implications for your health. Local produce is typically picked ripe and is fresher than supermarket produce, and for those reasons it should be tastier and more nutritious. As for supermarket organic produce, it too is likely to have come from far away — from the industrial organic farms of California or, increasingly, China.[1] And while it's true that the organic label guarantees that no synthetic pesticides or fertilizers have been used to produce the food, many, if not most, of the small farms that supply farmers' markets are organic in everything but name. To survive in the farmers' market or CSA economy, a farm will need to be highly diversified, and a diversified farm usually has little need for pesticides; it's the big monocultures that can't survive without them.[2]

---

[1]One recent study found that the average item of organic produce in the supermarket had actually traveled farther from the farm than the average item of conventional produce. [Pollan's note.]

[2]Wendell Berry put the problem of monoculture with admirable brevity and clarity in his essay "The Pleasures of Eating": "But as scale increases, diversity declines; as diversity declines, so does health; as health declines, the dependence on drugs and chemicals necessarily increases." [Pollan's note.]

If you're concerned about chemicals in your produce, you can simply   30
ask the farmer at the market how he or she deals with pests and fertility
and begin the sort of conversation between producers and consumers
that, in the end, is the best guarantee of quality in your food. So many of
the problems of the industrial food chain stem from its length and com-
plexity. A wall of ignorance intervenes between consumers and producers, and that wall fosters a certain carelessness on both sides. Farmers can
lose sight of the fact that they're growing food for actual eaters rather
than for middlemen, and consumers can easily forget that growing good
food takes care and hard work. In a long food chain, the story and identity of the food (Who grew it? Where and how was it grown?) disappear
into the undifferentiated stream of commodities, so that the only information communicated between consumers and producers is a price. In a
short food chain, eaters can make their needs and desires known to the
farmer, and farmers can impress on eaters the distinctions between ordinary and exceptional food, and the many reasons why exceptional food
is worth what it costs. Food reclaims its story, and some of its nobility,
when the person who grew it hands it to you. So here's a subclause to the
get-out-of-the-supermarket rule: *Shake the hand that feeds you.*

As soon as you do, accountability becomes once again a matter of relationships instead of regulation or labeling or legal liability. Food safety
didn't become a national or global problem until the industrialization of
the food chain attenuated° the relationships between food producers and
eaters. That was the story Upton Sinclair told about the Beef Trust in 1906, and
it's the story unfolding in China today, where the rapid industrialization of the
food system is leading to alarming breakdowns in food safety and integrity.
Regulation is an imperfect substitute for the accountability, and trust, built into a
market in which food producers meet the gaze of eaters and vice versa. Only
when we participate in a short food chain are we reminded every week that
we are indeed part of a food chain and dependent for our health on its
peoples and soils and integrity — on its health.

> "Only when we participate in a short food chain are we reminded every week that we are indeed part of a food chain and dependent for our health on its peoples and soils and integrity — on its health."

"Eating is an agricultural act," Wendell Berry famously wrote, by
which he meant that we are not just passive consumers of food but cocre-
ators of the systems that feed us. Depending on how we spend them, our

attenuated: made smaller, thinner, or weaker.

food dollars can either go to support a food industry devoted to quantity and convenience and "value" or they can nourish a food chain organized around *values* — values like quality and health. Yes, shopping this way takes more money and effort, but as soon as you begin to treat that expenditure not just as shopping but also as a kind of vote — a vote for health in the largest sense — food no longer seems like the smartest place to economize.

Understanding the Text

1. What is the "industrial food chain"?

2. What are "foodish products"? What reasons does Pollan offer for avoiding "foodish products"?

3. What are the differences between processed and whole foods? Why does this distinction matter to Pollan?

Reflection and Response

4. What does the advice to "just eat food" mean to you?

5. Does Pollan think we can trust food labels? Explain.

6. Select a packaged or processed food product that you like to eat, and examine the ingredients. Would Pollan classify your item as "food"? Why or why not? Do you classify it as "food"? Explain.

7. How would following Pollan's advice change your eating patterns? How might you benefit? What would you give up?

Making Connections

8. How might Pollan evaluate the Food Pyramid and Food Plate developed by the United States Department of Agriculture (p. 132)? Locate textual evidence to support your case.

9. Pollan quotes Wendell Berry, author of "The Pleasures of Eating" (p. 47), in the last paragraph of this selection. What ideals do Pollan and Berry share? What selections in this book complicate these ideals? How?

10. Rachel Laudan ("The Birth of the Modern Diet," p. 55) has said that her work as a food historian has made her an "unabashed, though not uncritical enthusiast about modern food." Compare her representation of the modern diet to Pollan's. What do they have in common? Where do they differ? How does Laudan complicate Pollan's prescription to eat only what your great-grandmother would recognize as food?

Why the Fries Taste Good

Eric Schlosser

Eric Schlosser is an award-winning journalist best known for his exhaustive research on the fast food industry and his best-selling book *Fast Food Nation* (2001), which began as a two-part article in *Rolling Stone.* Schlosser began his writing career as a fiction writer, then turned to nonfiction and became a correspondent for the *Atlantic Monthly*, where he is still a contributor. He appeared in the documentary *Food, Inc.* (2008), which draws on his searing critiques of the food industry to demonstrate their potential for damaging our health and environment. In this essay, excerpted from *Fast Food Nation*, Schlosser discusses how McDonald's flavors its fries as an example of larger industry flavoring practices. He offers an in-depth look at the flavor industry and how it differentiates "natural" and "artificial" flavorings.

The taste of McDonald's french fries has long been praised by customers, competitors, and even food critics. James Beard loved McDonald's fries. Their distinctive taste does not stem from the type of potatoes that McDonald's buys, the technology that processes them, or the restaurant equipment that fries them. Other chains buy their french fries from the same large processing companies, use Russet Burbanks, and have similar fryers in their restaurant kitchens. The taste of a fast food fry is largely determined by the cooking oil. For decades, McDonald's cooked its french fries in a mixture of about 7 percent cottonseed oil and 93 percent beef tallow. The mix gave the fries their unique flavor — and more saturated beef fat per ounce than a McDonald's hamburger.

Amid a barrage of criticism over the amount of cholesterol in their fries, McDonald's switched to pure vegetable oil in 1990. The switch presented the company with an enormous challenge: how to make fries that subtly taste like beef without cooking them in tallow. A look at the ingredients now used in the preparation of McDonald's french fries suggests how the problem was solved. At the end of the list is a seemingly innocuous, yet oddly mysterious phrase: "natural flavor." That ingredient helps to explain not only why the fries taste so good, but also why most fast food — indeed, most of the food Americans eat today — tastes the way it does.

Open your refrigerator, your freezer, your kitchen cupboards, and look at the labels on your food. You'll find "natural flavor" or "artificial flavor" in just about every list of ingredients. The similarities between these two broad categories of flavor are far more significant than their differences. Both are man-made additives that give most processed food its taste. The initial purchase of a food item may be driven by its packaging or appearance, but subsequent purchases are determined mainly by its taste. About 90 percent of the money that Americans spend on food is used to buy processed food. But the canning, freezing, and dehydrating techniques used to process food destroy most of its flavor. Since the end of World War II, a vast industry has arisen in the United States to make processed food palatable. Without this flavor industry, today's fast food industry could not exist. The names of the leading American fast food chains and their best-selling menu items have become famous worldwide, embedded in our popular culture. Few people, however, can name the companies that manufacture fast food's taste.

The flavor industry is highly secretive. Its leading companies will not divulge the precise formulas of flavor compounds or the identities of clients. The secrecy is deemed essential for protecting the reputation of beloved brands. The fast food chains, understandably, would like the public to believe that the flavors of their food somehow originate in their restaurant kitchens, not in distant factories run by other firms.

The New Jersey Turnpike runs through the heart of the flavor indus- 5 try, an industrial corridor dotted with refineries and chemical plants. International Flavors & Fragrances (IFF), the world's largest flavor company, has a manufacturing facility off Exit 8A in Dayton, New Jersey; Givaudan, the world's second-largest flavor company, has a plant in East Hanover. Haarmann & Reimer, the largest German flavor company, has a plant in Teterboro, as does Takasago, the largest Japanese flavor company. Flavor Dynamics has a plant in South Plainfield; Frutarom is in North Bergen; Elan Chemical is in Newark. Dozens of companies manufacture flavors in New Jersey industrial parks between Teaneck and South Brunswick. Indeed, the area produces about two-thirds of the flavor additives sold in the United States.

The IFF plant in Dayton is a huge pale blue building with a modern office complex attached to the front. It sits in an industrial park, not far from a BASF plastics factory, a Jolly French Toast factory, and a plant that manufactures Liz Claiborne cosmetics. Dozens of tractor-trailers were parked at the IFF loading dock the afternoon I visited, and a thin cloud of steam floated from the chimney. Before entering the plant, I signed a nondisclosure form, promising not to reveal the brand names of products that contain IFF flavors. The place reminded me of Willy Wonka's chocolate factory. Wonderful smells drifted through the hallways, men and women in neat white lab coats cheerfully went about their work, and hundreds of little glass bottles sat on laboratory tables and shelves. The bottles contained powerful but fragile flavor chemicals, shielded from light by the brown glass and the round plastic caps shut tight. The long chemical names on the little white labels were as mystifying to me as medieval Latin. They were the odd-sounding names of things that would be mixed and poured and turned into new substances, like magic potions.

I was not invited to see the manufacturing areas of the IFF plant, where it was thought I might discover trade secrets. Instead, I toured various laboratories and pilot kitchens, where the flavors of well-established brands are tested or adjusted, and where whole new flavors are created. IFF's snack and savory lab is responsible for the flavor of potato chips, corn chips, breads, crackers, breakfast cereals, and pet food. The confectionery lab devises the flavor for ice cream, cookies, candies, toothpastes, mouthwashes, and antacids. Everywhere I looked, I saw famous, widely advertised products sitting on laboratory desks and tables. The beverage lab is full of brightly colored liquids in clear bottles. It comes up with the flavor for popular soft drinks, sport drinks, bottled teas, and wine coolers, for all-natural juice drinks, organic soy drinks, beers, and malt liquors. In one pilot kitchen I saw a dapper chemist, a middle-aged man with an elegant tie beneath his lab coat, carefully preparing a batch of cookies with white frosting and pink-and-white sprinkles. In another pilot kitchen I saw a pizza oven, a grill, a milk-shake machine, and a french fryer identical to those I'd seen behind the counter at countless fast food restaurants.

In addition to being the world's largest flavor company, IFF manufactures the smell of six of the ten best-selling fine perfumes in the United States. It makes the smell of Estée Lauder's Beautiful, Clinique's Happy, Ralph Lauren's Polo, and Calvin Klein's Eternity. It also makes the smell of household products such as deodorant, dishwashing detergent, bath soap, shampoo, furniture polish, and floor wax. All of these aromas are made through the same basic process: the manipulation of volatile chemicals to create a particular smell. The basic science behind the scent of your shaving cream is the same as that governing the flavor of your TV dinner.

The aroma of a food can be responsible for as much as 90 percent of its flavor. Scientists now believe that human beings acquired the sense of taste as a way to avoid being poisoned. Edible plants generally taste sweet; deadly ones, bitter. Taste is supposed to help us differentiate food that's good for us from food that's not. The taste buds on our tongues can detect the presence of half a dozen or so basic tastes, including: sweet, sour, bitter, salty, astringent, and umami (a taste discovered by Japanese researchers, a rich and full sense of deliciousness triggered by amino acids in foods such as shellfish, mushrooms, potatoes, and seaweed). Taste buds offer a relatively limited means of detection, however, compared to the human olfactory system, which can perceive thousands of different chemical aromas. Indeed "flavor" is primarily the smell of gases being released by the chemicals you've just put in your mouth.

The act of drinking, sucking, or chewing a substance releases its 10 volatile gases. They flow out of the mouth and up the nostrils, or up the passageway in the back of the mouth, to a thin layer of nerve cells called the olfactory epithelium, located at the base of the nose, right between the eyes. The brain combines the complex smell signals from the epithelium with the simple taste signals from the tongue, assigns a flavor to what's in your mouth, and decides if it's something you want to eat.

Babies like sweet tastes and reject bitter ones; we know this because scientists have rubbed various flavors inside the mouths of infants and then recorded their facial reactions. A person's food preferences, like his or her personality, are formed during the first few years of life, through a process of socialization. Toddlers can learn to enjoy hot and spicy food, bland health food, or fast food, depending upon what the people around them eat. The human sense of smell is still not fully understood and can be greatly affected by psychological factors and expectations. The color of a food can determine the perception of its taste. The mind filters out the overwhelming majority of chemical aromas that surround us, focusing intently on some, ignoring others. People can grow accustomed to bad smells or good smells; they stop noticing what once seemed overpowering. Aroma and memory are somehow inextricably linked. A smell can suddenly evoke a long-forgotten moment. The flavors of childhood foods seem to leave an indelible mark, and adults often return to them, without always knowing why. These "comfort foods" become a source of pleasure and reassurance, a fact that fast food chains work hard to promote. Childhood memories of Happy Meals can translate into frequent adult visits to McDonald's, like those of the chain's "heavy users," the customers who eat there four or five times a week.

The human craving for flavor has been a largely unacknowledged and unexamined force in history. Royal empires have been built, unexplored lands have been traversed, great religions and philosophies have been forever changed by the spice trade. In 1492 Christopher Columbus set sail to find seasoning. Today the influence of flavor in the world marketplace is no less decisive. The rise and fall of corporate empires — of soft drink companies, snack food companies, and fast food chains — is frequently determined by how their products taste.

The flavor industry emerged in the mid-nineteenth century, as processed foods began to be manufactured on a large scale. Recognizing the need for flavor additives, the early food processors turned to perfume companies that had years of experience working with essential oils and volatile aromas. The great perfume houses of England, France, and the

Netherlands produced many of the first flavor compounds. In the early part of the twentieth century, Germany's powerful chemical industry assumed the technological lead in flavor production. Legend has it that a German scientist discovered methyl anthranilate, one of the first artificial flavors, by accident while mixing chemicals in his laboratory. Suddenly the lab was filled with the sweet smell of grapes. Methyl anthranilate later became the chief flavoring compound of grape Kool-Aid. After World War II, much of the perfume industry shifted from Europe to the United States, settling in New York City near the garment district and the fashion houses. The flavor industry came with it, subsequently moving to New Jersey to gain more plant capacity. Man-made flavor additives were used mainly in baked goods, candies, and sodas until the 1950s, when sales of processed food began to soar. The invention of gas chromatographs and mass spectrometers — machines capable of detecting volatile gases at low levels — vastly increased the number of flavors that could be synthesized. By the mid-1960s the American flavor industry was churning out compounds to supply the taste of Pop Tarts, Bac-Os, Tab, Tang, Filet-O-Fish sandwiches, and literally thousands of other new foods.

The American flavor industry now has annual revenues of about $1.4 billion. Approximately ten thousand new processed food products are introduced every year in the United States. Almost all of them require flavor additives. And about nine out of every ten of these new food products fail. The latest flavor innovations and corporate realignments are heralded in publications such as *Food Chemical News, Food Engineering, Chemical Market Reporter,* and *Food Product Design.* The growth of IFF has mirrored that of the flavor industry as a whole. IFF was formed in 1958, through the merger of two small companies. Its annual revenues have grown almost fifteenfold since the early 1970s, and it now has manufacturing facilities in twenty countries.

The quality that people seek most of all in a food, its flavor, is usually 15 present in a quantity too infinitesimal to be measured by any traditional culinary terms such as ounces or teaspoons. Today's sophisticated spectrometers, gas chromatographs, and headspace vapor analyzers provide a detailed map of a food's flavor components, detecting chemical aromas in amounts as low as one part per billion. The human nose, however, is still more sensitive than any machine yet invented. A nose can detect aromas present in quantities of a few parts per trillion — an amount equivalent to 0.000000000003 percent. Complex aromas, like those of coffee or roasted meat, may be composed of volatile gases from nearly a thousand different chemicals. The smell of a strawberry arises from the interaction of at least 350 different chemicals that are present in minute amounts. The chemical that provides the dominant flavor of bell pepper can be tasted in amounts as low as .02 parts per billion; one drop is sufficient to add flavor to five average size swimming pools. The flavor additive usually comes last, or second to last, in a processed food's list of ingredients (chemicals that add color are frequently used in even smaller amounts). As a result, the flavor of a processed food often costs less than its packaging. Soft drinks contain a larger proportion of flavor additives than most products. The flavor in a twelve-ounce can of Coke costs about half a cent.

The Food and Drug Administration does not require flavor companies to disclose the ingredients of their additives, so long as all the chemicals are considered by the agency to be GRAS (Generally Regarded As Safe). This lack of public disclosure enables the companies to maintain the secrecy of their formulas. It also hides the fact that flavor compounds sometimes contain more ingredients than the foods being given their taste. The ubiquitous phrase "artificial strawberry flavor" gives little hint of the chemical wizardry and manufacturing skill that can make a highly processed food taste like a strawberry.

A typical artificial strawberry flavor, like the kind found in a Burger King strawberry milk shake, contains the following ingredients: amyl acetate, amyl butyrate, amyl valerate, anethol, anisyl formate, benzyl acetate, benzyl isobutyrate, butyric acid, cinnamyl isobutyrate, cinnamyl valerate, cognac essential oil, diacetyl, dipropyl ketone, ethyl acetate,

Nutrition Facts

Serving Size 2.6 oz (75g)
Servings Per Container 1

Amount Per Serving

Calories 230   Calories from Fat 100

		% Daily Values*
Total Fat 11g		**17%**
Saturated Fat 1.5g		**8%**
Trans Fat 0g		
Sodium 130mg		**5%**
Total Carbohydrate 30g		**10%**
Dietary Fiber 2g		**8%**
Sugars 0g		
Protein 2g		**4%**

*Percent Daily Values are based on a 2,000 calorie diet.

INGREDIENTS: Potatoes, Vegetable Oil (Canola Oil, Soybean Oil, Hydrogenated Soybean Oil, Natural Beef Flavor [Wheat and Milk Derivatives]*, Citric Acid [Preservative]), Dextrose, Sodium Acid Pyrophosphate (Maintain Color), Salt. Prepared in Vegetable Oil (Canola Oil, Corn Oil, Soybean Oil, Hydrogenated Soybean Oil) with TBHQ and Citric Acid to preserve freshness of the oil and Dimethylpolysiloxane to reduce oil splatter when cooking.
CONTAINS: WHEAT AND MILK.
*Natural beef flavor contains hydrolyzed wheat and hydrolyzed milk as starting ingredients.

A nutrition label with ingredients for one small order of McDonald's french fries.

ethyl amylketone, ethyl butyrate, ethyl cinnamate, ethyl heptanoate, ethyl heptylate, ethyl lactate, ethyl methylphenylglycidate, ethyl nitrate, ethyl propionate, ethyl valerate, heliotropin, hydroxyphrenyl 2-butanone (10 percent solution in alcohol), α-ionone, isobutyl anthranilate, isobutyl butyrate, lemon essential oil, maltol, 4-methylacetophenone, methyl anthranilate, methyl benzoate, methyl cinnamate, methyl heptine carbonate, methyl naphthyl ketone, methyl salicylate, mint essential oil, neroli essential oil, nerolin, neryl isobutyrate, orris butter, phenethyl alcohol, rose, rum ether, γ-undecalactone, vanillin, and solvent.

Although flavors usually arise from a mixture of many different volatile chemicals, a single compound often supplies the dominant aroma. Smelled alone, that chemical provides an unmistakable sense of the food. Ethyl-2-methyl butyrate, for example, smells just like an apple. Today's highly processed foods offer a blank palette: whatever chemicals you add to them will give them specific tastes. Adding methyl-2-peridylketone makes something taste like popcorn. Adding ethyl-3-hydroxybutanoate makes it taste like marshmallow. The possibilities are now almost limitless. Without affecting the appearance or nutritional value, processed foods could even be made with aroma chemicals such as hexanal (the smell of freshly cut grass) or 3-methyl butanoic acid (the smell of body odor).

The 1960s were the heyday of artificial flavors. The synthetic versions of flavor compounds were not subtle, but they did not need to be, given the nature of most processed food. For the past twenty years food processors have tried hard to use only "natural flavors" in their products. According to the FDA, these must be derived entirely from natural sources — from herbs, spices, fruits, vegetables, beef, chicken, yeast, bark, roots, etc. Consumers prefer to see natural flavors on a label, out of a belief that they are healthier. The distinction between artificial and natural flavors can be somewhat arbitrary and absurd, based more on how the flavor has been made than on what it actually contains. "A natural flavor," says Terry Acree, a professor of food science technology at Cornell University, "is a flavor that's been derived with an out-of-date technology." Natural flavors and artificial flavors sometimes contain exactly the same chemicals, produced through different methods. Amyl acetate, for example, provides the dominant note of banana flavor. When you distill it from bananas with a solvent, amyl acetate is a natural flavor. When you produce it by mixing vinegar with amyl alcohol, adding sulfuric acid

> "The distinction between artificial and natural flavors can be somewhat arbitrary and absurd, based more on how the flavor has been made than on what it actually contains."

as a catalyst, amyl acetate is an artificial flavor. Either way it smells and tastes the same. The phrase "natural flavor" is now listed among the ingredients of everything from Stonyfield Farm Organic Strawberry Yogurt to Taco Bell Hot Taco Sauce.

A natural flavor is not necessarily healthier or purer than an artificial 20 one. When almond flavor (benzaldehyde) is derived from natural sources, such as peach and apricot pits, it contains traces of hydrogen cyanide, a deadly poison. Benzaldehyde derived through a different process — by mixing oil of clove and the banana flavor, amyl acetate — does not contain any cyanide. Nevertheless, it is legally considered an artificial flavor and sells at a much lower price. Natural and artificial flavors are now manufactured at the same chemical plants, places that few people would associate with Mother Nature. Calling any of these flavors "natural" requires a flexible attitude toward the English language and a fair amount of irony.

The small and elite group of scientists who create most of the flavor in most of the food now consumed in the United States are called "flavorists." They draw upon a number of disciplines in their work: biology, psychology, physiology, and organic chemistry. A flavorist is a chemist with a trained nose and a poetic sensibility. Flavors are created by blending scores of different chemicals in tiny amounts, a process governed by scientific principles but demanding a fair amount of art. In an age when delicate aromas, subtle flavors, and microwave ovens do not easily coexist, the job of the flavorist is to conjure illusions about processed food and, in the words of one flavor company's literature, to ensure "consumer likeability." The flavorists with whom I spoke were charming, cosmopolitan, and ironic. They were also discreet, in keeping with the dictates of their trade. They were the sort of scientist who not only enjoyed fine wine, but could also tell you the chemicals that gave each vintage its unique aroma. One flavorist compared his work to composing music. A well-made flavor compound will have a "top note," followed by a "dry-down," and a "leveling-off," with different chemicals responsible for each stage. The taste of a food can be radically altered by minute changes in the flavoring mix. "A little odor goes a long way," one flavorist said.

In order to give a processed food the proper taste, a flavorist must always consider the food's "mouthfeel" — the unique combination of textures and chemical interactions that affects how the flavor is perceived. The mouthfeel can be adjusted through the use of various fats, gums, starches, emulsifiers, and stabilizers. The aroma chemicals of a food can be precisely analyzed, but mouthfeel is much harder to measure. How does one quantify a french fry's crispness? Food technologists are now conducting basic research in rheology, a branch of physics that examines the flow and deformation of materials. A number of companies sell sophisticated devices that attempt to measure mouthfeel. The Universal TA-XT2 Texture Analyzer, produced by the Texture Technologies Corporation, performs calculations based on data derived from twenty-five separate probes. It is essentially a mechanical mouth. It gauges the most important rheological properties of a food — the bounce, creep, breaking point, density, crunchiness, chewiness, gumminess, lumpiness, rubberiness, springiness, slipperiness, smoothness, softness, wetness, juiciness, spreadability, spring-back, and tackiness.

Some of the most important advances in flavor manufacturing are now occurring in the field of biotechnology. Complex flavors are being made through fermentation, enzyme reactions, fungal cultures, and tissue cultures. All of the flavors being created through these methods — including the ones being synthesized by funguses — are considered natural flavors by the FDA. The new enzyme-based processes are responsible for extremely lifelike dairy flavors. One company now offers not just butter flavor, but also fresh creamy butter, cheesy butter, milky butter, savory melted butter, and super-concentrated butter flavor, in liquid or powder form. The development of new fermentation techniques, as well as new techniques for heating mixtures of sugar and amino acids, have led to the creation of much more realistic meat flavors. The McDonald's Corporation will not reveal the exact origin of the natural flavor added to its french fries. In response to inquiries from *Vegetarian Journal*, however, McDonald's did acknowledge that its fries derive some of their characteristic flavor from "animal products."

Other popular fast foods derive their flavor from unexpected sources. Wendy's Grilled Chicken Sandwich, for example, contains beef extracts. Burger King's BK Broiler Chicken Breast Patty contains "natural smoke flavor." A firm called Red Arrow Products Company specializes in smoke flavor, which is added to barbecue sauces and processed meats. Red Arrow manufactures natural smoke flavor by charring sawdust and capturing the aroma chemicals released into the air. The smoke is captured in water and then bottled, so that other companies can sell food which seems to have been cooked over a fire.

In a meeting room at IFF, Brian Grainger let me sample some of the company's flavors. It was an unusual taste test; there wasn't any food to taste. Grainger is a senior flavorist at IFF, a soft-spoken chemist with graying hair, an English accent, and a fondness for understatement. He could easily be mistaken for a British diplomat or the owner of a West End brasserie with two Michelin stars. Like many in the flavor industry, he has an Old World, old-fashioned sensibility which seems out of step 25 with our brand-conscious, egocentric age. When I suggested that IFF should put its own logo on the products that contain its flavors — instead of allowing other brands to enjoy the consumer loyalty and affection inspired by those flavors — Grainger politely disagreed, assuring me such a thing would never be done. In the absence of public credit or acclaim, the small and secretive fraternity of flavor chemists praises one another's work. Grainger can often tell, by analyzing the flavor formula of a product, which of his counterparts at a rival firm devised it. And he enjoys walking down supermarket aisles, looking at the many products that contain his flavors, even if no one else knows it.

Grainger had brought a dozen small glass bottles from the lab. After he opened each bottle, I dipped a fragrance testing filter into it. The filters were long white strips of paper designed to absorb aroma chemicals without producing off-notes. Before placing the strips of paper before my nose, I closed my eyes. Then I inhaled deeply, and one food after another was conjured from the glass bottles. I smelled fresh cherries, black olives, sautéed onions, and shrimp. Grainger's most remarkable creation took me by surprise. After closing my eyes, I suddenly smelled a grilled hamburger. The aroma was uncanny, almost miraculous. It smelled like someone in the room was flipping burgers on a hot grill. But when I opened my eyes, there was just a narrow strip of white paper and a smiling flavorist.

Understanding the Text

1. How are "artificial" and "natural" flavors similar? How are they different?

2. How does Schlosser describe the process through which food flavors are made?

3. According to Schlosser, what role does "taste" play in our health?

Reflection and Response

4. Why does Schlosser conclude that the distinction between artificial and natural flavors is often "arbitrary and absurd"? Do you agree or disagree? Explain.

5. Why is the production of flavors so secretive? What are the potential benefits of the secrecy to consumers? What are the potential drawbacks?

6. Does Schlosser's article make you think about french fries, fast food, or processed food flavors differently? Will his at-times searing critique change how you eat? Explain.

Making Connections

7. Why is the flavor industry so important? What role does the flavor industry play in what Michael Pollan calls the "industrial food chain" ("Eat Food: Food Defined," p. 10)? Using your campus library resources, locate two external sources to help support your response.

8. Compare Schlosser's description of the flavor industry to Donald L. Barlett and James B. Steele's description of Monsanto and the patented seed industry ("Monsanto's Harvest of Fear," p. 161). What commonalities exist? What differences do you see? How do these industries affect consumers?

Her Chee-to Heart

Jill McCorkle

Jill McCorkle is an award-winning novelist, essayist, and short story writer who has published many collections and novels, most recently *Life After Life* (2013). Several of her stories have been chosen for inclusion in *Best American Short Stories* collections. She teaches creative writing in the MFA Program at North Carolina State University and is a faculty member of the Bennington College Writing Seminars. In this essay, published in the collection *We Are What We Ate* (1998), McCorkle offers vivid memories of life as a "junk-food junkie."

If I could have a perfect day of eating, this would be it: I'd begin with pancakes and sausage patties drenched in Log Cabin syrup. Then I'd visit my grandmother's kitchen, where my sister and I used to watch ravenously as Gramma made her famous pound cake (a real pound cake — a pound of butter, a pound of sugar, egg after egg after egg swirled in Swans Down cake flour). We'd each slurp batter off the mixer whisks and then split what was left in the red-and-white Pyrex bowl. My grandmother also made chicken and pastry (her pastry was more like dumplings) and homemade biscuits (the secret ingredient is lard), which might be dipped in redeye gravy or covered in butter and Karo syrup (doughboys) and eaten as dessert. She made homemade apple pies (the fruit part of our diet) fried in Crisco and filled with sugar.

If I couldn't have homemade food, then I would settle for what could be bought. A foot-long hot dog at the B&R Drive-In, for example; french fries limp with grease and salt from the bowling alley; a barbecue sandwich (Carolina style — chopped fine and spiced up with hot sauce); a triple-chocolate milk shake from Tastee-Freez. Banana splits and hot-fudge sundaes. Maybe a frozen Zero candy bar or a Milky Way, a Little Debbie snack cake and a moon pie, too.

I am a junk-food junkie and always have been. My college roommate and my husband both blame me for their slides into high-fat, preservative-filled meals, like the frozen Mexican TV dinners that my roommate and I ate all the way through college, or the microwavable burritos I now stash at the back of my freezer for desperate moments (desperate meaning a craving for Tex-Mex or a need to drive a nail and not being able to find a hammer). Forget meals, anyway; the truly good treats for a junk-food junkie get served up in between: colorful Ben & Jerry's pints, natural in an ethical way (the money goes to good places, at least) that makes me feel healthy; names — Chubby Hubby, Chunky Monkey, Wavy Gravy — that make me laugh. Good Humor is what it's all about and has been since childhood: kids trained to respond to the ringing of a bell, to chase alongside trucks in neighborhood streets like so many pups for a Nutty Buddy. Ice cream is near the top of any junk-food junkie's list to be sure, but I haven't even begun to mention the Chee-tos, the Pecan Sandies.

There's something about unnatural food colors that has always attracted me. What tastes or looks better than the frosting on grocery-store-bakery birthday cakes? Hot pink or blue roses that melt in your mouth. The fluorescent brilliance of a crunchy Chee-to. Not too long ago my children (ages four and seven) were eating at a friend's. They were served a lovely meal of homemade macaroni and cheese, white, the way something without any additives and preservatives should be. I was on the other side of the room, helpless to defend myself when I heard my daughter say, "But my mom's macaroni and cheese is bright orange." Well? What can I say? I also love that fuchsia-colored sweet-and-sour sauce that you often find on Chinese food buffets.

> "There's something about unnatural food colors that has always attracted me. What tastes or looks better than the frosting on grocery-store-bakery birthday cakes?"

At the last big dinner party we had, my husband bought Yodels to 5 throw out on the dessert table along with a fresh-fruit concoction, which had taken me forever to cut up, and little cheesecakes. At the end of the night, there was not a Yodel in sight, but very few people had openly indulged. These scrumptious lunch-box treats (creme-filled chocolate rolls, 140 calories and 8 grams of fat each, which means, of course, that they are good) had instead been slyly tucked away into pockets and purses for the ride home. Yodels, Twinkies, Hostess Snoballs. They make people nostalgic for elementary school, those wonderful years when we were advised to eat beef and pork. Children thriving on sloppy joes and Saturday T-bones. Pork chops with applesauce. Sausage gravy over homemade biscuits. A good green vegetable in the South, where I grew up, was a green-bean casserole in which the beans were camouflaged in Campbell's cream of mushroom soup and canned fried onion rings. All the recipes in my favorite cookbooks begin with Campbell's cream-of-something soup.

I was enamored of a boy named Michael in the first grade who licked Kool-Aid powder from his palm whenever the teacher wasn't looking. He moved away before the end of the year, and yet thirty-one years later, I still remember him with a fond mixture of repulsion at the sticky red saliva that graced his notebook paper and admiration for the open ease with which he indulged his habit. I loved Pixy Stix straws, which, let's face it, were nothing more than dry Kool-Aid mix poured right into your mouth. Sweetarts. Jawbreakers. Firecrackers. Mary Janes. Any item that I was told was *very* bad for my teeth.

Maybe it's an oral-gratification thing. I'm sure that's why I smoked for fifteen years. When I quit nine years ago, I rediscovered my taste buds. I found flavors I had forgotten all about: Sugar Babies and Raisinets, that thick mashed-potato gravy that is the *real* secret ingredient at Kentucky Fried Chicken. I found flavors I had never had before, such as cheese blintzes and latkes smothered in sour cream. I found that wonderful, all-natural, fortified cereal Quaker 100% Natural Oats Honey and Raisins. I need oral participation, oral gratification. Despite what they will tell you on television, a little stick of Juicy Fruit is not going to get you there if you've been lighting up for years. But M&M's? Junior Mints? Those diablo-style peanuts thoroughly doused with cayenne pepper? Now, that's chewing satisfaction. A Coke (or diet Coke for the figure-minded; Jolt cola for the desperate-to-start-the-day-minded) chaser.

I could do a taste test. I can recognize all the sodas. The soda wanna-bes. I drink a good two to three cups of coffee when I get up, and by the time I drive the kids to school, I've switched over to diet Coke. People say, "Doesn't it keep you awake?" I wish! During one of my pregnancies I lost all taste for Coke. I couldn't believe it. I'd been drinking Coke for as long as I could remember. It was so sad; filling myself up on Hawaiian Punch (which is very good in its own right), Pop-Tarts, and ice cream, ice cream, ice cream. But I missed the Coke cans rolling around under the seat of my car. I missed the whoosh and zap of buying a Coke from a vending machine. And one day, like magic, it returned, this desire, like an old love resurfacing.

There are ways a junk-food junkie can feel less guilty about all this food, if indeed you ever do feel guilty. Did I mention caffeine? It's like air — essential for full enjoyment. And it burns calories. If that doesn't work, there are always things like the NordicTrack where I hang my clothes at the end of the day and the Suzanne Somers Thighmaster I keep in my closet for decoration.

Besides, I consider myself a purist; I don't like substitute things — like 10 these new clear sodas. Who cares? I went into the all-natural health-food grocery store not long ago only to discover that there are a lot of things in this world that are foreign to me. The produce section had products you might find growing in a neglected basement. There were name brands I'd never heard of; certainly they don't buy airtime on television. There were cereals without colored marshmallows or prizes in the box. They boasted of having no sugar (as if this were good). It did not take me long to get back to the familiar aisles of the Super Stop & Shop, the red-and-white Campbell's soup labels, the chip-and-cookie aisle (nothing there sweetened with fruit juice or carob imitating chocolate), and the candy bars at the checkout.

One of my fondest junk-food memories is of a rare snow day in Lumberton, North Carolina, when I was in the sixth grade, a wonderful age at which, though I liked boys, they were not nearly as exciting as the ice cream store nearby that served up an oversize cone called a Kitchen Sink. But that day, I sat with a couple of friends in the back of the Kwik-Pik (the South's version of the convenience store) and ate raw chocolate-chip-cookie dough while drinking Eagle Brand sweetened condensed milk straight from the can. My friends and I waddled home feeling sick but warmly nourished, our stomachs coated and glowing with sugar. I mean, really, there is no cake or cookie on earth that tastes as good as dough or batter.

My favorite food in the eighth grade was Slim Jim sausages. For the uninformed, these are the miniature pepperoni sticks usually found near the register of convenience stores, where you might also find the beef jerky and pickled eggs. When I was growing up, there was usually a big jar of pickled pig's feet too, but this was not a treat that ever caught my eye. No, I lived on Slim Jims, spicy and chewy. I kept them with me at all times, getting a good chew while at cheerleading practices. They re-minded me of being an even younger kid and getting a little bit of raw, salty country ham from my grandmother and chewing it all day like a piece of gum. (Sorry, Juicy Fruit; failed again.)

My husband, a doctor whose specialty is infectious diseases, is certain that I have been host to many parasites. Maybe, but what I'm certain that I have been host to are the junk-food parasites who refuse to admit that they indulge, but they do. Just put out a bowl of pistachios and check out the red fingertips leaving; chips, M&M's. Ah, M&M's. It was a sad day long ago when they retired the red ones. I had spent years being entertained by a pack; segregate and then integrate, close your eyes and guess which color. I was thrilled when the red ones returned, and now blue! Lovely blue M&M's. I love the pastel ones at Easter, along with those Cadbury eggs, and my own personal favorite: malted Easter eggs. These are actually Whoppers (malted-milk balls) covered in a speckled candy shell. Sometimes they are called robin eggs and sometimes simply malteds, but a Whopper is a Whopper is a Whopper. I like to bite one in half and then suck in. When the air is pulled out of a Whopper, what's left is more like a Milk Dud.

Of course there is also the Whopper from Burger King. Once, after a Friday night high-school football game, I sat down at a table with a bag of food that looked similar to those of all the guys on the team. I had a Whopper with everything, large fries, an apple pie, and a chocolate shake. Our cheerleading adviser told me that I wouldn't always be able to do that.

Thank God I didn't know she was right. It would have ruined the next 15
four years as I continued to down cream-filled Krispy Kreme doughnuts
and my own special high-protein omelette that was filled with mayon-
naise and cheese. I loved Funyuns, too, except that nobody wanted to sit
next to me on the bus when I ate them.

After all these years, I've made some adjustments. I now buy Hebrew
National for things like hot dogs and bologna. I figure the kosher laws
probably serve me well in this particular purchase, and try as I might to
dissuade them, my children love bologna with an absolute passion. They
can smell the reject turkey substitute from fifty paces. They don't like
real mac and cheese. They like the microwave kind. My niece (at age four)
once invited me into her playhouse for lunch. She said, "Would you like
a diet Coke while I cook lunch in the microwave?" So maybe it's a family
thing. Maybe it's the potassium benzoate.

I would love a diet Coke and a cream horn right about now. Some salt-
and-vinegar chips. Onion dip and Ruffles. S'mores. I like to get in bed to
read with a stash of something close by. I have found that I am especially
drawn to things with a high polyglycerol-ester-of-fatty-acids content. It
makes me feel *happy*. I think maybe this is the key to a true junk-food
junkie's heart: happiness. Just as Proust bit into his little madeleine and
had a flood of memories, I bite into my Devil Dog, my Ring-Ding,
Twinkie, Ho-Ho, Yodel. I bite into my Hostess Snoball and retreat to a
world where the only worry is what to ask your mother to put in your
lunch box the next day or which pieces of candy you will select at the
Kwik-Pik on your way home from school. Ahead of you are the wasteland
years: a pack of cigarettes, some Clearasil pads, a tube of Blistex, and
breath spray. But for now, reach back to those purer, those sugar-filled,
melt-in-your-mouth, forever-a-kid years. Who cares if there is a little
polysorbate 60 and some diglycerides, some carrageenan, some Red 40
and Blue 1, some agar-agar? I have a dream that somewhere out there in
the grown-up, low-fat world there is a boy named Michael licking his lips
and getting all the fumaric acid that he can.

Understanding the Text

1. What is a "junk-food junkie"?
2. What role does food play in McCorkle's life? Consider how food affects
   both her self-perception and her relationships with others.

Reflection and Response

3. Does McCorkle's diet fascinate or horrify you? Explain your reaction.

4. Do you think her eating habits are normal in our society? Why or why not?

5. Why do you think she wrote this essay? What do you think she hopes her readers will learn from her stories about food?

Making Connections

6. What attitudes or values do Michael Pollan ("Eat Food: Food Defined," p. 10) and McCorkle share? What would Pollan praise about McCorkle's relationship with food? What would he question?

7. Consider Eric Schlosser's description of the flavor industry ("Why the Fries Taste Good," p. 20). What role does the flavor industry play in McCorkle's diet?

8. Think about what Dhruv Khullar ("Why Shame Won't Stop Obesity," p. 135) and Masanobu Fukuoka ("Living by Bread Alone," p. 71) have to say about the role eating plays in our lives. How would they each analyze McCorkle's attitudes about food?

9. Make a list of what you have eaten in the last two days. In light of the views of Michael Pollan, Eric Schlosser, and Jill McCorkle, evaluate your diet.

Eating Made Simple

Marion Nestle

Marion Nestle is a professor in both the Department of Nutrition, Food Studies, and Public Health and the Department of Sociology at New York University. She has also spent much of her career in public service, consulting on government policies around food and health. She is the author of several books, including *What to Eat* (2007), *Food Politics: How the Food Industry Influences Nutrition and Health* (2007), *Safe Food: The Politics of Food Safety* (2010), *Why Calories Count: From Science to Politics* (2012), and *Eat Drink Vote: An Illustrated Guide to Food Politics* (2013). Nestle's research focuses on food and nutrition policy and analysis and the social, political, and environmental influences on food choice. She regularly writes about her work in the *San Francisco Chronicle*, the *Atlantic*, and her blog *Food Politics*. In this essay, which originally appeared in *Scientific American*, Nestle provides advice on how to sort out the often confusing and sometimes contradictory messages about nutrition and dietary advice.

As a nutrition professor, I am constantly asked why nutrition advice seems to change so much and why experts so often disagree. Whose information, people ask, can we trust? I'm tempted to say, "Mine, of course," but I understand the problem. Yes, nutrition advice seems endlessly mired in scientific argument, the self-interest of food companies, and compromises by government regulators. Nevertheless, basic dietary principles are not in dispute: eat less; move more; eat fruits, vegetables, and whole grains; and avoid too much junk food.

"Eat less" means consume fewer calories, which translates into eating smaller portions and steering clear of frequent between-meal snacks. "Move more" refers to the need to balance calorie intake with physical activity. Eating fruits, vegetables, and whole grains provides nutrients unavailable from other foods. Avoiding junk food means to shun "foods of minimal nutritional value" — highly processed sweets and snacks laden with salt, sugars, and artificial additives. Soft drinks are the prototypical° junk food; they contain sweeteners but few or no nutrients.

If you follow these precepts, other aspects of the diet matter much less. Ironically, this advice has not changed in years. The noted cardiologist Ancel Keys (who died in 2004 at the age of 100) and his wife, Margaret, suggested similar principles for preventing coronary heart disease nearly 50 years ago.

---

prototypical: serving as an example of a type.

But I can see why dietary advice seems like a moving target. Nutrition research is so difficult to conduct that it seldom produces unambiguous results. Ambiguity requires interpretation. And interpretation is influenced by the individual's point of view, which can become thoroughly entangled with the science.

Nutrition Science Challenges

This scientific uncertainty is not overly surprising given that humans eat   5
so many different foods. For any individual, the health effects of diets are modulated° by genetics but also by education and income levels, job satisfaction, physical fitness, and the use of cigarettes or alcohol. To simplify this situation, researchers typically examine the effects of single dietary components one by one.

Studies focusing on one nutrient in isolation have worked splendidly to explain symptoms caused by deficiencies of vitamins or minerals. But this approach is less useful for chronic conditions such as coronary heart disease and diabetes that are caused by the interaction of dietary, genetic, behavioral, and social factors. If nutrition science seems puzzling, it is because researchers typically examine single nutrients detached from food itself, foods separate from diets, and risk factors apart from other behaviors. This kind of research is "reductive" in that it attributes health effects to the consumption of one nutrient or food when it is the overall dietary pattern that really counts most.

> "If nutrition science seems puzzling, it is because researchers typically examine single nutrients detached from food itself, foods separate from diets, and risk factors apart from other behaviors."

For chronic diseases, single nutrients usually alter risk by amounts too small to measure except through large, costly population studies. As seen recently in the Women's Health Initiative, a clinical trial that examined the effects of low-fat diets on heart disease and cancer, participants were unable to stick with the restrictive dietary protocols. Because humans cannot be caged and fed measured formulas, the diets of experimental and control study groups tend to converge, making differences indistinguishable over the long run — even with fancy statistics.

modulate: modify or control.

It's the Calories

Food companies prefer studies of single nutrients because they can use the results to sell products. Add vitamins to candies, and you can market them as health foods. Health claims on the labels of junk foods distract consumers from their caloric content. This practice matters because when it comes to obesity — which dominates nutrition problems even in some of the poorest countries of the world — it is the calories that count. Obesity arises when people consume significantly more calories than they expend in physical activity.

America's obesity rates began to rise sharply in the early 1980s. Sociologists often attribute the "calories in" side of this trend to the demands of an overworked population for convenience foods — prepared, packaged products and restaurant meals that usually contain more calories than home-cooked meals.

But other social forces also promoted the calorie imbalance. The arrival of the Reagan administration in 1980 increased the pace of industry deregulation, removing controls on agricultural production and encouraging farmers to grow more food. Calories available per capita in the national food supply (that produced by American farmers, plus imports, less exports) rose from 3,200 a day in 1980 to 3,900 a day two decades later.

The early 1980s also marked the advent of the "shareholder value movement" on Wall Street. Stockholder demands for higher short-term returns on investments forced food companies to expand sales in a marketplace that already contained excessive calories. Food companies responded by seeking new sales and marketing opportunities. They encouraged formerly shunned practices that eventually changed social norms, such as frequent between-meal snacking, eating in book and clothing stores, and serving larger portions. The industry continued to sponsor organizations and journals that focus on nutrition-related subjects and intensified its efforts to lobby government for favorable dietary advice. Then and now food lobbies have promoted positive interpretations of scientific studies, sponsored research that can be used as a basis for health claims, and attacked critics, myself among them, as proponents of "junk science." If anything, such activities only add to public confusion.

Supermarkets as "Ground Zero"

No matter whom I speak to, I hear pleas for help in dealing with supermarkets, considered by shoppers as "ground zero" for distinguishing health claims from scientific advice. So I spent a year visiting supermarkets to help people think more clearly about food choices. The result was my book *What to Eat.*

Supermarkets provide a vital public service but are not social services agencies. Their job is to sell as much food as possible. Every aspect of store design — from shelf position to background music — is based on marketing research. Because this research shows that the more products customers see, the more they buy, a store's objective is to expose shoppers to the maximum number of products they will tolerate viewing.

If consumers are confused about which foods to buy, it is surely because the choices require knowledge of issues that are not easily resolved by science and are strongly swayed by social and economic considerations. Such decisions play out every day in every store aisle.

Are Organics Healthier?

Organic foods are the fastest-growing segment of the industry, in part 15 because people are willing to pay more for foods that they believe are healthier and more nutritious. The U.S. Department of Agriculture forbids producers of "Certified Organic" fruits and vegetables from using synthetic pesticides, herbicides, fertilizers, genetically modified seeds, irradiation, or fertilizer derived from sewage sludge. It licenses inspectors to ensure that producers follow those rules. Although the USDA is responsible for organics, its principal mandate is to promote conventional agriculture, which explains why the department asserts that it "makes no claims that organically produced food is safer or more nutritious than conventionally produced food. Organic food differs from conventionally grown food in the way it is grown, handled and processed."

This statement implies that such differences are unimportant. Critics of organic foods would agree; they question the reliability of organic certification and the productivity, safety, and health benefits of organic production methods. Meanwhile the organic food industry longs for research to address such criticisms, but studies are expensive and difficult to conduct. Nevertheless, existing research in this area has established that organic farms are nearly as productive as conventional farms, use less energy, and leave soils in better condition. People who eat foods grown without synthetic pesticides ought to have fewer such chemicals in their bodies, and they do. Because the organic rules require pretreatment of manure and other steps to reduce the amount of pathogens in soil treatments, organic foods should be just as safe — or safer — than conventional foods.

Similarly, organic foods ought to be at least as nutritious as conventional foods. And proving organics to be more nutritious could help justify their higher prices. For minerals, this task is not difficult. The mineral content of plants depends on the amounts present in the soil in which they are grown. Organic foods are cultivated in richer soils, so their mineral content is higher.

But differences are harder to demonstrate for vitamins or antioxidants (plant substances that reduce tissue damage induced by free radicals); higher levels of these nutrients relate more to a food plant's genetic strain or protection from unfavorable conditions after harvesting than to production methods. Still, preliminary studies show benefits: organic peaches and pears contain greater quantities of vitamins C and E, and organic berries and corn contain more antioxidants.

Further research will likely confirm that organic foods contain higher nutrient levels, but it is unclear whether these nutrients would make a measurable improvement in health. All fruits and vegetables contain useful nutrients, albeit in different combinations and concentrations. Eating a variety of food plants is surely more important to health than small differences in the nutrient content of any one food. Organics may be somewhat healthier to eat, but they are far less likely to damage the environment, and that is reason enough to choose them at the supermarket.

Dairy and Calcium

Scientists cannot easily resolve questions about the health effects of dairy foods. Milk has many components, and the health of people who consume milk or dairy foods is influenced by everything else they eat and do. But this area of research is especially controversial because it affects an industry that vigorously promotes dairy products as beneficial and opposes suggestions to the contrary. [20]

Dairy foods contribute about 70 percent of the calcium in American diets. This necessary mineral is a principal constituent of bones, which constantly lose and regain calcium during normal metabolism. Diets must contain enough calcium to replace losses, or else bones become prone to fracture. Experts advise consumption of at least one gram of calcium a day to replace everyday losses. Only dairy foods provide this much calcium without supplementation.

But bones are not just made of calcium; they require the full complement of essential nutrients to maintain strength. Bones are stronger in people who are physically active and who do not smoke cigarettes or drink much alcohol. Studies examining the effects of single nutrients in dairy foods show that some nutritional factors — magnesium, potassium, vitamin D, and lactose, for example — promote calcium retention in bones. Others, such as protein, phosphorus, and sodium, foster calcium excretion. So bone strength depends more on overall patterns of diet and behavior than simply on calcium intake.

Populations that do not typically consume dairy products appear to exhibit lower rates of bone fracture despite consuming far less calcium than recommended. Why this is so is unclear. Perhaps their diets contain less protein from meat and dairy foods, less sodium from processed foods, and less phosphorus from soft drinks, so they retain calcium more effectively. The fact that calcium balance depends on multiple factors could explain why rates of osteoporosis (bone density loss) are highest in countries where people eat the most dairy foods. Further research may clarify such counterintuitive observations.

In the meantime, dairy foods are fine to eat if you like them, but they are not a nutritional requirement. Think of cows: they do not drink milk after weaning, but their bones support bodies weighing 800 pounds or more. Cows feed on grass, and grass contains calcium in small amounts — but those amounts add up. If you eat plenty of fruits, vegetables and whole grains, you can have healthy bones without having to consume dairy foods.

A Meaty Debate

Critics point to meat as the culprit responsible for elevating blood choles- 25
terol, along with raising risks for heart disease, cancer, and other conditions. Supporters cite the lack of compelling science to justify such allegations; they emphasize the nutritional benefits of meat protein, vitamins, and minerals. Indeed, studies in developing countries demonstrate health improvements when growing children are fed even small amounts of meat.

But because bacteria in a cow's rumen attach hydrogen atoms to unsaturated fatty acids, beef fat is highly saturated — the kind of fat that increases the risk of coronary heart disease. All fats and oils contain some saturated fatty acids, but animal fats, especially those from beef, have more saturated fatty acids than vegetable fats. Nutritionists recommend eating no more than a heaping tablespoon (20 grams) of saturated fatty acids a day. Beef eaters easily meet or exceed this limit. The smallest McDonald's cheeseburger contains 6 grams of saturated fatty acids, but a Hardee's Monster Thickburger has 45 grams.

Why meat might boost cancer risks, however, is a matter of speculation. Scientists began to link meat to cancer in the 1970s, but even after decades of subsequent research they remain unsure if the relevant factor might be fat, saturated fat, protein, carcinogens,° or something else related to meat. By the late 1990s experts could conclude only that eating beef probably

carcinogen: any substance that directly causes cancer.

increases the risk of colon and rectal cancers and possibly enhances the odds of acquiring breast, prostate and perhaps other cancers. Faced with this uncertainty, the American Cancer Society suggests selecting leaner cuts, smaller portions, and alternatives such as chicken, fish, or beans — steps consistent with today's basic advice about what to eat.

Fish and Heart Disease

Fatty fish are the most important sources of long-chain omega-3 fatty acids. In the early 1970s Danish investigators observed surprisingly low frequencies of heart disease among indigenous populations in Greenland that typically ate fatty fish, seals, and whales. The researchers attributed the protective effect to the foods' content of omega-3 fatty acids. Some subsequent studies — but by no means all — confirm this idea.

Because large, fatty fish are likely to have accumulated methylmercury and other toxins through predation, however, eating them raises questions about the balance between benefits and risks. Understandably, the fish industry is eager to prove that the health benefits of omega-3s outweigh any risks from eating fish.

Even independent studies on omega-3 fats can be interpreted differently. In 2004 the National Oceanic and Atmospheric Administration — for fish, the agency equivalent to the USDA — asked the Institute of Medicine (IOM) to review studies of the benefits and risks of consuming seafood. The ensuing review of the research on heart disease risk illustrates the challenge such work poses for interpretation. 30

The IOM's October 2006 report concluded that eating seafood reduces the risk of heart disease but judged the studies too inconsistent to decide if omega-3 fats were responsible. In contrast, investigators from the Harvard School of Public Health published a much more positive report in the *Journal of the American Medical Association* that same month. Even modest consumption of fish omega-3s, they stated, would cut coronary deaths by 36 percent and total mortality by 17 percent, meaning that not eating fish would constitute a health risk.

Differences in interpretation explain how distinguished scientists could arrive at such different conclusions after considering the same studies. The two groups, for example, had conflicting views of earlier work published in March 2006 in the *British Medical Journal.* That study found no overall effect of omega-3s on heart disease risk or mortality, although a subset of the original studies displayed a 14 percent reduction in total mortality that did not reach statistical significance. The IOM team interpreted the "nonsignificant" result as evidence for the need for caution, whereas the Harvard group saw the data as consistent with studies reporting the benefits of omega-3s. When studies present inconsistent results, both interpretations are plausible. I favor caution in such situations, but not everyone agrees.

Because findings are inconsistent, so is dietary advice about eating fish. The American Heart Association recommends that adults eat fatty fish at least twice a week, but U.S. dietary guidelines say: "Limited evidence suggests an association between consumption of fatty acids in fish and reduced risks of mortality from cardiovascular disease for the general population . . . however, more research is needed." Whether or not fish uniquely protects against heart disease, seafood is a delicious source of many nutrients, and two small servings per week of the less predatory classes of fish are unlikely to cause harm.

Sodas and Obesity

Sugars and corn sweeteners account for a large fraction of the calories in many supermarket foods, and virtually all the calories in drinks — soft, sports, and juice — come from added sugars.

In a trend that correlates closely with rising rates of obesity, daily per 35 capita consumption of sweetened beverages has grown by about 200 calories since the early 1980s. Although common sense suggests that this increase might have something to do with weight gain, beverage makers argue that studies cannot prove that sugary drinks alone — independent of calories or other foods in the diet — boost the risk of obesity. The evidence, they say correctly, is circumstantial. But pediatricians often see obese children in their practices who consume more than 1,000 calories a day from sweetened drinks alone, and several studies indicate that children who habitually consume sugary beverages take in more calories and weigh more than those who do not.

Nevertheless, the effects of sweetened drinks on obesity continue to be subject to interpretation. In 2006, for example, a systematic review funded by independent sources found sweetened drinks to promote obesity in both children and adults. But a review that same year sponsored in part by a beverage trade association concluded that soft drinks have no special role in obesity. The industry-funded researchers criticized existing studies as being short-term and inconclusive, and pointed to studies finding that people lose weight when they substitute sweetened drinks for their usual meals.

These differences imply the need to scrutinize food industry sponsorship of research itself. Although many researchers are offended by suggestions that funding support might affect the way they design or interpret studies, systematic analyses say otherwise. In 2007 investigators classified studies of the effects of sweetened and other beverages on health according to who had sponsored them. Industry-supported studies were more likely to yield results favorable to the sponsor than those funded by independent sources. Even though scientists may not be able to prove that sweetened drinks cause obesity, it makes sense for anyone interested in losing weight to consume less of them.

The examples I have discussed illustrate why nutrition science seems so controversial. Without improved methods to ensure compliance with dietary regimens, research debates are likely to rage unabated. Opposing points of view and the focus of studies and food advertising on single nutrients rather than on dietary patterns continue to fuel these disputes. While we wait for investigators to find better ways to study nutrition and health, my approach — eat less, move more, eat a largely plant-based diet, and avoid eating too much junk food — makes sense and leaves you plenty of opportunity to enjoy your dinner.

Understanding the Text

1. What is nutrition science? Why is nutrition science "reductive"?
2. What nutritional principles do experts agree on, according to Nestle?
3. If the basic principles are not in dispute, why is there so much conflicting nutritional advice? How does Nestle suggest reconciling it?

Reflection and Response

4. Nestle explains that nutrition science is controversial. Why is it so difficult to conduct nutrition research, and what makes the results so controversial? Select three of her examples to illustrate your position.
5. Think about what you eat. What have you learned about your own overall nutrition from reading Nestle's essay? Are there changes you think you should make? Why or why not?

Making Connections

6. What possible connections exist between the flavor industry described by Eric Schlosser ("Why the Fries Taste Good," p. 20) and the nutrition research described by Nestle? How might Masanobu Fukuoka ("Living by Bread Alone," p. 71) analyze these connections?
7. Nestle served as a policy maker for the federal government nutrition guidelines. How do you think Nestle would interpret and evaluate the USDA's Food Pyramid in relation to the Food Plate guidelines (p. 132)? Which one do you think she would prefer and why?

8. Think about the story of nutrition in America that Nestle tells in relation to the argument David Freedman makes ("How Junk Food Can End Obesity," p. 139). How does Nestle's essay complicate the debate between Pollan and Freedman? How might they each use evidence presented by Nestle to support their views?

9. Messages regarding nutrition and dietary advice surround us, from stories in the media about cutting-edge studies to advertising and packaging labels (such as the FDA's proposed nutrition label, p. 133). Find several pieces of nutrition advice that employ nutrition science as evidence for why consumers should adopt the advice or buy the product. How do they use nutrition science? What would Nestle, Dhruv Khullar ("Why Shame Won't Stop Obesity," p. 135), and Wendell Berry ("The Pleasures of Eating," p. 47) say about the advice? What do you think of the advice? Would you follow it?

The Pleasures of Eating

Wendell Berry

Wendell Berry has spent his life as a poet and a farmer, drawing on his knowledge of and concern for the land, flora, and fauna in his more than thirty books of essays, poetry, and fiction. A prolific writer and man of letters, he uses his writing as a platform for speaking out about degradation of the land, environmental awareness, and conservation. He is well known for his essays on sustainable agriculture and food, many of which are collected in *Bringing It to the Table: On Farming and Food*, published in 2009. His many awards and lectures demonstrate his ability to connect with his audiences in meaningful ways. In this essay, Berry argues that we should think of eating as an "agricultural act" instead of thinking of food as an "agricultural product." He hopes that this will lead to a greater awareness of the complex relationships we have with our food and our responsibilities in its production.

M any times, after I have finished a lecture on the decline of American farming and rural life, someone in the audience has asked, "What can city people do?"

"Eat responsibly," I have usually answered. Of course, I have tried to explain what I mean by that, but afterwards I have invariably felt there was more to be said than I had been able to say. Now I would like to attempt a better explanation.

I begin with the proposition that eating is an agricultural act. Eating ends the annual drama of the food economy that begins with planting and birth. Most eaters, however, are no longer aware that this is true. They think of food as an agricultural product, perhaps, but they do not think of themselves as participants in agriculture. They think of themselves as "consumers." If they think beyond that, they recognize that they are passive consumers. They buy what they want — or what they have been persuaded to want — within the limits of what they can get. They pay, mostly without protest, what they are charged. And they mostly ignore certain critical questions about the quality and the cost of what they are sold: How fresh is it? How pure or clean is it, how free of dangerous chemicals? How far was it transported, and what did transportation add to the cost? How much did manufacturing or packaging or advertising add to the cost? When the food product has been manufactured or "processed" or "precooked," how has that affected its quality or price or nutritional value?

Most urban shoppers would tell you that food is produced on farms. But most of them do not know what farms, or what kinds of farms, or where the farms are, or what knowledge or skills are involved in farming. They apparently have little doubt that farms will continue to produce, but they do not know how or over what obstacles. For them, then, food is pretty much an abstract idea — something they do not know or imagine — until it appears on the grocery shelf or on the table.

The specialization of production induces specialization of consump- 5 tion. Patrons of the entertainment industry, for example, entertain themselves less and less and have become more and more passively dependent on commercial suppliers. This is certainly true also of patrons of the food industry, who have tended more and more to be mere consumers — passive, uncritical, and dependent. Indeed, this sort of consumption may be said to be one of the chief goals of industrial production. The food industrialists have by now persuaded millions of consumers to prefer food that is already prepared. They will grow, deliver, and cook your food for you and (just like your mother) beg you to eat it. That they do not yet offer to insert it, prechewed, into our mouth is only because they have found no profitable way to do so. We may rest assured that they would be glad to find such a way. The ideal industrial food consumer would be strapped to a table with a tube running from the food factory directly into his or her stomach.

Perhaps I exaggerate, but not by much. The industrial eater is, in fact, one who does not know that eating is an agricultural act, who no longer knows or imagines the connections between eating and the land, and who is therefore necessarily passive and uncritical — in short, a victim. When food, in the minds of eaters, is no longer associated with farming and with the land, then the eaters are suffering a kind of cultural amnesia that is misleading and dangerous. The current version of the "dream home" of the future involves "effortless" shopping from a list of available goods on a television monitor and heating precooked food by remote control. Of course, this implies and depends on a perfect ignorance of the history of the food that is consumed. It requires that the citizenry should give up their hereditary and sensible aversion to buying a pig in a poke. It wishes to make the selling of pigs in pokes an honorable and glamorous activity. The dreams in this dream home will perforce know nothing about the kind or quality of this food, or where it came from, or how it was produced and prepared, or what ingredients, additives, and residues it contains — unless, that is, the dreamer undertakes a close and constant study of the food industry, in which case he or she might as well wake up and play an active and responsible part in the economy of food.

There is, then, a politics of food that, like any politics, involves our freedom. We still (sometimes) remember that we cannot be free if our minds and voices are controlled by someone else. But we have neglected to understand that we cannot be free if our food and its sources are controlled by someone else. The condition of the passive consumer of food is not a democratic condition. One reason to eat responsibly is to live free.

But if there is a food politics, there are also a food esthetics and a food ethics, neither of which is dissociated from politics. Like industrial sex, industrial eating has become a degraded, poor, and paltry thing. Our kitchens and other eating places more and more resemble filling stations, as our homes more and more resemble motels. "Life is not very interesting," we seem to have decided. "Let its satisfactions be minimal, perfunctory, and fast." We hurry through our meals to go to work and hurry through our work in order to "recreate" ourselves in the evenings and on weekends and vacations. And then we hurry, with the greatest possible speed and noise and violence, through our recreation — for what? To eat the billionth hamburger at some fast-food joint hellbent on increasing the "quality" of our life? And all this is carried out in a remarkable obliviousness to the causes and effects, the possibilities and the purposes, of the life of the body in this world.

One will find this obliviousness represented in virgin purity in the advertisements of the food industry, in which food wears as much makeup as the actors. If one gained one's whole knowledge of food from these advertisements (as some presumably do), one would not know that the various edibles were ever living creatures, or that they all come from the soil, or that they were produced by work. The passive American consumer, sitting down to a meal of pre-prepared or fast food, confronts a platter covered with inert, anonymous substances that have been processed, dyed, breaded, sauced, gravied, ground, pulped, strained, blended, prettified, and sanitized beyond resemblance to any part of any creature that ever lived. The products of nature and agriculture have been made, to all appearances, the products of industry. Both eater and eaten are thus in exile from biological reality. And the result is a kind of solitude, unprecedented in human experience, in which the eater may think of eating as, first, a purely commercial transaction between him and a supplier and then as a purely appetitive transaction between him and his food.

And this peculiar specialization of the act of eating is, again, of obvi-   10
ous benefit to the food industry, which has good reasons to obscure the connection between food and farming. It would not do for the consumer to know that the hamburger she is eating came from a steer who spent much of his life standing deep in his own excrement in a feedlot, helping to pollute the local streams, or that the calf that yielded the veal cutlet on her plate spent its life in a box in which it did not have room to

turn around. And, though her sympathy for the slaw might be less tender, she should not be encouraged to meditate on the hygienic and biological implications of mile-square fields of cabbage, for vegetables grown in huge monocultures are dependent on toxic chemicals — just as animals in close confinements are dependent on antibiotics and other drugs.

The consumer, that is to say, must be kept from discovering that, in the food industry — as in any other industry — the overriding concerns are not quality and health, but volume and price. For decades now the entire industrial food economy, from the large farms and feedlots to the chains of supermarkets and fast-food restaurants, has been obsessed with volume. It has relentlessly increased scale in order to increase volume in order (probably) to reduce costs. But as scale increases, diversity declines; as diversity declines, so does health; as health declines, the dependence on drugs and chemicals necessarily increases. As capital replaces labor, it does so by substituting machines, drugs, and chemicals for human workers and for the natural health and fertility of the soil. The food is produced by any means or any shortcuts that will increase profits. And the business of the cosmeticians° of advertising is to persuade the consumer that food so produced is good, tasty, healthful, and a guarantee of marital fidelity and long life.

> "Eaters . . . must understand that eating takes place inescapably in the world, that it is inescapably an agricultural act, and how we eat determines, to a considerable extent, how the world is used."

It is possible, then, to be liberated from the husbandry and wifery of the old household food economy. But one can be thus liberated only by entering a trap (unless one sees ignorance and helplessness as the signs of privilege, as many people apparently do). The trap is the ideal of industrialism: a walled city surrounded by valves that let merchandise in but no consciousness out. How does one escape this trap? Only voluntarily, the same way that one went in: by restoring one's consciousness of what is involved in eating; by reclaiming responsibility for one's own part in the food economy. One might begin with the illuminating principle of Sir Albert Howard's, that we should understand "the whole problem of health in soil, plant, animal, and man as one great subject." Eaters, that is, must understand that eating takes place inescapably in the world, that it is inescapably an agricultural act, and how we eat determines, to a considerable extent, how the world is used. This is a simple way of describing

cosmetician: someone who sells or applies makeup.

a relationship that is inexpressibly complex. To eat responsibly is to understand and enact, so far as we can, this complex relationship. What can one do? Here is a list, probably not definitive:

1. Participate in food production to the extent that you can. If you have a yard or even just a porch box or a pot in a sunny window, grow something to eat in it. Make a little compost of your kitchen scraps and use it for fertilizer. Only by growing some food for yourself can you become acquainted with the beautiful energy cycle that revolves from soil to seed to flower to fruit to food to offal° to decay, and around again. You will be fully responsible for any food that you grow for yourself, and you will know all about it. You will appreciate it fully, having known it all its life.

2. Prepare your own food. This means reviving in your own mind and life the arts of kitchen and household. This should enable you to eat more cheaply, and it will give you a measure of "quality control": you will have some reliable knowledge of what has been added to the food you eat.

3. Learn the origins of the food you buy, and buy the food that is produced closest to your home. The idea that every locality should be, as much as possible, the source of its own food makes several kinds of sense. The locally produced food supply is the most secure, freshest, and the easiest for local consumers to know about and to influence.

4. Whenever possible, deal directly with a local farmer, gardener, or orchardist. All the reasons listed for the previous suggestion apply here. In addition, by such dealing you eliminate the whole pack of merchants, transporters, processors, packagers, and advertisers who thrive at the expense of both producers and consumers.

5. Learn, in self-defense, as much as you can of the economy and technology of industrial food production. What is added to the food that is not food, and what do you pay for those additions?

6. Learn what is involved in the best farming and gardening.

7. Learn as much as you can, by direct observation and experience if possible, of the life histories of the food species.

The last suggestion seems particularly important to me. Many people are now as much estranged from the lives of domestic plants and animals (except for flowers and dogs and cats) as they are from the lives of the

---

offal: scrap waste.

wild ones. This is regrettable, for these domestic creatures are in diverse ways attractive; there is such pleasure in knowing them, too.

It follows that there is great displeasure in knowing about a food economy that degrades and abuses those arts and those plants and animals and the soil from which they come. For anyone who does know something of the modern history of food, eating away from home can be a chore. My own inclination is to eat seafood instead of red meat or poultry when I am traveling. Though I am by no means a vegetarian, I dislike the thought that some animal has been made miserable in order to feed me. If I am going to eat meat, I want it to be from an animal that has lived a pleasant, uncrowded life outdoors, on bountiful pasture, with good water nearby and trees for shade. And I am getting almost as fussy about food plants. I like to eat vegetables and fruits that I know have lived happily and healthily in good soil, not the products of the huge, bechemicaled factory-fields that I have seen, for example, in the Central Valley of California. The industrial farm is said to have been patterned on the factory production line. In practice, it looks more like a concentration camp.

The pleasure of eating should be an extensive pleasure, not that of the 15 mere gourmet. People who know the garden in which their vegetables have grown and know that the garden is healthy and remember the beauty of the growing plants, perhaps in the dewy first light of morning when gardens are at their best. Such a memory involves itself with the food and is one of the pleasures of eating. The knowledge of the good health of the garden relieves and frees and comforts the eater. The same goes for eating meat. The thought of the good pasture and of the calf contentedly grazing flavors the steak. Some, I know, will think of it as bloodthirsty or worse to eat a fellow creature you have known all its life. On the contrary, I think it means that you eat with understanding and with gratitude. A significant part of the pleasure of eating is in one's accurate consciousness of the lives and the world from which food comes. The pleasure of eating, then, may be the best available standard of our health. And this pleasure, I think, is pretty fully available to the urban consumer who will make the necessary effort.

I mentioned earlier the politics, esthetics, and ethics of food. But to speak of the pleasure of eating is to go beyond those categories. Eating with the fullest pleasure — pleasure, that is, that does not depend on ignorance — is perhaps the profoundest enactment of our connection with the world. In this pleasure we experience and celebrate our dependence and our gratitude, for we are living from mystery, from creatures we did not make and powers we cannot comprehend. When I think of the meaning of food, I always remember these lines by the poet William Carlos Williams, which seem to me merely honest:

> There is nothing to eat,
> seek it where you will,
> but the body of the Lord.
> The blessed plants
> and the sea, yield it
> to the imagination intact.

Understanding the Text

1. What is an "industrial eater"?
2. Why does Berry think it is important to understand the connection between eating and the land?
3. According to Berry, how does the separation of food from farming and agriculture benefit the food industry?

Reflection and Response

4. Berry wrote this essay in 1989. Do you notice substantial changes from what he describes? Do you think he would be pleased with how farming and agricultural practices have changed since then? Why or why not?
5. Berry suggests that freedom depends on eating responsibly and understanding our place in the agricultural economy. Why does he think eating responsibly is a necessary condition of democracy? Explain your answer. Do you agree? Why or why not?
6. Why do you think Berry includes the poem by William Carlos Williams at the end of his essay? What does it add? How does it connect to the larger purpose of Berry's essay?

Making Connections

7. What is the "pleasure of eating," according to Berry? Compare the way Berry describes the purpose of food to the ways Jill McCorkle ("Her Chee-to Heart," p. 31) and Jean Anthelme Brillat-Savarin ("The Physiology of Taste," p. 68) describe it.
8. Berry argues that eating is necessarily an "agricultural act" and makes seven suggestions for responsible eating. Compare them to Michael Pollan's rules for choosing foods to eat ("Eat Food: Food Defined," p. 10). What values do they share? Are they rules or suggestions you have tried or would consider trying? Which ones? What might you gain (or lose)? What might you learn about your food (and yourself)?

9. Berry argues that there is a "food politics" that is impossible to separate from a "food esthetics" and a "food ethics." What is a "food politics"? Think about the community in which you live. What kinds of local food movements, organizations, programs, or activities exist that could be identified as political in nature (overtly or subtly)? Research at least one of them, and use the views of Berry, Eliot Coleman ("Real Food, Real Farming," p. 266), and Bill McKibben ("The Only Way to Have a Cow," p. 229) to analyze its potential for contributing to awareness of the public's relationships with and responsibilities to food production.

The Birth of the Modern Diet

Rachel Laudan

Rachel Laudan grew up on a farm before studying history and philosophy of science at the University of London, where she received her PhD. After a lengthy academic career of writing and teaching on the history and foundations of modern science, Laudan turned her focus to the history of food. She won the Sophie Coe Prize of the Oxford Symposium on Food and Cookery for an extended essay on which this article is based. She also won awards for her books *The Food of Paradise: Exploring Hawaii's Culinary Heritage* (1996) and *Cuisine and Empire: Cooking in World History* (2013). Her recent works examine how politics, economics, religion, and technology have led humans to create and recreate their varied relationships with food. This selection offers a glimpse into the history of the modern diet by tracing seventeenth-century notions about food and nutrition.

Were we to attend a sixteenth-century court banquet in France or England, the food would seem strange indeed to anyone accustomed to traditional Western cooking. Dishes might include blancmange°, a thick puree of rice and chicken moistened with milk from ground almonds and then sprinkled with sugar and fried pork fat. Roast suckling pig might be accompanied by a cameline sauce, a side dish made of sour grape juice thickened with bread crumbs, ground raisins and crushed almonds and spiced with cinnamon and cloves. Other offerings might include fava beans cooked in meat stock and sprinkled with chopped mint — or quince° paste, a sweetmeat of quinces and sugar or honey. To wash it all down, we would probably drink hypocras, a mulled red wine seasoned with ground ginger, cinnamon, cloves and sugar.

Fast-forward 100 years, however, and the food would be reassuringly familiar. On the table in the late 1600s might be beef bouillon°, oysters, anchovies and a roast turkey with gravy. These dishes might be served alongside mushrooms cooked in cream and parsley, a green salad with a dressing of oil and vinegar, fresh pears, lemon sherbet, and even cool, sparkling white wine.

Before 1650, the elite classes throughout the Islamic and Christian worlds from Delhi to London shared pretty much the same diet: thick purees, lots of spices, sweet and sour sauces, cooked vegetables, warmed

---

blancmange: a sweet French dessert usually made will milk and sugar, flavored with almonds, thickened with gelatin, set in a mold, and served cold.
quince: a yellow fruit that is usually used for making jelly.
bouillon: a clear, flavorful broth used to make soups or sauces.

wine, and of course bread — white, raised breads in the West and mainly flat breads in northern India and the Middle East. Sugar was ubiquitous as a seasoning in savory dishes.

But in the middle of the seventeenth century, the northern European diet began to change. This new regimen relied on fewer spices, based its sauces on fats such as butter and olive oil, and incorporated raw fruits and vegetables. Sugar appeared only at the end of a meal.

What happened? Economic considerations cannot account for the dif- 5
ference: for the upper class, money was no object. For the poor, both meals would have been far out of reach. Well into the nineteenth century, those in the lower economic classes subsisted on vegetable soups and gruels with bread or porridge. Novel foodstuffs from the New World do not explain the shift in diet either, because with the exception of turkey, the dishes at the second banquet depended not on new ingredients but on new uses of long familiar ones. The clue to this transformation in eating habits between the sixteenth and seventeenth centuries must be sought instead in evolving ideas about diet and nutrition — which is to say, in the history of chemistry and medicine.

Medicine in the Sixteenth Century

Eating healthy food was extremely important to people of earlier eras, perhaps even more so than it is today. Activity in the kitchen mattered so much because physicians had so few other options. To avoid resorting to unpleasant therapies such as purging or bloodletting, doctors carefully monitored their wealthy patients' daily habits: their emotional state, for example, or how much sleep, exercise and fresh air they got. Most crucially, doctors advised their patients on the food and drink they should consume.

"Eating healthy food was extremely important to people of earlier eras, perhaps even more so than it is today. Activity in the kitchen mattered so much because physicians had so few other options."

Every court had a bevy of physicians who were schooled in the physiology of human digestion, the nutritive properties of foodstuffs and the nature of a healthy meal. Offering dietary advice to their affluent patrons was a major part of their work.

The actual task of transforming abstract dietary theory into dishes appropriate for the courtly table fell to the master cooks, as executive chefs were then called. In a popular medical text written in 1547, *Breviary of Health*, author Andrew Boorde noted, "A good coke is halfe a physycyon."

Sixteenth-century cooks, physicians and their patrons shared a common notion of diet and nutrition that can be traced to classical antiquity. First formulated around 400 B.C. as part of the Hippocratic Collection, the ideas were systematized by the great Roman doctor Galen in the early second century A.D. After the collapse of classical civilization, Islamic intellectuals eagerly took up these beliefs (along with many other scientific theories of the ancient world). By the twelfth century, European scholars had translated key Arabic texts into Latin; teachers at the major medical schools, such as Montpellier in the south of France, relied extensively on these texts. In the late fifteenth century, experts began translating newly discovered Greek manuscripts as well as retranslating known texts.

These documents formed the basis of a host of popular manuals and 10 mnemonic jingles. Particularly well liked were the numerous vernacular variations on a Latin poem, the *Regimen Sanitatis Salernitanum*, which was apparently composed around the end of the eleventh century but still widely circulated in the sixteenth and even seventeenth centuries:

> *Peaches, apples, pears, milk,*
> *cheese, and salted meat,*
> *Deer, hare, goat, and veal,*
> *These engender black bile and are*
> *enemies of the sick*

The prevailing dietary wisdom of the sixteenth century, as presented in these medical guidebooks, relied on two assumptions. The first axiom was that the process of digesting foods was actually a form of cooking. Indeed, cooking stood as the basic metaphor for the systems that sustained all life. Seeds were "cooked" into plants; when the plants appeared above the ground, the heat of the sun cooked them into ripe fruits and grains. If humans gathered these foodstuffs, they could cook them further to create edible dishes. Finally, the internal heat of the body turned the food into blood. The body then expelled as feces what was not digestible. Excrement joined putrefying dead animals and plants to begin the life cycle again.

The second assumption underlying sixteenth-century medical advice was that eating a suitably balanced diet helped to maintain a proper equilibrium of bodily fluids. Doctors and chefs of the time believed that four fluids, or humors, circulated in the body: blood, phlegm, yellow bile and black bile. These humors corresponded to the four Aristotelian° elements — air, water, fire and earth. Blood, being hot and moist, was analogous to air. Phlegm was cold and moist and therefore resembled water. Yellow bile

---

Aristotelian: relating to the philosophy of the Greek philosopher Artistotle.

was hot and dry, similar to fire, whereas black bile was cold, dry and thus connected to earth.

In this theory, a human body in perfect health was slightly warm and slightly moist, although in practice the exact balance varied from individual to individual, depending on variables such as age, sex and geographic location. Older people were thought to be colder and drier than younger ones; menstruating women colder and wetter than men; southern Europeans hot-blooded compared with their neighbors to the north.

The perfect meal, like the perfect human temperament, was thought to be slightly warm and slightly moist. But combinations away from this center could be used as mild dietary correctives to warm and moisten the elderly, dry out the moister sex, and calm down the southerner or perk up the northerner.

The master cook, then, had the challenge of selecting and preparing   15 meals adjusted to the temperament of the eater. The properties of any given food item were common knowledge: pepper, for example, was hot and dry in the third degree, and vinegar was cold and wet in the second degree. Root vegetables such as turnips were by nature earthy — dry and cold — and thus better left to peasants. If chefs should decide to prepare them, however, they would make sure to stew them to add warmth and moisture. In contrast, chard, marrow (a watery, squashlike vegetable) and especially onions were very wet and had to be fried.

Certain foods were deemed completely unacceptable: Guy Patin, a doctor at the University of Paris and author of *Treatise on the Conservation of Health*, published in 1632, cautioned that mushrooms, being cold and wet, should be avoided entirely. Melons and other fresh fruit were not much better, being very moist and liable to putrefy. In general, though, cooking not only helped achieve proper culinary balance — dry foods were boiled, wet foods fried or roasted — but the process also, in effect, partially predigested the foods, thus making them easier for the body to assimilate.

According to these medical theories, the blancmange on our sixteenth-century table was close to perfect. The wise chef had combined chicken, rice and almond milk, all slightly warm and moist, and the sugar on top — also warm and moist — was the crowning touch. The naturally moist suckling pig had been roasted. The cameline sauce balanced cool, moist vinegar with the warmth of raisins and hot, dry spices. The chef was careful not to serve quinces and grapes fresh, and hence dangerously cold and moist, but instead offered them dried or cooked with added sugar (in the quince paste).

Health experts approved of wine served with a meal, viewing it as an ideal nutrient — provided, of course, that diners did not drink to excess.

The Book of Wine, written around 1310, printed in 1478 and widely attributed to Arnald of Villanova (a leading medical writer and physician to King James II of Aragon), had only high praise for the beverage. Wine is not only good for flatulence and infertility, the book asserts, but it also "fortifies the brain and the natural strength . . . causes foods to be digested and produces good blood."

Even so, because red wine tended to be cold and dry, chefs often served it warm with added sugar and spices, creating hypocras. With these options before them, the members of the sixteenth-century court could rest assured that they were getting a healthy meal.

Seventeenth-Century Cooking

By the middle of the seventeenth century, however, physicians of a quite 20 different persuasion began to join the courts of northern Europe. These scholars derived their ideas from Paracelsus, an itinerant doctor from Germany who, in the 1520s, began to mock the structure of classical medicine. Paracelsus's abrasive personality and radical religious beliefs gave him a dreadful reputation, so few physicians admitted to this heritage. But acknowledged or not, the link was clear: these court doctors argued, as Paracelsus had, that the idea of a cosmic life cycle based on cooking and the Aristotelian elements was wrong and had to be revised.

Historians of science still debate the causes of this shift, but the technology of distillation seems to have contributed to it. As the practice became more important from the late Middle Ages on, chemists experimented with heating a great variety of natural substances, many of them edible, such as fennel, nutmeg and cloves. They noted that in every case the original material separated into three parts: a volatile, or "spirituous," fluid; an oily substance; and a solid residue.

Drawing on such observations, these chemists proposed three new elements in place of Aristotle's four: mercury, sulfur and salt. Although each of these is familiar to us today as a common element or compound, the early chemists used the terms to connote things quite unrelated to a specific liquid metal, yellow powder or white crystal. Mercury was considered to be the essence of the vaporous fluids, sulfur was the essence of the oily substances, and salt was the essence of all solids.

In such a scheme, salt dictated the taste and consistency of foods. Mercury was the source of smells and aromas. Sulfur, or oil, carried the properties of moistness and sweetness; it also bound together the other two, usually antagonistic, elements.

Physicians of this era also believed that human digestion involved fermentation rather than cooking, and they began to investigate the familiar yet mysterious process more closely. Because fermentation included gentle heat and the production of vapors, it seemed to resemble (or was possibly the same as) putrefaction°, distillation, and the interaction of acids and salts. Vapors, spirits or airs (soon to be dubbed "gases" by Dutch scientist and mystic Johannes Baptista van Helmont) excited chemists of the time, as they appeared to be the very essences of the substances from which they originated.

Several prominent physicians of the seventeenth century advocated this new understanding of digestion as a kind of fermentation, among them van Helmont, Franciscus Sylvius, a physician at the University of Leiden, and Thomas Willis, then the best-known doctor in England and a founding member of the Royal Society of London. According to this view, gastric juices, considered acid and sharp, acted on foods to turn them into a white, milky fluid, which then mixed with alkaline bile in the digestive tract. The mixture fermented and bubbled, producing a salty substance that the body could transform into blood and other fluids.

Like their sixteenth-century predecessors, these later physicians presented a cosmic cycle of life that reflected their view of digestion. Seeds became plants as a result of the "ferments of the earth," in the words of John Evelyn, a keen horticulturist who spoke before the Royal Society in 1675. Fermentation° turned grains and fruits into bread, beer and wine, which the digestive system could ferment further. Putrefaction of waste material started the cycle all over again.

"Vegetable putrefaction resembles very much Animal Digestion," wrote John Arbuthnot, member of the Royal Society and physician to Queen Anne, in a popular handbook on foodstuffs that appeared in 1732. The cosmos was still a kitchen but was now equipped with brewers' vats, and the human body held miniature copies of that equipment.

These changes in the understanding of the digestive process put seventeenth-century chefs on guard. Alert cooks seized the opportunity to establish their good reputations by thinking up dishes that were healthful by the new standards — and, of course, also tasty. For instance, chefs welcomed oysters, anchovies, green vegetables, mushrooms and fruits because they fermented so readily and thus did not need complicated preparation in the kitchen to be predigested.

As cooks began to incorporate fresh produce into many of their dishes, horticulture and botanical gardens became the rage. Scientists and scholarly gentlemen exchanged seeds, translated gardening books and developed

---

putrefaction: decomposition of organic matter resulting in decay and characterized by a foul smell.
fermentation: a chemical change that turns sugar or another carbohydrate into an alcohol or acid.

hothouses for tender vegetables. They began cultivating mushrooms on beds of putrefying dung. In England, the well-to-do put even such previously distasteful dishes as eggplant on their tables.

The First Restaurants

Substances rich in oil, such as butter, lard or olive oil, all with the useful 30 sulfurous property of binding the components of salt and mercury, became the basis of a variety of sauces. They were combined with ingredients containing the element salt — such as flour and table salt — and other ingredients high in mercury — such as vinegar, wine, spirits, and essences of meat or fish. The first recipe for roux, a combination of fat and flour moistened with wine or stock to produce a single delicious taste, appeared in the cookbook *The French Chef,* written in 1651 by François Pierre de la Varenne.

Salads, which combined oil-based dressings and readily digestible greens, also became quite fashionable. Evelyn, for example, promoted vinaigrette salad dressing in his *Acetaria: A Discourse of Sallets,* published in 1699.

As fruits, herbs and vegetables assumed a more prominent place in the main meal, sugar, formerly lauded as a panacea, came in for rough treatment at the hands of the chemical physicians. Some wanted to banish it altogether.

"Under its whiteness," hissed Joseph Duchesne, physician to King Henry IV of France, in 1606, "sugar hides a great blackness" — doctors knew that it blackened the teeth — "and under its sweetness a very great acrimony, such that it equals agua fortis [nitric acid]."

British physician Willis, who had noticed the sugary urine of patients suffering from what doctors later termed diabetes, concurred: "Sugar, distilled by itself, yields a liquor scarcely inferior to aqua fortis. . . . Therefore it is very probable that mixing sugar with almost all our food, and taken to so great a degree, from its daily use, renders the blood and humours salt and acrid; and consequently scorbutic [tainted by scurvy]."

The moral was clear: sugar was dangerous, perhaps even a poison. 35 Such dire warnings would surely have given any chef second thoughts about sprinkling it over the main dishes of the meal, leaving the diner no choice but to eat it. Thus, sugar moved to the periphery of the menu, served only in desserts, which were prepared in a separate kitchen. Sugar became the subject of a distinct genre of books dedicated to its decorative, not medical, properties.

Physicians regarded alcoholic spirits and other distilled essences as useful medicines. They and their patients, though, considered a cordial° or an

---

cordial: a sweet liqueur.

THE THREE PRINCIPLES by which foods were classified in the seventeenth century
The Mercury Principle Makes food volatile or gaseous, gives it smell (vinegar, wine, meat essence)
The Sulfur Principle Makes food oily, binds foods high in salt and mercury (oil, butter, lard)
The Salt Principle Gives food taste (salt, flour)

eau-de-vie° fine for the occasional sip but too strong for everyday use. Less powerful extractions, made from such nutritive foods as meats that had been concentrated by boiling or fermenting, could be more easily digested.

Sometimes the concentrated goodness of a food even showed up as desirable gas bubbles that nourished the brain. Sparkling mineral waters gained immense popularity as spas opened across Europe. At the table, hot and spicy hypocras yielded to cool wines, even to sparkling champagne, which was most likely first produced in the late seventeenth century.

Chefs made essences of meat or fish from the "musculous Flesh, which is of all [parts of the animal] the most nourishing, that which produces the best juice." They then served this healthy fare in the form of stock, bouillon or jellies made from these liquids. Land animals, they believed, had more nutritious juices than fish or birds did — and of the land animals, beef produced the most restorative extracts.

By 1733 Vincent la Chapelle, a French chef who worked for the earl of Chesterfield in England, had assembled a variety of recipes for delicately garnished beef bouillon in his book *The Modern Cook*, which was quickly translated into French. Before long, entrepreneurs saw an opportunity in this new cuisine, selling "restaurants" — which in French means "restoratives" — to those who could not afford their own chefs.

Eventually Europe's middle classes emulated the aristocracy, develop-   40
ing a taste not only for restaurants but for all the new cuisine. Such foods seemed to offer a certain refinement, not just in the sense of good taste but also in a chemical sense, as the meals represented the most enhanced form of food. As the authors of the gastronomic treatise *The Gifts of Comus*, published in Paris in 1739, put it: "Modern cookery is a kind of chemistry. The cook's science consists today of analyzing, digesting, and

eau-de-vie: a clear brandy made from fermented juice.

extracting the quintessence of foods, drawing out the light and nourishing juices, mingling and blending them together."

This new diet gradually spread across Europe as it simultaneously made its way down the social scale. By the mid- to late nineteenth century it had become the standard for the English- and French-speaking worlds in Europe, the U.S., Canada and Australia. Other regions, however — the Islamic world and Spanish-speaking parts of the Americas, for example — remained isolated from the chemistry derived from Paracelsus and adopted neither the dietary theory nor the resultant cuisine. (The modern curries of India and moles of Mexico, for instance, resemble the cuisine of pre-Paracelsian northern Europe.)

The Western cuisine born in the seventeenth century long outlived the dietary theory that inspired it. By the end of the eighteenth century, chemists and physicians had embarked on the research that was to lead to the modern theories of the role of calories, carbohydrates, proteins, vitamins and minerals in the biochemical processes of digestion. Notably, during the nineteenth and early twentieth centuries, when most of these studies were carried out, nutritionists focused on developing a cheap but adequate diet for factory workers, soldiers and other less affluent people. The shift of emphasis in the medical community from the rich to the poor, though, meant that chefs catering to the well-heeled continued to develop Western cuisine along the lines established in the seventeenth century.

In the last third of the twentieth century, when everyone in the West could afford the cuisine formerly restricted to the wealthy, many became concerned about its dietary foundations. Although they gave fresh fruits and vegetables high marks, they worried about the centrality of fat in sauces such as espagnole, béchamel and more homely gravy. As a result, those sauces have waned in importance, their place taken by other ways of adding flavor such as rubs of herbs and spices and tomato sauce.

Meanwhile sugar has again fallen from favor, derided as little more than "empty" calories. Once more, cooks are shifting to conform to the latest thinking in physiology and nutrition.

Understanding the Text

1. What was the relationship between nutrition and medicine in the sixteenth century?

2. In the sixteenth century, what was the perfect meal?

3. Describe the difference between Aristotle's four elements and those proposed by seventeenth-century chemists to replace them.

Reflection and Response

4. Why do you think physicians and chemists of earlier eras relied on analogies like fermentation and cooking to describe digestion?

5. Compare the similarities and differences between seventeenth-century perceptions of salt and our modern-day conception of salt. Why do you think these differences exist?

6. Analyze the shift in thinking about sugar that occurred in the seventeenth century. How do earlier views of sugar compare to views we hold today?

Making Connections

7. Laudan explains that healthy eating "was extremely important to people of earlier eras, perhaps even more so than it is today. Activity in the kitchen mattered so much because physicians had so few other options" (par. 6). Explain how Laudan supports this idea. Then connect it to Marion Nestle's ("Eating Made Simple," p. 37) view of the relationship between health, nutrition, and food choices. How would Nestle view the advice of physicians and scientists from the sixteenth and seventeenth centuries? According to Nestle, has the purpose of food changed, and if so, how?

8. Laudan argues that "sugar has again fallen from favor, derided as little more than 'empty' calories" (par. 44). Select two other authors in this book who offer evidence that would support or refute this, and analyze their positions in relation to Laudan's claim. How do the authors support their positions? Do you find their evidence and reasoning convincing? Why or why not?

9. Compare Michael Pollan's advice ("Eat Food: Food Defined," p. 10) for eating to the advice of physicians and scientists of earlier eras. Research examples of eating advice, and find at least one more expert who offers a different perspective than these. Make a presentation that explains the various kinds of advice and offers an analysis of their similarities and differences. Conclude your analysis by arguing for which advice you think is most sound and why. Be sure to consider various ways of presenting your ideas, and select the one that you think will be most effective.

2

If You Are
What You Eat,
Who Are You?

We eat food to stay alive, of course. Yet, while food provides the calories and nutrients we need to maintain our bodies, sustenance is far from the only reason we eat. What we eat reflects aspects of who we are, as the selections in this chapter — by a gastronome, linguist, economist, food writer, urban farmer, food justice advocate, science writer, and farmer-turned-philosopher — show.

We have all heard the aphorism "You are what you eat." But we seldom stop to think about what it really means. Is it the notion that to be healthy, we need to eat healthy, nutritious food? Or is there a deeper, more complex meaning? How does what we eat reflect and shape our identities — who we are and how we are perceived by others?

What you eat and why you eat can vary greatly depending on your position in society, your goals and values, your culture and country of origin, and your spiritual and political beliefs. Eating with family and friends — sharing meals while sharing company and conversation — is a custom worldwide and reflects values of community and belonging (and, implicitly, privilege or exclusion). Particular foods also hold traditional places in the daily lives of those who prepare and consume them. While we eat for health, pleasure, and social purposes, we also communicate something about who we are through our food choices and preferences.

The selections in this chapter examine the complex relationships among food, culture, language, and identity from various academic and popular perspectives. Brillat-Savarin's aphorisms (short, witty observations) on the physiology of taste offer suggestions for maximizing the pleasures of eating and displaying proper food etiquette that contrast Masanobu Fukuoka's prescription for a diet that can nourish bodies and souls. While Erica Strauss demonstrates that what makes food "good" or "authentic" is deeply individual and personal, Daniel Jurafsky explains our relationships to food via linguistics — by looking at the names of foods and how they reflect cultural aspects of eating. Lily Wong describes her food choices

photo: Bhaskar Dutta/Getty Images

as a window into aspects of her Asian-American cultural identity, while Questlove, in conversation with an accomplished chef, explores the complex relationships among culture, food, race, and identity. Brian Wansink and Collin Payne look at how classic recipes have changed over time, reflecting on what this says about our culture's changing values — and waistlines. And Mary Roach looks to linguistics, history, and science to help us see just how complicated — and, at times, funny — our relationships with the foods we eat are.

Taken together, these authors complicate the view of food as simply sustenance and draw attention to the myriad ways food might be said to nourish us. Defining food inevitably requires us to consider how our food defines us. Roach encourages us to recognize that we come from the same environment and are made of the same matter (and organs!) as our food. We are, very literally, what we eat. As you read this chapter, think about the various ways you choose your foods and what your food choices say about who you are.

The Physiology of Taste

Jean Anthelme Brillat-Savarin

Jean Anthelme Brillat-Savarin (1755–1826) lived in France during the French Revolution and is said to have barely escaped with his life during the Reign of Terror. He traveled through Europe and to the United States before returning to France, where he served as a judge. He was educated as a lawyer, played and taught violin, and studied chemistry and medicine. While he wrote extensively about the law and political economy, he is now best remembered for witty meditations about the pleasure of food and the appropriate way to enjoy it, and for a kind of cheese and a pastry named for him. His famous *The Physiology of Taste* (from which this selection comes) was first published in 1825, translated into English in 1884, and has remained in print since it first appeared. Brillat-Savarin published the work anonymously and at his own expense after spending twenty-five years writing it. In it, he offers us aphorisms that demonstrate how closely tied to culture our food preferences, habits—even prejudices—are.

Aphorisms of the Professor

To Serve as Prolegomena° to His Work and Eternal Basis to the Science

I. The universe would be nothing were it not for life and all that lives must be fed.

II. Animals fill themselves; man eats. The man of mind alone knows how to eat.

III. The destiny of nations depends on the manner in which they are fed.

IV. Tell me what kind of food you eat, and I will tell you what kind of man you are.

V. The Creator, when he obliges man to eat, invites him to do so by appetite, and rewards him by pleasure.

VI. Gourmandise° is an act of our judgment, in obedience to which, we grant a preference to things which are agreeable, over those which have not that quality.

prolegomena: opening remarks; an introduction to a critical essay or discussion.
gourmandise: from French, appreciation of good food and drink.

VII. The pleasure of the table belongs to all ages, to all conditions, to all countries, and to all eras; it mingles with all other pleasures, and remains at last to console us for their departure.

VIII. The table is the only place where one does not suffer, from ennui° during the first hour.

IX. The discovery of a new dish confers more happiness on humanity, than the discovery of a new star.

X. Those persons who suffer from indigestion, or who become drunk, are utterly ignorant of the true principles of eating and drinking.

XI. The order of food is from the most substantial to the lightest.

XII. The order of drinking is from the mildest to the most foamy and perfumed.

XIII. To say that we should not change our drinks is a heresy; the tongue becomes saturated, and after the third glass yields but an obtuse sensation.

XIV. A dessert without cheese is like a beautiful woman who has lost an eye.

XV. A cook may be taught, but a man who can roast, is born with the faculty.

XVI. The most indispensable quality of a good cook is promptness. It should also be that of the guests.

XVII. To wait too long for a dilatory guest, shows disrespect to those who are punctual.

XVIII. He who receives friends and pays no attention to the repast prepared for them, is not fit to have friends.

XIX. The mistress of the house should always be certain that the coffee be excellent; the master that his liquors be of the first quality.

XX. To invite a person to your house is to take charge of his happiness as long as he be beneath your roof.

---

ennui: feeling of dissatisfaction, lack of enthusiasm or interest.

Understanding the Text

1. What is an aphorism?
2. What is the "physiology of taste"?
3. What does Brillat-Savarin mean in Aphorism XVIII when he writes, "He who receives friends and pays no attention to the repast prepared for them, is not fit to have friends"?

Reflection and Response

4. Why do you think Brillat-Savarin decided to develop his explanation of "the physiology of taste" with a list of aphorisms? Would his thoughts have been more effective in a different form — say, told as short fiction stories?
5. What do the aphorisms say about the social customs of the time in which Brillat-Savarin was living and writing? What does Brillat-Savarin suggest about the relationship between food and culture? Use at least two of the aphorisms to support and develop your response.
6. Select an aphorism that you have heard before — or one that suggests a sentiment similar to a saying that you have heard before. Where and when did you hear it? How did you interpret it? What does it suggest about the purpose of food that you think is important? Explain what that purpose is and why it is important in your own culture.

Making Connections

7. Aphorism IV ("Tell me what kind of food you eat, and I will tell you what kind of man you are.") suggests a relationship between food and identity. Use this aphorism to analyze the essays by Jill McCorkle ("Her Chee-to Heart," p. 31), Erica Strauss ("Zombies vs. The Joy of Canning," p. 77), and Lily Wong ("Eating the Hyphen," p. 93). How and why do each of them tell us what kind of person they are via their food choices and preferences?
8. Aphorism X suggests that there are "true principles of eating and drinking." What principles do Brillat-Savarin's aphorisms promote? Compare them to the principles advocated by Michael Pollan ("Eat Food: Food Defined," p. 10) and Wendell Berry ("The Pleasures of Eating," p. 47).
9. Research the life and work of Brillat-Savarin. Why do you think his writings are still valued and quoted today? What notions about food and culture do we share with him? What has changed?

Living by Bread Alone

Masanobu Fukuoka

Masanobu Fukuoka was a Japanese philosopher and farmer dedicated to natural farming practices. As a young man, he had a profound spiritual experience while recovering from a serious illness, which led him to leave his work as a research scientist and return to his family's farm on an island in southern Japan. Here he began experimenting with organic farming practices, even after World War II, when he lost most of his farmland to the forced redistribution policies of the American occupying forces. He began writing books and traveling the world to give lectures to share his agricultural philosophy of natural farming. He received many awards and much recognition worldwide for his important contributions to the international organic farming movement. He died in 2008 at the age of 95. His 1975 book *The One-Straw Revolution* has sold more than one million copies and has been translated into more than 20 languages. In this excerpt from it, he argues that our spiritual health is connected to what we eat and that to truly nourish ourselves and live healthy lives, we need to eat what he calls a natural diet.

There is nothing better than eating delicious food, but for most people eating is just a way to nourish the body, to have energy to work and to live to an old age. Mothers often tell their children to eat their food — even if they do not like the taste — because it is "good" for them.

But nutrition cannot be separated from the sense of taste. Nutritious foods, good for the human body, whet the appetite and are delicious on their own account. Proper nourishment is inseparable from good flavor.

Not too long ago the daily meal of the farmers in this area consisted of rice and barley with *miso*° and pickled vegetables. This diet gave long life, a strong constitution, and good health. Stewed vegetables and steamed rice with red beans was a once-a-month feast. The farmer's healthy, robust body was able to nourish itself well on this simple rice diet.

The traditional brown-rice-and-vegetable diet of the East is very different from that of most Western societies. Western nutritional science believes that unless certain amounts of starch, fat, protein, minerals, and vitamins are eaten each day, a well-balanced diet and good health cannot be preserved. This belief produced the mother who stuffs "nutritious" food into her youngster's mouth.

miso: a traditional Japanese seasoning made from fermented soybeans.

One might suppose that Western dietetics, with its elaborate theories 5 and calculations, could leave no doubts about proper diet. The fact is, it creates far more problems than it resolves.

One problem is that in Western nutritional science there is no effort to adjust the diet to the natural cycle. The diet that results serves to isolate human beings from nature. A fear of nature and a general sense of insecurity are often the unfortunate results.

Another problem is that spiritual and emotional values are entirely forgotten, even though foods are directly connected with human spirit and emotions. If the human being is viewed merely as a physiological° object, it is impossible to produce a coherent understanding of diet. When bits

> "Nutrition cannot be separated from the sense of taste."

and pieces of information are collected and brought together in confusion, the result is an imperfect diet which draws away from nature.

"Within one thing lie all things, but if all things are brought together not one thing can arise." Western science is unable to grasp this precept of Eastern philosophy. A person can analyze and investigate a butterfly as far as he likes, but he cannot make a butterfly.

If the Western scientific diet were put into practice on a wide scale, what sort of practical problems do you suppose would occur? High-quality beef, eggs, milk, vegetables, bread, and other foods would have to be readily available all year around. Large-scale production and long-term storage would become necessary. Already in Japan, adoption of this diet has caused farmers to produce summer vegetables such as lettuce, cucumbers, eggplants, and tomatoes in the winter. It will not be long before farmers are asked to harvest persimmons in spring and peaches in the autumn.

It is unreasonable to expect that a wholesome, balanced diet can be 10 achieved simply by supplying a great variety of foods regardless of the season. Compared with plants which ripen naturally, vegetables and fruits grown out-of-season under necessarily unnatural conditions contain few vitamins and minerals. It is not surprising that summer vegetables grown in the autumn or winter have none of the flavor and fragrance of those grown beneath the sun by organic and natural methods.

Chemical analysis, nutritional ratios, and other such considerations are the main causes of error. The food prescribed by modern science is far from the traditional Oriental diet, and it is undermining the health of the Japanese people.

---

physiological: relating to the functions of the body.

Summing Up Diet

In this world there exist four main classifications of diet:

1. A lax diet conforming to habitual desires and taste preferences. People following this diet sway back and forth erratically in response to whims and fancies. This diet could be called self-indulgent, empty eating.

2. The standard nutritional diet of most people, proceeding from biological conclusions. Nutritious foods are eaten for the purpose of maintaining the life of the body. It could be called materialist, scientific eating.

3. The diet based on spiritual principles and idealistic philosophy. Limiting foods, aiming toward compression, most "natural" diets fall into this category. This could be called the diet of principle.

4. The natural diet, following the will of heaven. Discarding all human knowledge, this diet could be called the diet of non-discrimination.

People first draw away from the empty diet which is the source of countless diseases. Next, becoming disenchanted with the scientific diet, which merely attempts to maintain biological life, many proceed to a diet of principle. Finally, transcending this, one arrives at the non-discriminating diet of the natural person.

The Diet of Non-Discrimination

Human life is not sustained by its own power. Nature gives birth to human beings and keeps them alive. This is the relation in which people stand to nature. Food is a gift of heaven. People do not create foods from nature; heaven bestows them.

Food is food and food is not food. It is a part of man and is apart 15 from man.

When food, the body, the heart, and the mind become perfectly united within nature, a natural diet becomes possible. The body as it is, following its own instinct, eating if something tastes good, abstaining if it does not, is free.

It is impossible to prescribe rules and proportions for a natural diet.* This diet defines itself according to the local environment, and the various needs and the bodily constitution of each person.

---

*A definite code or system by which one can consciously decide these questions is impossible. Nature, or the body itself, serves as a capable guide. But this subtle guidance goes unheard by most people because of the clamor caused by desire and by the activity of the discriminating mind. [Fukuoka's note.]

The Diet of Principle

Everyone should be aware that nature is always complete, balanced in perfect harmony within itself. Natural food is whole and within the whole are nourishment and subtle flavors.

It appears that, by applying the system of yin and yang°, people can explain the origin of the universe and the transformations of nature. It may also seem that the harmony of the human body can be determined and consciously sustained. But if the doctrines are entered into too deeply (as is necessary in the study of Eastern medicine) one enters the domain of science and fails to make the essential escape from discriminating perception.

Swept along by the subtleties of human knowledge without recogniz- 20 ing its limits, the practitioner of the diet of principle comes to concern himself only with separate objects. But when trying to grasp the meaning of nature with a wide and far-reaching vision, he fails to notice the small things happening at his feet.

The Typical Sick Person's Diet

Sickness comes when people draw apart from nature. The severity of the disease is directly proportional to the degree of separation. If a sick person returns to a healthy environment often the disease will disappear. When alienation from nature becomes extreme, the number of sick people increases. Then the desire to return to nature becomes stronger. But in *seeking* to return to nature, there is no clear understanding of what nature is, and so the attempt proves futile.

Even if one lives a primitive life back in the mountains, one may still fail to grasp the true objective. If you *try* to do something, your efforts will never achieve the desired result.

People living in the cities face tremendous difficulty in trying to attain a natural diet. Natural food is simply not available, because farmers have stopped growing it. Even if they could buy natural food, people's bodies would need to be fit to digest such hearty fare.

In this sort of situation, if you try to eat wholesome meals or attain a balanced yin-yang diet, you need practically supernatural means and powers of judgment. Far from a return to nature, a complicated, strange sort of "natural" diet arises and the individual is only drawn further away from nature.

If you look inside "health food" stores these days you will find a bewil- 25 dering assortment of fresh foods, packaged foods, vitamins, and dietary

---

yin and yang: in Eastern philosophy, two complementary forces that are opposite extremes yet make up all aspects of life.

supplements. In the literature many different types of diets are presented as being "natural," nutritious, and the best for health. If someone says it is healthful to boil foods together, there is someone else who says foods boiled together are only good for making people sick. Some emphasize the essential value of salt in the diet, others say that too much salt causes disease. If there is someone who shuns fruit as yin and food for monkeys, there is someone else who says fruit and vegetables are the very best foods for providing longevity and a happy disposition.

At various times and in various circumstances all of these opinions could be said to be correct, and so people come to be confused. Or rather, to a confused person, all of these theories become material for creating greater confusion.

Nature is in constant transition, changing from moment to moment. People cannot grasp nature's true appearance. The face of nature is unknowable. Trying to capture the unknowable in theories and formalized doctrines is like trying to catch the wind in a butterfly net.

If you hit the mark on the wrong target, you have missed.

Humanity is like a blind man who does not know where he is heading. He gropes around with the cane of scientific knowledge, depending on yin and yang to set his course.

What I want to say is, don't eat food with your head, and that is to say 30 get rid of the discriminating mind.

The prime consideration is for a person to develop the sensitivity to allow the body to choose food by itself. Thinking only about the foods themselves and leaving the spirit aside, is like making visits to the temple, reading the sutras°, and leaving Buddha on the outside. Rather than studying philosophical theory to reach an understanding of food, it is better to arrive at a theory from *within* one's daily diet.

Doctors take care of sick people; healthy people are cared for by nature. Instead of getting sick and then becoming absorbed in a natural diet to get well, one should live in a natural environment so that sickness does not appear.

The young people who come to stay in the huts on the mountain and live a primitive life, eating natural foods and practicing natural farming, are aware of man's ultimate purpose, and they have set out to live in accordance with it in the most direct way.

---

sutras: ancient Indian texts that provide rules of conduct.

Understanding the Text

1. What does Fukuoka argue is the purpose of food?
2. What does Fukuoka argue is the best way to nourish the body?
3. According to Fukuoka, what causes the number of sick people to increase?

Reflection and Response

4. What do the foods we eat say about our spiritual values? In what ways might eating be called a spiritual act?
5. Why does Fukuoka critique modern science's food prescriptions? What beliefs about food does Western nutrition science privilege? What does it ignore?
6. What would change in your life if you decided to follow Fukuoka's advice? What would you have to do differently in your daily life to live by a "diet of principle"?

Making Connections

7. Compare Fukuoka's concerns about nutrition science to Marion Nestle's ("Eating Made Simple," p. 37). What values do they share? How are they different? Which approach do you think is more effective? Why?
8. How might Questlove and chef Donald Link ("Something to Food About," p. 98) respond to Fukuoka's philosophy about nourishing the body? Is it possible to follow Fukuoka's advice in the culture and climate that Questlove and Link discuss in places like New Orleans? Provide textual examples from both readings to support your conclusions.
9. Fukuoka argues that Western nutrition science "with its elaborate theories and calculations" actually "creates far more problems than it resolves" (par. 5). Using library resources, identify and research two or three of the problems it creates. Analyze the problems using the argument made by Fukuoka and at least one other author from this book. Do you agree that they are "problems"? Why or why not?

Zombies vs. The Joy of Canning: Motivation in the Productive Home

Erica Strauss

After attending culinary school and working in restaurants in the Seattle area for ten years, Erica Strauss took her interest in food and gardening to a new level. Her garden includes an impressive array of amazing fruits and vegetables, much of which she cooks fresh, using elaborate recipes that she shares on her Web site and some of which she dries, pickles, and freezes for later use. She keeps an exhaustive blog, *Northwest Edible Life: Life on Garden Time,* that documents her gardening triumphs (and defeats); her impressive growing, food storage, and cooking knowledge; and her tips on motherhood, daily living, and the cultivation of a slower life in a fast-paced world. With an impressive and exhaustive array of food knowledge and advice, a political edge that keeps it interesting, and an authorial voice that aims to delight on a regular basis, her blog and her recently published book *The Hands-On Home: A Seasonal Guide to Cooking, Preserving and Natural Homekeeping* (2015) captures in writing what she lives, thinks, and values in her life as a self-described "urban farmer" and "radical homemaker." In this blog post, Strauss talks about why she grows and stores her own food.

"Hey, we were planning on getting together later today, right?" I asked my friend.

"Yeah, but after dinner."

"Can we push that back to later in the week?" I was exhausted from *Can-o-Rama* and the idea of a social commitment after dinner was more than I could handle.

"Sure. What's up?"

"I'm pretty tired. I stayed up until 2 in the morning yesterday wrap- 5 ping up a weekend of canning."

Long pause.

"Um . . . *why*?!?" my friend laughed.

I muttered something about trying to have my year's supply of canned tomatoes be home-canned.

"Wow, ok. You're really crazy!"

Why? Why do I do this? 10

I ask myself this question with some frequency, actually. When I have a list of a million things that all need doing and very short windows of time in which to do them, I ask myself what the point of playing urban farmer really is.

Chickens, crops, children, canning, cooking — not necessarily in that order.

Chickens, crops, cooking and canning are entirely optional (children are optional too, I suppose, but only *before* you have them). Most people don't do these things. I have realized this lately. Most people don't even cook. Maybe they heat stuff up, but balls-to-the-wall, from-scratch cooking? That's more unusual than the popularity of cookbooks and *Food TV* shows and cooking blogs would lead you to believe.

Most people consider real, honest-to-God, from-scratch food to be entertainment, not a thrice-daily reality.

So, *why?* Why can my own tomatoes? Why grow my own lettuce?   15
Why make my own deodorant? Why use cloth diapers on my son? Why cook from scratch? Why check the thrift store first?

In a nutshell: why voluntarily take on the complications and efforts of the productive home when the economic system I live in means I simply don't have to? Why make life harder?

There's a lot of answers to that question floating around the world of the self-proclaimed Radical Homemakers, Urban Householders, and Punk Domestic badasses.

A lot of the answers are political-economic. You'll hear that we owe it to local farmers to source directly from them and provide them with a market for their goods. You'll hear that rejecting industrial food undermines soul-less corporate interests and is, therefore, a radical political statement. At the micro-economic level you'll hear about the money that can be saved if you can your own tomatoes (a dubious claim unless your garden is putting out *a lot* of excellent-quality canning tomatoes).

There's rallying cries about supporting different markets — local markets, sustainable markets, alternative markets. Anything but the international, corporate-dominated, local-to-nowhere market we currently enjoy.

"Occupy your food supply! Make your own jam!"

"Be prepared for zombies! Grow a garden!"

"Take out insurance against midwestern crop failures — support your local farmers!"

These claims are how the lifestyle of the productive home is sold.   20
They say: be a part of something bigger. Be a part of a movement. Help to change the world. Join our gang, we jump you in with homemade scones and really delicious bing cherry jam. You'll love our global fight for justice! We wage our battle at the fair-trade, shade-grown coffee shop!

All these motivations are very good reasons to attempt to make your home a place of greater productivity and less consumption. And I'm not saying the world couldn't use a little changing.

But all that political spitfire, as much as I enjoy it occasionally, isn't *really* why I do any of this. I don't bake my own bread to fuck over Wonder Bread (owned by Hostess) or can my own tomatoes to stick it to Muir Glen (owned by General Mills).

While I do have some grave concerns about the just-in-time food distribution system that connects most people with their calories, I don't expect hoards of zombies to suck my brains out or neighbors to take my butternut squash at gunpoint any time soon.

The drought in the Midwest is bad. It's going to be very, very bad for farmers and ranchers and very bad for companies and consumers that rely on cheap cereal grains and products made from them. It's going to cost taxpayers a bundle, even though most will have no idea that they are paying for it, and the knock-on to the supply/demand curve will send grocery prices higher more or less across the board.

> *"You have to love food enough to work for it."*

But that has almost *nothing* to do with why I visit the farmer's market, 25 or buy boxes of fruit in season from the family farmer just over the mountains in Central Washington.

Really, I can my tomatoes, make jam, keep chickens, bake bread and — perhaps most consumingly — grow a rather large garden — because I *enjoy* doing these things. Even if once a year in late August that means a few late-nights in front of the canning pot, I still *enjoy* this life.

I think, against the backdrop of big reasons why productive home-keeping is *A Very Important Movement* and all that, the simple pleasures that come from nurturing and creating in the home are sometimes lost.

When we feel like we are obligated to do something, because doing that thing is how we make our political statement in a world gone mad, or keep our families safe against unseen, unknown, and as-yet-unrealized threats, or protect our assets against the vagaries of a complicated global economic system, we are acting from fear or from anger.

We are stretching out our hand to try to take some measure of control back from that which seems so out-of-control.

We are saying with clenched fist, "You and your peak oil and BPA 30 and your global banking crisis and your housing collapse and your high-fructose-corn-syrup, pink-slime, diabetes-nation food system, you can push me into the dirt. But I will rise back up and when I do, I'll be holding these homegrown, organic cantaloupes, motherfucker! Yeah!"

There's nothing wrong with this, to a point. Anger that changes behaviors and fear that motivates people to examine their deep values can be a catalyst for great and positive change. But at the end of a long, long, long day of canning, or weeding, or sowing, something greater than fear and anger has to carry you along.

After 16 hours of processing tomatoes, if you have the energy to be fist-raising, passionately upset about anything, you should look really into anger management classes.

Nah, when push comes to shove, you have to do this stuff because you like it. You have to *like* patiently reducing strawberry syrup to get just the right texture in your jam. You have to *like* bullshitting with farmers and ranchers and going out on field trips to where the food is grown. You have to get a small thrill when you harvest an egg that is still warm, or find yourself covered with sticky gold from the beehives you've helped along.

You have to be in love with the miracle that is a squash seed — no bigger than a fingernail but able to produce hundreds of pounds of food in a single summer with only a little help from you, the gardener. You have to find a certain calm prayerfulness in the act of working your earth, even as your To Do list presses in on you ceaselessly.

You have to love food enough to work for it, and not in an abstract 35 trade-space kind of way. Not in the, "An hour writing this code for the latest version of Microsoft Excel pays me enough to buy a month's worth of hamburgers on the road!" kind of way.

You have to be okay getting your hands dirty, and your brow sweaty, and your forearms scratched from the cuts of a thousand blackberry brambles. You have to not just survive that kind of labor, but revel in it.

Right now, we do have a choice — those #10 cans of tomatoes are cheap and easy to buy. Those pears from Argentina are available in June. That feedlot ground beef is on special for $2.49 a pound. McDonald's is on the way and Hot Pockets and Lean Cuisines are in the freezer section.

So why go to all that trouble? Why not run out and grab a can of crushed tomatoes and a jar of jam right alongside the Lean Cuisines and Hot Pockets?

Why?

Because I have a pantry that reflects a summer spent in relaxing work 40 and joyful creation.

Because cooking dinner makes me proud.

Because the food is delicious.

Because this kind of work makes me happy.

That's why. And that's enough.

Understanding the Text

1. Why does Strauss can her own tomatoes? shop at the farmer's market? keep chickens? What purposes do these practices serve in her life and the life of her family?

2. What is an urban farmer? Why does Strauss identify as one?

3. What is a "productive home"?

Reflection and Response

4. Strauss writes a blog about her life, her gardening practices, her food production, and her values. If you were to write a blog documenting your "food life," what would we learn about you and your food?

5. The way Strauss describes it, canning tomatoes sounds like a lot of hard work. Why does it make her happy? What intrinsic pleasures does it bring? Why might we conclude that she "love[s] food enough to work for it" (par. 24)?

6. If food is a mirror through which we can better understand ourselves — that is, if "we are what we eat" — what kind of reflection would Strauss see? Explain your answer.

Making Connections

7. Think about Strauss's depiction of the urban farming movement in relation to Troy Johnson's ("Farm to Fable," p. 191) depiction of the farm-to-table movement. Research both movements. What values do they share? Are there important differences? Do you think Strauss would eat at the restaurants described by Johnson? Why or why not?

8. Strauss is not the only blogger writing about food, cooking, and gardening. Search the Internet for blogs about food, cooking, eating, and gardening. Find blogs that support a movement or advocate a practice. Select two or three and analyze what they tell us (implicitly or explicitly) about the food values and food politics they are promoting. Compare them to Strauss's blog and to one another. Use specific textual examples to support your analysis.

Does This Name Make Me Sound Fat?

Dan Jurafsky

Dan Jurafsky studied linguistics and computer science at the University of California, Berkeley before winning a MacArthur Fellowship and becoming a professor of linguistics and of computer science at Stanford University. He studies computational linguistics and its applications to the behavioral and social sciences and has published numerous academic articles and books in this field. Jurafsky also writes and teaches about the language of food; in this work, he applies linguistics to food studies in ways that illuminate the relationships among language, food, psychology, and culture. His book *The Language of Food: A Linguist Reads the Menu* (2014), from which this selection comes, demonstrates how much history and culture resides in our daily food choices.

So far, we've seen a lot hidden in the language of food. The Chinese history of ketchup and the Muslim histories of sherbet, macaroons, and escabeche tell us about the crucial role of the East in the creation of the West. The way we use words like *heirloom, a la, delicious*, or *exotic* on menus tells us about how we think about social class and about the nature of food advertising. But although we've talked about food words in terms of their history and the adjectives we use to describe them, I've said nothing so far about the sound of the food words themselves.

Why would the sound of a food word tell us anything? It's not obvious why the sounds in the name of a word might be suggestive of, say, the taste or smell of the food. Shakespeare expressed this skepticism most beautifully in *Romeo and Juliet*:

What's in a name? that which we call a rose

By any other name would smell as sweet;

Juliet is expressing the theory we call *conventionalism*: that a name for something is just an agreed upon convention. English uses the word *egg*, but Cantonese calls it *daan*, and Italian *uovo*, but if accidentally it had evolved the other way around, it would be fine as long as everyone agreed. The alternative view, that there is something about a name that fits the object naturally, that some names might naturally "sound more sweet" than others, is called *naturalism*.

Conventionalism is the norm in modern linguistics, because we have found that the sounds that make up a word don't generally tell you what

the word means. Linguists phrase this by saying that the relation between sound and meaning is "arbitrary," a word first used by political
philosopher John Locke in *An Essay Concerning Human Understanding.*
Locke pointed out that if there were a necessary relationship between
sound and meaning, all languages would have the same words for everything, and the word for egg in English and Italian would be the same as
the Chinese word.

A moment's thought suggests another reason that conventionalism
makes more sense than naturalism, at least for spoken (as opposed to
signed) languages: spoken languages only have around 50 or so distinct
"phones" (the distinct sounds that make up the sound structure of a language) and obviously have a lot more ideas to express than 50.

But 2500 years ago in the *Cratylus*, Plato points out that there are reason- 5
able arguments for naturalism as well as conventionalism. Socrates first
agrees with Cratylus's position that there is an "inherently correct" name
for everything for "both Greeks and barbarians." One way to be natural or
"inherently correct" is to use letters consistent with the meaning of the
word. For example the letter o (omicron) is round, and "therefore there is
plenty of omicron mixed up in the word *goggulon* (round)." Similarly, words
with the sound r (Greek rho, ρ, which was pronounced as a rolling trilled r
like modern Spanish) often mean something related to motion (*rhein* [flow],
rhoe [current], *tromos* [trembling]).

But then Socrates turns right around and argues for the conventional-
ist position of Hermogenes by noting, for example, that even in different
dialects of Greek words are pronounced differently, suggesting that convention is needed after all.

Linguistics as a discipline followed this latter line of reasoning, and
Ferdinand de Saussure, the Geneva professor who is one of the fathers of
modern linguistics, made the principle of the "arbitrariness of the sign"
a foundation of our field. But research in the last few decades, following
the earlier lead of giants of linguistics from the past century like Otto
Jespersen and Roman Jakobson, has shown us that there was something
to naturalism after all: sometimes the sounds of a name are in fact associated with the tastes of food.

We call the phenomenon of sounds carrying meaning *sound symbolism*. Sound symbolism has ramifications beyond its deep philosophical
and linguistic interest. Like other linguistic cues to marketing strategies
sounds are crucial to food marketing and branding.

Sound symbolism has been most deeply studied with vowels, and in
particular the difference between two classes of vowels, *front vowels* and
back vowels, which are named depending on the position of the tongue
when articulating the vowels.

The vowels i (the vowel in the words *cheese* or *teeny*) and I (pronounced 10 as in *mint* or *thin*) are front vowels. Front vowels, roughly speaking, are made by holding the tongue high up in the front part of the mouth. The figure below left shows a very schematic cutaway of the head, with the lips and teeth on the left, and the tongue high up toward the front of the mouth.

By contrast, the vowel α (as in *large, pod,* or *on*) is a low back vowel; this sound is made by holding the tongue lower in the back part of the mouth; other back vowels are o (as in *bold*) and ɔ (as in the word *coarse* or my mother's New York pronunciation of *caught*). The figure below right shows a very schematic tongue position for these vowels; lower in general, and more toward the back of the throat.

A number of studies over the last 100 years or so have shown that front vowels in many languages tend to be used in words that refer to small, thin, light things, and back vowels in words that refer to big, fat, heavy things. It's not always true — there are certainly exceptions — but it's a tendency that you can see in any of the stressed vowels in words like *little, teeny,* or *itsy-bitsy* (all front vowels) versus *humongous* or *enormous* (back vowels). Or the i vowel in Spanish *chico* (front vowel, meaning "small") versus the ɔ in *gordo* (back vowel, meaning "fat"). Or French *petit* (front vowel) versus *grand* (back vowel).

In one marketing study, for example, Richard Klink created pairs of made-up product brand names that were identical except for having front vowels (*detal*) or back vowels (*dutal*) and asked participants to answer:

Which brand of laptop seems bigger, Detal or Dutal?

Which brand of vacuum cleaner seems heavier, Keffi or Kuffi?

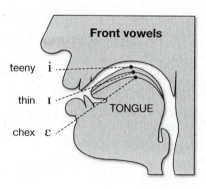

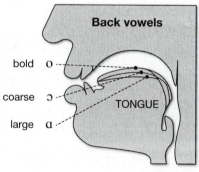

Which brand of ketchup seems thicker, Nellen or Nullen?

Which brand of beer seems darker, Esab or Usab?

In each case, the product named with back vowels (Dutal, Nullen) was chosen as the larger, heavier, thicker product.

Since ice cream is a product whose whole purpose is to be rich, creamy, and heavy, it is not surprising that people seem to prefer ice creams that are named with back vowels. Eric Yorkston and Geeta Menon at New York University asked participants to read a press release describing a new ice cream about to be released. For half, the ice cream was called "Frish" (front vowel) while for the other half it was called "Frosh" (back vowel). Asked their opinions, the "Frosh" people rated this hypothetical ice cream as smoother, creamier, and richer than other participants rated "Frish," and were more likely to say they would buy it.

In a final twist, Yorkston and Menon distracted some participants by 15 having them perform another task simultaneously, so they couldn't fully concentrate on reading about the ice cream. The distracted participants were even more influenced by the vowels, suggesting that the response to the vowels was automatic, at a subconscious° level.

I wondered whether commercial ice creams make use of this subconscious association of ice cream names with back vowels as richer and creamier. To find out, I ran what University of Pennsylvania linguist Mark Liberman calls a Breakfast Experiment. Liberman — a tenacious° advocate for bringing linguistics to bear on public affairs — often runs a quick experiment on a linguistic tip in the news before breakfast, posting the results on *Language Log*, the "blog of record" in linguistics. He is legendary for his ability to run complex linguistic statistical analyses in minutes, which he says comes from his days as a piano tuner.

My hypothesis was that we would see more back vowels in names of ice cream brands or flavors, and conversely that thin, light foods like crackers would have more front vowels.

I tested the hypothesis on two lists of food names from the web, the 81 ice cream flavors sold by either Haagen Dazs or Ben & Jerry's, and a list of 592 cracker brands from a dieting website. For each list, I counted the total number of front vowels (i, I, ε, e, æ) and the total number of back vowels.

The result? I found more back vowels in ice cream names like Rocky Road, Jamoca Almond Fudge, Chocolate, Caramel, Cookie Dough, Coconut

---

subconscious: existing in the mind, but in a part of the mind that is not available to the person.
tenacious: firm or strong.

and front vowels in cracker names (note the extraordinary number of I vowels) like Ch*ee*se N*i*ps, Ch*ee*z *I*t, Wh*ea*t Th*i*ns, Pr*e*tzel Th*i*ns, R*i*tz, Kr*i*spy, Tr*i*scuit, Th*i*n Cr*i*sps, Ch*ee*se Cr*i*sps, Ch*i*cken in a B*i*skit, Snack St*i*cks, R*i*tz b*i*ts.

Of course there are exceptions: van*i*lla (the orange blossom of our 20 day), has an I. But most of the front vowels in ice cream flavors tend to be the names of small, thin ingredients in the ice cream (th*i*n m*i*nt, ch*i*p, p*ea*nut br*i*ttle).

> "Sound symbolism is thus an important device in the toolbox of modern advertisers and designers of brand names, and in fact branding companies often get their insights from linguists."

Sound symbolism is thus an important device in the toolbox of modern advertisers and designers of brand names, and in fact branding companies often get their insights from linguists.

While our ice cream and cracker connections might be subconscious, they are systematic, and linguists have theories about the underlying cause: about why front vowels are associated with small, thin, light things, and back vowels with big, solid, heavy things.

The most widely accepted theory, the *frequency code*, suggests that low frequencies (sounds with low pitch) and high frequencies (sounds with high pitch) are associated with particular meanings. The frequency code was developed by linguist John Ohala (my phonetics professor as an undergraduate at Berkeley) by extending work by Eugene Morton of the Smithsonian.

Morton noticed that mammals and birds tend to use low-frequency (deeper) sounds when they are aggressive or hostile, but use higher-frequency (higher-pitched) sounds when frightened, appeasing, or friendly. Because larger animals naturally make deeper sounds (the roar of lions) and smaller animals naturally make high-pitched sounds (the tweet of birds), Morton's idea is that animals try to appear larger when they are competing or aggressive, but smaller and less threatening otherwise.

Morton and Ohala thus suggest that humans instinctively associate 25 the pitch of sounds with size. All vowels are composed of different frequency resonances. When the tongue is high and in the front of the mouth, it creates a small cavity in front. Small cavities cause higher-pitched resonances (the smaller the space for vibration, the shorter the wavelength, hence the higher the frequency). One particular resonance (called the second formant) is much higher for front vowels and lower for back vowels.

Thus the frequency code suggests that front vowels like I and i are associated with small, thin, things, and back vowels like a and o with big heavy things because front vowels have higher-pitched resonances, and we instinctively associate higher pitch with smaller animals, and by extension smaller things in general.

Researchers have extended this idea to show that raising pitch or "fronting" vowels (moving the tongue a bit toward the front of mouth to make all vowels have a slightly higher second formant pitch) are both especially associated with babies or children. In an early paper I examined more than 60 languages around the world and proposed that the word endings used in many languages to indicate smallness or lightness come historically from a word originally meaning "child" or associated with names of children, like the *y* in pet names Barbie and Robby. My linguistics colleague Penny Eckert shows that front vowels are associated with positive affect, and that preadolescent girls sometimes use vowel fronting to subtly imbue° their speech with sweetness or childhood innocence. Linguist Katherine Rose Geenberg found that speakers of American English move their vowels toward the front when using baby talk, and psychologist Anne Fernald shows that, across languages, talk to babies tends to have high pitch.

The frequency code isn't the only kind of sound symbolism in food. To see why, we'll need a brief digression. Consider these two pictures:

Suppose I told you that in the Martian language one of these two was called bouba and the other was called kiki and you had to guess which was which. Think for a second. Which picture is bouba? Which kiki? How about maluma versus takete?

---

imbue: to permeate or deeply influence.

If you're like most people, you called the jagged picture on the left *kiki* (or *takete*) and the round one on the right *bouba* (or *maluma*). This test was invented by German psychologist Wolfgang Köhler, one of the founders of Gestalt psychology, in 1929. Linguists and psychologists have repeated this experiment using all sorts of made-up words with sounds like bouba and kiki, and no matter what language they study, from Swedish to Swahili to a remote nomadic° population of northern Namibia, and even in toddlers two and a half years old, the results are astonishingly consistent. There seems to be something about jagged shapes that makes people call them *kiki* and rounder curvy shapes that is somehow naturally *bouba*.

The link to food comes from the lab of Oxford psychologist Charles 30 Spence, one of the world's foremost researchers in sensory perception. In a number of recent papers, Spence and his colleagues have studied the link between the taste of different foods, the curved and jagged pictures, and words like *maluma/takete.*

In one paper, for example, Spence, Mary Kim Ngo, and Reeva Misra asked people to eat a piece of chocolate and say whether the taste better matched the words *maluma* or *takete.* People eating milk chocolate (Lindt extra creamy 30 percent cocoa) said the taste fit the word *maluma* (and also matched the curvier figure). People eating dark chocolate (Lindt 70 percent and 90 percent cocoa) instead chose the word *takete* (and matched the jagged figure). In another paper they found similar results for carbonation; carbonated water was perceived as more "kiki" (and spiky) and still water was perceived as more "bouba" (and curvy). In other words, words with m and l sounds like *maluma* were associated with creamier or gentler tastes and words with t and k sounds like *takete* were associated with bitter or carbonated tastes.

These associations are very similar to what I also found with consonants in ice cream and cracker names. I found that l and m occurred more often in ice cream names, while t and d occurred more often in cracker names.

So what is it about bouba and maluma that people associate with visual images of round and curvy, or tastes of creamy and smooth, while kiki and takete are associated with jagged visual images and sharp, bitter, and sour tastes? Recent work by a number of linguists studied exactly which sounds seem to be causing the effects.

One reasonable proposal for what's going on has to do with continuity and smoothness. Sounds like m, l, and r, called *continuants* because

---

nomadic: roaming about from place to place, usually without a fixed plan or pattern of movement.

they are continuous and smooth acoustically (the sound is pretty consistent across its whole length), are more closely associated with smoother figures. By contrast, *strident* sounds that abruptly start and stop, like t and k, are associated with the spiky figures. The consonant t has the most distinct jagged burst of energy of any consonant in English.

To help you visualize this, look at the display below of the sound 35 waves from a recording that I made of myself saying "maluma" followed by "takete." Note the relatively smooth wave for maluma, which has a relatively smooth flow of air. By contrast, the three sharp discontinuities in takete on the right occurred when I said the sounds t and k; for each of these consonants, the airflow is briefly blocked by the tongue in the mouth, and then a little burst of air explodes out.

What I call the synesthetic hypothesis suggests that the perception of acoustic smoothness by one of our five senses, hearing, is somehow linked to the perception of smoothness by two other senses: vision (seeing a curvy figure instead of a jagged one) and taste (tasting a creamy instead of sharp taste).

Synesthesia is the general name for the phenomenon of strong associations between the different senses. Some people, like Dan Slobin, a Berkeley professor of psychology and linguistics, are very strong synesthetes. For Slobin, each musical key is associated with a color: C major is pink, C minor is dark red tinged with black. But the bouba/kiki results suggest that, to at least some extent, we are all a little bit synesthetic. Something about our senses of taste/smell, vision, and hearing are linked at least enough so that what is smooth in one is associated with being smooth in another, so that we feel the similarity between sharpness detected by smell (as in cheddar),

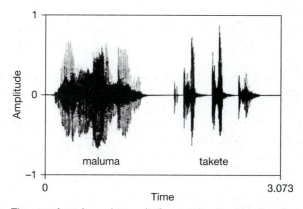

The waveform (sound waves) of me saying "maluma" and "takete"

sharpness detected by touch or vision (like acute angles), and sharpness detected by hearing (abrupt changes in sound).

We can see this link between the senses even in our daily vocabulary. The words *sharp* and *pungent* both originally meant something tactile and visual: something that feels pointy or subtends a small visual angle, but both words can be applied to tastes and smells as well.

It's not clear to what extent these synesthetic links are innate or genetic, and to what extent they are cultural. For example, nomadic tribes in Namibia do associate takete with spiky pictures, but, unlike speakers of many other languages, they don't associate either the word or the pictures with the bitterness of dark chocolate or with carbonation. This suggests that the fact that we perceive bitter chocolate as "sharper" than milk chocolate or carbonated water as "sharper" than flat water is a metaphor that we learn culturally to associate with these foods. But we really don't know yet, because we are just at the beginning of understanding these aspects of perception.

There are, however, some evolutionary implications of the synesthetic 40 smoothness hypothesis and of the frequency code.

John Ohala suggests that the link of high pitch with deference or friendliness may explain the origin of the smile, which is similarly associated with appeasing or friendly behavior. The way we make a smile is by retracting the corners of the mouth. Animals like monkeys also retract the corners of their mouths to express submission, and use the opposite facial expression (Ohala calls it the "o-face"), in which the corners of the mouth are drawn forward with the lips possibly protruding, to indicate aggression.

Retracting the corners of the mouth shrinks the size of the front cavity in the mouth, just like the vowels I or i. In fact, the similarity in mouth position between smiling and the vowel i explains why we say "cheese" when we take pictures; i is the smiling vowel.

Ohala's theory is thus that smiling was originally an appeasement gesture, meaning something like "don't hurt little old me." It evolved when mammals were in competitive situations as a way to make the voice sound more high pitched and the smiler appear smaller and less aggressive, and hence friendlier.

Both the frequency code and the synesthetic smoothness hypothesis may also be related to the origin of language. If some kinds of meaning are iconically related to sounds in the way that these hypotheses suggest, it might have been a way for speakers to get across concepts to hearers early on in the evolution of language. The origins of language remain a deep mystery. We do, however, have some hypotheses, like the "bow-wow" theory of language evolution, the idea that language emerged at least partly by copying nature, naming dogs after their bark and cats after their meow and so on. The frequency code suggests that perhaps one of the earliest words created by some cavewoman had high pitched *i* sounds that meant "baby," or low pitched α sounds that meant "big," or perhaps was an acoustically abrupt *kikiki* meaning "sharp." Such iconic concepts are only a small part of the vast number of things we talk about using language, but iconicity° still may help us understand some of these crucial early bootstrappings of human language.

Whatever their early origins, vowels and consonants have become 45 part of a rich and beautiful system for expressing complex meanings by combining sounds into words, just as smiling has evolved into a means of expressing many shades of happiness, love, and much else.

Whatever hidden meanings words and smiles may have, in the end there is always ice cream, as a much later bard, Wallace Stevens, told us:

Let be be finale of seem.

The only emperor is the emperor of ice-cream.

iconicity: resemblance between form and meaning; an iconic sign resembles its meaning.

Understanding the Text

1. What is the difference between conventionalism and naturalism?
2. Who is Ferdinand de Saussure, and why is he important to the history of modern linguistics? How has the field moved away from the early foundation he established?
3. What is *sound symbolism*?
4. What is *synaesthesia*, and how is it relevant to how we name foods?

Reflection and Response

5. What are back vowels? Why do people prefer ice creams with back vowels? Can you think of some examples of food names with back vowels that Jurafsky does not mention?
6. Why do you think Jurafsky named this essay "Does This Name Make Me Sound Fat?" Explain your answer using evidence from the text and from the world around you.
7. What is the Breakfast Experiment? What did Jurafsky learn from it? Is this kind of research compelling to you? Why or why not?

Making Connections

8. Do you think certain food names "sound more sweet" than others? Why or why not? Use Jurafsky's argument to analyze the various foods named by Jill McCorkle ("Her Chee-to Heart," p. 31). Can you use her essay to explain why ice cream and crackers have different names?

9. Go online and research the *kiki* and *bouba* test developed by Wolfgang Köhler. How does this test work? What kind of experiments have academics used it to do? Why is it useful for studying the relationship between the tastes of food and what we call them? How does an understanding of this research change how you think about the names of the foods you enjoy?

10. Jurafsky, Mary Roach ("Liver and Opinions," p. 118), and Rachel Laudan ("The Birth of the Modern Diet," p. 55) present various kinds of academic research as evidence to support the arguments that they make. Analyze the kinds of evidence they rely on. What does it say about the kinds of arguments they are making?

Eating the Hyphen

Lily Wong

Lily Wong wrote this essay in a class she took on food and society when she was an undergraduate student at Williams College. After earning a bachelor's degree in history and Asian studies there, she has dabbled in food writing, taught English in Hong Kong, and worked in a museum conducting research and planning exhibits. This essay first appeared in *Gastronomica: The Journal of Food and Culture*, an academic journal that uses food as a source of knowledge about culture; it was selected for inclusion in *Best Food Writing 2013*. Wong loves food and cooking, and thinking and writing about food continue to intrigue her. Here she describes her love of dumplings eaten with a fork, a knife, a pair of chopsticks, and ketchup to illustrate the important relationship between food and identity.

Fork? Check. Knife? Check. Chopsticks? Check. It may seem odd to have all three of these eating utensils side by side for the consumption of a single meal, but for me, there's just no other way. Oh, and ketchup, that's key. Definitely need to have the ketchup, pre-shaken to avoid an awkward first squirt of pale red water. There's no place for that on my plate, not when I'm eating dumplings. Yes, that is what I said: I need a fork, a knife, a pair of chopsticks, and ketchup before I eat my dumplings.

Now I've just looked up "dumpling" on the online *Oxford English Dictionary* and discovered that it is "a kind of pudding consisting of a mass of paste or dough, more or less globular in form, either plain and boiled, or enclosing fruit and boiled or baked." I am definitely not talking about whatever unappetizing-sounding food that dumpling is supposed to be. I'm talking about Chinese dumplings, pot stickers, Peking ravioli, *jiaozi*, whatever you want to call them. Do you know what I mean yet? Maybe you've gotten a vague idea, but let me explain, because I am *very* picky about my dumplings.

To begin with, the skin has to be thick. I mean really thick. Thick and chewy and starchy and the bottom should be a bit burnt and dark golden brown from the pan-frying. Have you ever had *gyoza*, the Japanese dumplings? Yes, those thin, almost translucent skins just won't do it for me. Hands-down, no question, until my dying day, I will vouch that the skin is the make-or-break feature of a dumpling. Bad skin equals bad dumpling. Those boiled dumplings that are also a type of Chinese dumplings? The skin is too thin, too soggy, and frankly, rather flavorless. If I had to call it names, I'd say it was limp and weak and characterless. The thick-skinned dumplings that I know and love absorb more of the meaty-flavored goodness inside the dumplings. Also, because they are pan-fried (a key aspect of delicious dumplings), the bottom gets its own texture — a slightly charred crispiness to add that perfect smidgen of crunch. So, if you were to eat just the skin of the dumpling, it would be simultaneously chewy and crispy, with a bit of savory meat flavor mixed in with a burnt taste off the bottom — a wonderfulness that the words of the English language are hard-pressed to capture.

But what about the filling? To me, it's a bit peripheral. The dumplings I'm talking about have a standard pork filling with "Chinese vegetables." I've never been entirely sure what these elusively named Chinese vegetables actually are, but I imagine that they are some combination of leeks and Chinese cabbage. They're not too salty and they don't have cilantro. These dumplings also have enough savory broth secretly sequestered inside the skin so that when you cut them open, you get some oil spatterings, pretty much all over your clothes, plate, and table. That's the sign of a good, moist, and juicy meat section.

I should mention before you envision me slaving away in a kitchen to 5 create the perfect dumpling that the ones I like come out of the freezer. In plastic bags of fifty each. Imported to my house from Boston's Chinatown. It's strange, considering that most days I like the home-grown version of foods more than the store-bought version, but these are the exception. Even though I know they're hand made by a small company, so you get that same small-batch feel as if you made them at home, they're still store-bought and frozen rather than fresh.

But enough about finding the right dumplings; you're probably still confused as to why it's so imperative that I have a fork, knife, chopsticks, and ketchup. Here is your step-by-step guide to an entirely new dumpling eating experience.

1. On a large white plate, place six or seven dumplings (or more if you're particularly ravenous) and add some broccoli or beans for color and nutrition.

2. Squirt a glop of ketchup in one of the empty white spaces on your plate (as in not touching the broccoli or the dumplings). This is where it's key that the ketchup has been shaken a bit, otherwise that red ketchup juice runs all over your plate ruining everything.

3. Take that fork and knife on the side and cut each dumpling in half width-wise. Make sure to cut completely through the skin and meat.

4. Take the backside of your fork and push down on the top of each dumpling half until the meat abruptly pops out in a pool of brothy juice.

5. Once you've finished systematically cutting and squishing, you'll have lots of skins and meat pieces separated and you can put that knife and fork away. Grab the chopsticks.

6. Pick up a piece of the meat (just the meat now, no trying to get some skin in on this too) and dip it into the ketchup. Eat and repeat. If at any point you want to indulge in that steamed broccoli, it's a good idea. You wouldn't want to leave it all to the end. But don't dip it in ketchup. That's weird.

7. Now this is the best part. Use your chopsticks to one-by-one eat every last half dumpling's worth of skin. Savor every part because this is what it's all really been about. No ketchup or meat to obscure the flavor and chewiness, just pure starchy goodness.

And that's how it goes. Every single time. Confused? So was I the first time I really sat down to think about how I eat dumplings. It sounds a little like a grand mutilation of how a dumpling should be eaten for it to be "authentic" (using only chopsticks and with the dumpling left whole and dipped in black vinegar, no ketchup in sight). And I have unabashedly criticized and ridiculed Americanized Chinese food for being fake and something of a disgrace to "authentic" Chinese food. Yet here I am, still eating my dumplings with ketchup and a fork, unceremoniously and quite literally butchering my dumplings before I eat them. My grandmother meanwhile takes small bites out of whole dumplings, careful not to lose any of that broth from inside (with a face only three-quarters filled with disgust as I rush from the table to grab my ketchup from the fridge).

Bottled up in this entirely strange ritual is my status as a Chinese American. It is unclear to me where I ever came up with the idea that dumplings should be cut in half, or that the meat would taste better with ketchup (particularly since this is literally the only time that I use ketchup). Perhaps this combination has something to do with the fact that since both my parents grew up in the States, we've embraced many American traditions while abandoning or significantly modifying many Chinese ones. But even so, I have always embraced my Chinese culture and heritage. It gives me something larger to cling to when I'm feeling ostracized by American culture for looking "different." The suburb I grew up in is mostly white, but it's not as if I didn't have Chinese people around me; after all, there was always Chinatown. But Chinatown was full of people who spoke the language — whether Cantonese or Mandarin — who somehow just seemed so much more Chinese than I ever could be. And perhaps that's true. Maybe that's why I feel so gosh-darned American when I eat my dumplings with ketchup while holding my chopsticks "incorrectly."

The notion that this somehow takes away from my ability to identify with Chinese culture is, I rationally understand, flawed. But in my pursuit to try and discover who I am, it's taken an oddly large place.

I'm not sure why I often think that to be a Chinese American means that you relish authentic Chinese food — and by authentic I mostly mean strictly what your grandmother cooks for you — but I do. I've told friends that they don't know what real Chinese food is because all they know is Panda Express. I pride myself on my Cantonese background, which leads me to look favorably on pig's ears and fungus of all shapes and sizes. My innate territorialism regarding my particular definition of what Chinese food is makes the choice to continue eating my dumplings in such a strange fashion slightly fraught. I'm not even sure that anyone besides my family knows that this is how I eat dumplings. In part, I think my reticence derives precisely from a fear that it would make me "less" Chinese.

> "I'm not sure why I often think that to be a Chinese American means that you relish authentic Chinese food — and by authentic I mostly mean strictly what your grandmother cooks for you — but I do."

Somehow, I've come to strange terms with these contradictions. Somewhere along the way, dumplings, cut in half with ketchup on the meat and the skin separated as a special entity of its own, have become my comfort food. So whether or not it perverts some thousand-year-old tradition of the "proper" way to eat dumplings, this is what makes me happy. Although I sometimes catch myself overcompensating with extra delight in Chinese delicacies involving jellyfish and sea cucumber that cause most Americans to squirm, eating dumplings in my own style has become the hyphen between Chinese and American in my identity.

Understanding the Text

1. How does Wong define "food"? How does she define "Chinese food"?
2. How does Wong feel that her food preferences define her? Do you agree?
3. What constitutes an "authentic" food experience for Wong?

Reflection and Response

4. Why do you think Wong includes the dictionary definition of "dumpling"? What effect does it have on the rest of the piece?
5. How do you explain the significance of the title? What does it emphasize about Wong's story?

Making Connections

6. Compare Wong's love of dumplings to Jean Anthelme Brillat-Savarin's love of food and etiquette ("The Physiology of Taste," p. 68) and Questlove's exploration of regional identity, race, and food ("Something to Food About," p. 98). What do they suggest about the relationships between food, emotion, and pleasure? Find some images, photographs, or illustrations to help support your analysis.

7. Reflect on the relationship between your food preferences and your identity. Do your food choices express something about your identity or aspects of it? Why or why not?

8. Wong and Michael Pollan ("Eat Food: Food Defined," p. 10) define food in relation to what grandmothers would consider authentic. Why do you think this is? Do you connect certain foods to your grandmother or to other family members? Explain.

Something to Food About

Questlove

Questlove (or ?uestlove), who was born Ahmir Khalib Thompson, is well-known as a drummer, musician, producer, musical journalist, and author. His musician parents took him on tour when he was a child, and he grew up backstage at doo-wop shows, first drumming on stage at seven years old. After attending a performing arts school, he became a musical director, actor, and DJ, and he is perhaps best known for his performances with the band The Roots, which performs on *The Tonight Show Starring Jimmy Fallon*. Questlove pursues creativity in many forms and venues; he recently departed from writing about music to publish a book about food: *somethingtofoodabout: Exploring Creativity with Innovative Chefs*. The book depicts the creative side of cooking, exploring how chefs use cooking to develop their understanding of culture and their role in the world. While his conversation with each chef begins with food, Questlove often relates working with food to his own artistic pursuits in music and other venues. In this excerpt from *somethingtofoodabout*, Questlove interviews Donald Link, a New Orleans-based chef.

For years, I thought of New Orleans as a music city first — more than that, as America's first city of music. In 2005, the Roots were playing a gig, and we struck up a relationship with a local band called the To Be Continued Brass Band. They were teenagers from Carver High. Rich° and I talked about it and decided that the city had a rich enough music history that we should move there and record our next record. We had the idea of doing something like a domestic Graceland, where we would mix musicology and cultural exploration. A few months later, Hurricane Katrina came along and ended that dream.

While we were there, though, my sense of the city changed. Going in, I knew that my knowledge of the city's culture beyond music was pretty narrow. Whenever anyone comes to Philly, the first thing I do is keep them from going to the Top Five typical cheesesteak spots — the Geno's and the Pat's, etc. I'm always looking for that person in each city, the guide who will steer me away from the predictable. And so, when we were in New Orleans, I made some new friends who introduced me to the true local spots. That's a kind of tricky process, because you start a game of oneupsmanship. If you go to a great hole in the wall, the food

---

Richard Nichols: longtime manager and producer of The Roots; he died in 2014.

snobs will try to outdo you and come up with an even more secret one. That year, I tried local cooking in ways I hadn't before. I went into deep swamp food, meats like alligator, crocodile, frogs.

New Orleans is a great example of what I have started to learn [. . .]: food is much more than taste. A real experience has to be immersive in all five senses. It has to smell awesome. It has to feel awesome. It has to have a distinctive look. Donald Link is an expert at paying homage to his culture while also building away from it. He picked up a thread that . . . others spun out — how does a creative professional know when to double down on success and when to cut loose and start something new? I have eaten at his places, from Herbsaint to Butcher to Cochon, and I have eaten with him, and every experience is a master class in how regional cuisines can survive and change, or change to survive.

Deep South food has one scary dimension, which is that you can only go back so many years before you bump into something dark in history. It's not Cochon's responsibility, and I feel it more in other places than in Louisiana, but it's really a factor. I was in Mobile, Alabama, recently, and there was a diner there that had a big plate-glass window in front. It was about to be dusk. There were these great old trees outside, and as the sun went down, the trees started to look haunting and threatening. I asked my tour manager how old the trees were and the answer came back: hundreds of years old. So these are the trees that my forefathers hanged from? I felt like they were going to come to life and chase me. It was too authentic. I didn't tell Donald Link that story before I spoke to him. I guess he knows it now, if he's reading this.

[Questlove:] Some chefs are transplants, in the sense they're cooking 5 far from where they grew up. Ludo Lefebvre comes from France to open a restaurant in Los Angeles, or Ryan Roadhouse goes from Iowa to Canada to Tulsa, Oklahoma, to Denver to Portland. You're more or less back where you started in Louisiana. What was the first restaurant you remember going to?

[Link:] Well, I was born in Bossier City, Louisiana, on an air force base. I grew up in Sulphur, Louisiana, which is named for the sulfur mines, and then spent a few years abroad when my dad was in the military. We came back to the States when I was six or seven, I went to college in Baton Rouge, at LSU, and then I settled in New Orleans. That was about twenty years ago. This is a long way of saying that I ate in Louisiana my whole life. And most of our eating was in people's homes. There weren't that many restaurants around. If we did go to a restaurant, it was probably a Chinese restaurant. That's all we had: a Chinese restaurant and McDonald's and cooking at home.

[Q:] So who did the cooking? I remember my grandmother making us her version of down-home cuisine. Sometimes she would cook up what my dad's brothers would bring in from hunting. Sometimes she would make food to stockpile in the refrigerator.

[L:] Both sets of my grandparents cooked, though it wasn't equally distributed. My dad's dad didn't cook shit. In that family, it was my grandmother, and she might make a pork roast or a gumbo. But on my mom's side, there were ten kids who lived in-state, and my grandfather on that side cooked everything. He hunted and fished and he would have eight things on the stove: collard greens and creamed corn and rabbit and dumplings. They were these huge spreads.

[Q:] Right now, when you talk, I'm picturing a huge Louisiana meal. I'm including all the things that you mentioned, the collard greens and creamed corn, but I'm including other things, too, things that probably make it much more like a movie cliché. When most people mention Philly food, they're not thinking much past cheesesteaks. Louisiana must have food clichés, and they're probably connected to cultural clichés in general. Even with new, more sophisticated shows like *True Detective* or *Treme*, there's always a *Big Easy*-type stereotype lurking in the background where people can't stop talking about beignets and jambalaya and po'boys and gumbo.

[L:] I don't think Louisiana is ever represented that well. I thought *True Detective* was a great show in terms of the cinematography and the screenwriting, but it didn't get points for cultural accuracy. Louisiana's a tough place to describe to outsiders. Most people's idea of our food comes from Paul Prudhomme in the eighties. Back then, he was everywhere, and so people got the idea that Louisiana food was Cajun food — and more specifically than that, a version of Cajun food that was really Paul's interpretation. But what does that mean? If you go back a little bit in history, Cajun is a blend of the cultures of the French, the Caribbean, and the Spanish. And so you start with things like Puerto Rican rice casseroles, then the Caribbean French come along and add roux, and others added okra, and gradually the cuisine became what it is today. When I grew up, it was never called Cajun. It was just food to us.

[Q:] There's a comedian who has that joke for Chinese food, that in China they just call it food.[1]

[L:] As a kid, I never really thought about food in this formal professional way, where I would track influences and map cuisines. Now I can see the whole thing a little more clearly. That's what gave me the original idea for Cochon. I spent lots of time in culinary school doing fine-dining French. It wasn't that I had forgotten my heritage, only that there wasn't so much call for it. When I moved back to New Orleans in 2000, everyone kept asking me where to get good Cajun and there really wasn't a place. I decided to open Cochon to connect it to my upbringing.

[Q:] The idea of upbringing is brought up all the time. . . . I grew up surrounded by music, not just as a consumer but also as the son of musicians, and I got the idea early that music was something that required hard work but yielded amazing results. Did you feel that as a Louisianan, you somehow had access to a more evolved sense of eating? There must be places where food isn't really woven into the fabric of everyday life.

[L:] I went to debate camp in California at fifteen, and I'll never forget that first meal in the cafeteria. I was just shocked: This is what y'all eat? I may have even said it out loud. Even our school lunches were good when I was a kid — we had homemade rolls and greens and smothered hamburgers with onions and gravy. That was one of my early recognitions that there was a food culture at home, though that didn't point me toward the food business.

[Q:] What did?

10

[L:] It's a winding path, probably like everyone. In high school, I had some rough times, and I cooked and washed dishes in burger joints. Then in the early nineties, in my early twenties, I moved to San Francisco with this girl I met at LSU and got a job at a place called Spaghetti Western. At first I was doing breakfast, but they asked me if I could add some Louisiana food. It was pretty basic stuff: dirty rice, some gumbo. I

---

[1] I have a vague memory of hearing this in a stand-up special or seeing it in a movie, but it's proving very difficult to source that joke. It's all over message boards and seems to be part of the overall comic mind.

moved on to a Caribbean restaurant in the Upper Haight that was owned by a Cuban guy, and I remember how exciting that food was. It had a bigger flavor profile, bigger seasonings. Then I went on to a place called the Flying Saucer, where I worked with a guy named Albert Tordjman. He was half-Moroccan, half-French, and all crazy. There's an urban legend about a chef who stabs a knife into the table of the food critic and tells him to get the fuck out of his place. Well, Albert was the guy who really did that. I had just started culinary school out there, and all the instructors said that nobody could work with Albert. Anyone who can make it through one night with him, they said, can make it through anything. That was enough for me. I showed up at his door, and it's a good thing I did. In addition to being crazy, he was a genius. People who said he was the best chef in California weren't exaggerating. If anything, they were underselling. He's deceased now.

[Q:] That's not the first story I have heard about an extreme personality in a kitchen. The restaurant business seems to work on people that way. Some comedian says that about cocaine: whatever your personality is, it just intensifies it. If you're a jerk, you become that much more of a jerk.[2]

[L:] It wasn't great behavior, but it showed me that the restaurant business is so much about passion. A guy came up to me one night, not even Albert, and shook me and screamed at me and said "You gotta be a fucking gladiator!" Albert was a gladiator. He was passionate to a fault. His cooking techniques were obsessively perfect. He wouldn't let us use a potato peeler. We had to do it with a knife. And when you cut vegetables, there was no hacking away at them. You had to do perfect dice. He would watch everything. He was meticulous and unyielding. And even though it was only a thirty-five-seat restaurant, it felt like we were doing a thousand covers a night. That's where I really found this deep love and appreciation for techniques and skills and seasoning — and, obviously, shutting the fuck up and keeping your head down and staying out of the line of fire.

[Q:] That's the very definition of an apprenticeship, and it's something I have also heard from lots of chefs. You're not ready until you're ready. Dale Talde told me a story of working at a restaurant, I won't say which, and having a spoon thrown at him so hard it hit a pot next to him and dented it. Those things seem like violence, but

---

[2]Again, I can't source this quote. Richard Pryor? This is part of a larger comedian intellectual-property issue: jokes just make the rounds and people claim them.

they're also measures of commitment. So how did that travel with you back from California?

[L:] When I made my way back to New Orleans, I didn't want to be known as a Cajun chef. There was a bit of backlash in me in terms of not blackening catfish. I had an attitude that it just wasn't what I did. I opened Herbsaint at the very end of 2000, and that whole first year, I fought against anything that seemed like local color and tried to go traditional Continental instead. I remember making a foie gras terrine that was very French-based. Over time, I loosened up a bit and started to realize that it was okay to embrace my roots. I had a skill, which was that I had this built-in experience with boudin and gumbos. I could make them with soul and character. I stopped resisting. I realized that I didn't have to exactly re-create the dishes of my childhood, but that they were an amazing foundation. I returned to Southern cooking with some of the ideas from California — big flavors and brightness and local ingredients. But that took changing what was around here.

[Q:] What do you mean?

[L:] It took changing attitudes, for starters. At one point, I opened a second branch of Cochon in Lafayette, in Cajun country, and that didn't work out well. People out there had an even more specific and conservative idea of what the cuisine is and what it's not. They accepted only the most traditional dishes: gumbo, jambalaya, etouffee.

[Q:] I had those battles with my father all the time, where his idea of music clashed with new things that were happening and he was stubborn about moving off his spot. I remember when he first saw Prince on TV. "Is that boy in his diapers?" he said. Another time, we were in a van and the Police were playing — it was that song where Andy Summers is screaming.[3] My father didn't like that and he said so to the guy who was playing it. "Turn that devil shit off in front of my son," he said. And hip-hop, well, he didn't think much of it. I think in *Mo' Meta Blues* my description of his description is "a bunch of nonmusical nutgrabbing."

[L:] Right. And I don't think that with most of these customers, their resistance to my food was hugely considered. It was simply that their moms cooked it a certain way, and so that's the only way, and everything else is

---

[3]It's "Mother," and he even says the word *screaming* as he screams: "The telephone is screaming." It's on *Synchronicity*, which was the first rock record I bought on my own, without my sister's help, so it has a special place in my heart.

crap. For me, I like different gumbos. I love that there are so many versions and variations and experiments. When I'm out, I always order it to see what that particular restaurant is doing. Take something like catfish courtbouillion. It's still a fairly conservative dish: fish cooked in white wine, tomatoes, bones in. But there are discrepancies in how it should be made. I had a guy once who came up to me in Lafayette. "I want to see how you make that," he said. I started to show him and he stopped me. "No, no," he said. "What you gotta do is get the seasoning in a can."

[Q:] **So how do you start connecting to simplicity without resorting to** 15 **seasoning in a can? It's like a form of innovation that looks backwards instead of forward. It's like the opposite of** *Back to the Future***. It's more like** *The Wiz* **— or, as other people insist on calling it,** *The Wizard of Oz***.[4] You need to teach people that they had the power to go home all along.**

[L:] The first thing you have to do is to realize that ingredients matter. Let's take pork. When I first got back to New Orleans and started calling purveyors for pork, what I got was this bland dry cheek and chemical laden pork shoulder. It was fucking nasty. We found our own farmer and made a deal to start raising a certain breed. We did lots of research on what kind of hogs would produce the best fat and meat without sacrificingtheamountofmeat.Nowwesustainthatfarmer.Webuyeighttwo-hundred-and-fifty-pound hogs a week. The same thing is true with produce. I'd go to markets and wonder why we're only getting these bell peppers when chiles grow like weeds. In fact, they're one of the only things that will grow around here. I had been to Spain and had these amazing chile peppers. I got a catalog and found a farmer and said "Hey, let's try these." In traditional Creole, or Cajun, the spices are really just these mediocre chiles in a shitty dry form. We get these amazing chiles, and then dry them and I keep them in a Ziploc bag.

[Q:] **Are you always receiving transmissions on the food frequency? Can you go to a country without thinking about the way they're eating? I ask, obviously, because I can't really go places without thinking about the local music culture.**

[L:] Well, I've been fortunate enough to travel extensively, and I always pick up something new. I've been to France, to Italy, to Uruguay, to Peru,

---

[4]I just learned that *The Wiz* will return to TV as one of those live-action network musicals, like *The Sound of Music* or *Peter Pan*. It will already have aired by the time this book comes out, but let me just say for the record that I'm not sure how I feel about a *Wiz* without Michael Jackson.

to Puerto Rico. I pick up ideas or rather bits of ideas. It's not like if I go to Mexico I'm going to come back and suddenly start cooking Mexican. But I had this ceviche in Mexico that I loved. I don't generally like Peruvian ceviches. They're too acidic and sharp. This Mexican one had a nice balance. It had spices that were not too extreme in terms of heat level but had great flavors that worked well together. That kind of thing is perfect for Creole cooking. Creole cooking is just waiting for it.

[Q:] **When you have a discipline in any of the arts, music or food, there's so much training that goes into it before you're equipped to have your own ideas. You might have glimmerings before then, but not fully formed ideas. I do remember the period where I started to move from re-creating other people's beats to thinking that maybe the things I was playing were my own. Do you remember when you first felt that moment of invention?**

[L:] It was probably at Elite Cafe in San Francisco in 1997 or 1998. I was serving this eighties version of bad Cajun food from a steam table. I went in and asked if they wanted to get rid of it and do some exciting Cajun. The owner called me to talk it through. I was very clear with him that my plan was to throw everything away and write a new menu. He agreed. I started inventing — in other words, finding these routes to arriving at the food I wanted. For example, at that time I couldn't find good sausage, so I started making my own. I began to combine French dishes like duck confit with traditional Louisiana staples like dirty rice. It got so popular that the general manager was concerned that I had set up something that nobody else would be able to follow if I left. To me, at the time, that was funny. I was twenty-seven and I didn't give a shit. You're telling me it's too good? That's not my problem.

[Q:] **When you talk about American culture, you're talking at least partly about race. Sometimes the issue is right there on top, and sometimes you have to peel away layers to get to it. What's the history of black food and black chefs in New Orleans as it relates to the broader community?**

[L:] That's a tricky and complicated question. Think of the music of New Orleans. It came through Africa and the Caribbean, with black creators and black messengers. Lots of the food arrived along the same route, of course. It was Spanish and French food bouncing in and out of these New World locations. They weren't eating Creole food because it didn't exist yet. And the slaves created their own food because of what they had to cook with: different ingredients, different tools. But their food didn't get written about very much. Lafcadio Hearn was eloquent about Creole culture when he wrote about it in the nineteenth century, but he limited his sense of things to white colonists. So lots of black cooks and black food got written out of the process.

[Q:] Does that process continue to this day in some ways? As I was researching for this book, and thinking about how race plays a role in music, in food, in the visual arts, I noticed that despite the fact that the food world includes so many kinds of dishes, so many influences, most chefs are still white men. Why is that?

[L:] It's something that's impossible not to think about. I have taken field trips to Baltimore and to Washington, D.C., and they have some of the same issues as New Orleans. When you look at large urban African-American communities, there's a lack of food and a lack of access, and it's hard not to feel like it's part of a bigger systemic problem with education and opportunity. When I was growing up in Louisiana, most people in black communities still cooked, especially in rural areas. Everyone was a home cook. That happened without it becoming a profession or an industry, really. I think the same is true with music.

"Thinking about how race plays a role in music, in food, in the visual arts, I noticed that despite the fact that the food world includes so many kinds of dishes, so many influences, most chefs are still white men. Why is that?"

If you go to the Mississippi Delta, there are these musicians there that are just phenomenal, like nothing you've ever heard, and maybe they're making forty bucks a night. You just can't believe how good they are and they're in this Podunk fucking town, how skilled and advanced, but it doesn't necessarily translate to being able to make a living. And then in urban areas, there's not even that level of skill.

[Q:] This is part of the much larger crisis in urban black communities. There probably isn't cooking because that depends on some kind of stability. Tariq° and I both went to CAPA, this performing arts school in Philadelphia, and we've tried to keep a hand in sponsoring students and raising scholarship money and making sure that kids who show talent have at least a chance of turning it into something more permanent. 20

[L:] The terrible parts of this system seem to grow. There's poor education and too much violence and drugs. Households are busted up. Not quite

Tariq Luqmaan Trotter: better known as Black Thought, the co-founder and lead MC of The Roots.

forty percent of black males in New Orleans finish high school. There's not opportunity, and because of that, young people in those communities aren't looking for jobs in the same way. At my restaurants, for example, we don't get many black applicants. That makes the problem even harder to attack. It backs up the problem to a more basic level. You can't even have discussions about black-owned restaurants, or black chefs, until you have black cooks. And getting black cooks means getting black workers in your kitchens, and that's going to take some basic job training: how to look for a job. When you go into the Quarter, you see black cooks there, but they're older. I want to restart some of that among younger people.

[Q:] You also hear about all the problems with urban diets. Other chefs have talked about that, too — how there's not really a problem with food scarcity in poor neighborhoods. There's a problem with a surplus of the wrong kinds of foods; foods that are cheap, but not nutritional.

[L:] When I was in Baltimore, I went to a market to shop. I got ten dollars to buy food for four people. I can do that all day long. But the woman in front of me had the same budget, and she was spending it all on donuts and soda. That's an urban poverty issue that has consequences for food culture.[5] I try to deal with it by staying focused on local issues. We get offered all kinds of opportunities to participate in national charities. People from out of town are calling all the time to ask us to join up with this nutrition program or that local sourcing program. We've had to give up all of that to focus on just one thing, which is the problem of urban communities here in New Orleans. We have a job-training program called Liberty's Kitchen. I tell kids that if you want to come hang out in the restaurant, let me know. If you want to take an apprenticeship and show up and work, we can work on that, too. There's ways we can be directly involved, and not just by raising money.

---

[5] A few weeks after this interview, in April 2015, Baltimore was in crisis as a result of other urban poverty issues: police brutality, entrenched gangs, underclass frustration, and more. I thought of Donald's point when I read the eloquent remarks of John Angelos, whose family owns the Baltimore Orioles. He wished for peaceful protests and hoped that unrest would not interfere with baseball games, but he said he was much more concerned with something else: "The past four-decade period during which an American political elite have shipped middle-class and working-class jobs away from Baltimore and cities and towns around the U.S. to third-world dictatorships like China and others, plunged tens of millions of good, hard-working Americans into economic devastation, and then followed that action around the nation by diminishing every American's civil rights protections in order to control an unfairly impoverished population living under an ever-declining standard of living." It's a messy sentence, but it's a messy situation.

[Q:] This is a heavy issue. I feel like I'm Charlie Rose. Let's talk about lighter stuff for a little while. What's your favorite guilty-pleasure food?

[L:] I'm pretty fond of chicken wings, or, for that matter, any kind of fried chicken. Fried rice and fried chicken seem to be my greatest weaknesses.

[Q:] Are there any foods that you hate?

[L:] Anything that's badly prepared. But I have a problem with bell peppers. And cranberries. I don't get it. I don't see the appeal at all. Maybe it's the tartness. And I'm not a huge fan of pineapple in hot food.

[Q:] For me, it's beets. I've had so many horrible experiences with them. And then I ate at this vegan spot in Philly called Vedge and had no idea I was eating beets. The chef came out to explain the dish and I was stunned. "Beets?" I said. What's a food you want to eat in its native environment?

[L:] Vietnam is the number one place I want to go. It's just so fresh and vibrant and interesting. It's more like what we think of as street food, with incredibly inventive spices and herbs. Many cooks here go and eat Vietnamese food whenever they get the chance.

[Q:] If you could invent one thing to make your life in the kitchen easier, what would it be?   25

[L:] A line cook. Everybody wants to be a chef these days. I want some actual cooks.

[Q:] Many of the chefs in this book are at the same point creatively that I'm at: early middle age, I guess you'd call it. And one of the things I keep hearing is that as chefs get older they cook more simply. They set aside the impulse they had early in their careers to make a stand, or make a show.

[L:] Without a doubt, that's true for me. When you eat the food of some young chefs, it's like reading a fucking novel. What are you trying to accomplish? It's too ego-driven. These days, if I cook fish, I want to taste the fish. You shouldn't be serving it if it's not beautiful. So why put so much shit on the plate? And if you try for simplicity, that also helps you avoid cliché. We opened Cochon eight or nine years ago, and in that span we've seen the growth of lots of Southern food, but it has become so trite. Everything has bourbon or pecan or molasses. Everything has glaze. Do you need those same techniques piled on top of everything?

[Q:] It's like the EPCOT problem. When you go there, there are all these international plazas that boil down countries to a few ideas: schnitzel in Austrialand, or tulip soup in Hollandland. Those are bad examples, but you know what I mean.

[L:] Pêche is a good illustration of this. We went to Uruguay, and I fell in love with this simple cooking there. It was brilliant. You have great meat and you have fire. After four bottles of wine I wrote out a two-page menu of my vision, based on that. Then I was talking to my partners and we decided we should go to San Sebastian, where they do the same thing but with seafood. We wanted to change the way people think of Gulf Coast seafood. The result was this Spanish South American style of roast meats and cooking over fire. How do you make it a New Orleans restaurant? Well, it is one, by default, because it's here. You don't need po'boys.

[Q:] But do people clamor for them? Is the tourist jones still so strong that they want the cartoon version of New Orleans? You'd think that diners in general would be better informed because of the Internet — not that their taste would be better, necessarily, but that they would have a better sense of the tastes that are available to them.

[L:] The more people eat out around the world, the more they learn about international foods and world cuisines, the more sophisticated their palates become. You do see more and more people come to New Orleans looking for something special or distinctive. There was a time in the beginning of Cochon when everyone wanted fish blackened. That doesn't happen as much anymore.

[Q:] Do you like the Internet in general for its effect on restaurants?

[L:] No. I hate it. Especially when it comes to the ways that it lets people weigh in critically. I don't know if you've seen that YouTube series "Real Actors Read Yelp Reviews." They're just ridiculous. There are some legitimate concerns. But honestly, the validity of the negative experiences that people have are maybe .02 percent. The most common thing you see is people getting pissed off because they were made to wait. What they don't tell you is that they had an eight o'clock reservation on a busy night and they show up at 7:40 or so and got seated at 8:08. Or someone else claims that they got food poisoning and there's no accounting for why the two hundred other people who ate at that same restaurant that same night were fine.

[Q:] **Other chefs have said that they read the reviews, sift through** 30 **them, and find things that they can learn from.**

[L:] I can't say I learn anything from Yelp. We look once every six months, and I get angry and say, what a bunch of morons. There's never anything good in there. I'm in the restaurant all the time. I see how it works. I have a system of managers and chefs that are trained to look out for exactly the kinds of things that people on Yelp are claiming to have noticed. And they're good at their jobs. Managers can walk around and look at expressions, at the visual cues people give.

[Q:] **Michael Solomonov° was talking about the Internet's criticism culture and said that for him the biggest problem is that it takes away the face-to-face component of desires, demands, and disappointments. It's one thing, he says, to go and talk to the chef and say that you were unhappy with your meal. It's another one to scurry home and carp about it.**

[L:] In the restaurant, that's absolutely true. Feedback, especially negative feedback, is one of the most important things. People come up after meals all the time and say they loved everything. I'm glad to hear that but I'm more interested in what people didn't like. I mean, I know our food is good but at the same time I want to understand why some people didn't have a good experience so that we can turn that around. If someone orders pork belly and complains about it being too fatty, we'll give you something else. In the end, our only goal is to please diners. Still, I use the Internet all the time. I look up other restaurants. I look at menus and research different ingredients. I get images for plates and presentations. It's incredibly useful if I'm traveling: not to read reviews, but to get a list of new places in a city.

[Q:] **We're asking chefs not only to be innovators, but also futurists. Where do you see the food world going in the next decade?**

[L:] I think you'll see food really become more intertwined with other culture, to the point where there might not be cuisines in the traditional sense. When I look back ten years, or twenty, food was very specific. There was Mexican or French or Chinese. If you wanted to bring one to the other, it took some doing. Now the food blends more and more. You almost cannot locate or recognize the actual source of a dish. It all melds together.

Michael Solomonov: Israeli-born, Philadelphia-based chef and restauranteur.

[Q:] How about the future of ingredients? Will there be fewer and fewer good ingredients? Many chefs have said that fish, for instance, are in shorter and shorter supply.

[L:] We're lucky here, because we're on the water and have lots of connections. The Gulf is a pretty well-maintained fishery. But worldwide, I do think that farm fish will come into play. With other meats, like pork, there has been lots of movement. When we started making bacon, it sucked, so we got a relationship with one pig farm, and we sustain them. Our business alone accounts for about $7,000 a week. And there are lots of local farms that profit from those kinds of arrangements. We have a girl on staff who does nothing but work with farmers. She'll go and say this is how much we'll buy, this is our usage, this is how it's spaced out. The result might be fifteen cases of arugula every week, or ten pounds of squash, and we can start directing them as to what to plant and when. But the truth is that this is only a sliver of the larger picture. We're not going back to Wendell Berry's utopia of small farms. The best that can happen is that this kind of behavior from restaurants will pressure the bigger producers to behave more responsibly and make better food. You're not going to feed millions and millions of people with small community farms. I would like to tell everyone to buy chicken from local farmers, but that's not economically realistic. You're only going to make a big-picture difference when the major agricultural industry starts to shift, when labeling is more honest, when politicians get past rhetoric.

[Q:] Do they ever? Plus, there's the matter that bespoke eating isn't for everyone. Think of audio equipment. I might know that a certain audio system sounds good, but the truth of the matter is that most people are going to be listening to music on their computer speakers, or through earbuds.

[L:] You can't be a stickler and say that there are only two choices — either locally produced organics or starvation. And while you can tell kids to eat healthy all day long, imagine a single mother in the middle of the country with no access to ingredients. Most urban farmers' markets are for yuppies, for hobby cooks. There are exceptions. When I was in San Francisco, I would go to the market, and it was large and cheap — there were lots of Asian foods that were being used by real people. You could cook for twenty people for five bucks or less. Some Latino communities are the same way. There's a way to stretch food and eat better, and it's not necessarily this utopian yuppie idea of local and organic.

[Q:] Maybe the answer is in bringing food back into the home. I've 35 been asking people about their earliest meals, both in restaurants and at home, and every time I ask I think about my own answer. Much of the cooking was done by my grandmother. She used to make us bacon, or prepare what my uncles caught when they went hunting. She did it all for cheap. Those are the same kinds of dishes you might see now in a restaurant as part of a $500 meal.

[L:] We went to Belize and ate in these shacks in Mayan villages. One of the places was an Indian restaurant, and that was one of the best meals I've ever had. It was nothing fancy at all — a hacked-up chicken with chiles and curry — but it was out of this world, and cheap as hell. There is a way to cook well with no money. You say you think of your grand-mother. I think about my grandfather, who I mentioned at the beginning of our conversation. It's almost the same thing. He's up there laughing, seeing what restaurants now charge for ham hocks and collard greens. That food was born out of poverty. Now it's haute cuisine. It's ironic.

Understanding the Text

1. What do you learn about Questlove and Donald Link from reading this interview?
2. According to Questlove, what is a "real" food experience?
3. Questlove explains, "When you have a discipline in any of the arts, music or food, there's so much training that goes into it before you're equipped to have your own ideas" (par. 17). What does he mean by this?
4. According to Questlove and Link in the interview, what is the problem of urban diets and urban communities in places like New Orleans, and how have they tried to solve the problem?

Reflection and Response

5. What does it mean to think of food as an art form? How does that change the way you think about chefs — or eating in a restaurant or at home?
6. Questlove asks Donald Link if he thinks he "had access to a more evolved sense of eating" (par. 9) while growing up in Louisiana. What do you think he means by this? Do you think your upbringing gave you access to "a more evolved sense of eating"? Why or why not?

Making Connections

7. Questlove argues that Donald Link's cooking demonstrates "how regional cuisines can survive and change, or change to survive" (par. 3). Research

cuisines in your region, examining their history and how they are enjoyed now. What has helped them survive? How have they changed? Compare a local cuisine in your region to one discussed in the interview. What kinds of observations might Questlove make about food in your region?

8. In his conversation with Donald Link, Questlove offers this observation: "There must be places where food isn't really woven into the fabric of everyday life" (par. 9). Select one or two sources in this book that discuss places where food seems to be part of the cultural and social fabric. Then select one or two sources that discuss places where it is not. Use these sources to develop an analysis of what you think Questlove means by this observation.

9. Donald Link tells Questlove that in cooking, "ingredients matter." Which other authors in this book would agree with this view? Locate passages in their texts to support your response.

10. Think about Questlove and Donald Link's discussion about food and race in American culture. Then locate at least three other sources that discuss this relationship. Why is it important to think about the relationship between food and race? Write a research-based paper in response to this question.

The Joy of Cooking Too Much: 70 Years of Calorie Increases in Classic Recipes

Brian Wansink and Collin R. Payne

Brian Wansink is the John Dyson Professor of Consumer Behavior at Cornell University and the award-winning author of more than 150 academic articles and books, including *Mindless Eating: Why We Eat More Than We Think* (2006). His areas of expertise include eating behavior, nutrition science, and food psychology. His research has contributed to marketing changes and policies, some of which are aimed at reducing portion sizes and preventing overeating. Collin R. Payne was a postdoctoral research associate at Cornell University before becoming a professor of marketing in the College of Business at New Mexico State University. He specializes in consumer behavior and social marketing. In this academic article, originally published in *Annals of Internal Medicine* in 2009, Wansink and Payne examine the classic recipes in various editions of *The Joy of Cooking*, concluding that serving sizes and calories have increased since 1936.

B*ackground:* Obesity has been associated with the expanding portion sizes of away-from-home foods (1). Although portion size norms and calorie density have increased outside the home, they could also have a parallel or referred impact on serving sizes in the home (2, 3). Cookbook recipes might provide a longitudinal° gauge of how serving sizes and calorie density have changed inside homes. One cookbook, Th*e Joy of Cooking*, has been updated approximately every 10 years since 1936 (4) and could provide a glimpse into the changing norms of U.S. food preparation and serving sizes over the past 70 years (5).

Objective: To assess changes in calorie density and serving sizes of household meals since 1936, as reflected in recipes in *The Joy of Cooking.*

Methods: We content-analyzed the seven editions of *The Joy of Cooking* (1936, 1946, 1951, 1963, 1975, 1997, and 2006) to determine how serving sizes and calorie density have changed over the past 70 years [see the table on p. 115]. Since the first edition in 1936, only 18 recipes have been continuously published in each subsequent edition. By using standard nutritional analysis techniques, we determined serving size calorie levels for each recipe in each edition.

longitudinal: involving information gathered over a long period of time.

We performed all analyses of variance by using SPSS statistical software, version 12.0 (SPSS, Chicago, Illinois). We considered a P value less than 0.05 to be statistically significant.

Results: Over the past 70 years, the total caloric content increased for 14 of the 18 recipes. Because of changes in ingredients, the mean average calories in a recipe increased by 928.1 (from 2123.8 calories [95% CI, 1638.7 to 2608.9 calories] to 3051.9 calories [CI, 2360.7 to 3743.1 calories]), representing a 43.7% increase ($P < 0.001$). As the table indicates, mean average calories per serving increased for 17 of 18 recipes and was influenced by both changes in ingredients and changes in serving size. The resulting increase of 168.8 calories (from 268.1 calories [CI, 210.4 to 325.8 calories] to 436.9 calories [CI, 359.1 to 514.7 calories]) represents a 63.0% increase ($P < 0.001$) in calories per serving. Given that the average 2006 recipe had 1.1 fewer servings than in 1936, the average calorie density per serving size has increased by 37.4% ($P < 0.001$).

Over the 70-year history of *The Joy of Cooking*, the recommended serving sizes were altered at 3 points. Between 1946 and 1951, 3 of 18 recipes increased their serving size by an average of 32.5%. Between 1951 and 1963, 4 recipes increased their serving size by an average of 20.0%. Between 1997 and 2006, 5 recipes increased their serving size by an average of 21.1%. Only 3 recipes decreased their serving size at any point in the past 70 years, but all three were compensated by subsequent increases in later years.

Average Caloric Content and Number of Servings in
***The Joy of Cooking*, by Publication Year**

Characteristic	Publication Year			
	1936	**1946**	**1951**	**1963**
Mean total calories	2123.8	2122.3	2089.9	2250.0
per recipe (SD)	(1050.0)	(1002.3)	(1009.6)	(1078.6)
Mean average calories	268.1	271.1	280.9	294.7
per serving (SD)	(124.8)	(124.2)	(116.2)	(117.7)
Mean number of servings	12.9	12.9	13.0	12.7
per recipe (SD)	(13.3)	(13.3)	(14.5)	(14.6)
	1975	**1997**	**2006**	
Mean total calories	2234.2	2249.6	3051.9	
per recipe (SD)	(1089.2)	(1094.8)	(1496.2)	
Mean average calories	285.6	288.6	384.4	
per serving (SD)	(118.3)	(122.0)	(168.3)	
Mean number of servings	12.4	12.4	12.7	
per recipe (SD)	(14.3)	(14.3)	(13.0)	

Discussion: The mean average calorie density in 18 classic recipes has increased 35.2% per serving over the past 70 years. This is due mostly to the use of higher-calorie ingredients and partly to serving sizes that showed small increases in the late 1940s and early 1960s and a 33.2% increase since 1996.

The calories and portion sizes of classic recipes may reflect prevailing tastes and norms. Yet, they may also establish or reinforce exaggerated norms in other settings, such as new families. Although this study is largely descriptive, it implies a prescriptive recommendation for families. The serving size and calorie composition of classic recipes need to be downsized to counteract growing waistlines.

> "The serving size and calorie composition of classic recipes need to be downsized to counteract growing waistlines."

Conclusion: Calorie density and serving sizes in recipes from *The Joy of Cooking* have increased since 1936.

References

Nielsen SJ, Popkin BM. Patterns and trends in food portion sizes, 1977–1998. JAMA. 2003;289:450–3. [PMID: 12533124]

Wansink B, van Ittersum K. Portion size me: downsizing our consumption norms. J Am Diet Assoc. 2007;107:1103–6. [PMID: 17604738]

Smiciklas-Wright H, Mitchell DC, Mickle SJ, Goldman JD, Cook A. Foods commonly eaten in the United States, 1989–1991 and 1994–1996: are portion sizes changing? J Am Diet Assoc. 2003;103:41–7. [PMID: 12525792]

Rombauer IS, Becker MR, Becker E, eds. The Joy of Cooking. New York: Bobbs-Merrill; 1936, 1946, 1951, 1963, 1975; New York: Scribner; 1997, 2006.

Wansink B. Environmental factors that increase the food intake and consumption volume of unknowing consumers. Annu Rev Nutr. 2004;24:455–79. [PMID: 15189128]

Understanding the Text

1. What did Wansink and Payne set out to learn in their study of *The Joy of Cooking* recipes? What method did they use?
2. What conclusion did they reach? On what is this conclusion based?
3. What does the table show?

Reflection and Response

4. This article was published in an academic journal. What do you learn about academic research from reading this article? What is the value of this kind of research about food? What are some practical uses of such research?

5. Why did they choose to analyze recipes from *The Joy of Cooking*? Are you familiar with this cookbook? Do you know anyone who uses it?

Making Connections

6. What would Marion Nestle ("Eating Made Simple," p. 37) and Rachel Laudan ("Birth of the Modern Diet," p. 55) think of this study? Use textual evidence to support your response.

7. What do our recipes say about who we are? Think about how Wansink and Payne, Questlove (p. 98), and Mary Roach (p. 118) would answer this question. Then, select a favorite recipe of your own, and explain what it says about who you are.

Liver and Opinions: Why We Eat What We Eat and Despise the Rest

Mary Roach

Mary Roach is known for her lively, humorous, and illuminating treatment of taboo subjects about the human body. She graduated from Wesleyan with a degree in psychology before heading to San Francisco, where she worked as a freelance copy editor and a public relations consultant for the San Francisco Zoological Society. Eventually she began writing humor pieces and first-person essays in a variety of popular magazines, including *Vogue*, *National Geographic*, *Outside Magazine*, and the *New York Times Magazine*. She has published five highly regarded books, including *Gulp: Adventures on the Alimentary Canal* (2013), *Packing for Mars: The Curious Science of Life in the Void* (2010), and *Stiff: The Curious Lives of Human Cadavers* (2003). Roach's gift as a writer is her ability to turn complex subjects into something average readers can understand and enjoy reading about, despite her having no formal academic background in science. In this excerpt from *Gulp*, Roach does just that.

The Northern Food Tradition and Health Resource Kit contains a deck of forty-eight labeled photographs of traditional Inuit foods. Most are meat, but none are steaks. Seal Heart, one is labeled. Caribou Brain, says another. The images, life-size where possible, are printed on stiff paper and die-cut, like paper dolls that you badly want to throw some clothes on. The kit I looked through belonged to Gabriel Nirlungayuk, a community health representative from Pelly Bay, a hamlet in Canada's Nunavut territory. Like me, he was visiting Igloolik — a town on a small island near Baffin Island — to attend an Arctic athletic competition.* With him was Pelly Bay's mayor at the time, Makabe Nartok. The three of us met by chance in the kitchen of Igloolik's sole lodgings, the Tujormivik Hotel.

---

*The Inuit Games. Most are indoor competitions originally designed to fit in igloos. Example: the Ear Lift: "On a signal, the competitor walks forward lifting the weight off the floor and carrying it with his ear for as far a distance as his ear will allow." For the Mouth Pull, opponents stand side by side, shoulders touching and arms around each other's necks as if they were dearest friends. Each grabs the outside corner of his opponent's mouth with his middle finger and attempts to pull him over a line drawn in the snow between them. As so often is the case in life, "strongest mouth wins."

Nirlungayuk's job entailed visiting classrooms to encourage young Inuit "chip-aholics and pop-aholics" to eat like their elders. As the number of Inuit who hunt has dwindled, so has the consumption of organs (and other anatomy not available for purchase at the Igloolik Co-op: tendons, blubber, blood, head).

I picked up the card labeled Caribou Kidney, Raw. "Who actually eats this?"

"I do," said Nirlungayuk. He is taller than most Inuit, with a prominent, thrusting chin that he used to indicate Nartok. "He does."

Anyone who hunts, the pair told me, eats organs. Though the Inuit (in   5 Canada, the term is preferred over *Eskimo*) gave up their nomadic existence in the 1950s, most adult men still supplemented the family diet with hunted game, partly to save money. In 1993, when I visited, a small can of Spork, the local Spam, cost $2.69. Produce arrives by plane. A watermelon might set you back $25. Cucumbers were so expensive that the local sex educator did his condom demonstrations on a broomstick.

I asked Nartok to go through the cutouts and show me what he ate. He reached across the table to take them from me. His arms were pale to the wrist, then abruptly brown. The Arctic suntan could be mistaken, at a glance, for gloves. He peered at the cutouts through wire-rim glasses. "Caribou liver, yes. Brain. Yes, I eat brain. I eat caribou eyes, raw and cooked." Nirlungayuk looked on, nodding.

"I like this part very much." Nartok was holding a cutout labeled Caribou Bridal Veil. This is a prettier way of saying "stomach membrane." It was dawning on me that eating the whole beast was a matter not just of economics but of preference. At a community feast earlier in the week, I was offered "the best part" of an Arctic char. It was an eye, with fat and connective tissue dangling off the back like wiring on a headlamp. A cluster of old women stood by a chain-link fence digging marrow from caribou bones with the tilt-headed focus nowadays reserved for texting.

For Arctic nomads, eating organs has, historically, been a matter of survival. Even in summer, vegetation is sparse. Little beyond moss and lichen° grows abundantly on the tundra. Organs are so vitamin-rich, and edible plants so scarce, that the former are classified, for purposes of Arctic health education, both as "meat" and as "fruits and vegetables." One serving from the Fruits and Vegetables Group in Nirlungayuk's materials is "½ cup berries or greens, or 60 to 90 grams of organ meats."

Nartok shows me an example of Arctic "greens": cutout number 13, Caribou Stomach Contents. Moss and lichen are tough to digest, unless, like caribou, you have a multichambered stomach in which to ferment

---

lichen: a plantlike organism that grows on rocks or walls in a symbiotic relationship.

them. So the Inuit let the caribou have a go at it first. I thought of Pat Moeller and what he'd said about wild dogs and other predators eating the stomachs and stomach contents of their prey first. "And wouldn't we all," he'd said, "be better off."

If we could strip away the influences of modern Western culture and   10
media and the high-fructose, high-salt temptations of the junk-food sellers, would we all be eating like Inuit elders, instinctively gravitating to the most healthful, nutrient-diverse foods? Perhaps. It's hard to say. There is a famous study from the 1930s involving a group of orphanage babies who, at mealtimes, were presented with a smorgasbord of thirty-four whole, healthy foods. Nothing was processed or prepared beyond mincing or mashing. Among the more standard offerings — fresh fruits and vegetables, eggs, milk, chicken, beef — the researcher, Clara Davis, included liver, kidney, brains, sweetbreads°, and bone marrow. The babies shunned liver and kidney (as well as all ten vegetables, haddock°, and pineapple), but brains and sweetbreads did *not* turn up among the low-preference foods she listed. And the most popular item of all? Bone marrow.

At half past ten, the sky was princess pink. There was still enough light to make out the walrus appliqués on the jacket of a young girl riding her bicycle on the gravel road through town. We were joined in the kitchen by a man named Marcel, just back from a hunting camp where a pod of narwhal° had been spotted earlier in the day. The narwhal is a medium-sized whale with a single tusk protruding from its head like a birthday candle.

Marcel dropped a white plastic bag onto the table. It bounced slightly on landing. "Muktuk," Nirlungayuk said approvingly. It was a piece of narwhal skin, uncooked. Nartok waved it off. "I ate muktuk earlier. Whole lot." In the air he outlined a square the size of a hardback book.

Nirlungayuk speared a chunk on the tip of a pocketknife blade and held it out for me. My instinct was to refuse it. I'm a product of my upbringing. I grew up in New Hampshire in the 1960s, when meat meant muscle. Breast and thigh, burgers and chops. Organs were something you donated. Kidney was a shape for coffee tables. It did not occur to my people to fix innards for supper, especially raw ones. Raw outards seemed even more unthinkable.

I pulled the rubbery chunk from Nirlungayuk's knife. It was cold from the air outside and disconcertingly narwhal-colored. The taste of muktuk is hard to pin down. Mushrooms? Walnut? There was plenty of time to think about it, as it takes approximately as long to chew narwhal as it

sweetbreads: pancreas of a sheep or calf that is eaten as food.
haddock: a type of fish that is eaten as food, from the cod family.
narwhal: a medium-sized, toothed whale found in the Arctic; the males grow a large sword-like tusk.

does to hunt them. I know you won't believe me, because I didn't believe Nartok, but muktuk is exquisite (and, again, healthy: as much vitamin A as in a carrot, plus a respectable amount of vitamin C).

I like chicken skin and pork rinds. Why the hesitation over muktuk? 15 Because to a far greater extent than most of us realize, culture writes the menu. And culture doesn't take kindly to substitutions.

What Gabriel Nirlungayuk was trying to do with organs for health, the United States government tried to do for war. During World War II, the U.S. military was shipping so much meat overseas to feed troops and allies that a domestic shortage loomed. According to a 1943 *Breeder's Gazette* article, the American soldier consumed close to a pound of meat a day. Beginning that year, meat on the homefront was rationed — but only the mainstream cuts. You could have all the organ meats you wanted. The army didn't use them because they spoiled more quickly and because, as *Life* put it, "the men don't like them."

Civilians didn't like them any better. Hoping to change this, the National Research Council (NRC) hired a team of anthropologists, led by the venerable Margaret Mead, to study American food habits. How do people decide what's good to eat, and how do you go about

> "To a far greater extent than most of us realize, culture writes the menu. And culture doesn't take kindly to substitutions."

changing their minds? Studies were undertaken, recommendations drafted, reports published — including Mead's 1943 opus "The Problem of Changing Food Habits: Report of the Committee on Food Habits," and if ever a case were to be made for word-rationing, there it was.

The first order of business was to come up with a euphemism. People were unlikely to warm to a dinner of "offal" or "glandular meats," as organs were called in the industry.* "Tidbits" turned up here and there — as in *Life's* poetic "Plentiful are these meats called 'tidbits' " — but "variety meats" was the standout winner. It had a satisfactorily vague and cheery air, calling to mind both protein and primetime programming with dance numbers and spangly getups. In the same vein — ew! Sorry. Similarly, meal planners and chefs were encouraged "to give special attention to the naming" of new organ-meat entrées. A little French was thought to help things go down easier. A 1944 *Hotel Management* article included recipes for "Brains à la King" and "Beef Tongue Piquant."

---

*Among themselves, meat professionals speak a jolly slang. "Plucks" are thoracic viscera: heart, lungs, trachea. Spleens are "melts," rumens are "paunch," and unborn calves are "slunks." I once saw a cardboard box outside a New York meat district warehouse with a crude sign taped to it: FLAPS AND TRIANGLES.

A promotional poster by John E. Sheridan,
sponsored by the United States Food
Administration during war time.
N.Y. : Heywood Strasser & Voight Litho. Co., [1918(?)]

Another strategy was to target kids. "The human infant enters the world without information about what is edible and what is not," wrote psychologist Paul Rozin, who studied disgust for many years at the University of Pennsylvania. Until kids are around two, you can get them to try pretty much anything, and Rozin did. In one memorable study, he tallied the percentage of children aged sixteen to twenty-nine months who ate or tasted the following items presented to them on a plate: fish eggs (60 percent), dish soap (79 percent), cookies topped with ketchup (94 percent), a dead (sterilized) grasshopper (30 percent), and artfully coiled peanut butter scented with Limburger cheese and presented as "dog-doo" (55 percent). The lowest-ranked item, at 15 percent acceptance, was a human hair.*

---

*The children were wise to be wary. Compulsive hair-eaters wind up with trichobezoars — human hairballs. The biggest ones extend from stomach into intestine and look like otters or big hairy turds and require removal by stunned surgeons who run for their cameras and publish the pictures in medical journal articles about "Rapunzel syndrome." Bonus points for reading this footnote on April 27, National Hairball Awareness Day.

By the time children are ten years old, generally speaking, they've 20 learned to eat like the people around them. Once food prejudices are set, it is no simple task to dissolve them. In a separate study, Rozin presented sixty-eight American college students with a grasshopper snack, this time a commercially prepared honey-covered variety sold in Japan. Only 12 percent were willing to try one.

So the NRC tried to get elementary schools involved. Home economists were urged to approach teachers and lunch planners. "Let's do more than say 'How do you do' to variety meats; let's make friends with them!" chirps Jessie Alice Cline in the February 1943 *Practical Home Economics*. The War Food Administration pulled together a *Food Conservation Education* brochure with suggested variety-meat essay themes ("My Adventures in Eating New Foods"). Perhaps sensing the futility of trying to get ten-year-olds to embrace brains and hearts, the administration focused mainly on not wasting food. One suggested student activity took the form of "a public display of wasted edible food actually found in the garbage dump," which does more than say "How do you do" to a long night of parental phone calls.

The other problem with classroom-based efforts to change eating habits was that children don't decide what's for dinner. Mead and her team soon realized they had to get to the person they called the "gatekeeper" — Mom. Nirlungayuk reached a similar conclusion. I tracked him down, seventeen years later, and asked him what the outcome of his country-foods campaign had been. "It didn't really work," he said, from his office in the Nunavut department of wildlife and environment. "Kids eat what parents make for them. That's one thing I didn't do is go to the parents."

Even that can flop. Mead's colleague Kurt Lewin, as part of the NRC research, gave a series of lectures to homemakers on the nutritional benefits of organ meats, ending with a plea for patriotic cooperation.* Based on follow-up interviews, just 10 percent of the women who'd attended had gone home and prepared a new organ meat for the family. Discussion groups were more effective than lectures, but guilt worked best of all. "They said to the women, 'A lot of people are making a lot of sacrifices in this war,'" says Brian Wansink, author of "Changing Eating Habits on the Home Front." "'You can do your part by trying organ meats.' All of a sudden, it was like, 'Well, I don't want to be the only person not doing my part.'"

Also effective: pledges. Though it now seems difficult to picture it, Wansink says government anthropologists had PTA members stand up and recite, "I will prepare organ meats at least ___ times in the coming

---

*Meat and patriotism do not fit naturally together, and sloganeering proved a challenge. The motto "Food Fights for Freedom" would seem to inspire cafeteria mayhem more than personal sacrifice.

two weeks." "The act of making a public commitment," said Wansink, "was powerful, powerful, powerful." A little context here: The 1940s was the heyday of pledges and oaths.* In Boy Scout halls, homerooms, and Elks lodges, people were accustomed to signing on the dotted line or standing and reciting, one hand raised. Even the Clean Plate Club — dreamed up by a navy commander in 1942 — had an oath: "I, ___, being a member in good standing . . . , hereby agree that I will finish all the food on my plate . . . and continue to do so until Uncle Sam has licked the Japs and Hitler" — like, presumably, a plate.

To open people's minds to a new food, you sometimes just have to get   25
them to open their mouths. Research has shown that if people try something enough times, they'll probably grow to like it. In a wartime survey conducted by a team of food-habits researchers, only 14 percent of the students at a women's college said they liked evaporated milk. After serving it to the students sixteen times over the course of a month, the researchers asked again. Now 51 percent liked it. As Kurt Lewin put it, "People like what they eat, rather than eat what they like."

The phenomenon starts early. Breast milk and amniotic fluid° carry the flavors of the mother's foods, and studies consistently show that babies grow up to be more accepting of flavors they've sampled while in the womb and while breastfeeding. (Babies swallow several ounces of amniotic fluid a day.) Julie Mennella and Gary Beauchamp of the Monell Chemical Senses Center have done a great deal of work in this area, even recruiting sensory panelists to sniff† amniotic fluid° (withdrawn during

---

amniotic fluid: liquid in the womb of a pregnant woman that surrounds and provides nutrients to the fetus.

---

*Pledge madness peaked in 1942. The June issue of *Practical Home Economics* reprinted a twenty-item Alhambra, California, Student Council anti-waste pledge that included a promise to "drive carefully to conserve rubber" and another to "get to class on time to save paper on tardy slips." Perhaps more dire than the shortages in metal, meat, paper, and rubber was the "boy shortage" mentioned in an advice column on the same page. "Unless you do something about it, this means empty hours galore!" Luckily, the magazine had some suggestions. An out-of-fashion bouclé suit could be "unraveled, washed, tinted and reknitted" to make baby clothes. Still bored? "Take two worn rayon dresses and combine them to make one Sunday-best that looks brand new" — and fits like a dream if you are a giant insect or person with four arms.

†They are to be excused for not tasting it too. Amniotic fluid contains fetal urine (from swallowed amniotic fluid) and occasionally meconium: baby's first feces, composed of mucus, bile, epithelial cells, shed fetal hair, and other amniotic detritus. The *Wikipedia* entry helpfully contrasts the tarry, olive-brown smear of meconium — photographed in a tiny disposable diaper — with the similarly posed yellowish excretion of a breast-fed newborn, both with an option for viewing in the magnified resolution of 1,280 × 528 pixels.

amniocentesis) and breast milk from women who had and those who hadn't swallowed a garlic oil capsule. Panelists agreed: the garlic-eaters' samples smelled like garlic. (The babies didn't appear to mind. On the contrary, the Monell team wrote, "Infants . . . sucked more when the milk smelled like garlic.")

As a food marketing consultant, Brian Wansink was involved in efforts to increase global consumption of soy products. Whether one succeeds at such an undertaking, he found, depends a great deal on the culture whose diet you seek to change. Family-oriented countries where eating and cooking are firmly bound by tradition — Wansink gives the examples of China, Colombia, Japan, and India — are harder to infiltrate. Cultures like the United States and Russia, where there's less cultural pressure to follow tradition and more emphasis on the individual, are a better bet.

Price matters too, though not always how you think it would. Saving money can be part of the problem. The well-known, long-standing cheapness of offal, Mead wrote, condemned it to the wordy category "edible for human beings but not by own kind of human being." Eating organs, in 1943, could degrade one's social standing. Americans preferred bland preparations of muscle meat partly because for as long as they could recall, that's what the upper class ate.

So powerful are race- and status-based disgusts that explorers have starved to death rather than eat like the locals. British polar exploration suffered heavily for its mealtime snobbery. "The British believed that Eskimo food . . . was beneath a British sailor and certainly unthinkable for a British officer," wrote Robert Feeney in *Polar Journeys: The Role of Food and Nutrition in Early Exploration.* Members of the 1860 Burke and Wills expedition to cross Australia fell prey to scurvy or starved in part because they refused to eat what the indigenous Australians ate. Bugong-moth abdomen and witchetty grub may sound revolting, but they have as much scurvy-battling vitamin C as the same size serving of cooked spinach, with the additional benefits of potassium, calcium, and zinc.

Of all the so-called variety meats, none presents a steeper challenge to 30 the food persuader than the reproductive organs. Good luck to Deanna Pucciarelli, the woman who seeks to introduce mainstream America to the culinary joys of pig balls. "I am indeed working on a project on pork testicles," said Pucciarelli, director of the Hospitality and Food Management Program at — fill my heart with joy! — Ball State University. Because she was bound by a confidentiality agreement, Pucciarelli could not tell me who would be serving them or why or what form they would take. Setting aside alleged fertility enhancers and novelty dare items (for example, "Rocky Mountain oysters"), the reproductive equipment seem to have managed to stay off dinner plates world-wide. Neither I nor Janet Riley, spokesperson for the American Meat Institute, could come up with a contemporary culture that regularly partakes of ovaries, uterus, penis, or vagina simply as something good to eat.

Historically, there was ancient Rome. Bruce Kraig, president of the Culinary Historians of Chicago, passed along a recipe from *Apicius*, for sow uterus sausage. For a cookbook, *Apicius* has a markedly gladiatorial style. "Remove the entrails° by the throat before the carcass hardens immediately after killing," begins one recipe. Where a modern recipe might direct one to "salt to taste," the uterus recipe says to "add cooked brains, as much as is needed." Sleeter Bull,* the author of the 1951 book *Meat for the Table*, claims the ancient Greeks had a taste for udders. Very specifically, "the udders of a sow just after she had farrowed but before she had suckled her pigs." That is either the cruelest culinary practice in history or so much Sleeter bull.

I would wager that if you look hard enough, you will find a welcoming mouth for any safe source of nourishment, no matter how unpleasant it may strike you. "If we consider the wide range of foods eaten by all human groups on earth, one must . . . question whether any edible material that provides nourishment with no ill effects can be considered inherently disgusting," writes the food scientist Anthony Blake. "If presented at a sufficiently early age with positive reinforcement from the childcarer, it would become an accepted part of the diet." As an example, Blake mentions a Sudanese condiment made from fermented cow urine and used as a flavor enhancer "very much in the way soy sauce is used in other parts of the world."

The comparison was especially apt in the summer of 2005, when a small-scale Chinese operation was caught using human hair instead of soy to make cheap ersatz° soy sauce. Our hair is as much as 14 percent L-cysteine, an amino acid commonly used to make meat flavorings and to elasticize dough in commercial baking. How commonly? Enough to merit debate among scholars of Jewish dietary law, or kashrut.° "Human hair, while not particularly appetizing, is Kosher," states Rabbi Zushe Blech, the author of *Kosher Food Production*, on Kashrut.com. "There is no 'guck' factor," Blech maintained, in an e-mail. Dissolving hair in hydrochloric acid, which creates the L-cysteine, renders it unrecognizable and sterile. The

---

entrails: internal organs of an animal.
ersatz: artificial or inferior imitation or copy.
kashrut: the state of being kosher, in accordance with Jewish dietary laws.

---

*Bull was chief of the University of Illinois Meats Division and founding patron of the Sleeter Bull Undergraduate Meats Award. Along with meat scholarship, Bull supported and served as grand registrar of the Alpha Gamma Rho fraternity, where they knew a thing or two about undergraduate meats.

rabbis' primary concern had not to do with hygiene but with idol worship. "It seems that women would grow a full head of hair and then shave it off and offer it to the idol," wrote Blech. Shrine attendants in India have been known to surreptitiously collect the hair and sell it to wigmakers, and some in kashrut circles worried they might also be selling it to L-cysteine* producers. This proved not to be the case. "The hair used in the process comes exclusively from local barber shops," Blech assures us. *Phew.*

---

*The other common source of L-cysteine is feathers. Blech has a theory that this might explain the medicinal value of chicken soup, a recipe for which can be found in the Gemorah (shabbos 145b) portion of the Talmud. L-cysteine, he says, is similar to the mucus-thinning drug acetylcysteine. And it is found, albeit in lesser amounts, in birds' skin. "Chicken soup and its L-cysteine," Blech said merrily, may indeed be "just what the doctor ordered."

Understanding the Text

1. Why did Arctic nomads eat organs?
2. What does research suggest is the best way to get people to be open to a new food?
3. According to Roach, where do our food preferences come from?

Reflection and Response

4. Locate three places in her essay where Roach comments on the relationship between our food choices and culture, and analyze them. What conclusions can you draw about Roach's understanding of this relationship?
5. Would you try a "grasshopper snack" (par. 19) if you were offered one? Why or why not? What does your answer say about who you are?

Making Connections

6. Look up the study conducted by Clara Davis that Mary Roach mentions. What does it suggest about the relationship between what we eat and who we are? Why do you think Roach finds it so compelling? Do you?
7. Roach discusses a research project led by anthropologist Margaret Mead. Consider Mead's project that Roach mentions and Mead's essay in this book ("The Changing Significance of Food," p. 200). What contributions can anthropology make to our understanding of the expression "we are what we eat"?
8. Roach is known for humor writing in which she writes about taboo subjects using raunchy, distasteful, and unpleasant descriptions to draw readers into her explanations of complex scientific descriptions of bodily functions. Consider the use of humor as a rhetorical strategy. When and why is it useful? Compare Roach's use of humor to Jill McCorkle's (p. 31) and Barbara Kingsolver's (p. 218).

Bhaskar Dutta/Getty Images

3 | What Forces Affect Our Food Choices?

We wake up in the morning and decide what to eat for breakfast. We go to the cafeteria or the fridge or a restaurant, and we make choices about what to select from the display or order from the menu. We might select an apple or some raspberries, or we might opt for a doughnut or a granola bar. In one sense, then, *we* determine what we eat. But our food choices aren't made in a vacuum; many larger political, social, economic, environmental, and cultural factors help direct what choices are available (and where) and if they are affordable (and for whom).

A variety of factors, then, affect what we eat — whether we realize it or not. Various laws, policies, patents, and trade agreements play a role in determining what food choices are available to us. Federal guidelines make recommendations about health. Restaurant options and portion sizes help dictate what we choose, and various food movements work to influence our habits and choices. Government agencies regulate buying and selling options. International trade agreements affect what is available and where. Corporate interests and farming practices — and disputes between corporations and farmers — play a part in determining what is planted and harvested, and how it is processed and made available for public consumption.

We are thus surrounded by institutions, agencies, corporations, and businesses that affect our food choices, as the readings in this chapter demonstrate. The federal government develops nutritional graphics and guidelines for us to use to decide what and how much to eat. Dhruv Khullar demonstrates that these guidelines are not always easy to follow in his discussion of the prevalence of readily available junk food and how this reality helps determine what we eat. David H. Freedman wonders if "junk food" is really so harmful as he critiques the wholesome-food movement and considers its relationship to the obesity epidemic. Donald Barlett and James Steele investigate the role of corporations and the courts in food production and food availability, and Raj Patel challenges us to understand

photo: Bhaskar Dutta/Getty Images

both our place in the food distribution system and the way it affects the farmers who suffer under its rigid constraints. Vandana Shiva discusses how globalization affects food availability and food choices in her account of the effects of global food markets on local food cultures in India, and Troy Johnson investigates farm-to-table culture, questioning whether it's really as wholesome as people believe.

The complex mix of laws, social realities, health guidelines, seed patents, and trade agreements discussed in these selections are not usually on our minds when we ask "What's for dinner?" But international trade, federal health recommendations, corporate interests, globalization, farming practices, local trends, and even seed patents impact the answer in important ways. The readings in this chapter ask us to attend to this broad range of forces that affect our food choices.

Nutritional Guidelines

United States Government

The U.S. Department of Agriculture established the Center for Nutrition Policy and Promotion in 1994 to promote the nutrition and well-being of Americans. One of the core ways the center supports this objective is through the advancement of dietary guidelines and the promotion of guidance systems like MyPyramid and MyPlate. The Food Pyramid was introduced in 1992, updated in 2005, and replaced in 2010 by MyPlate. These visual diagrams are widely used as educational tools for translating nutritional guidelines into simple images of how much to eat and what kinds of food to eat on a daily basis. More recently, the U.S. Food and Drug Administration has updated the Nutrition Facts labels on food packages sold in the United States. The update reflects new scientific research and public health concerns and represents another method by which the federal government works to promote health and nutrition.

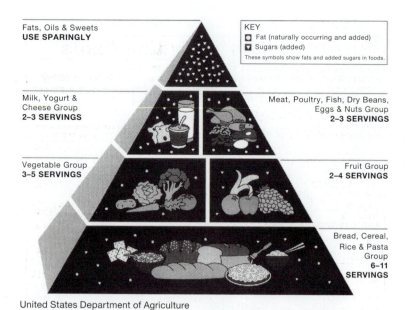

Fats, Oils & Sweets
USE SPARINGLY

KEY
☐ Fat (naturally occurring and added)
☑ Sugars (added)
These symbols show fats and added sugars in foods.

Milk, Yogurt & Cheese Group
2–3 SERVINGS

Meat, Poultry, Fish, Dry Beans, Eggs & Nuts Group
2–3 SERVINGS

Vegetable Group
3–5 SERVINGS

Fruit Group
2–4 SERVINGS

Bread, Cereal, Rice & Pasta Group
6–11 SERVINGS

United States Department of Agriculture

United States Department of Agriculture

Current Label

Nutrition Facts
Serving Size 2/3 cup (55g)
Servings Per Container About 8

Amount Per Serving

Calories 230	Calories from Fat 72

	% Daily Values*
Total Fat 8g	**12%**
Saturated Fat 1g	**5%**
Trans Fat 0g	
Cholesterol 0mg	**0%**
Sodium 160mg	**7%**
Total Carbohydrate 37g	**12%**
Dietary Fiber 4g	**16%**
Sugars 1g	
Protein 3g	

Vitamin A	10%
Vitamin C	8%
Calcium	20%
Iron	45%

*Percent Daily Values are based on a 2,000 calorie diet.
Your daily value may be higher or lower depending on
your calorie needs

	Calories:	2,000	2,500
Total Fat	Less than	65g	80g
Sat Fat	Less than	20g	25g
Cholesterol	Less than	300mg	300mg
Sodium	Less than	2,400mg	2,400mg
Total Carbohydrate		300g	375g
Dietary Fiber		25g	30g

New Label

Nutrition Facts
8 servings per container
Serving size   2/3 cup (55g)

Amount per serving
Calories   230

	% Daily Value*
Total Fat 8g	**10%**
Saturated Fat 1g	**5%**
Trans Fat 0g	
Cholesterol 0mg	**0%**
Sodium 160mg	**7%**
Total Carbohydrate 37g	**13%**
Dietary Fiber 4g	**14%**
Total Sugars 12g	
Includes 10g Added Sugars	**20%**
Protein 3g	

Vitamin D 2mcg	10%
Calcium 260mg	20%
Iron 8mg	45%
Potassium 235mg	6%

* The % Daily Value (DV) tells you how much a nutrient in
a serving of food contributes to a daily diet. 2,000 calories
a day is used for general nutrition advice.

Understanding the Text

1. What did the Food Pyramid prioritize? What kinds of recommendations did it give?
2. How is the MyPlate different in scope and purpose than the Food Pyramid? What goals do they share?
3. What changes are most prominent in the new Nutrition Facts label?

Reflection and Response

4. Why do you think the USDA continues to rely on visual images to promote nutrition? Which visual do you think will lead to better health education? To healthier eating? Why?
5. What social, cultural, and economic tendencies are the federal nutritional guidelines and Nutrition Facts labels working against?
6. Were you aware of these nutrition guidelines and labels before reading them here? Where did you encounter them? Have you studied them in school? Have you tried to live by them?

Making Connections

7. Review Michael Pollan's "rules" ("Eat Food: Food Defined," p. 10). How do they compare to the advice of the USDA and the FDA? What would he applaud in this advice? What might he question? Would he see this as a good way to decide what to eat? Why or why not?
8. Do you think the federal government should play a role in nutrition education? Why or why not? Select two or three selections in this collection and two or three sources you find through library research to help you construct your argument. Select at least one source that presents a challenge to your position. Refute that challenge as part of your support for your position.

Why Shame Won't Stop Obesity

Dhruv Khullar

Dhruv Khullar wrote this piece in 2012 for the *Bioethics Forum*, the blog published by the *Hastings Center Report*, while studying medicine at Yale University and public policy at the John F. Kennedy School of Government at Harvard University as a Zuckerman Fellow. Khullar's interest in public health and social justice has led him to do research that bridges the gap between medicine and public policy. He considers obesity a public health as well as a social justice issue, one that disproportionately affects minority groups and the poor. He is particularly interested in publishing his research for the general public in the hope that sound research can play a larger role in public discussion of health policies. In this essay, Khullar offers specific suggestions for reversing the trend of junk food and fast food as being more readily available and cheaper than healthy food choices.

I am still in medical school, but today I sigh the frustrated, disapproving sigh of a fully trained doctor. "You know," I scold the middle-aged man in front of me, "you really should start eating better."

Like many patients I saw in clinic that morning, this man is obese. His diabetes is poorly controlled. His blood pressure is through the roof. And he hasn't lost a single pound in months.

Oh well, it's lunchtime and I'm hungry. I slip off to the hospital cafeteria and begin to ponder why these patients can't seem to lead a healthier lifestyle. As I wait in line, I consider a more pressing problem: should I get the fried chicken or the four-cheese pizza? I settle on popcorn shrimp and some curly fries. Only then do I ask myself what exactly I would have recommended my patients eat — besides maybe a side of cheesy broccoli and some bruised bananas — had they joined me for lunch.

This, sadly, is the case in the cafeteria of a major hospital, an institution devoted to preserving and promoting health. It is a stark and telling microcosm of a much broader issue — one in large part responsible for the skyrocketing rates of obesity and associated disease in this country.

Americans today are exposed to an unprecedented amount of readily available high-fat, high-calorie, and low-nutrient foods. We are saturated with junk food advertising. We are eating more and more meals outside the home, and portion sizes are bigger than ever. Healthy options are more frequently the exception than the rule. 5

It is hardly surprising, then, that we find ourselves in the midst of an obesity epidemic. Nearly three-quarters of Americans are overweight or obese, and a report by United Healthcare predicts that half of all

American adults will develop diabetes or prediabetes by the end of the decade. The report further estimates that diabetes — which increases one's risk of stroke, cardiovascular disease, kidney failure, blindness, and amputations — will cost our society $500 billion a year by 2020.

In an effort to combat this disturbing trend, Georgia — the state with the nation's second highest obesity rates — recently launched a provocative and controversial ad campaign. It emphasizes the role of parents in failing to recognize and address childhood obesity. In the commercials, obese children sullenly ask questions like, "Mom, why am I fat?" and drive home poignant messages like, "It's hard to be a little girl, when you're not," or "Being fat takes the fun out of being a kid."

One might argue that Georgia's campaign is a bold and necessary step in the right direction, and to the extent that it raises awareness and sparks constructive conversation, it may be. However, these commercials miss the point. Shaming children and parents into losing weight is unlikely to be an effective strategy. It increases stigma on those already struggling with the psychosocial° consequences of being overweight, and shifts the focus of obesity control efforts to personal responsibility at a time when, for many individuals, options for improving eating habits may be limited.

"While taking responsibility for one's health is certainly part of the solution, we must also recognize that we have created a food environment so ripe for obesity that to expect anything else would be irrational."

While taking responsibility for one's health is certainly part of the solution, we must also recognize that we have created a food environment so ripe for obesity that to expect anything else would be irrational. Even for the most knowledgeable and resourceful among us, consistently eating well is a challenge. It is difficult to distinguish healthy options from unhealthy ones, and purchasing the right foods once they are identified is no cakewalk. Furthermore, people living in low-income areas have limited access to healthy food options for a variety of reasons, a barrier that contributes to their particularly high risk for being obese.

There is much we can and should do to reverse the current trend. An important step would be to provide monetary incentives to promote the production of and access to fresh, healthy food. By subsidizing fresh fruits and vegetables and supporting restaurants and vendors that offer

10

psychosocial: relating to the interconnection of individual thoughts and behavior and external social factors.

healthy alternatives, we might create an economic environment more conducive to healthy eating. Making healthy options more accessible and affordable, especially for those living in low-income areas of the country, is a vital component of reducing the burden of obesity. When you can buy 2,000 calories for under $10 at your neighborhood McDonald's, but have trouble getting your hands on an apple, it's difficult to justify trying to shame anyone into skinniness.

Another important measure would be to minimize junk food advertising, especially to children. Each year, the food industry spends nearly $2 billion marketing its products to children, and evidence suggests that children exposed to junk food advertising express greater preference for these types of foods. Asking the industry to refrain from advertising foods that contain unhealthful amounts of sugar, salts, and fats to youth could also encourage the production of healthier options. I think that initially the guidelines should be voluntary, but significant public and political pressure should be placed on the food industry to adopt them. If it becomes clear over time that they are unwilling to do so, then federal regulations may be needed.

A third initiative might center on education and empowering youth to make informed decisions. Instituting nutrition and health curriculums into public schools would help children learn how to read nutrition labels and identify healthy foods, as well as understand the negative long-term consequences of obesity. Today's youth may be the first generation of Americans to live shorter, more disease-riddled lives than their parents — a staggering prediction based largely on the rapid rise in childhood obesity. Let this not be our legacy.

Understanding the Text

1. What realization does Khullar have when he makes his trip to the cafeteria?
2. What dilemma does Khullar describe? What solutions does he propose?

Reflection and Response

3. Why does Khullar claim that shame will not help reduce the obesity epidemic? Does he make a good case? Why or why not? Do you agree with him? Why or why not?
4. Khullar indicates that personal responsibility for food choices is not the only factor that affects what people eat. On what does he base this conclusion? What evidence does he give?

Making Connections

5. David H. Freedman ("How Junk Food Can End Obesity," p. 139) quotes Robert Kushner, obesity scientist and clinical director at Northwestern University, who says, "The difference between losing weight and not losing weight is a few hundred calories a day" (par. 44). How do the essays by Khullar and Brian Wansink and Collin Payne ("The Joy of Cooking Too Much," p. 114) support this statement? How do they complicate it? What does each author suggest about the relationship between weight, calories, and eating practices? Are there other authors in this collection who would argue for a different view?

6. Do your eating habits and food choices reflect your values regarding food, or are they determined by other factors? Explain your answer using Khullar's argument, at least one other source from this book, and at least two other sources located in your campus library.

How Junk Food Can End Obesity

David H. Freedman

David H. Freedman studied physics at Oberlin College. As a Boston-based journalist, he writes about science, technology, medicine, and business for the *New York Times, Inc. Magazine*, the *Atlantic*, *Wired*, *Scientific American*, and many other publications. He is known for offering skeptical critiques of some popular scientific findings and how they are portrayed in the popular media. He blogs (fatandskinner.org) on medical findings that get reported to the public, taking a critical look at the way they are presented and used. He also consults with university medical centers, working with them to improve health systems. Freedman has published several books, including *Wrong: Why Experts* Keep Failing Us — and How to Know When Not to Trust Them* (2010). In this essay, Freedman launches a strong critique of proponents of the wholesome-food movement and suggests that technology might have an important role to play in solving the obesity crisis.

Late last year, in a small health-food eatery called Cafe Sprouts in Oberlin, Ohio, I had what may well have been the most wholesome beverage of my life. The friendly server patiently guided me to an apple-blueberry-kale-carrot smoothie-juice combination, which she spent the next several minutes preparing, mostly by shepherding farm-fresh produce into machinery. The result was tasty, but at 300 calories (by my rough calculation) in a 16-ounce cup, it was more than my diet could regularly absorb without consequences, nor was I about to make a habit of $9 shakes, healthy or not.

Inspired by the experience nonetheless, I tried again two months later at L.A.'s Real Food Daily, a popular vegan restaurant near Hollywood. I was initially wary of a low-calorie juice made almost entirely from green vegetables, but the server assured me it was a popular treat. I like to brag that I can eat anything, and I scarf down all sorts of raw vegetables like candy, but I could stomach only about a third of this oddly foamy, bitter concoction. It smelled like lawn clippings and tasted like liquid celery. It goes for $7.95, and I waited 10 minutes for it.

I finally hit the sweet spot just a few weeks later, in Chicago, with a delicious blueberry-pomegranate smoothie that rang in at a relatively modest 220 calories. It cost $3 and took only seconds to make. Best of all, I'll be able to get this concoction just about anywhere. Thanks, McDonald's!

If only the McDonald's smoothie weren't, unlike the first two, so fattening and unhealthy. Or at least that's what the most-prominent voices in our food culture today would have you believe.

An enormous amount of media space has been dedicated to promot- 5 ing the notion that all processed food, and only processed food, is making us sickly and overweight. In this narrative, the food-industrial complex — particularly the fast-food industry — has turned all the powers of food-processing science loose on engineering its offerings to addict us to fat, sugar, and salt, causing or at least heavily contributing to the obesity crisis. The wares of these pimps and pushers, we are told, are to be universally shunned.

Consider *The New York Times*. Earlier this year, *The Times Magazine* gave its cover to a long piece based on Michael Moss's about-to-be-bestselling book, *Salt Sugar Fat: How the Food Giants Hooked Us*. Hitting bookshelves at about the same time was the former *Times* reporter Melanie Warner's *Pandora's Lunchbox: How Processed Food Took Over the American Meal*, which addresses more or less the same theme. Two years ago *The Times Magazine* featured the journalist Gary Taubes's "Is Sugar Toxic?," a cover story on the evils of refined sugar and high-fructose corn syrup. And most significant of all has been the considerable space the magazine has devoted over the years to Michael Pollan, a journalism professor at the University of California at Berkeley, and his broad indictment of food processing as a source of society's health problems.

"The food they're cooking is making people sick," Pollan has said of big food companies. "It is one of the reasons that we have the obesity and diabetes epidemics that we do . . . If you're going to let industries decide how much salt, sugar and fat is in your food, they're going to put [in] as much as they possibly can . . . They will push those buttons until we scream or die." The solution, in his view, is to replace Big Food's engineered, edible evil — through public education and regulation — with fresh, unprocessed, local, seasonal, *real* food.

Pollan's worldview saturates the public conversation on healthy eating. You hear much the same from many scientists, physicians, food activists, nutritionists, celebrity chefs, and pundits. *Foodlike substances*, the derisive term Pollan uses to describe processed foods, is now a solid part of the elite vernacular. Thousands of restaurants and grocery stores, most notably the Whole Foods chain, have thrived by answering the call to reject industrialized foods in favor of a return to natural, simple, nonindustrialized — let's call them "wholesome" — foods. The two newest restaurants in my smallish Massachusetts town both prominently tout wholesome ingredients; one of them is called the Farmhouse, and it's usually packed.

A new generation of business, social, and policy entrepreneurs is rising to further cater to these tastes, and to challenge Big Food. Silicon Valley, where tomorrow's entrepreneurial and social trends are forged, has spawned a small ecosystem of wholesome-friendly venture-capital firms (Physic Ventures, for example), business accelerators (Local Food Lab), and Web sites (Edible Startups) to fund, nurture, and keep tabs on young companies such as blissmo (a wholesome-food-of-the-month club), Mile High Organics (online wholesome-food shopping), and Wholeshare (group wholesome-food purchasing), all designed to help reacquaint Americans with the simpler eating habits of yesteryear.

In virtually every realm of human existence, we turn to technology to 10 help us solve our problems. But even in Silicon Valley, when it comes to food and obesity, technology — or at least food-processing technology — is widely treated as if it *is* the problem. The solution, from this viewpoint, necessarily involves turning our back on it.

If the most-influential voices in our food culture today get their way, we will achieve a genuine food revolution. Too bad it would be one tailored to the dubious health fantasies of a small, elite minority. And too bad it would largely exclude the obese masses, who would continue to sicken and die early. Despite the best efforts of a small army of wholesome-food heroes, there is no reasonable scenario under which these foods could become cheap and plentiful enough to serve as the core diet for most of the obese population — even in the unlikely case that your typical junk-food eater would be willing and able to break lifelong habits to embrace kale and yellow beets. And many of the dishes glorified by the wholesome-food movement are, in any case, as caloric and obesogenic° as anything served in a Burger King.

Through its growing sway over health-conscious consumers and policy makers, the wholesome-food movement is impeding the progress of the one segment of the food world that is actually positioned to take effective, near-term steps to reverse the obesity trend: the processed-food industry. Popular food producers, fast-food chains among them, are already applying various tricks and technologies to create less caloric and more satiating versions of their junky fare that nonetheless retain much of the appeal of the originals, and could be induced to go much further. In fact, these roundly demonized companies could do far more for the public's health in five years than the wholesome-food movement is likely to accomplish in the next 50. But will the wholesome-food advocates let them?

Michael Pollan Has No Clothes

Let's go shopping. We can start at Whole Foods Market, a critical link in the wholesome-eating food chain. There are three Whole Foods stores within 15 minutes of my house — we're big on real food in the suburbs west of

obesogenic: tending to cause excessive weight gain.

Boston. Here at the largest of the three, I can choose from more than 21 types of tofu, 62 bins of organic grains and legumes, and 42 different salad greens.

Much of the food isn't all that different from what I can get in any other supermarket, but sprinkled throughout are items that scream "wholesome." One that catches my eye today, sitting prominently on an impulse-buy rack near the checkout counter, is Vegan Cheesy Salad Booster, from Living Intentions, whose package emphasizes the fact that the food is enhanced with spirulina°, chlorella°, and sea vegetables. The label also proudly lets me know that the contents are raw — no processing! — and that they don't contain any genetically modified ingredients. What the stuff does contain, though, is more than three times the fat content per ounce as the beef patty in a Big Mac (more than two-thirds of the calories come from fat), and four times the sodium.

After my excursion to Whole Foods, I drive a few minutes to a Trader 15 Joe's, also known for an emphasis on wholesome foods. Here at the register I'm confronted with a large display of a snack food called "Inner

RubberBall / Alamy

spirulina: blue-green algae, used as a health food because it is loaded with good nutrients.
chlorella: green algae, recognized as a super food because of its high protein and Vitamin B content.

Peas," consisting of peas that are breaded in cornmeal and rice flour, fried in sunflower oil, and then sprinkled with salt. By weight, the snack has six times as much fat as it does protein, along with loads of carbohydrates. I can't recall ever seeing anything at any fast-food restaurant that represents as big an obesogenic crime against the vegetable kingdom. (A spokesperson for Trader Joe's said the company does not consider itself a "'wholesome food' grocery retailer." Living Intentions did not respond to a request for comment.)

This phenomenon is by no means limited to packaged food at upscale supermarkets. Back in February, when I was at Real Food Daily in Los Angeles, I ordered the "Sea Cake" along with my green-vegetable smoothie. It was intensely delicious in a way that set off alarm bells. RFD wouldn't provide precise information about the ingredients, but I found a recipe online for "Tofu 'Fish' Cakes," which seem very close to what I ate. Essentially, they consist of some tofu mixed with a lot of refined carbs (the RFD version contains at least some unrefined carbs) along with oil and soy milk, all fried in oil and served with a soy-and-oil-based tartar sauce. (Tofu and other forms of soy are high in protein, but per 100 calories, tofu is as fatty as many cuts of beef.) L.A. being to the wholesome-food movement what Hawaii is to Spam, I ate at two other mega-popular wholesome-food restaurants while I was in the area. At Café Gratitude I enjoyed the kale chips and herb-cornmeal-crusted eggplant parmesan, and at Akasha I indulged in a spiced-lamb-sausage flatbread pizza. Both are pricey orgies of fat and carbs.

I'm not picking out rare, less healthy examples from these establishments. Check out their menus online: fat, sugar, and other refined carbs abound. (Café Gratitude says it uses only "healthy" fats and natural sweeteners; Akasha says its focus is not on "health food" but on "farm to fork" fare.) In fact, because the products and dishes offered by these types of establishments tend to emphasize the healthy-sounding foods they contain, I find it much harder to navigate through them to foods that go easy on the oil, butter, refined grains, rice, potatoes, and sugar than I do at far less wholesome restaurants. (These dishes also tend to contain plenty of sea salt, which Pollanites hold up as the wholesome alternative to the addictive salt engineered by the food industry, though your body can't tell the difference.)

One occasional source of obesogenic travesties is *The New York Times Magazine*'s lead food writer, Mark Bittman, who now rivals Pollan as a shepherd to the anti-processed-food flock. (*Salon*, in an article titled "How to Live What Michael Pollan Preaches," called Bittman's 2009 book, *Food Matters*, "both a cookbook and a manifesto that shows us how to eat better — and save the planet.") I happened to catch Bittman on the

Today show last year demonstrating for millions of viewers four ways to prepare corn in summertime, including a lovely dish of corn sautéed in bacon fat and topped with bacon. Anyone who thinks that such a thing is much healthier than a Whopper just hasn't been paying attention to obesity science for the past few decades.

That science is, in fact, fairly straightforward. Fat carries more than twice as many calories as carbohydrates and proteins do per gram, which means just a little fat can turn a serving of food into a calorie bomb. Sugar and other refined carbohydrates, like white flour and rice, and high-starch foods, like corn and potatoes, aren't as calorie-dense. But all of these "problem carbs" charge into the bloodstream as glucose in minutes, providing an energy rush, commonly followed by an energy crash that can lead to a surge in appetite.

Because they are energy-intense foods, fat and sugar and other prob- 20 lem carbs trip the pleasure and reward meters placed in our brains by evolution over the millions of years during which starvation was an ever-present threat. We're born enjoying the stimulating sensations these ingredients provide, and exposure strengthens the associations, ensuring that we come to crave them and, all too often, eat more of them than we should. Processed food is not an essential part of this story: recent examinations of ancient human remains in Egypt, Peru, and elsewhere have repeatedly revealed hardened arteries, suggesting that pre-industrial diets, at least of the affluent, may not have been the epitome of healthy eating that the Pollanites make them out to be. People who want to lose weight and keep it off are almost always advised by those who run successful long-term weight-loss programs to transition to a diet high in lean protein, complex carbs such as whole grains and legumes, and the sort of fiber vegetables are loaded with. Because these ingredients provide us with the calories we need without the big, fast bursts of energy, they can be satiating without pushing the primitive reward buttons that nudge us to eat too much.

(A few words on salt: Yes, it's unhealthy in large amounts, raising blood pressure in many people; and yes, it makes food more appealing. But salt is not obesogenic — it has no calories, and doesn't specifically increase the desire to consume high-calorie foods. It can just as easily be enlisted to add to the appeal of vegetables. Lumping it in with fat and sugar as an addictive junk-food ingredient is a confused proposition. But let's agree we want to cut down on it.)

To be sure, many of Big Food's most popular products are loaded with appalling amounts of fat and sugar and other problem carbs (as well as salt), and the plentitude of these ingredients, exacerbated by large portion sizes, has clearly helped foment the obesity crisis. It's hard to find anyone anywhere who disagrees. Junk food is bad for you because it's full of fat and problem carbs. But will switching to wholesome foods free us from this scourge? It could in theory, but in practice, it's hard to see how. Even putting aside for a moment the serious questions about whether wholesome foods could be made accessible to the obese public, and whether the obese would be willing to eat them, we have a more immediate stumbling block: many of the foods served up and even glorified by the wholesome-food movement are themselves chock full of fat and problem carbs.

Some wholesome foodies openly celebrate fat and problem carbs, insisting that the lack of processing magically renders them healthy. In singing the praises of clotted cream and lard-loaded cookies, for instance, a recent *Wall Street Journal* article by Ron Rosenbaum explained that "eating basic, earthy, fatty foods isn't just a supreme experience of the senses — it can actually be good for you," and that it's "too easy to conflate eating fatty food with eating industrial, oil-fried junk food." That's right, we wouldn't want to make the same mistake that all the cells in our bodies make. Pollan himself makes it clear in his writing that he has little problem with fat — as long as it's not in food "your great-grandmother wouldn't recognize."

> "Many of the foods served up and even glorified by the wholesome-food movement are themselves chock full of fat and problem carbs."

Television food shows routinely feature revered chefs tossing around references to healthy eating, "wellness," and farm-fresh ingredients, all the while spooning lard, cream, and sugar over everything in sight. (A study published last year in the *British Medical Journal* found that the recipes in the books of top TV chefs call for "significantly more" fat per portion than what's contained in ready-to-eat supermarket meals.) Corporate wellness programs, one of the most promising avenues for getting the population to adopt healthy behaviors, are falling prey to this way of thinking as well. Last November, I attended a stress-management seminar for employees of a giant consulting company, and listened to a high-powered professional wellness coach tell the crowded room that it's okay to eat anything as long as its plant or animal origins aren't obscured by processing. Thus, she explained, potato chips are perfectly healthy, because they plainly come from potatoes, but Cheetos will make you sick and fat, because what plant or animal is a Cheeto? (For the record, typical potato chips and Cheetos have about equally nightmarish amounts of fat calories per ounce; Cheetos have fewer carbs, though more salt.)

The Pollanites seem confused about exactly what benefits their way of 25
eating provides. All the railing about the fat, sugar, and salt engineered
into industrial junk food might lead one to infer that wholesome food,
having not been engineered, contains substantially less of them. But
clearly you can take in obscene quantities of fat and problem carbs while
eating wholesomely, and to judge by what's sold at wholesome stores and
restaurants, many people do. Indeed, the more converts and customers the
wholesome-food movement's purveyors seek, the stronger their incentive
to emphasize foods that light up precisely the same pleasure centers as a 3
Musketeers bar. That just makes wholesome food stealthily obesogenic.

Hold on, you may be thinking. Leaving fat, sugar, and salt aside, what
about all the nasty things that wholesome foods do not, by definition,
contain and processed foods do? A central claim of the wholesome-food
movement is that wholesome is healthier because it doesn't have the
artificial flavors, preservatives, other additives, or genetically modified
ingredients found in industrialized food; because it isn't subjected to the
physical transformations that processed foods go through; and because it
doesn't sit around for days, weeks, or months, as industrialized food
sometimes does. (This is the complaint against the McDonald's smoothie,
which contains artificial flavors and texture additives, and which is
pre-mixed.)

The health concerns raised about processing itself — rather than the
amount of fat and problem carbs in any given dish — are not, by and
large, related to weight gain or obesity. That's important to keep in mind,
because obesity is, by an enormous margin, the largest health problem
created by what we eat. But even putting that aside, concerns about processed food have been magnified out of all proportion.

Some studies have shown that people who eat wholesomely tend to be
healthier than people who live on fast food and other processed food
(particularly meat), but the problem with such studies is obvious: substantial nondietary differences exist between these groups, such as pro-
pensity to exercise, smoking rates, air quality, access to health care, and
much more. (Some researchers say they've tried to control for these factors, but that's a claim most scientists don't put much faith in.) What's
more, the people in these groups are sometimes eating entirely different
foods, not the same sorts of foods subjected to different levels of processing. It's comparing apples to Whoppers, instead of Whoppers to hand-
ground, grass-fed-beef burgers with heirloom tomatoes, garlic aioli, and
artisanal cheese. For all these reasons, such findings linking food type
and health are considered highly unreliable, and constantly contradict
one another, as is true of most epidemiological studies that try to tackle
broad nutritional questions.

The fact is, there is simply no clear, credible evidence that any aspect of food processing or storage makes a food uniquely unhealthy. The U.S. population does not suffer from a critical lack of any nutrient because we eat so much processed food. (Sure, health experts urge Americans to get more calcium, potassium, magnesium, fiber, and vitamins A, E, and C, and eating more produce and dairy is a great way to get them, but these ingredients are also available in processed foods, not to mention supplements.) Pollan's "foodlike substances" are regulated by the U.S. Food and Drug Administration (with some exceptions, which are regulated by other agencies), and their effects on health are further raked over by countless scientists who would get a nice career boost from turning up the hidden dangers in some common food-industry ingredient or technique, in part because any number of advocacy groups and journalists are ready to pounce on the slightest hint of risk.

The results of all the scrutiny of processed food are hardly scary, 30 although some groups and writers try to make them appear that way. The Pew Charitable Trusts' Food Additives Project, for example, has bemoaned the fact that the FDA directly reviews only about 70 percent of the ingredients found in food, permitting the rest to pass as "generally recognized as safe" by panels of experts convened by manufacturers. But the only actual risk the project calls out on its Web site or in its publications is a quote from a *Times* article noting that bromine°, which has been in U.S. foods for eight decades, is regarded as suspicious by many because flame retardants containing bromine have been linked to health risks. There is no conclusive evidence that bromine itself is a threat.

In *Pandora's Lunchbox*, Melanie Warner assiduously catalogs every concern that could possibly be raised about the health threats of food processing, leveling accusations so vague, weakly supported, tired, or insignificant that only someone already convinced of the guilt of processed food could find them troubling. While ripping the covers off the breakfast-cereal conspiracy, for example, Warner reveals that much of the nutritional value claimed by these products comes not from natural ingredients but from added vitamins that are chemically synthesized, which must be bad for us because, well, they're *chemically synthesized*. It's the tautology° at the heart of the movement: processed foods are unhealthy because they aren't natural, full stop.

---

bromine: chemical element with an extremely offensive odor and recently the subject of much controversy over its safety.
tautology: redundant expression or needless repetition of an idea.

In many respects, the wholesome-food movement veers awfully close to religion. To repeat: there is no hard evidence to back any health-risk claims about processed food — evidence, say, of the caliber of several studies by the Centers for Disease Control and Prevention that have traced food poisoning to raw milk, a product championed by some circles of the wholesome-food movement. "Until I hear evidence to the contrary, I think it's reasonable to include processed food in your diet," says Robert Kushner, a physician and nutritionist and a professor at Northwestern University's medical school, where he is the clinical director of the Comprehensive Center on Obesity.

There may be other reasons to prefer wholesome food to the industrialized version. Often stirred into the vague stew of benefits attributed to wholesome food is the "sustainability" of its production — that is, its longterm impact on the planet. Small farms that don't rely much on chemicals and heavy industrial equipment may be better for the environment than giant industrial farms — although that argument quickly becomes complicated by a variety of factors. For the purposes of this article, let's simply stipulate that wholesome foods are environmentally superior. But let's also agree that when it comes to prioritizing among food-related public-policy goals, we are likely to save and improve many more lives by focusing on cutting obesity — through any available means — than by trying to convert all of industrial agriculture into a vast constellation of small organic farms.

The impact of obesity on the chances of our living long, productive, and enjoyable lives has been so well documented at this point that I hate to drag anyone through the grim statistics again. But let me just toss out one recent dispatch from the world of obesity-havoc science: a study published in February in the journal *Obesity* found that obese young adults and middleagers in the U.S. are likely to lose almost a decade of life on average, as compared with their non-obese counterparts. Given our obesity rates, that means Americans who are alive today can collectively expect to sacrifice 1 billion years to obesity. The study adds to a river of evidence suggesting that for the first time in modern history — and in spite of many health-related improvements in our environment, our health care, and our nondietary habits — our health prospects are worsening, mostly because of excess weight.

By all means, let's protect the environment. But let's not rule out the 35 possibility of technologically enabled improvements to our diet — indeed, let's not rule out *any* food — merely because we are pleased by images of pastoral family farms. Let's first pick the foods that can most plausibly make us healthier, all things considered, and then figure out how to make them environmentally friendly.

The Food Revolution We Need

The one fast-food restaurant near [a] busy East L.A. intersection otherwise filled with bodegas was a Carl's Jr. I went in and saw that the biggest and most prominent posters in the store were pushing a new grilled-cod sandwich. It actually looked pretty good, but it wasn't quite lunchtime, and I just wanted a cup of coffee. I went to the counter to order it, but before I could say anything, the cashier greeted me and asked, "Would you like to try our new Charbroiled Atlantic Cod Fish Sandwich today?" Oh, well, sure, why not? (I asked her to hold the tartar sauce, which is mostly fat, but found out later that the sandwich is normally served with about half as much tartar sauce as the notoriously fatty Filet-O-Fish sandwich at McDonald's, where the fish is battered and fried.) The sandwich was delicious. It was less than half the cost of the Sea Cake appetizer at Real Food Daily. It took less than a minute to prepare. In some ways, it was the best meal I had in L.A., and it was probably the healthiest.

We know perfectly well who within our society has developed an extraordinary facility for nudging the masses to eat certain foods, and for making those foods widely available in cheap and convenient forms. The Pollanites have led us to conflate the industrial processing of food with the adding of fat and sugar in order to hook customers, even while pushing many faux-healthy foods of their own. But why couldn't Big Food's processing and marketing genius be put to use on genuinely healthier foods, like grilled fish? Putting aside the standard objection that the industry has no interest in doing so — we'll see later that in fact the industry has plenty of motivation for taking on this challenge — wouldn't that present a more plausible answer to America's junk-food problem than ordering up 50,000 new farmers' markets featuring locally grown organic squash blossoms?

According to Lenard Lesser, of the Palo Alto Medical Foundation, the food industry has mastered the art of using in-store and near-store promotions to shape what people eat. As Lesser and I drove down storied Telegraph Avenue in Berkeley and into far less affluent Oakland, leaving behind the Whole Foods Markets and sushi restaurants for gas-station markets and barbecued-rib stands, he pointed out the changes in the billboards. Whereas the last one we saw in Berkeley was for fruit juice, many in Oakland tout fast-food joints and their wares, including several featuring the Hot Mess Burger at Jack in the Box. Though Lesser noted that this forest of advertising may simply reflect Oakland residents' preexisting preference for this type of food, he told me lab studies have indicated that the more signs you show people for a particular food product or dish, the more likely they are to choose it over others, all else being equal.

We went into a KFC and found ourselves traversing a maze of signage that put us face-to-face with garish images of various fried foods that presumably had some chicken somewhere deep inside them. "The more they want you to buy something, the bigger they make the image on the menu board," Lesser explained. Here, what loomed largest was the $19.98 fried-chicken-and-corn family meal, which included biscuits and cake. A few days later, I noticed that McDonald's places large placards showcasing desserts on the trash bins, apparently calculating that the best time to entice diners with sweets is when they think they've finished their meals.

Trying to get burger lovers to jump to grilled fish may already be a bit of 40 a stretch — I didn't see any of a dozen other customers buy the cod sandwich when I was at Carl's Jr., though the cashier said it was selling reasonably well. Still, given the food industry's power to tinker with and market food, we should not dismiss its ability to get unhealthy eaters — slowly, incrementally — to buy better food.

That brings us to the crucial question: Just how much healthier could fast-food joints and processed-food companies make their best-selling products without turning off customers? I put that question to a team of McDonald's executives, scientists, and chefs who are involved in shaping the company's future menus, during a February visit to McDonald's surprisingly bucolic° campus west of Chicago. By way of a partial answer, the team served me up a preview tasting of two major new menu items that had been under development in their test kitchens and high-tech sensory-testing labs for the past year, and which were rolled out to the public in April. The first was the Egg White Delight McMuffin ($2.65), a lower-calorie, less fatty version of the Egg McMuffin, with some of the refined flour in the original recipe replaced by whole-grain flour. The other was one of three new Premium McWraps ($3.99), crammed with grilled chicken and spring mix, and given a light coating of ranch dressing amped up with rice vinegar. Both items tasted pretty good (as do the versions in stores, I've since confirmed, though some outlets go too heavy on the dressing). And they were both lower in fat, sugar, and calories than not only many McDonald's staples, but also much of the food served in wholesome restaurants or touted in wholesome cookbooks.

In fact, McDonald's has quietly been making healthy changes for years, shrinking portion sizes, reducing some fats, trimming average salt content by more than 10 percent in the past couple of years alone, and

---

bucolic: pastoral, relating to an idyllic rural or country life.

adding fruits, vegetables, low-fat dairy, and oatmeal to its menu. In May, the chain dropped its Angus third-pounders and announced a new line of quarter-pound burgers, to be served on buns containing whole grains. Outside the core fast-food customer base, Americans are becoming more health-conscious. Public backlash against fast food could lead to regulatory efforts, and in any case, the fast-food industry has every incentive to maintain broad appeal. "We think a lot about how we can bring nutritionally balanced meals that include enough protein, along with the tastes and satisfaction that have an appetite-tiding effect," said Barbara Booth, the company's director of sensory science.

Such steps are enormously promising, says Jamy Ard, an epidemiology° and preventive-medicine researcher at Wake Forest Baptist Medical Center in Winston-Salem, North Carolina, and a co-director of the Weight Management Center there. "Processed food is a key part of our environment, and it needs to be part of the equation," he explains. "If you can reduce fat and calories by only a small amount in a Big Mac, it still won't be a health food, but it wouldn't be as bad, and that could have a huge impact on us." Ard, who has been working for more than a decade with the obese poor, has little patience with the wholesome-food movement's call to eliminate fast food in favor of farm-fresh goods. "It's really naive," he says. "Fast food became popular because it's tasty and convenient and cheap. It makes a lot more sense to look for small, beneficial changes in that food than it does to hold out for big changes in what people eat that have no realistic chance of happening."

According to a recent study, Americans get 11 percent of their calories, on average, from fast food — a number that's almost certainly much higher among the less affluent overweight. As a result, the fast-food industry may be uniquely positioned to improve our diets. Research suggests that calorie counts in a meal can be trimmed by as much as 30 percent without eaters noticing — by, for example, reducing portion sizes and swapping in ingredients that contain more fiber and water. Over time, that could be much more than enough to literally tip the scales for many obese people. "The difference between losing weight and not losing weight," says Robert Kushner, the obesity scientist and clinical director at Northwestern, "is a few hundred calories a day."

Which raises a question: If McDonald's is taking these sorts of steps, 45 albeit in a slow and limited way, why isn't it more loudly saying so to deflect criticism? While the company has heavily plugged the debut of its new egg-white sandwich and chicken wraps, the ads have left out

---

epidemiology: the study of causes, effects, and patterns of health and disease across defined populations.

even a mention of health, the reduced calories and fat, or the inclusion of whole grains. McDonald's has practically kept secret the fact that it has also begun substituting wholegrain flour for some of the less healthy refined flour in its best-selling Egg McMuffin.

The explanation can be summed up in two words that surely strike fear into the hearts of all fast-food executives who hope to make their companies' fare healthier: McLean Deluxe.

Among those who gleefully rank such things, the McLean Deluxe reigns as McDonald's worst product failure of all time, eclipsing McPasta, the McHotdog, and the McAfrica (don't ask). When I brought up the McLean Deluxe to the innovation team at McDonald's, I faced the first and only uncomfortable silence of the day. Finally, Greg Watson, a senior vice president, cleared his throat and told me that neither he nor anyone else in the room was at the company at the time, and he didn't know that much about it. "It sounds to me like it was ahead of its time," he added. "If we had something like that in the future, we would never launch it like that again."

Introduced in 1991, the McLean Deluxe was perhaps the boldest single effort the food industry has ever undertaken to shift the masses to healthier eating. It was supposed to be a healthier version of the Quarter Pounder, made with extra-lean beef infused with seaweed extract. It reportedly did reasonably well in early taste tests — for what it's worth, my wife and I were big fans — and McDonald's pumped the reduced-fat angle to the public for all it was worth. The general reaction varied from lack of interest to mockery to revulsion. The company gamely flogged the sandwich for five years before quietly removing it from the menu.

The McLean Deluxe was a sharp lesson to the industry, even if in some ways it merely confirmed what generations of parents have well known: if you want to turn off otherwise eager eaters to a dish, tell them it's good for them. Recent studies suggest that calorie counts placed on menus have a negligible effect on food choices, and that the less-health-conscious might even use the information to steer clear of low-calorie fare — perhaps assuming that it tastes worse and is less satisfying, and that it's worse value for their money. The result is a sense in the food industry that if it is going to sell healthier versions of its foods to the general public — and not just to that minority already sold on healthier eating — it is going to have to do it in a relatively sneaky way, emphasizing the taste appeal and not the health benefits. "People expect something to taste worse if they believe it's healthy," says Charles Spence, an Oxford University neuroscientist who specializes in how the brain perceives food. "And that expectation affects how it tastes to them, so it actually *does* taste worse."

Thus McDonald's silence on the nutritional profiles of its new menu 50 items. "We're not making any health claims," Watson said. "We're just saying it's new, it tastes great, come on in and enjoy it. Maybe once the product is well seated with customers, we'll change that message." If customers learn that they can eat healthier foods at McDonald's without even realizing it, he added, they'll be more likely to try healthier foods there than at other restaurants. The same reasoning presumably explains why the promotions and ads for the Carl's Jr. grilled-cod sandwich offer not a word related to healthfulness, and why there wasn't a whiff of health cheerleading surrounding the turkey burger brought out earlier this year by Burger King (which is not yet calling the sandwich a permanent addition).

If the food industry is to quietly sell healthier products to its mainstream, mostly non-health-conscious customers, it must find ways to deliver the eating experience that fat and problem carbs provide in foods that have fewer of those ingredients. There is no way to do that with farm-fresh produce and wholesome meat, other than reducing portion size. But processing technology gives the food industry a potent tool for trimming unwanted ingredients while preserving the sensations they deliver.

I visited Fona International, a flavor-engineering company also outside Chicago, and learned that there are a battery of tricks for fooling and appeasing taste buds, which are prone to notice a lack of fat or sugar, or the presence of any of the various bitter, metallic, or otherwise unpleasant flavors that vegetables, fiber, complex carbs, and fat or sugar substitutes can impart to a food intended to appeal to junk-food eaters. Some 5,000 FDA-approved chemical compounds — which represent the base components of all known flavors — line the shelves that run alongside Fona's huge labs. Armed with these ingredients and an array of state-of-the-art chemical-analysis and testing tools, Fona's scientists and engineers can precisely control flavor perception. "When you reduce the sugar, fat, and salt in foods, you change the personality of the product," said Robert Sobel, a chemist, who heads up research at the company. "We can restore it."

For example, fat "cushions" the release of various flavors on the tongue, unveiling them gradually and allowing them to linger. When fat is removed, flavors tend to immediately inundate the tongue and then quickly flee, which we register as a much less satisfying experience. Fona's experts can reproduce the "temporal profile" of the flavors in fattier foods by adding edible compounds derived from plants that slow the release of flavor molecules; by replacing the flavors with similarly flavored compounds that come on and leave more slowly; or by enlisting "phantom aromas" that create the sensation of certain tastes even when those tastes are not present on the tongue. (For example, the smell of vanilla can essentially mask reductions in sugar of up to 25 percent.) One triumph of this sort of engineering is the modern protein drink, a staple of many successful weight-loss programs and a favorite of those trying to build muscle. "Seven years ago they were unpalatable," Sobel said. "Today we can mask the astringent flavors and eggy aromas by adding natural ingredients."

I also visited Tic Gums in White Marsh, Maryland, a company that engineers textures into food products. Texture hasn't received the attention that flavor has, noted Greg Andon, Tic's boyish and ebullient° president, whose family has run the company for three generations. The result, he said, is that even people in the food industry don't have an adequate vocabulary for it. "They know what flavor you're referring to when you say 'forest floor,' but all they can say about texture is 'Can you make it more creamy?'" So Tic is inventing a vocabulary, breaking textures down according to properties such as "mouth coating" and "mouth clearing." Wielding an arsenal of some 20 different "gums" — edible ingredients mostly found in tree sap, seeds, and other plant matter — Tic's researchers can make low-fat foods taste, well, creamier; give the same full body that sugared drinks offer to sugar-free beverages; counter chalkiness and gloopiness; and help orchestrate the timing of flavor bursts. (Such approaches have nothing in common with the ill-fated Olestra, a fat-like compound engineered to pass undigested through the body, and billed in the late 1990s as a fat substitute in snack foods. It was made notorious by widespread anecdotal complaints of cramps and loose bowels, though studies seemed to contradict those claims.)

Fona and Tic, like most companies in their industry, won't identify 55 customers or product names on the record. But both firms showed me an array of foods and beverages that were under construction, so to speak, in the name of reducing calories, fat, and sugar while maintaining mass appeal. I've long hated the taste of low-fat dressing — I gave up on it a few years ago and just use vinegar — but Tic served me an in-development version of a low-fat salad dressing that was better than any I've ever had. Dozens of companies are doing similar work, as are the big food-ingredient manufacturers, such as ConAgra, whose products are in 97 percent of American homes, and whose whole-wheat flour is what McDonald's is relying on for its breakfast sandwiches. Domino Foods, the sugar manufacturer, now sells a low-calorie combination of sugar and the nonsugar sweetener stevia that has been engineered by a flavor company to mask the sort of nonsugary tastes driving many consumers

ebullient: enthusiastic.

away from diet beverages and the like. "Stevia has a licorice note we were able to have taken out," explains Domino Foods CEO Brian O'Malley. High-tech anti-obesity food engineering is just warming up. Oxford's Charles Spence notes that in addition to flavors and textures, companies are investigating ways to exploit a stream of insights that have been coming out of scholarly research about the neuroscience of eating. He notes, for example, that candy companies may be able to slip healthier ingredients into candy bars without anyone noticing, simply by loading these ingredients into the middle of the bar and leaving most of the fat and sugar at the ends of the bar. "We tend to make up our minds about how something tastes from the first and last bites, and don't care as much what happens in between," he explains. Some other potentially useful gimmicks he points out: adding weight to food packaging such as yogurt containers, which convinces eaters that the contents are rich with calories, even when they're not; using chewy textures that force consumers to spend more time between bites, giving the brain a chance to register satiety; and using colors, smells, sounds, and packaging information to create the belief that foods are fatty and sweet even when they are not. Spence found, for example, that wine is perceived as 50 percent sweeter when consumed under a red light.

> "Candy companies may be able to slip healthier ingredients into candy bars without anyone noticing. . . . 'We tend to make up our minds about how something tastes from the first and last bites, and don't care as much what happens in between.'"

Researchers are also tinkering with food ingredients to boost satiety. Cargill has developed a starch derived from tapioca that gives dishes a refined-carb taste and mouthfeel, but acts more like fiber in the body — a feature that could keep the appetite from spiking later. "People usually think that processing leads to foods that digest too quickly, but we've been able to use processing to slow the digestion rate," says Bruce McGoogan, who heads R&D for Cargill's North American food-ingredient business. The company has also developed ways to reduce fat in beef patties, and to make baked goods using half the usual sugar and oil, all without heavily compromising taste and texture.

Other companies and research labs are trying to turn out healthier, more appealing foods by enlisting ultra-high pressure, nanotechnology°, vacuums, and edible coatings. At the University of Massachusetts at

---

nanotechnology: the science of manipulating matter on a very small (atomic or molecular) scale.

Amherst's Center for Foods for Health and Wellness, Fergus Clydesdale, the director of the school's Food Science Policy Alliance — as well as a spry 70-something who's happy to tick off all the processed food in his diet — showed me labs where researchers are looking into possibilities that would not only attack obesity but also improve health in other significant ways, for example by isolating ingredients that might lower the risk of cancer and concentrating them in foods. "When you understand foods at the molecular level," he says, "there's a lot you can do with food and health that we're not doing now."

The Implacable Enemies of Healthier Processed Food

What's not to like about these developments? Plenty, if you've bought into the notion that processing itself is the source of the unhealthfulness of our foods. The wholesome-food movement is not only talking up dietary strategies that are unlikely to help most obese Americans; it is, in various ways, getting in the way of strategies that could work better.

The Pollanites didn't invent resistance to healthier popular foods, as the fates of the McLean Deluxe and Olestra demonstrate, but they've greatly intensified it. Fast food and junk food have their core customer base, and the wholesome-food gurus have theirs. In between sit many millions of Americans — the more the idea that processed food should be shunned no matter what takes hold in this group, the less incentive fast-food joints will have to continue edging away from the fat-and-problem-carb-laden fare beloved by their most loyal customers to try to broaden their appeal.

Pollan has popularized contempt for "nutritionism," the idea behind   60 packing healthier ingredients into processed foods. In his view, the quest to add healthier ingredients to food isn't a potential solution, it's part of the problem. Food is healthy not when it contains healthy ingredients, he argues, but when it can be traced simply and directly to (preferably local) farms. As he resonantly put it in *The Times* in 2007: "If you're concerned about your health, you should probably avoid food products that make health claims. Why? Because a health claim on a food product is a good indication that it's not really food, and food is what you want to eat."

In this way, wholesome-food advocates have managed to pre-damn the very steps we need the food industry to take, placing the industry in a no-win situation: If it maintains the status quo, then we need to stay away because its food is loaded with fat and sugar. But if it tries to moderate these ingredients, then it is deceiving us with nutritionism. Pollan explicitly counsels avoiding foods containing more than five ingredients, or any hard-to-pronounce or unfamiliar ingredients. This rule eliminates almost anything the industry could do to produce healthier foods that retain mass appeal — most of us wouldn't get past xanthan gum — and that's perfectly in keeping with his intention.

By placing wholesome eating directly at odds with healthier processed foods, the Pollanites threaten to derail the reformation of fast food just as it's starting to gain traction. At McDonald's, "Chef Dan" — that is, Dan Coudreaut, the executive chef and director of culinary innovation — told me of the dilemma the movement has caused him as he has tried to make the menu healthier. "Some want us to have healthier food, but others want us to have minimally processed ingredients, which can mean more fat," he explained. "It's becoming a balancing act for us." That the chef with arguably the most influence in the world over the diet of the obese would even consider adding fat to his menu to placate wholesome foodies is a pretty good sign that something has gone terribly wrong with our approach to the obesity crisis.

Many people insist that the steps the food industry has already taken to offer less-obesogenic fare are no more than cynical ploys to fool customers into eating the same old crap under a healthy guise. In his 3,500-word *New York Times Magazine* article on the prospects for healthier fast food, Mark Bittman lauded a new niche of vegan chain restaurants while devoting just one line to the major "quick serve" restaurants' contribution to better health: "I'm not talking about token gestures, like the McDonald's fruit-and-yogurt parfait, whose calories are more than 50 percent sugar." Never mind that 80 percent of a farm-fresh apple's calories come from sugar; that almost any obesity expert would heartily approve of the yogurt parfait as a step in the right direction for most fast-food-dessert eaters; and that many of the desserts Bittman glorifies in his own writing make the parfait look like arugula, nutrition-wise. (His recipe for corn-and-blueberry crisp, for example, calls for adding two-thirds of a cup of brown sugar to a lot of other problem carbs, along with five tablespoons of butter.)

Bittman is hardly alone in his reflexive dismissals. No sooner had McDonald's and Burger King rolled out their egg-white sandwich and turkey burger, respectively, than a spate of articles popped up hooting that the new dishes weren't healthier because they trimmed a mere 50 and 100 calories from their standard counterparts, the Egg McMuffin and the Whopper. Apparently these writers didn't understand, or chose to ignore, the fact that a reduction of 50 or 100 calories in a single dish places an eater exactly on track to eliminate a few hundred calories a day from his or her diet — the critical threshold needed for long-term weight loss. Any bigger reduction would risk leaving someone too hungry to stick to a diet program. It's just the sort of small step in the right direction we should be aiming for, because the obese are much more likely to take it than they are to make a big leap to wholesome or very-low-calorie foods.

Many wholesome foodies insist that the food industry won't make serious progress toward healthier fare unless forced to by regulation. I, for one, believe regulation aimed at speeding the replacement of obesogenic foods with appealing healthier foods would be a great idea. But what a lot of foodies really want is to ban the food industry from selling junk food altogether. And that is just a fantasy. The government never managed to keep the tobacco companies from selling cigarettes, and banning booze (the third-most-deadly consumable killer after cigarettes and food) didn't turn out so well. The two most health-enlightened, regulation-friendly major cities in America, New York and San Francisco, tried to halt sales of two of the most horrific fast-food assaults on health — giant servings of sugared beverages and kids' fast-food meals accompanied by toys, respectively — and neither had much luck. Michelle Obama is excoriated by conservatives for asking schools to throw more fruits and vegetables into the lunches they serve. Realistically, the most we can hope for is a tax on some obesogenic foods. The research of Lisa Powell, the University of Illinois professor, suggests that a 20 percent tax on sugary beverages would reduce consumption by about 25 percent. (As for fatty foods, no serious tax proposal has yet been made in the U.S., and if one comes along, the wholesome foodies might well join the food industry and most consumers in opposing it. Denmark did manage to enact a fatty-food tax, but it was deemed a failure when consumers went next door into Germany and Sweden to stock up on their beloved treats.)

Continuing to call out Big Food on its unhealthy offerings, and loudly, is one of the best levers we have for pushing it toward healthier products — but let's call it out intelligently, not reflexively. Executives of giant food companies may be many things, but they are not stupid. Absent action, they risk a growing public-relations disaster, the loss of their more affluent and increasingly health-conscious customers, and the threat of regulation, which will be costly to fight, even if the new rules don't stick. Those fears are surely what's driving much of the push toward moderately healthier fare within the industry today. But if the Pollanites convince policy makers and the health-conscious public that these foods are dangerous by virtue of not being farm-fresh, that will push Big Food in a different direction (in part by limiting the profit potential it sees in lower-fat, lower-problem-carb foods), and cause it to spend its resources in other ways.

Significant regulation of junk food may not go far, but we have other tools at our disposal to prod Big Food to intensify and speed up its efforts to cut fat and problem carbs in its offerings, particularly if we're smart about it. Lenard Lesser points out that government and advocacy groups could start singling out particular restaurants and food products for praise or shaming — a more official version of "eat this, not that" — rather than sticking to a steady drumbeat of "processed food must go away." Academia could do a much better job of producing and highlighting solid research into less obesogenic, high-mass-appeal foods, and could curtail its evidence-light anti-food-processing bias, so that the next generation of social and policy entrepreneurs might work to narrow the gap between the poor obese and the well-resourced healthy instead of inadvertently widening it. We can keep pushing our health-care system to provide more incentives and support to the obese for losing weight by making small, painless, but helpful changes in their behavior, such as switching from Whoppers to turkey burgers, from Egg McMuffins to Egg White Delights, or from blueberry crisp to fruit-and-yogurt parfaits.

And we can ask the wholesome-food advocates, and those who give them voice, to make it clearer that the advice they sling is relevant mostly to the privileged healthy — and to start getting behind realistic solutions to the obesity crisis.

Understanding the Text

1. What is the wholesome food movement, and what does Freedman think is wrong with it?

2. How does Freedman think that the fast-food and processed-food industries could improve public health?

3. What happened with the McLean Deluxe? Why does it matter to Freedman's argument?

Reflection and Response

4. Freedman argues that telling people to eat more fruits and vegetables and less fat and calories hasn't and won't work. How does he support this assertion? Do you agree with his line of reasoning? Why or why not?

5. Freedman rejects the claim that "processed foods are unhealthy because they aren't natural" (par. 31) in favor of the idea that we could engineer healthier processed foods that are popular and tasty and actually have the potential to help the poor and the obese lose weight. How does he support his rejection of the "processed foods are unhealthy" view? Based on your analysis of this essay, as well as your own experience, which position do you think is more valid? Why?

6. How does Freedman depict the media's role in building brand reputations? How does the media affect how you see brands? Does your experience support or complicate Freedman's depiction?

Making Connections

7. Compare Freedman's description of the texture industry to Eric Schlosser's description of the flavor industry ("Why the Fries Taste Good," p. 20), and then go online and research both industries. Write a descriptive essay about their influences on food choices.

8. Imagine that Freedman and Jill McCorkle ("Her Chee-to Heart," p. 31) are discussing the pleasures of food. How might their perspectives on eating complicate each other?

9. Compare Rachel Laudan's historical portrait of sugar and salt ("The Birth of the Modern Diet," p. 55) to Freedman's contemporary view. How has scientific thinking on sugar and salt changed? What has remained the same? Consider the FDA's Nutrition Facts (p. 132) as you develop your analysis.

10. Freedman offers a harsh critique of Michael Pollan and the wholesome-food movement. He not only objects to Pollan's position, he criticizes it as impractical and goes so far as to accuse him of hypocrisy. Does Freedman offer a fair critique of Pollan? Does Freedman's critique hold up to scrutiny? Might some of his ideas be called impractical and hypocritical, too? How do we make sense of the debate they are having? Join their conversation, supporting your ideas with concrete evidence and strong analysis that helps your reader understand how you are interpreting the evidence and why you think it is support for your position. You may want to visit Pollan's Web site, read "Eat Food: Food Defined" on p. 10, or look at other essays that he has written to develop your response.

11. Frances Moore Lappé ("Biotechnology Isn't the Key to Feeding the World," p. 294) argues that democracy, not technology, is the answer to solving global hunger issues. Freedman argues for the benefits of using technology to solve the obesity crisis. Research the relationship between food production and new technologies. Select a few recent innovations, and explore if and how they might help us improve our health or make our food supply more sustainable, stable, or healthy. Evaluate the positives and negatives of the innovations you select.

Monsanto's Harvest of Fear

Donald L. Barlett and James B. Steele

Donald L. Barlett and James B. Steele have reported and written together for more than four decades. As a widely acclaimed and award-winning investigative reporting team, these two American journalists have wowed audiences with their in-depth reporting and careful research and analysis of the complex issues and institutions of their times. They began working together in the 1970s at the *Philadelphia Inquirer*, then moved to *Time*, and now are contributing editors at *Vanity Fair*. They have won many prominent journalism awards, including the Pulitzer Prize (twice) and the National Magazine Award (twice). They have also coauthored eight books, including *The Betrayal of the American Dream* (2012). In this selection from a longer article that first appeared in *Vanity Fair* in May 2008, Barlett and Steele investigate the role of the Monsanto corporation and the legal system in American food production.

G ary Rinehart clearly remembers the summer day in 2002 when the stranger walked in and issued his threat. Rinehart was behind the counter of the Square Deal, his "old-time country store," as he calls it, on the fading town square of Eagleville, Missouri, a tiny farm community 100 miles north of Kansas City.

The Square Deal is a fixture in Eagleville, a place where farmers and townspeople can go for lightbulbs, greeting cards, hunting gear, ice cream, aspirin, and dozens of other small items without having to drive to a big-box store in Bethany, the county seat, 15 miles down Interstate 35.

Everyone knows Rinehart, who was born and raised in the area and runs one of Eagleville's few surviving businesses. The stranger came up to the counter and asked for him by name.

"Well, that's me," said Rinehart.

As Rinehart would recall, the man began verbally attacking him, say- 5 ing he had proof that Rinehart had planted Monsanto's genetically modified (G.M.) soybeans in violation of the company's patent. Better come clean and settle with Monsanto, Rinehart says the man told him — or face the consequences.

Rinehart was incredulous, listening to the words as puzzled customers and employees looked on. Like many others in rural America, Rinehart knew of Monsanto's fierce reputation for enforcing its patents and suing anyone who allegedly violated them. But Rinehart wasn't a farmer.

He wasn't a seed dealer. He hadn't planted any seeds or sold any seeds. He owned a small — a *really* small — country store in a town of 350 people. He was angry that somebody could just barge into the store and embarrass him in front of everyone. "It made me and my business look bad," he says. Rinehart says he told the intruder, "You got the wrong guy."

When the stranger persisted, Rinehart showed him the door. On the way out the man kept making threats. Rinehart says he can't remember the exact words, but they were to the effect of: "Monsanto is big. You can't win. We will get you. You will pay."

Scenes like this are playing out in many parts of rural America these days as Monsanto goes after farmers, farmers' co-ops, seed dealers — anyone it suspects may have infringed its patents of genetically modified seeds. As interviews and reams of court documents reveal, Monsanto relies on a shadowy army of private investigators and agents in the American heartland to strike fear into farm country. They fan out into fields and farm towns, where they secretly videotape and photograph farmers, store owners, and co-ops; infiltrate community meetings; and gather information from informants about farming activities. Farmers say that some Monsanto agents pretend to be surveyors. Others confront farmers on their land and try to pressure them to sign papers giving Monsanto access to their private records. Farmers call them the "seed police" and use words such as "Gestapo" and "Mafia" to describe their tactics.

When asked about these practices, Monsanto declined to comment specifically, other than to say that the company is simply protecting its patents. "Monsanto spends more than $2 million a day in research to identify, test, develop, and bring to market innovative new seeds and technologies that benefit farmers," Monsanto spokesman Darren Wallis wrote in an e-mailed letter to *Vanity Fair*. "One tool in protecting this investment is patenting our discoveries and, if necessary, legally defending those patents against those who might choose to infringe upon them." Wallis said that, while the vast majority of farmers and seed dealers follow the licensing agreements, "a tiny fraction" do not, and that Monsanto is obligated to those who do abide by its rules to enforce its patent rights on those who "reap the benefits of the technology without paying for its use." He said only a small number of cases ever go to trial.

Some compare Monsanto's hard-line approach to Microsoft's zealous 10 efforts to protect its software from pirates. At least with Microsoft the buyer of a program can use it over and over again. But farmers who buy Monsanto's seeds can't even do that.

The Control of Nature

For centuries — millennia — farmers have saved seeds from season to season: they planted in the spring, harvested in the fall, then reclaimed and cleaned the seeds over the winter for re-planting the next spring. Monsanto has turned this ancient practice on its head.

Monsanto developed G.M. seeds that would resist its own herbicide, Roundup, offering farmers a convenient way to spray fields with weed killer without affecting crops. Monsanto then patented the seeds. For nearly all of its history the United States Patent and Trademark Office had refused to grant patents on seeds, viewing them as life-forms with too many variables to be patented. "It's not like describing a widget," says Joseph Mendelson III, the legal director of the Center for Food Safety, which has tracked Monsanto's activities in rural America for years.

Indeed not. But in 1980 the U.S. Supreme Court, in a five-to-four decision, turned seeds into widgets, laying the groundwork for a handful of corporations to begin taking control of the world's food supply. In its decision, the court extended patent law to cover "a live human-made microorganism." In this case, the organism wasn't even a seed. Rather, it was a *Pseudomonas* bacterium developed by a General Electric scientist to clean up oil spills. But the precedent was set, and Monsanto took advantage of it. Since the 1980s, Monsanto has become the world leader in genetic modification of seeds and has won 674 biotechnology patents, more than any other company, according to U.S. Department of Agriculture data.

Farmers who buy Monsanto's patented Roundup Ready seeds are required to sign an agreement promising not to save the seed produced after each harvest for re-planting, or to sell the seed to other farmers. This means that farmers must buy new seed every year. Those increased sales, coupled with ballooning sales of its Roundup weed killer, have been a bonanza for Monsanto.

This radical departure from age-old practice has created turmoil in 15
farm country. Some farmers don't fully understand that they aren't supposed to save Monsanto's seeds for next year's planting. Others do, but ignore the stipulation rather than throw away a perfectly usable product. Still others say that they don't use Monsanto's genetically modified seeds, but seeds have been blown into their fields by wind or deposited by birds. It's certainly easy for G.M. seeds to get mixed in with traditional varieties when seeds are cleaned by commercial dealers for re-planting. The seeds look identical; only a laboratory analysis can show the difference. Even if a farmer doesn't buy G.M. seeds and doesn't want

them on his land, it's a safe bet he'll get a visit from Monsanto's seed police if crops grown from G.M. seeds are discovered in his fields.

Most Americans know Monsanto because of what it sells to put on our lawns — the ubiquitous weed killer Roundup. What they may not know is that the company now profoundly influences — and one day may virtually control — what we put on our tables. For most of its history Monsanto was a chemical giant, producing some of the most toxic substances ever created, residues from which have left us with some of the most polluted sites on earth. Yet in a little more than a decade, the company has sought to shed its polluted past and morph into something much different and more far-reaching — an "agricultural company" dedicated to making the world "a better place for future generations." Still, more than one Web log claims to see similarities between Monsanto and the fictional company "U-North" in the movie *Michael Clayton*, an agribusiness giant accused in a multibillion-dollar lawsuit of selling an herbicide that causes cancer.

> "Most Americans know Monsanto because of what it sells to put on our lawns — the ubiquitous weed killer Roundup. What they may not know is that the company now profoundly influences — and one day may virtually control — what we put on our tables."

Monsanto's genetically modified seeds have transformed the company and are radically altering global agriculture. So far, the company has produced G.M. seeds for soybeans, corn, canola, and cotton. Many more products have been developed or are in the pipeline, including seeds for sugar beets and alfalfa. The company is also seeking to extend its reach into milk production by marketing an artificial growth hormone for cows that increases their output, and it is taking aggressive steps to put those who don't want to use growth hormone at a commercial disadvantage.

Even as the company is pushing its G.M. agenda, Monsanto is buying up conventional-seed companies. In 2005, Monsanto paid $1.4 billion for Seminis, which controlled 40 percent of the U.S. market for lettuce, tomatoes, and other vegetable and fruit seeds. Two weeks later it announced the acquisition of the country's third-largest cottonseed company, Emergent Genetics, for $300 million. It's estimated that Monsanto seeds now account for 90 percent of the U.S. production of soybeans, which are used in food products beyond counting. Monsanto's acquisitions have fueled explosive growth, transforming the St. Louis–based corporation into the largest seed company in the world.

In Iraq, the groundwork has been laid to protect the patents of Monsanto and other G.M.-seed companies. One of L. Paul Bremer's last acts as head of the Coalition Provisional Authority was an order stipulating that "farmers shall be prohibited from re-using seeds of protected varieties." Monsanto has said that it has no interest in doing business in Iraq, but should the company change its mind, the American-style law is in place.

To be sure, more and more agricultural corporations and individual 20 farmers are using Monsanto's G.M. seeds. As recently as 1980, no genetically modified crops were grown in the U.S. In 2007, the total was 142 million acres planted. Worldwide, the figure was 282 million acres. Many farmers believe that G.M. seeds increase crop yields and save money. Another reason for their attraction is convenience. By using Roundup Ready soybean seeds, a farmer can spend less time tending to his fields. With Monsanto seeds, a farmer plants his crop, then treats it later with Roundup to kill weeds. That takes the place of labor-intensive weed control and plowing.

Monsanto portrays its move into G.M. seeds as a giant leap for mankind. But out in the American countryside, Monsanto's no-holds-barred tactics have made it feared and loathed. Like it or not, farmers say, they have fewer and fewer choices in buying seeds.

And controlling the seeds is not some abstraction. Whoever provides the world's seeds controls the world's food supply.

Under Surveillance

After Monsanto's investigator confronted Gary Rinehart, Monsanto filed a federal lawsuit alleging that Rinehart "knowingly, intentionally, and willfully" planted seeds "in violation of Monsanto's patent rights." The company's complaint made it sound as if Monsanto had Rinehart dead to rights:

During the 2002 growing season, Investigator Jeffery Moore, through surveillance of Mr. Rinehart's farm facility and farming operations, observed Defendant planting brown bag soybean seed. Mr. Moore observed the Defendant take the brown bag soybeans to a field, which was subsequently loaded into a grain drill and planted. Mr. Moore located two empty bags in the ditch in the public road right-of-way beside one of the fields planted by Rinehart, which contained some soybeans. Mr. Moore collected a small amount of soybeans left in the bags which Defendant had tossed into the public right-of-way. These samples tested positive for Monsanto's Roundup Ready technology.

Faced with a federal lawsuit, Rinehart had to hire a lawyer. Monsanto eventually realized that "Investigator Jeffery Moore" had targeted the wrong man, and dropped the suit. Rinehart later learned that the company had been secretly investigating farmers in his area. Rinehart never heard from Monsanto again: no letter of apology, no public concession that the company had made a terrible mistake, no offer to pay his attorney's fees. "I don't know how they get away with it," he says. "If I tried to do something like that it would be bad news. I felt like I was in another country."

Gary Rinehart is actually one of Monsanto's luckier targets. Ever since 25 commercial introduction of its G.M. seeds, in 1996, Monsanto has launched thousands of investigations and filed lawsuits against hundreds of farmers and seed dealers. In a 2007 report, the Center for Food Safety, in Washington, D.C., documented 112 such lawsuits, in 27 states.

Even more significant, in the Center's opinion, are the numbers of farmers who settle because they don't have the money or the time to fight Monsanto. "The number of cases filed is only the tip of the iceberg," says Bill Freese, the Center's science-policy analyst. Freese says he has been told of many cases in which Monsanto investigators showed up at a farmer's house or confronted him in his fields, claiming he had violated the technology agreement and demanding to see his records. According to Freese, investigators will say, "Monsanto knows that you are saving Roundup Ready seeds, and if you don't sign these information-release forms, Monsanto is going to come after you and take your farm or take you for all you're worth." Investigators will sometimes show a farmer a photo of himself coming out of a store, to let him know he is being followed.

Lawyers who have represented farmers sued by Monsanto say that intimidating actions like these are commonplace. Most give in and pay Monsanto some amount in damages; those who resist face the full force of Monsanto's legal wrath. . . .

The Milk Wars

Jeff Kleinpeter takes very good care of his dairy cows. In the winter he turns on heaters to warm their barns. In the summer, fans blow gentle breezes to cool them, and on especially hot days, a fine mist floats down to take the edge off Louisiana's heat. The dairy has gone "to the ultimate end of the earth for cow comfort," says Kleinpeter, a fourth-generation dairy farmer in Baton Rouge. He says visitors marvel at what he does: "I've had many of them say, 'When I die, I want to come back as a Kleinpeter cow.'"

Monsanto would like to change the way Jeff Kleinpeter and his family do business. Specifically, Monsanto doesn't like the label on Kleinpeter Dairy's milk cartons: "From Cows *Not* Treated with rBGH." To consumers, that means the milk comes from cows that were not given artificial bovine growth hormone, a supplement developed by Monsanto that can be injected into dairy cows to increase their milk output.

No one knows what effect, if any, the hormone has on milk or the 30 people who drink it. Studies have not detected any difference in the quality of milk produced by cows that receive rBGH, or rBST, a term by which it is also known. But Jeff Kleinpeter — like millions of consumers — wants no part of rBGH. Whatever its effect on humans, if any, Kleinpeter feels certain it's harmful to cows because it speeds up their metabolism and increases the chances that they'll contract a painful illness that can shorten their lives. "It's like putting a Volkswagen car in with the Indianapolis 500 racers," he says. "You gotta keep the pedal to the metal the whole way through, and pretty soon that poor little Volkswagen engine's going to burn up."

Kleinpeter Dairy has never used Monsanto's artificial hormone, and the dairy requires other dairy farmers from whom it buys milk to attest that they don't use it, either. At the suggestion of a marketing consultant, the dairy began advertising its milk as coming from rBGH-free cows in 2005, and the label began appearing on Kleinpeter milk cartons and in company literature, including a new Web site of Kleinpeter products that proclaims, "We treat our cows with love . . . not rBGH."

The dairy's sales soared. For Kleinpeter, it was simply a matter of giving consumers more information about their product.

But giving consumers that information has stirred the ire of Monsanto. The company contends that advertising by Kleinpeter and other dairies touting their "no rBGH" milk reflects adversely on Monsanto's product. In a letter to the Federal Trade Commission in February 2007, Monsanto said that, notwithstanding the overwhelming evidence that there is no difference in the milk from cows treated with its product, "milk processors persist in claiming on their labels and in advertisements that the use of rBST is somehow harmful, either to cows or to the people who consume milk from rBST-supplemented cows."

Monsanto called on the commission to investigate what it called the "deceptive advertising and labeling practices" of milk processors such as Kleinpeter, accusing them of misleading consumers "by falsely claiming that there are health and safety risks associated with milk from rBST-supplemented cows." As noted, Kleinpeter does not make any such claims — he simply states that his milk comes from cows not injected with rBGH.

Monsanto's attempt to get the F.T.C. to force dairies to change their   35
advertising was just one more step in the corporation's efforts to extend
its reach into agriculture. After years of scientific debate and public controversy, the F.D.A. in 1993 approved commercial use of rBST, basing its
decision in part on studies submitted by Monsanto. That decision allowed
the company to market the artificial hormone. The effect of the hormone
is to increase milk production, not exactly something the nation needed
then — or needs now. The U.S. was actually awash in milk, with the government buying up the surplus to prevent a collapse in prices.

Monsanto began selling the supplement in 1994 under the name
Posilac. Monsanto acknowledges that the possible side effects of rBST for
cows include lameness, disorders of the uterus, increased body tempera-
ture, digestive problems, and birthing difficulties. Veterinary drug reports
note that "cows injected with Posilac are at an increased risk for mastitis,"
an udder infection in which bacteria and pus may be pumped out with
the milk. What's the effect on humans? The F.D.A. has consistently said
that the milk produced by cows that receive rBGH is the same as milk from
cows that aren't injected: "The public can be confident that milk and meat
from BST-treated cows is safe to consume." Nevertheless, some scientists
are concerned by the lack of long-term studies to test the additive's impact,
especially on children. A Wisconsin geneticist, William von Meyer,
observed that when rBGH was approved the longest study on which
the F.D.A.'s approval was based covered only a 90-day laboratory test with
small animals. "But people drink milk for a lifetime," he noted. Canada
and the European Union have never approved the commercial sale of the
artificial hormone. Today, nearly 15 years after the F.D.A. approved rBGH,
there have still been no long-term studies "to determine the safety of milk
from cows that receive artificial growth hormone," says Michael Hansen,
senior staff scientist for Consumers Union. Not only have there been no
studies, he adds, but the data that does exist all comes from Monsanto.
"There is no scientific consensus about the safety," he says.

However F.D.A. approval came about, Monsanto has long been wired
into Washington. Michael R. Taylor was a staff attorney and executive
assistant to the F.D.A. commissioner before joining a law firm in
Washington in 1981, where he worked to secure F.D.A. approval of
Monsanto's artificial growth hormone before returning to the F.D.A. as
deputy commissioner in 1991. Dr. Michael A. Friedman, formerly
the F.D.A.'s deputy commissioner for operations, joined Monsanto in
1999 as a senior vice president. Linda J. Fisher was an assistant

administrator at the E.P.A. when she left the agency in 1993. She became a vice president of Monsanto, from 1995 to 2000, only to return to the E.P.A. as deputy administrator the next year. William D. Ruckelshaus, former E.P.A. administrator, and Mickey Kantor, former U.S. trade representative, each served on Monsanto's board after leaving government. Supreme Court justice Clarence Thomas was an attorney in Monsanto's corporate-law department in the 1970s. He wrote the Supreme Court opinion in a crucial G.M.-seed patent-rights case in 2001 that benefited Monsanto and all G.M.-seed companies. Donald Rumsfeld never served on the board or held any office at Monsanto, but Monsanto must occupy a soft spot in the heart of the former defense secretary. Rumsfeld was chairman and C.E.O. of the pharmaceutical maker G. D. Searle & Co. when Monsanto acquired Searle in 1985, after Searle had experienced difficulty in finding a buyer. Rumsfeld's stock and options in Searle were valued at $12 million at the time of the sale.

From the beginning some consumers have consistently been hesitant to drink milk from cows treated with artificial hormones. This is one reason Monsanto has waged so many battles with dairies and regulators over the wording of labels on milk cartons. It has sued at least two dairies and one co-op over labeling.

Critics of the artificial hormone have pushed for mandatory labeling on all milk products, but the F.D.A. has resisted and even taken action against some dairies that labeled their milk "BST-free." Since BST is a natural hormone found in all cows, including those not injected with Monsanto's artificial version, the F.D.A. argued that no dairy could claim that its milk is BST-free. The F.D.A. later issued guidelines allowing dairies to use labels saying their milk comes from "non-supplemented cows," as long as the carton has a disclaimer saying that the artificial supplement does not in any way change the milk. So the milk cartons from Kleinpeter Dairy, for example, carry a label on the front stating that the milk is from cows not treated with rBGH, and the rear panel says, "Government studies have shown no significant difference between milk derived from rBGH-treated and non-rBGH-treated cows." That's not good enough for Monsanto.

The Next Battleground

As more and more dairies have chosen to advertise their milk as "No 40 rBGH," Monsanto has gone on the offensive. Its attempt to force the F.T.C. to look into what Monsanto called "deceptive practices" by dairies trying to distance themselves from the company's artificial hormone was the most recent national salvo. But after reviewing Monsanto's claims, the F.T.C.'s Division of Advertising Practices decided in August 2007 that a "formal investigation and enforcement action is not warranted at this time." The agency found some instances where dairies had made "unfounded health and safety claims," but these were mostly on Web sites, not on milk cartons. And the F.T.C. determined that the dairies Monsanto had singled out all carried disclaimers that the F.D.A. had found no significant differences in milk from cows treated with the artificial hormone.

Blocked at the federal level, Monsanto is pushing for action by the states. In the fall of 2007, Pennsylvania's agriculture secretary, Dennis Wolff, issued an edict prohibiting dairies from stamping milk containers with labels stating their products were made without the use of the artificial hormone. Wolff said such a label implies that competitors' milk is not safe, and noted that non-supplemented milk comes at an unjustified higher price, arguments that Monsanto has frequently made. The ban was to take effect February 1, 2008.

Wolff's action created a firestorm in Pennsylvania (and beyond) from angry consumers. So intense was the outpouring of e-mails, letters, and calls that Pennsylvania governor Edward Rendell stepped in and reversed his agriculture secretary, saying, "The public has a right to complete information about how the milk they buy is produced."

On this issue, the tide may be shifting against Monsanto. Organic dairy products, which don't involve rBGH, are soaring in popularity. Supermarket chains such as Kroger, Publix, and Safeway are embracing them. Some other companies have turned away from rBGH products, including Starbucks, which has banned all milk products from cows treated with rBGH. Although Monsanto once claimed that an estimated 30 percent of the nation's dairy cows were injected with rBST, it's widely believed that today the number is much lower.

But don't count Monsanto out. Efforts similar to the one in Pennsylvania have been launched in other states, including New Jersey, Ohio, Indiana, Kansas, Utah, and Missouri. A Monsanto-backed group called AFACT — American Farmers for the Advancement and Conservation of Technology — has been spearheading efforts in many of these states. AFACT describes itself as a "producer organization" that decries "questionable labeling tactics and activism" by marketers who have convinced some consumers to "shy away from foods using new technology." AFACT reportedly uses the same St. Louis public-relations firm, Osborn & Barr, employed by Monsanto. An Osborn & Barr spokesman told the *Kansas City Star* that the company was doing work for AFACT on a pro bono basis.

Even if Monsanto's efforts to secure across-the-board labeling changes 45
should fall short, there's nothing to stop state agriculture departments
from restricting labeling on a dairy-by-dairy basis. Beyond that,
Monsanto also has allies whose foot soldiers will almost certainly keep
up the pressure on dairies that don't use Monsanto's artificial hormone.
Jeff Kleinpeter knows about them, too.

He got a call one day from the man who prints the labels for his milk
cartons, asking if he had seen the attack on Kleinpeter Dairy that had
been posted on the Internet. Kleinpeter went online to a site called
StopLabelingLies, which claims to "help consumers by publicizing examples of false and misleading food and other product labels." There, sure
enough, Kleinpeter and other dairies that didn't use Monsanto's product
were being accused of making misleading claims to sell their milk.

There was no address or phone number on the Web site, only a list of
groups that apparently contribute to the site and whose issues range from
disparaging organic farming to downplaying the impact of global warming. "They were criticizing people like me for doing what we had a right to
do, had gone through a government agency to do," says Kleinpeter. "We
never could get to the bottom of that Web site to get that corrected."

As it turns out, the Web site counts among its contributors Steven
Milloy, the "junk science" commentator for FoxNews.com and operator
of junkscience.com, which claims to debunk "faulty scientific data and
analysis." It may come as no surprise that earlier in his career, Milloy,
who calls himself the "junkman," was a registered lobbyist for Monsanto.

Understanding the Text

1. What are genetically modified seeds? What are Roundup Ready seeds?

2. Why is Monsanto trying to protect its patent?

3. How has Monsanto changed farming practices? What ancient practices are
   being eliminated?

Reflection and Response

4. What's at stake in the legal battles between Monsanto and the farmers
   accused of misusing patented seeds? Why is Monsanto trying to protect its
   interests so vigorously? Why and how are some farmers fighting back?

5. Barlett and Steele's investigative reporting is aimed at exposing Monsanto's
   ruthless tactics, legal and otherwise. How do they do this? What rhetorical
   strategies do they employ? How and why are their strategies effective?

6. Why does Monsanto care about how dairy farmers advertise their
   products? Should Monsanto have a say? Who should decide?

Making Connections

7. Describe Monsanto's tactics for protecting its own interests. Are they justified? Why or why not? Which authors in this collection would critique Monsanto's tactics? Would any defend them? Use textual evidence to support your answers.

8. Barlett and Steele claim that Monsanto "profoundly influences — and one day may virtually control — what we put on our tables" (par. 16). How do they support this argument? What evidence is presented in Vandana Shiva's essay ("Soy Imperialism and the Destruction of Local Food Cultures," p. 179) that could be used to support this claim? What evidence could be used to complicate or argue against it? Using your campus library resources, locate at least two other sources that discuss the impact of Monsanto on food production to develop your response to these questions. Use textual evidence to support your responses.

Stuffed and Starved

Raj Patel

Raj Patel is a prolific and award-winning writer, respected scholar, and celebrated activist. He is known for his outspoken and carefully researched social justice writing. With degrees from the University of Oxford, the London School of Economics, and Cornell University, Patel has studied and taught around the world, including a gig co-teaching a course at the University of California, Berkeley, with Michael Pollan. He has both worked for and protested against the World Bank and the World Trade Organization. His particular interest in food policy is evident in his media appearances, articles, podcasts, books, and documentaries, and his position as a fellow at The Institute for Food and Development Policy (also known as Food First). His latest book, *The Value of Nothing* (2009), was a *New York Times* best seller. In his first book, *Stuffed and Starved: The Hidden Battle for the World Food System* (2007), excerpted here, Patel uncovers the shocking reasons for our global condition in which half the world is malnourished while the other half is obese. His account also provides hope as he explores potential solutions, ones that are more democratic and more sustainable. This selection examines the food distribution system, which favors big business over consumers and farmers.

An Hourglass Figure

There is a superabundance of coffee farmers and coffee drinkers, there are many millers, and a good few exporters. But there's a bottleneck in the distribution chain, and what is true for coffee also holds for a range of other foods. At some stages in the chain that links field to plate, power is concentrated in very few hands. If there had to be a picture or two showing where power is concentrated in the way food is grown and sold, Figure 1.1 (p. 174) would do the trick. The first figure shows aggregated data from the Netherlands, Germany, France, UK, Austria and Belgium. The second shows similar but not entirely comparable data from the United States. The numbers need to be taken with a pinch of salt. For instance, the total number of farmers who grow food for Europeans and North Americans is far higher than indicated here. After all, millions of farmers and farmworkers, growing all kinds of tropical fruits and vegetables for export, live *outside* the wealthiest countries in the world.

As far as power is concerned, the bottleneck is the central clue. Somehow, we've ended up at a world with a few corporate buyers and sellers. The process of shipping, processing and trucking food across distances demands a great deal of capital — you need to be rich to play this game. It is also a game that has economies of scale. This means that the bigger a company is, and the more transport and logistics it does, the cheaper it is for that company to be in the business. There are, after all, no mom-and-pop international food distribution companies. The small fish have been devoured by the Leviathans of distribution and supply. And when the number of companies controlling the gateways from farmers to consumers is small, this gives them market power both over the people who grow the food *and* the people who eat it.

One measure of the power wielded by these "bottleneck corporations" is the size of the industry, and of the biggest players in it. The retailers turned over US$4 trillion in 2009, the seed-sellers US$31 billion a year, the agrochemical industry in 2007 sold US$38.6 billion, food-processors' revenue was US$1.3 trillion in 2007. (Just for comparison's sake, the total

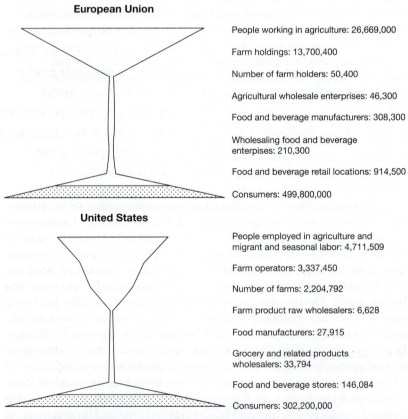

European Union

People working in agriculture: 26,669,000

Farm holdings: 13,700,400

Number of farm holders: 50,400

Agricultural wholesale enterprises: 46,300

Food and beverage manufacturers: 308,300

Wholesaling food and beverage enterpises: 210,300

Food and beverage retail locations: 914,500

Consumers: 499,800,000

United States

People employed in agriculture and migrant and seasonal labor: 4,711,509

Farm operators: 3,337,450

Number of farms: 2,204,792

Farm product raw wholesalers: 6,628

Food manufacturers: 27,915

Grocery and related products wholesalers: 33,794

Food and beverage stores: 146,084

Consumers: 302,200,000

Figure 1.1 **Hourglasses: the concentration of power and players in the food system**
Sources: "European Union": EU, 2010; Eurostat, 2009; Marcu, 2009; "United States": Passel, 2009; Population Reference Bureau, 2007; US Census Bureau, 2007; USDA, 2007.

GDP of Mexico in 2007 was US$1.02 trillion.) If the output of these industries feels a little rich, the US$390.3 billion a year global weight loss industry is happy to help. And for those countries unable to find enough to eat, well, the US$2 billion food aid industry can step in there too. (And that doesn't factor in the oil industry that stands behind them.) Meanwhile, those who can afford to consume are left with calories too cheap to meter.

The giants in the corporate food system are big enough that they don't have to play by the rules. They can tilt the playing field. At home and at venues such as the World Trade Organization, these corporations lobby governments for an economic environment conducive to their activities. Trade agreements are one among many routes through which governments help the corporations at the waist of the food system hourglass. Other support is available too. If an overseas investment seems a bit risky, a public-funded export credit agency or perhaps the World Bank can help shoulder the risk directly, or persuade a country to underwrite the risk itself. If a country refuses to accept a particular product on grounds of health, safety or environmental concerns, direct diplomatic pressure can be applied.

*"*To put it slightly differently, the current food system isn't an arrangement dropped from the sky. It's a compromise between different demands and anxieties, of corporations pushing for higher profit in food, of governments concerned with social unrest or, occasionally, a drubbing at the polls, and of urban consumers.*"*

Against accusations that they are merely selling favors to the highest 5 bidder, governments have gone to great lengths to ensure that interventions in the food system can be seen as functioning in the national interest. Often, these views are genuinely held by the people who provide governmental support, and the public undoubtedly benefited from initiatives such as the US New Deal, the European welfare state and the Indian Public Distribution system. Yet governments' motives are rarely pure. Governmental concerns about poverty, for example, have historically been driven by fear, not least because of their concerns of what large groups of politically organized, angry and hungry urban poor people might do to the urban rich. In the UK, back at the beginning of the twentieth century, Cecil Rhodes was a passionate advocate of colonialism as a means to hush the speeches of angry workers on street corners who wanted for bread. And, in different ways, the countries of Europe and North America set their food policies in order to ensure that the cries of the urban hungry didn't lead to civil war.

To put it slightly differently, the current food system isn't an arrangement dropped from the sky. It's a compromise between different demands and anxieties, of corporations pushing for higher profit in food, of governments concerned with social unrest or, occasionally, a drubbing° at the polls, and of urban consumers. Written out of this story are the rural communities, who seem to be suffering silently. And yet it is they who are leading the way in forging a new and different food system. They do it out of necessity, for they are dying.

Ways of Being Free

To none do countryside hymns sound flatter than to people in dying rural communities. As lands have fallen before the banks, repossessed and repurposed, suicide rates for farmers across the world have soared. Yet farmers and the dispossessed are not going quietly. There have always been, and continue to be, rebels. The food system is a battlefield, though few realize quite how many casualties there have been. While consumers have been only recently wrestling with the problems of how to eat well, farmers have long been fighting against the vanishing of their freedoms, and their battle continues today. From the ten-million-strong Karnataka State Farmers' Association (Karnataka Rajya Raitha Sangha or KRRS) in India, to the *campesinos* (translated as "peasant" but without the pejorative° association in English) in and from Mexico — there's a fistful of organizations not only fighting against this food system, and sometimes dying in protest, but building alternatives to it, and living in dignity.

Farmers' groups in the US, India and Mexico, for example, have taken their grievances about low prices from their fields to the barricades outside the World Trade Organization, or to the offices of companies that end up buying the fruits of their labor, like Taco Bell, or to the offices of the corporations who profit from the sale of seeds and pesticides, like the Monsanto Company, or to the governments which have abetted rural privation°.

In Brazil, over one million landless people have organized and occupied disused farmland. As a result, they are living healthier, longer and better-educated lives than those in comparable schemes elsewhere. The members of this movement, the Brazilian Landless Rural Workers Movement, are part of arguably the world's largest independent social movement organization — La Via Campesina (The Peasant Way), claiming a membership of 200 million people worldwide. Incorporating groups

drubbing: a beating, thrashing, or resounding defeat.
pejorative: disparaging or disapproving.
privation: the state of being deprived of things that are essential for well-being, such as food and water.

from the KRRS, with an estimated membership of twenty million in India, to the National Farmers Union in Canada, the Korean Women Farmers Association, the Confédération Paysanne in France and the União Nacional de Camponeses in Mozambique, it's nearly as globalized as the forces against which it ranges itself. It's a mixed bag of movements. Some of its members are landless, some own land and hire the landless; some are small producers, some are medium-sized; what counts as a small farm in Canada is an estate in India. Clearly not all farmers are equal, and neither are their social organizations. Even within countries, there are important differences. In the US, for example, black farmers have consistently had it harder than white. One of the largest anti-discrimination lawsuits was settled in 1999 by the US Department of Agriculture, in restitution for consistent and ongoing discrimination against black farmers in the distribution of federal funding.

In the places where they fight, each movement confronts specific conditions, constraints, opposition and arms. Yet they are able to unite around a common understanding of the international food system. These movements don't restrict themselves to joint analytical work. They are also able to come together in action, in complex and sophisticated ways. When the 2004 Indian Ocean tsunami struck farmers and fishing communities in Indonesia and Sri Lanka, the movement was there helping them to rebuild.

As the hourglass shows, though, the food system doesn't just put farmers at the blunt end of abuses of power. Consumers are also subject to the market power of corporations. Of course, as consumers our position is slightly different — as consumers we can shape the market, however slightly, by taking our wallets elsewhere. But the choice between Coke and Pepsi is a pop freedom — it's choice lite. Community organizations are fighting back for a deeper kind of choice. The ways such organizations have tried to reimagine our choices range from the creation of alternative food distribution mechanisms for people of color, such as the Peoples' Grocery in Oakland, California, to the struggle to redefine what food means, as the gastronomic° grammarians at the Slow Food movement are trying to do. Groups around the world have been trying to broaden the food system to give back the choices that have been taken away from the people who grow, and the people who eat.

Of course, no group is without contradiction. There is no pure ideology made flesh, no holier-than-thou land in which resistance is perfect and untrammeled°. We all make our politics with the tools we have at hand, in the places we find them.

---

gastronomic: relating to the art or practice of good eating.
untrammeled: completely free, not restricted.

Understanding the Text

1. What are economies of scale, and how does that help you understand the food distribution system?

2. Where in the food distribution chain is power concentrated? Use Patel's images of the hourglasses to compare and contrast the concentration of power in the European Union and United States food systems.

3. According to Patel, what role does government play in the current food system?

Reflection and Response

4. Patel claims that corporate food giants don't have to play by the rules. What does he mean by "the rules" in this context? Who makes the rules?

5. Patel uses several metaphors to describe the food distribution chain — a bottleneck, an hourglass, and a battlefield. What makes these metaphors compelling? Why do you think he uses them? Which one do you think supports his argument most effectively, and why?

6. Patel argues that rural farmers who are suffering the most under the current food system are also the ones who are leading the efforts to reform the system. Does this surprise you? Why or why not? What reasons does Patel offer for why this is so?

Making Connections

7. Patel argues that as consumers, we can shape the market, even if only slightly. Research efforts in your local community that have this aim. What kinds of actions are consumers or other community groups taking by "taking [their] wallets elsewhere" (par. 11)? Are they succeeding? Be sure to explain how you are measuring success. Select one of two other authors in this book to help you support and contextualize your analysis.

8. Compare Patel's description of the relations of power present in the food distribution system to the descriptions offered by Troy Johnson ("Farm to Fable," p. 191) and Richard Marosi ("Hardship on Mexico's Farms, A Bounty for U.S. Tables," p. 283). Who has power? Who is powerless? How do these relations of power affect us as consumers? How do they affect farmers?

9. Patel suggests, "We all make our politics with the tools we have at hand, in the places we find them" (par. 12). Many authors in this book support this notion as they offer a view of the politics of food production and distribution. Compare and contrast the ways Patel, Wendell Berry ("The Pleasures of Eating," p. 47), Dhruv Khullar ("Why Shame Won't Stop Obesity," p. 135), and Frances Moore Lappé ("Biotechnology Isn't the Key to Feeding the World," p. 294) portray the politics of food.

Soy Imperialism and the Destruction of Local Food Cultures

Vandana Shiva

Vandana Shiva was a leading physicist in India before she became an internationally known environmental and antiglobalization activist. She is particularly dedicated to the protection of local food cultures and the preservation of heirloom seeds in India. She is the recipient of many international awards and the author of more than 20 books, including *Staying Alive: Women, Ecology, and Development* (1988); *Stolen Harvest: The Hijacking of the Global Food Supply* (2000); *Earth Democracy: Justice, Sustainability, and Peace* (2005) and *Making Peace with the Earth* (2013). She is a leader in the International Forum on Globalization and director of the Research Foundation on Science, Technology, and Ecology. In this selection from *Stolen Harvest*, Shiva issues a stinging critique of the way global food markets are destroying local food cultures. She argues that particular economic and political trends of globalization are threatening India's local food culture.

The diversity of soils, climates, and plants has contributed to a diversity of food cultures across the world. The maize-based food systems of Central America, the rice-based Asian systems, the teff-based Ethiopian diet, and the millet-based foods of Africa are not just a part of agriculture; they are central to cultural diversity. Food security is not just having access to adequate food. It is also having access to culturally appropriate food. Vegetarians can starve if asked to live on meat diets. I have watched Asians feel totally deprived on bread, potato, and meat diets in Europe.

India is a country rich in biological diversity and cultural diversity of food systems. In the high Himalayan mountains, people eat pseudocereals such as amaranth, buckwheat, and chenopods. The people of the arid areas of Western India and semiarid tracts of the Deccan live on millets. Eastern India is home to rice and fish cultures, as are the states of Goa and Kerala. Each region also has its culturally specific edible oil used as a cooking medium. In the North and East it is mustard, in the West it is [peanut], in the Deccan it is sesame, and in Kerala it is coconut.

The diversity of oilseeds has also contributed to diversity of cropping systems. In the fields, oilseeds have always been mixed with cereals. Wheat is intercropped with mustard and sesame is intercropped with millets. A typical home garden could have up to 100 different species growing in cooperation.

The story of how the soybean displaced mustard in India within a few months of open imports is a story being repeated with different foods, crops, and cultures across the world, as subsidized exports from industrialized countries are dumped on agricultural societies, destroying livelihoods, biodiversity, and cultural diversity of food. The flooding of domestic markets with artificially cheap imports is stealing local markets and livelihoods from local farmers and local food processors. The expansion of global markets is taking place by extinguishing local economies and cultures.

"Mustard Is Our Life"

For Bengalis, Hilsa fish fried in mustard oil is the ultimate delight, and 5
North Indians like their *pakoras* fried in it because of the unique taste and aroma. In the South, mustard seeds are the preferred seasoning for many dishes. Mustard oil is used as the cooking medium in the entire North Indian belt — the standard oil of Bihar, Bengal, Orissa, and East Uttar Pradesh, used for flavoring and cooking.

Mustard, which was developed as a crop in India, is not just useful as an edible oil. It is an important medicine in the indigenous system of health care. It is used for therapeutic massages and for muscular and joint problems. Mustard oil with garlic and turmeric is used for rheumatism and joint pains. Mustard oil is also used as a mosquito repellent, a significant contribution in a region where the resurgence of malaria is responsible for the death of thousands.

There are many other personal and health care uses for mustard seeds and oil, and diverse varieties and species of mustard are grown and used for different purposes.[1] During the Deepavali celebration, mustard oil is used to light *diya* lamps. This is not just a celebratory tradition, but an ecological method of pest control at a time when the change in seasons causes an outbreak of disease and pests. The smoke from the mustard oil used to light the *deepavali* lamp acts as an environmental purifier and pest-control agent, reducing the spread of diseases that destroy stored grains and cleaning the atmosphere of homes and villages. As these mustard-oil lamps have been replaced by candles made of paraffin wax, an environmentally cleansing festival is transformed into an environmentally polluting one.

Indigenous° oilseeds, being high in oil content, are easy to process at small-scale, decentralized levels with eco-friendly and health-friendly technologies. These oils are thus available to the poor at low cost.

indigenous: occurring naturally in a particular place.

Hundreds and thousands of artisans are self-employed in rural India by extracting oil from locally produced crops for oil edible by humans and oil cake edible by cattle. The bulk of oilseed processing is done by over 1 million *ghanis* (expellers) and 20,000 small and tiny crushers that account for 68 percent of edible oils processed.[2] The oil extracted through these cold-pressing indigenous technologies is fresh, nutritious, unadulterated, and contains natural flavor.[3]

Women in the *bastis*, or slums, usually buy small quantities of mustard oil extracted on their local *ghani* in front of their eyes. This direct, community supervision over processing is the best guarantee for food safety. Yet these community-based systems of food and health safety were quickly dismantled in the name of food safety in 1998, when local processing of mustard oil was banned and free imports of soybean oil were installed in response to a mysterious contamination of Delhi's edible-oil supply.

The sudden lack of availability of mustard oil posed serious problems 10 for poor women. Their children would not eat food cooked in imported palm oil or soybean oil, and were going to bed hungry. Being poor, they could not afford to buy the packaged oil that was the only form in which oil was available after the ban on local processors. For although the Chinese and Japanese eat soybean products as fermented foods, in most cultures outside East Asia, soybean products are not eaten. In spite of decades of promotion through free distribution in schools, soybean has not been adopted in India as a preferred choice for either oil or protein.

The Dropsy Epidemic

During August 1998, a tragedy unfolded in Delhi due to a massive adulteration° of mustard oil with seeds of the weed *Argemone mexicana*, as well as other adulterants such as diesel, waste oil, and industrial oil.

Consumption of the adulterated oil had led to an epidemic of what was called "dropsy" and referred to a range of signs and symptoms affecting multiple organs and systems. These included nausea, vomiting, diarrhea, abdominal swelling, liver toxicity, kidney damage, cardio-toxicity, breathlessness due to retention of fluids in the lungs, and death due to heart failure. The link between dropsy and adulterated edible oil was first established by an Indian doctor in Bengal in 1926. By early September 1998, the official death toll was 41, and 2,300 people had been affected.

Mustard-oil sales were banned in Delhi, Assam, Bihar, Haryana, Madhya Pradesh, Orissa, Uttar Pradesh, West Bengal, Arunachal Pradesh,

adulteration: the process of adding extraneous or inferior ingredients.

Sikkum, Tripura, and Karnataka. In July, India announced that it would import 1 million tons of soybeans for use as oilseeds, over the protests of citizen groups and the Agriculture Ministry, which challenged the necessity and safety of the imports. Later, free imports of soybeans were instituted. Not only was there no guarantee that these soybeans would not be contaminated with genetically engineered soybeans, the moves profoundly jeopardized the local oil-processing industry and with it the food culture and economy that depended on it.

On September 4, the government banned the sale of all unpackaged edible oils, thus ensuring that all household and community-level processing of edible oils stopped, and edible oil became fully industrialized. The food economy of the poor, who depend on unpackaged oil since it is cheaper and they can buy it in small quantities, was completely destroyed.

> "The highest-level political and economic conflicts between freedom and slavery, democracy and dictatorship, diversity and monoculture have thus entered into the simple acts of buying edible oils and cooking our food."

The adulteration that triggered these dire effects remains mysterious in origin. First, in the past local traders had adulterated particular brands of oils in remote and marginalized regions to cheat consumers in a way that would go unnoticed; however, the mustard-oil adulteration affected nearly all brands, and India's capital, Delhi, was the worst-affected region. Such an adulteration triggered an immediate response and could not have been initiated by an individual local trader. 15

Second, while corrupt traders had adulterated mustard oil with argemone° in the past, before the 1998 tragedy, the adulterating agent was never found to be more than 1 percent of the oil. This time, contaminated oil contained up to 30 percent argemone and other agents. The high level of adulteration with argemone and other toxic substances such as diesel and waste oil clearly indicated that the tragedy was not the result of the normal business of adulteration.

According to the health minister of Delhi, the adulteration was not possible without an organized conspiracy. It was done in such a way that it could kill people quickly and conspicuously, and an immediate ban on mustard oil and free import of soybeans and other oilseeds for oil became inevitable. The Rajasthan Oil Industries Association claimed that a "conspiracy" was being hatched to undermine the mustard-oil trade, and felt that "invisible hands of the multinationals" were involved.

argemone: a flowering plant commonly known as prickly poppy; its oil is sometimes mixed with edible oils even though it is considered toxic.

Multinational Companies Gain from the Mustard-Oil Tragedy

During the oil crisis, the Indian soybean lobby organized a major conference, "Globoil India 98," to promote the globalization and monoculturization of India's edible-oil economy. The U.S. Soybean Association was present at this conference to push for soybean imports.[4] According to *Business Line*, "U.S. farmers need big new export markets. . . . India is a perfect match."[5]

Multinational companies (MNCs) did gain from the mustard-oil tragedy. The ban on local processing has destroyed the domestic, small-scale edible-oil economy. It has criminalized the small-scale oil processor. It has criminalized the small trader. And it has destroyed the local market for farmers. Mustard prices have crashed from Rs.° 2,200 to Rs. 600–800 per 100 kilograms.

The dangers of this destruction are tremendous. If traders cannot sell 20 mustard oil, they will not buy mustard from farmers, and farmers will stop growing mustard. This will lead to the extinction of a crop that is the very symbol of spring. Once mustard oil has gone out of cultivation, even after the ban is lifted on mustard oil, we will be forced to continue an enforced dependence on soybeans for edible oil.

Calgene, now owned by Monsanto, has patented the Indian mustard plant, the *India brassica*. If India wanted to reintroduce mustard later, it would have to depend on genetically engineered, patented mustard varieties. Farmers and consumers would be dependent on Monsanto for patented seeds of both soybean and mustard.

Such a reliance on imported oilseeds can easily trigger violence and instability. The food riots in Indonesia in the late 1990s were largely based on the fact that Indonesia had been made cripplingly dependent on imported soybeans for oil. When the Indonesian currency collapsed, the price of cooking oils shot up, and violence was the result.

Nor does the destruction of the domestic oil industry ensure greater food safety, as is argued by the government. It is an established fact that U.S. exports are heavily adulterated through what has been called purposeful contamination, or "blending." The toxic weed parthenium, which has spread across India, has been traced to wheat shipments from the United States.

More significantly, the adulteration of genetic engineering takes place at the genetic level and is hence invisible. Instead of toxic seeds like those of argemone being added *externally*, genetic engineering in effect allows food adulteration to be done *internally* by introducing genes for toxins

Rs.: Rupees (the currency of India).

from bacteria, viruses, and animals into crops. Genetic engineering is adulterating foods with toxins from rats and scorpions.

It is estimated that over 18 million acres were planted with genetically 25 engineered Roundup Ready soybeans in 1998. The soybeans are engineered by Monsanto to contain a bacterial gene that confers tolerance to the herbicide Roundup, also manufactured by Monsanto. This soybean has been genetically engineered not in order to improve its yield or healthfulness. The sole purpose of Roundup Ready soybeans is to sell more chemicals for seeds tailored to these chemicals.

The United States has been unable to sell its genetically engineered soybeans to Europe because of European consumers' demands that such foods be labeled, something that is ardently opposed by agribusiness interests and their allies. According to former U.S. president Jimmy Carter, such labeling would make U.S. exports rot at ports around the world. (A wide-ranging coalition of U.S. scientists, health professionals, consumers, farmers, and religious leaders have filed a lawsuit demanding mandatory labeling.)

U.S. companies are therefore desperate to dump their genetically engineered soybeans on countries such as India. The mustard-oil tragedy is a perfect "market opening." For while the Indian government lost no time imposing packaging and labeling restrictions on the indigenous edible-oil industry, it has taken no steps to require segregation and labeling of genetically engineered soybeans.

A new soybean-futures exchange has been opened in India. According to Harsh Maheshwari of the Soya Association, the most conservative estimate of its activity is a turnover of $2.3 billion. Some say it will be five times more. The Council for Scientific Research and the Technology Mission on oilseeds have announced steps to promote the use of soybeans for food. Every agency of government in the United States and India is being used by the soybean lobby to destroy agricultural and food diversity in order to spread the soybean monoculture.

While the profits for agribusiness grow, the prices U.S. farmers receive for soybeans have been crashing. Both U.S. farmers and Indian farmers are losers in a globalized free-trade system that benefits global corporations.

Global Merchants of Soybeans

In 1921, 36 firms accounted for 85 percent of U.S. grain exports. By the 30 end of the 1970s, six giant "Merchants of Grain" controlled more than 90 percent of exports from the United States, Canada, Europe, Argentina, and Australia. Today, Cargill and Continental each control 25 percent of the grain trade.

Referring to this concentration of power, former Representative James Weaver (D-OR) said,

These companies are giants. They control not only the buying and the selling of grain but the shipment of it, the storage of it, and everything else. It's obscene. I have rallied against them again and again. I think food is the most — hell, whoever controls the food supply has really got the people by the scrotum. And yet we allow six corporations to do this in secret. It's mind-boggling![6]

The United States is the world's biggest producer of soybeans, an East Asian crop that is also the United States' biggest export commodity. Twenty-six percent of U.S. acreage is under soybean cultivation. This production doubled between 1972 and 1997, from 34.6 million to 74.2 million metric tons. More than half of this crop is exported as soybeans or as soybean oil.

The U.S. acreage planted with genetically engineered soybeans has shot up from 0.5 million hectares in 1996 to 18 million hectares° in 1998, accounting for 40 percent of the country's genetically engineered crops.[7] It is thus becoming inevitable that conventional soybeans will be mixed with genetically engineered soybeans in export shipments.

In the United States, soybeans are used for cattle feed, fish feed, adhesives, pesticides, plastics, solvents, soaps, paints, and inks.[8] Eighty percent of industrially processed foods now have soybeans in them, as European consumers discovered when they tried to boycott foods with Monsanto Roundup Ready soybeans.

Brazil follows the United States in soybean production, producing 30.7 million metric tons in 1997. Argentina is the third-biggest producer. Acreage in Argentina under soybean cultivation has increased from none in the 1960s to nearly 7 million hectares in 1998, with more than half planted with transgenic varieties. India's acreage under soybean cultivation has also increased from zero in the 1960s to nearly 6 million hectares in 1998.

The soybean trade, like trade in other agricultural commodities, is controlled by six Merchants of Grain: Cargill, Continental (now owned by Cargill), Louis Dreyfus, Bunge, Mitsui Cook, and Andre & Company.[9] These companies also control the storage and transport facilities, and hence the prices of commodities.

35

---

hectare: a metric unit of measure equal to 10,000 square meters.

Soybean Patents and Seed Monopoly

Not only is the soybean trade controlled by multinational corporations; soybean cultivation is becoming increasingly monopolized through control over the seed itself.

Monsanto has bought up the seed business of corporations such as Cargill, Agracetus, Calgene, Asgrow Seed, Delta and Pine Land, Holden, Unilever, and Sementes Agrocetes. It owns the broad species patents on soybean. A subsidiary of W. R. Grace, Agracetus owns patent on all transgenic° soybean varieties and seeds, regardless of the genes used, and all methods of transformation.

Agracetus's extraordinarily broad soybean patent has been challenged by Rural Advancement Foundation International, a public-interest group. Dr. Geoffrey Hawtin, director-general of the International Plant Genetic Resources Institute in Rome, Italy, expressed his concern at such patenting:

The granting of patents covering all genetically engineered varieties of a species, irrespective of the genes concerned or how they were transferred, puts in the hands of a single inventor the possibility to control what we grow on our farms and in our gardens. At a stroke of a pen the research of countless farmers and scientists has potentially been negated in a single, legal act of economic hijack.[10]

While Monsanto had originally challenged the patent, it has withdrawn the challenge after buying Agracetus. 40

Monsanto also owns a patent on herbicide-resistant plants. This patent covers herbicide-resistant corn, wheat, rice, soybean, cotton, sugar beet, oilseed, rape, canola, flax, sunflower, potato, tobacco, alfalfa, poplar, pine, apple, and grape. It also covers methods for weed control, planting of seeds, and application of glyphosate (a herbicide). Thus Monsanto controls the entire production process of these plants, from breeding to cultivation to sale.

The Roundup Ready soybean has been genetically engineered to be resistant to Monsanto's broad-spectrum herbicide Roundup. The three new genes genetically engineered into the soybean — from a bacterium, a cauliflower virus, and a petunia — don't do a thing for the taste or nutritional value of the bean. Instead, the unusual genetic combination — which would never be created by nature — makes the soybean resistant to a weed-killer. Normally soybeans are too delicate to spray once they start sprouting from the ground. But now, since two of its products — the bean and the weed-killer — are so closely linked, Monsanto gets to sell

transgenic: containing genetic material into which DNA from another organism has been introduced.

more of both.[11] Monsanto claims this will mean more soybean yields from each crop, but they cannot guarantee it.

Industrial Processing

From seed to distribution to processing, soybeans are associated with concentration of power. While the oil content of coconut is 75 percent, [peanut] 55 percent, sesame 50 percent, castor 56 percent, and niger 40 percent, the oil content of soybeans is only 18 percent. However, text-books state that "soybean yields abundant supply of oil" and "soybeans have oil content higher than other pulses."[12]

Being low in oil content, soybean oil is extracted at large solvent-extraction plants. (Solvent extraction was first applied in the United States to extract grease from garbage, bones, and cracking and packing house waste.) Chlorinated solvents such as chloroethylene are used to extract the oil.

Food safety is necessarily sacrificed in large-scale industrial process- 45 ing since:

- the processing allows mixing of non-edible oils with edible oils,
- the processing is based on the use of chemicals,
- processing creates saturated fats,
- the long-distance transport lends itself to risks of adulteration, adds "food miles" in the form of CO_2 pollution, and contributes to climate change, and
- consumers are denied the right to know what ingredients have been used and what processing has been used to produce industrial oils.

Are Soy Products Healthy?

Soybeans and soybean products are being pushed as global substitutes for diverse sources of foods in diverse cultures. They are being promoted as substitutes for the diverse oilseeds and pulses of India and for cereals and dairy products worldwide. The American Soybean Association is promoting "analogue" dals — soybean extrusions shaped into pellets that look like black gram, green gram, pigeon pea, lentil, and kidney bean. The diet they envision would be a monoculture of soybean; only its appearance would be diverse.

However, even though the promotion of soybean-based foods is justi-fied on grounds of health and nutrition, studies show that this sudden shift to soybean-based diets can be harmful to health. Soybean foods, in both raw and processed form, contain a number of toxic substances at concentration levels that pose significant health risks to humans and animals.

Soybeans have trypsin inhibitors that inhibit pancreatic processes, cause an increase in pancreatic size and weight, and can even lead to cancer.[13] In the United States, pancreatic cancer is the fifth most common fatal cancer, and its incidence is rising. The highest concentrations of trypsin inhibitors are found in soybean flour, which is a soy-based product that is not consumed in traditional soybean-eating cultures, which specialize in the consumption of fermented soybean products.[14]

Soybeans also have lectins that interfere with the immune system and the microbial ecology of the gut. When injected into rats, lectins isolated from soybeans were found to be lethal. When administered orally, these lectins inhibited rat growth.[15] Soybeans also contain phytic acid, which interferes in the absorption of essential minerals such as calcium, magnesium, zinc, copper, and iron. Given that deficiencies in calcium and iron are major symptoms of malnutrition in women and children in countries such as India, compromising the body's absorption of these essential minerals can have serious consequences.[16]

The most significant health hazard posed by diets rich in soybeans is 50
due to their high estrogen content, especially in genetically engineered soybeans. The devastating impact of estrogenic compounds was highlighted when women born to mothers who took synthetic estrogens were found to have three times more miscarriages than other women and a greater incidence of a rare form of malignant vaginal cancer. Men born to mothers who took these synthetic estrogens had higher infertility levels than other men.[17]

Since soybeans are being used widely in all food products, including baby food, high doses of estrogen are being consumed by children, women, and men. Infants fed with soy-based formula are daily ingesting a dose of estrogens equivalent to that of 8 to 12 contraceptive pills.[18] According to New Zealand ecologist Richard James, soybean products are "unsafe at any speed and in any form."[19] The globalization of soybean-based foods is a major experiment being carried out on present and future generations. It is an unnecessary experiment, since nature has given us a tremendous diversity of safe foods, and diverse cultures have selected and evolved nutritious foods from nature's diversity.

During the mustard-oil crisis in 1998, women from the slums of Delhi, organized by a women's group called "Sabla Sangh," invited me to discuss with them the roots of the crisis. They said that "mustard is our life. . . . We want our cheap and safe mustard oil back." Ultimately, a women's alliance for food rights was formed. We held protests and distributed pure organic mustard oil as part of the Sarson Satyagraha, a program of non-cooperation against laws and policies that were denying people safe, cheap, and culturally appropriate foods.

The National Alliance for Women's Food Rights has challenged the ban on small-scale processing and local sales of open oil in the Supreme Court of India. We are building direct producer-consumer alliances to defend the livelihood of farmers and the diverse cultural choices of consumers. We protest soybean imports and call for a ban on the import of genetically engineered soybean products. As the women from the slums of Delhi sing, "Sarson Bachao, Soya Bhagao," or "Save the Mustard, Dump the Soya."

The highest-level political and economic conflicts between freedom and slavery, democracy and dictatorship, diversity and monoculture have thus entered into the simple acts of buying edible oils and cooking our food. Will the future of India's edible-oil culture be based on mustard and other edible oilseeds, or will it become part of the globalized monoculture of soybean, with its associated but hidden food hazards?

Notes

1. Some of these diverse varieties include Indian mustard, *Brassica juncea*; black mustard, *Brassica nigra*; turnip rape; brown and yellow *Brassica campestris*; Indian rape; and rocket cross.

2. "Conspiracy in Mustard Oil Adulteration," *The Hindu*, September 17, 1998.

3. Status Paper on "Ghani Oil Industry," Mumbai: KVIC.

4. "Oilseeds Sector Needs to Be Liberalized: U.S. Soya Body," *Economic Times*, September 22, 1998.

5. *Business Line*, October 12, 1998.

6. A. V. Krebs, "The Corporate Reapers: The Book of Agribusiness," Washington, DC: Essential Books, 1992.

7. Clive James, "Global Status of Transgenic Crops in 1997," ISAAA Briefs, Cambridge, MA: MIT Press, 1996. Also, Greg D. Horstmeier, "Lessons from Year One: Experience Changes How Farmers Will Grow Roundup Ready Beans in 98," *Farm Journal*, January 1998, p. 16.

8. American Soybean Association, "Soy Stats, 1998."

9. A. V. Krebs.

10. Brian Belcher and Geoffrey Hawtin, "A Patent on Life Ownership of Plant and Animal Research," Ottawa, Canada: International Development Research Centre, 1991.

11. Vandana Shiva, *Mustard or Soya? The Future of India's Edible Oil Culture*, New Delhi: Navdanya, 1998.

12. Dr. Irfan Khan, *Genetic Improvement of Oilseed Crops*, New Delhi: Ukaaz Publications, 1996, p. 334.

13. M. G. Fitzpatrick, "Report on Soybeans and Related Products: An Investigation into Their Toxic Effects," New Zealand: Allan Aspell and Associates, Analytical Chemists and Scientific Consultants, March 31, 1994, p. 5.

14. B. A. Charpentier and D. E. Lemmel, "A Rapid Automated Procedure for the Determination of Trypsin Inhibitor Activity in Soy Products and Common Food Stuffs," *Journal of Agricultural and Food Chemistry,* Vol. 32, 1984, p. 908.

15. I. E. Liener and M. J. Pallansch, "Purification of a Toxic Substance from Defatted Soy Bean Flour," *Journal of Biological Chemistry,* Vol. 197, 1952, p. 29.

16. S. L. Fitzgerald et al., "Trace Element Intakes and Dietary Phytat/Zn and Caz Phytate/Zn Millimolar Ratios in Periurban Guatemalan Women During the Third Trimester of Pregnancy," *American Journal of Clinical Nutrition,* Vol. 57, 1993, p. 725. See also J. W. Erdman and E. J. Fordyce, "Soy Products and the Human Diet," *American Journal of Clinical Nutrition,* Vol. 49, 1989, p. 725.

17. F. A. Kinil, "Hormone Toxicity in the Newborn," *Monographs on Endocrinology,* Vol. 31, 1990. See also R. J. Apfel and S. M. Fisher, *To Do No Harm: DES and the Dilemmas of Modern Medicine,* New Haven: Yale University Press, 1984.

18. A. Axelsol et al., "Soya — A Dietary Source of the Non-Steroidal Oestregen Equal in Man and Animals," *Journal of Endocrinology,* Vol. 102, 1984, p. 49. See also K. D. R. Setchell et al., "Non-Steroidal Estrogens of Dietary Origin: Possible Roles in Hormone-Dependent Disease," *American Journal of Clinical Nutrition,* Vol. 40, 1984, p. 569.

19. Richard James, "The Toxicity of Soy Beans and Their Related Products," unpublished manuscript, 1994, p. 1.

Understanding the Text

1. What does it mean to have access to "culturally appropriate food"?
2. What role does mustard — in its various manifestations — play in Indian culture? Why was the lack of mustard oil such a serious problem?

Reflection and Response

3. What does Shiva mean by "soy imperialism"? Does this term serve as a valid description of the dynamics she is describing? Why or why not?
4. What kinds of grassroots efforts are being made to protect India's edible-oil culture? Do you think they will succeed? Why or why not?
5. Why is Shiva critical of Monsanto's business practices? What evidence does she provide? Is her criticism justified? Why or why not?

Making Connections

6. Review Michael Pollan's argument "in defense of food" ("Eat Food: Food Defined," p. 10). What kinds of conclusions do you think he would draw about Monsanto? In what ways would he agree with Shiva and the farmers? Do you consider theirs a compelling argument? Why or why not?
7. What goals and values do Shiva and Raj Patel ("Stuffed and Starved," p. 173) share? What brings you to this conclusion? Use specific textual references to support your answer.

Farm to Fable

Troy Johnson

Troy Johnson studied Speech Communications and poetry at Chico State University in California before embarking on a career in writing. After writing about music and culture for magazines such as *Rolling Stone* and *Surfer*, he turned to writing about food. Johnson is known for his program *Crave* on the Food Network, and he is currently a dining critic at *San Diego Magazine*. He writes restaurant reviews along with more hard-hitting essays about food trends and issues. In this essay, Johnson tells the story of fraud and deception in the farm-to-table movement in San Diego, recounting stories of rampant abuse and creative advertising that mislead the restaurant-going public into thinking they are supporting local farms when they often are not.

"A new restaurant opened in La Jolla," says San Diego farmer Tim Connelly, renown for his tomatoes. "I went in to try to sell them my food. They didn't buy any. Eight years later, a friend called to say 'Hey, I just had your salad at that restaurant!' The restaurant had been claiming to sell a 'Connelly Farms Salad' for eight years. They never bought a thing from me."

The farm-to-table movement is (or was) a very good thing. Restaurants buy from local farmers, supporting the area economy and serving their customers the freshest possible produce grown in season. Knowing your farmer also lets you ensure you're buying from people whose methods match your restaurant's and customers' values, whether that means organic, sustainable, non-GMO, fair trade, etc.

Like any good movement, farm-to-table has now been severely co-opted. The stories of restaurants deceiving their customers — or flat-out lying to them — have increased. Multiple San Diego restaurants claim to serve Respected Local, Organic, Sustainable Farm X when in fact they're serving nameless commodity produce that could be from Chile, for all they know.

Call it farm-to-fable.

Restaurants have learned that aligning themselves with local, organic, 5 sustainable farms makes them seem to be all those things by association. It's the old practice of greenwashing — co-opting an eco-friendly brand in order to "wash" your own not-so-friendly brand.

Recently, a San Diego restaurant sold tickets to a dinner advertised as using Suzie's Farms produce. Suzie's owner, Robin Taylor, was surprised to learn about the dinner — especially since he wasn't growing the produce listed on the menu. When he relayed word to the restaurant, the chef called to yell at him and swore to never use their produce again.

When farm-to-table was at its height a few years ago, David Barnes of Crows Pass Farms was famous for calling out dishonest restaurants. For instance, the time George's at the Cove chef Trey Foshee — one of the city's honest farm-to-table chefs — asked why he wasn't offered Crows Pass cauliflower.

Barnes doesn't grow cauliflower.

"Trey showed me a menu from another restaurant, and it had 'Crows Pass cauliflower soup' on it," says Barnes. "I went straight to the restaurant. A sous chef saw me walk in and he went out the other door. The chef was a little embarrassed. He got caught red-handed. I told him, 'I'd love to sell you produce, but don't use my name.'

"Like any good movement, farm-to-table has now been severely co-opted. The stories of restaurants deceiving their customers — or flat out lying to them — have increased. Multiple San Diego restaurants claim to serve Respected Local, Organic, Sustainable Farm X when in fact they're serving nameless commodity produce that could be from Chile, for all they know."

"Another restaurant in North County — "a big, old fancy place," says Barnes — hired a new sous chef who was a friend of Barnes. The friend called to say, "I had no idea you sold here — Crows Pass is all over the menu!"

"They hadn't bought a thing from us," Barnes explains. "I walked into the place with an invoice for $1,400. If you're going to use my name, here's an invoice for that."

Barnes raises a bigger issue: "Then I went down the menu and saw Kobe beef. I wondered, 'How many other lies are on this menu?'"

Multiple industry insiders tell the same story of a famous San Diego restaurant claiming to serve an equally famous farm's corn. (It could be legend, but the specifics — including the chef and the farm — are known to many sources.) One particular customer thought it seemed odd, since it wasn't corn season. He asked the chef to come out. The chef became indignant and defended himself: "Yes, that's from Famous Farm X." The customer replied, "I'm from Famous Farm X, and we're not growing corn right now." He banned the chef from the farm.

Chino Farms is one of America's most iconic operations. Alice Waters helped kick off the whole farm-to-table movement in the 1970s using bounty from Chino. They are the Apple, Inc. of produce — one of the most iconic brand names, with a cult following. Tom Chino's family has earned that reputation over 70 years, and their produce naturally costs more. Makes sense, then, that Chino is the farm most often fibbed about.

Insiders say a common farm-to-fable practice involving Chino goes 15
like this: A restaurant will claim to sell a "Chino Farms Salad." The price
is significantly higher. In reality, it's a bowl of commodity lettuce and
vegetables, lightly garnished with Chino peppers or edible flowers.

At his roadside farm stand in Rancho Santa Fe, the soft-spoken, wry
Tom Chino reluctantly agrees to talk about the issue. He's obviously
experienced it many times. "But I'm hesitant to say anything because,
well," he says, pausing for a long while, "I don't want to be a horse's ass."

He laughs, though, at some of the more egregious examples.
"Sometimes it can be very blatant," he says. "Chefs will come look [at
what we're selling that day], write down notes, leave without buying
anything, and then say they're serving our food at their restaurants."

Is fibbing about a farm really such a crime? It's just a salad, after all.

"I've busted my ass for 23 years to get a reputation," Barnes of Crows
Pass told me over a year ago. "I'm not making a ton of money. No one's
forcing me to live this life; I choose it. But if someone's going to use my
name, charge their customers extra money because of my name, and
then pocket the money?"

It's fraud. 20

Seafood fraud is rife in the restaurant industry; a 2012 study by watch-
dog group Oceana found that 39 percent of seafood in New York City
restaurants was mislabeled.

Farm-to-fable defrauds a few different people. First, it defrauds the
customers, who pay more for local, sustainable, organic produce.
Restaurants that cheat are preying on food lovers' good intentions. It also
defrauds the local farm, by using its hard-earned "brand name" without
paying it, or its workers, a penny. Finally, it defrauds other honest restaurants in the market.

"The restaurateurs that really do make the effort to buy direct from
farmers, it's tough for them," says Catt White, farmers market manager at
Little Italy Mercato. "You often have to get the stuff to the restaurant
because smaller farmers aren't equipped to do deliveries. It's definitely
more costly. Smaller farmers aren't subsidized like big farms. So the real
cost comes into play. It's expensive and admirable. For people to say
they're doing it but they're not really — that's really frustrating for the
folks who are doing right."

Just ask Trish Watlington, owner of the Red Door and Wellington
Steak House. She and chef Karrie Hills grow about half of their restaurants' produce on Watlington's small farm. They've spent hundreds of
hours developing relationships with local purveyors for most of the rest.

"Farm-to-table is hip," Watlington says. "People want to think they're 25
eating locally sourced food. Restaurants are definitely leveraging that as

a marketing technique. You have people claiming farm-to-table who have no idea where their product comes from. I could spend a lot more time being resentful, but it's not really worth it. I just don't like people who lie. Sell yourself for what you are. If you have a great interior and swank place, that's okay."

The worst kind of farm-to-fable is the pure, intentional deception. There are less obvious ways of using the farm's name. "What you see on menus and grocery stores is 'We buy Suzie's Farms,'" says White. "When in reality a couple of heads of lettuce do come from Suzie's, but the rest doesn't. By implication, customers assume the rest is coming from the farmer."

"You'll find a lot of people say they use local produce," says Barnes. "They'll buy $5,000 worth of produce, but only $100 is local."

Or a restaurant will throw a "Famous Farm X Dinner." They'll buy all the produce from that farm for the special event, reap all of the positive brand association with postings all over Facebook and social media. Afterward, they'll never buy anything else from the farm.

In restaurants' defense, sometimes it's an understandable oversight. Maybe the restaurant did buy produce from X Farms and simply hasn't updated its menu since it stopped. And let's not overstate the controversy. Let's assume a majority of restaurants and chefs are honest. But it's apparent that this sort of thing happens enough to affect the livelihood of farmers and the people they employ.

A few years ago, Suzie's Farms was selling $7,000 to $10,000 a week to   30
local restaurants. Now they're down to about 30 percent of that. "But a lot of people still seem to be using our name," Taylor says. Suzie's will soon have to cut back their operations. As for Barnes, who started selling Crows Pass out of his van directly to San Diego restaurants 20 years ago (at the height, he was doing a half-million dollars a year in revenue) — he now sells direct to only two restaurants.

"We're so done with that shit, farm-to-table," says Barnes, who now works as a general manager at Mountain Meadow Mushrooms.

As Connelly told me, "When you're talking true farm-to-table, only a handful of people are doing it, but a lot of people talk about it."

There's no solution in sight for farm-to-table. New restaurants are just slapping "farm-to-table" on their signage, without any clear indication of what that means. Media is also to blame, often blindly using "farm-to-table" as an adjective for food that looks fresh.

A program by the SD Farm Bureau pushed by the County Health and Human Services — called San Diego Grown 365 — seeks to verify the origin of food. Restaurants can sign a contract and guarantee that any dish they label with San Diego Grown 365 brand contains at least

80 percent to 85 percent food produced locally. But it's been around since 2004, and only 87 individuals have signed up for the labeling, says Farm Bureau Membership & Project Manager Casey Anderson.

Tom Chino takes a grin-and-bear-it approach. "The old joke is some- 35 one will say, 'Oh, I had some of your asparagus at this really great restaurant!' Then I'll tell them we don't grow asparagus. So I'll ask, 'Well, was it good?' They'll say, 'Oh yes, everything was great.' 'Well, then I guess it's okay!'"

But on the flip side, if Restaurant X serves a really mediocre, out-of-season tomato and claims it's from Chino Farms, customers aren't going to have the highest impression of Chino Farms. That's doing damage to a farm's name.

Taylor has kind of thrown up his hands. "We've been thinking about maybe a licensing fee," he jokes. "If you want to just use our name and not our produce, you pay a fee."

Most restaurant professionals say it's up to public education. If diners see tomatoes in the winter, they're probably not from San Diego. If a restaurant is selling asparagus in summer, it's probably not local, either.

Because of the fraud, many restaurants have stopped mentioning local farms at all. Which is a shame, since that should be something to celebrate and brag about. But whether it's farm-to-table or farm-to-fable, White looks on the bright side.

"The good news is that people are getting more into greenwashing 40 because there's a perception that people care that they're eating things that haven't been loaded with pesticides," she says. "So that's very motivational, that people are jumping on the bandwagon."

Understanding the Text

1. What is the farm-to-table movement?
2. What does Johnson mean by "farm to fable"?
3. What groups of people are negatively affected by the fraudulent behavior and deceptive practices described by Johnson?

Reflection and Response

4. Johnson suggests that the fraudulent practices of some chefs and restaurants prey on the good intentions of those who dine in the restaurants in question. Why do you think they do this? What larger social and economic forces play a role in these dynamics?
5. Robin Taylor of Suzie's Farms jokes with Johnson that they have "been thinking about maybe a licensing fee . . . If you want to just use our name

and not our produce, you pay a fee" (par. 37). What does this comment say about what diners seek when they eat in farm-to-table restaurants? What does it say about the larger cultural and economic forces at work in the farm-to-table movement?

6. Why is eating locally produced food important to some people? Is it important to you? Why or why not? How is its importance (or lack thereof) evident in your life and eating habits?

Making Connections

7. Think about Johnson's essay in relation to the essays by Barbara Kingsolver ("You Can't Run Away on Harvest Day," p. 218) and Eliot Coleman ("Real Food, Real Farming," p. 266). What do they say about the relationship between local eating and farming practices? Do their views support or complicate Wendell Berry's ("The Pleasures of Eating," p. 47) assertion that eating is an "agricultural act"?

8. Research the farm-to-table movement in your area. What is the relationship between local farms and restaurants? Do you and your neighbors eat locally produced food — or have the option to do so? Why or why not? What larger social, economic, and political forces help determine what's eaten in your community?

9. Johnson exposes fraudulent behavior in the farm-to-table movement, David H. Freedman ("How Junk Food Can End Obesity," p. 139) critiques the wholesome-food movement, and Michael Pollan ("Eat Food: Food Defined," p. 10) and others write about the local-food movement, the slow-food movement, and the organic food movement. What's up with all of these food movements? Research two or three different food movements online, and listen to a few podcasts or view some TED talks that highlight particular movements. Then, analyze the social, cultural, and political forces that create and help produce these trends. What do various food movements say about the people who advocate them? What do they say about culture more broadly?

Bhaskar Dutta/Getty Images

4

What Does It Mean to Eat Ethically?

W hile larger political, cultural, and socioeconomic factors may play a significant role in determining what we eat, we do make our own food choices. And thus, what we eat is at least partially a moral choice, whether we are cognizant of it or not. What are our ethical responsibilities when we make food choices? Does it matter *morally* what we choose to eat? What does it mean to eat ethically? What moral principles should guide our food choices and ways of eating?

In this section, various authors weigh in on what it means to eat ethically and raise issues that can play a role in the ethics of food: animal rights, environmental concerns, world hunger, farmer rights, and worker rights. These authors offer varied and sometimes conflicting views on the obligations we necessarily take on when we make dietary choices and offer a range of potential responsibilities — social, political, personal, environmental, spiritual, global. And they make suggestions about what principles and priorities should affect our ethical obligations related to food.

Beginning with a focus on global hunger and its relation to food production, Margaret Mead encourages Americans to develop a "world conscience" and to think of the ways that our ability to produce enough food to feed the world changes the ethical position of those who can or do overconsume. Peter Singer and Barbara Kingsolver offer moral perspectives on the ethics of eating meat, suggesting varying and complex views on human responsibility in animal consumption, and Bill McKibben brings environmental factors into the equation. And while Yuval Noah Harari suggests that the treatment of domesticated animals on industrial farms is among the worst crimes in history, Blake Hurst takes issue with critiques of industrial farming by proponents of organic farming. On top of these concerns, Eric Holt-Giménez explains racial and class inequities that he argues plague the global food system. By making arguments in support of various ethical positions, the authors in this section argue for the moral principles they think should motivate our choices.

photo: Bhaskar Dutta/Getty Images

We do not eat in isolation. An ethics of eating, then, must take into account a variety of factors: what we eat, its ability to nourish us, how much we eat, where and how it is produced, who produces it, how they are compensated, and how food production and consumption affect our environment and natural resources. Moral obligations and responsibilities related to an ethics of food exist for consumers, producers, farmers, law and policy makers, regulators, and communities. They exist for the affluent and the poor. This chapter asks us to consider what it means to declare that eating is necessarily a moral act.

The Changing Significance of Food

Margaret Mead

Margaret Mead (1901–1978) was a highly respected, often controversial, cultural anthropologist. She is best known for her book *Coming of Age in Samoa* (1928), which she wrote after conducting fieldwork there. She received her doctoral degree from Columbia University and served as curator of ethnology at the American Museum of Natural History in New York and executive secretary of the National Research Council's Committee on Food Habits. She popularized anthropological discoveries through her extensive writing and speaking engagements, in which she sometimes shared her view that small groups of committed individuals could, in fact, change the world. President Jimmy Carter awarded Mead the Presidential Medal of Freedom posthumously in 1979. In this essay, originally published in *American Scientist*, Mead provides a historical look at our relationship with food, examining how it has changed over time and been affected by economic, political, and cultural trends. She argues that Americans need to think about the relationship between the American diet and their capacity to feed the poor and the hungry both at home and abroad.

We live in a world today where the state of nutrition in each country is relevant and important to each other country, and where the state of nutrition in the wealthy industrialized countries like the United States has profound significance for the role that such countries can play in eliminating famine and providing for adequate nutrition throughout the world. In a world in which each half knows what the other half does, we cannot live with hunger and malnutrition in one part of the world while people in another part are not only well nourished, but over-nourished. Any talk of one world, of brotherhood, rings hollow to those who have come face to face on the television screen with the emaciation° of starving children and to the people whose children are starving as they pore over month-old issues of glossy American and European magazines, where full color prints show people glowing with health, their plates piled high with food that glistens to match the shining textures of their clothes. Peoples who have resolutely tightened their belts and put up with going to bed hungry, peoples who have seen their children die because they did not have the strength to resist disease, and called it fate or the will of God, can no longer do so, in the vivid visual realization of the amount and quality of food eaten — and wasted — by others.

emaciation: extreme thinness.

Through human history there have been many stringent taboos on watching other people eat, or on eating in the presence of others. There have been attempts to explain this as a relationship between those who are involved and those who are not simultaneously involved in the satisfaction of a bodily need, and the inappropriateness of the already satiated watching others who appear — to the satisfied — to be shamelessly gorging. There is undoubtedly such an element in the taboos, but it seems more likely that they go back to the days when food was so scarce and the onlookers so hungry that not to offer them half of the little food one had was unthinkable, and every glance was a plea for at least a bite.

In the rural schools of America when my grandmother was a child, the better-off children took apples to school and, before they began to eat them, promised the poor children who had no apples that they might have the cores. The spectacle of the poor in rags at the rich man's gate and of hungry children pressing their noses against the glass window of the rich man's restaurant have long been invoked to arouse human compassion. But until the advent of the mass media and travel, the sensitive and sympathetic could protect themselves by shutting themselves away from the sight of the starving, by gifts of food to the poor on religious holidays, or perpetual bequests for the distribution of a piece of meat "the size of a child's head" annually. The starving in India and China saw only a few feasting foreigners and could not know how well or ill the poor were in countries from which they came. The proud poor hid their hunger behind a façade that often included insistent hospitality to the occasional visitor; the beggars flaunted their hunger and so, to a degree, discredited the hunger of their respectable compatriots.

"We cannot live with hunger and malnutrition in one part of the world while people in another part are not only well nourished, but over-nourished."

But today the articulate cries of the hungry fill the air channels and there is no escape from the knowledge of the hundreds of millions who are seriously malnourished, of the periodic famines that beset whole populations, or of the looming danger of famine in many other parts of the world. The age-old divisions between one part of the world and another, between one class and another, between the rich and the poor everywhere, have been broken down, and the tolerances and insensitivities of the past are no longer possible.

But it is not only the media of communication which can take a man 5 sitting at an overloaded breakfast table straight into a household where some of the children are too weak to stand. Something else, something even more significant, has happened. Today, for the first time in the history of mankind, we have the productive capacity to feed everyone in the world, and the technical knowledge to see that their stomachs are not only filled but that their bodies are properly nourished with the essential ingredients for growth and health. The progress of agriculture — in all its complexities of improved seed, methods of cultivation, fertilizers and pesticides, methods of storage, preservation, and transportation — now make it possible for the food that is needed for the whole world to be produced by fewer and fewer farmers, with greater and greater certainty. Drought and flood still threaten, but we have the means to prepare for and deal with even mammoth shortages — if we will. The progress of nutritional science has matched the progress of agriculture; we have finer and finer-grained knowledge of just which substances — vitamins, minerals, proteins — are essential, especially to growth and full development, and increasing ability to synthesize many of them on a massive scale.

These new twentieth-century potentialities have altered the ethical position of the rich all over the world. In the past, there were so few who lived well, and so many who lived on the edge of starvation, that the well-to-do had a rationale and indeed almost a necessity to harden their hearts and turn their eyes away. The jewels of the richest rajah° could not have purchased enough food to feed his hungry subjects for more than a few days; the food did not exist, and the knowledge of how to use it was missing also. At the same time, however real the inability of a war-torn and submarine-ringed Britain to respond to the famine in Bengal, this inability was made bearable in Britain only by the extent to which the British were learning how to share what food they had among all the citizens, old and young. "You do not know," the American consul, who had come to Manchester from Spain, said to me: "you do not know what it means to live in a country where no child has to cry itself to sleep from hunger." But this was only achieved in Britain in the early 1940s. Before, the well-fed turned away their eyes, in the feeling that they were powerless to alleviate the perennial poverty and hunger of most of their own people and the peoples in their far-flung commonwealth. And such turning away the eyes, in Britain and in the United States and elsewhere, was accompanied by the rationalizations, not only of the inability of the well-to-do — had they given all their wealth — to feed the poor, but of the undeservingness of the poor, who had they only been industrious and saving would have had enough, although of course of a lower quality, to keep "body and soul together."

rajah: a ruler in India or the East Indies.

When differences in race and in cultural levels complicated the situation, it was only too easy to insist that lesser breeds somehow, in some divinely correct scheme, would necessarily be less well fed, their alleged idleness and lack of frugality combining with such matters as sacred cows roaming over the landscapes — in India — or nights spent in the pub or the saloon — at home in Britain or America — while fathers drank up their meager pay checks and their children starved. So righteous was the assumed association between industriousness and food that, during the Irish famine, soup kitchens were set up out of town so that the starving could have the moral advantage of a long walk to receive the ration that stood between them and death. (The modern version of such ethical acrobatics can be found in the United States, in the mid-1960s, where food stamps were so expensive, since they had to be bought in large amounts, that only those who had been extraordinarily frugal, saving, and lucky could afford to buy them and obtain the benefits they were designed to give.)

The particular ways in which the well-to-do of different great civilizations have rationalized the contrast between rich and poor have differed dramatically, but ever since the agricultural revolution, we have been running a race between our capacity to produce enough food to make it possible to assemble great urban centers, outfit huge armies and armadas, and build and elaborate the institutions of civilization and our ability to feed and care for the burgeoning population which has always kept a little, often a great deal, ahead of the food supply.

In this, those societies which practiced agriculture contrasted with the earlier simpler societies in which the entire population was engaged in subsistence activities. Primitive peoples may be well or poorly fed, feasting seldom, or blessed with ample supplies of fish or fruit, but the relations between the haves and the have-nots were in many ways simpler. Methods by which men could obtain permanent supplies of food and withhold them from their fellows hardly existed. The sour, barely edible breadfruit mash which was stored in breadfruit pits against the ravages of hurricanes and famines in Polynesia was not a diet for the table of chiefs but a stern measure against the needs of entire communities. The chief might have a right to the first fruits, or to half the crop, but after he had claimed it, it was redistributed to his people. The germs of the kinds of inequities that later entered the world were present: there was occasional conspicuous destruction of food, piled up for prestige, oil poured on the flames of self-glorifying feasts, food left to rot after it was offered to the gods. People with very meager food resources might use phrases that made it seem that each man was the recipient of great generosity on the part of his fellows, or on the other hand always to be giving away a whole animal, and always receiving only small bits.

The fear of cannibalism that hovered over northern peoples might be 10 elaborated into cults of fear, or simply add to the concern that each member of a group had for all, against the terrible background that extremity might become so great that one of the group might in the end be sacrificed. But cannibalism could also be elaborated into a rite of vengeance or the celebration of victories in war, or even be used to provision an army in the field. Man's capacity to elaborate man's inhumanity to man existed before the beginning of civilization, which was made possible by the application of an increasingly productive technology to the production of food.

With the rise of civilizations, we also witness the growth of the great religions that made the brotherhood of all men part of their doctrine and the gift of alms or the life of voluntary poverty accepted religious practices. But the alms were never enough, and the life of individual poverty and abstinence was more efficacious for the individual's salvation than for the well-being of the poor and hungry, although both kept alive an ethic, as yet impossible of fulfillment, that it was right that all should be fed. The vision preceded the capability.

But today we have the capability. Whether that capability will be used or not becomes not a technical but an ethical question. It depends, in enormous measure, on the way in which the rich, industrialized countries handle the problems of distribution, of malnutrition and hunger, within their own borders. Failure to feed their own, with such high capabilities and such fully enunciated statements of responsibility and brotherhood, means that feeding the people of other countries is almost ruled out, except for sporadic escapist pieces of behavior where people who close their eyes to hunger in Mississippi can work hard to send food to a "Biafra." The development of the international instruments to meet food emergencies and to steadily improve the nutrition of the poorer countries will fail, unless there is greater consistency between ideal and practice at home.

And so, our present parlous° plight in the United States, with the many pockets of rural unemployment, city ghettos, ethnic enclaves, where Americans are starving and an estimated tenth of the population malnourished, must be viewed not only in its consequences for ourselves, as a viable political community, but also in its consequences for the world. We need to examine not only the conditions that make this possible, to have starving people in the richest country in the world, but also the repercussions of American conditions on the world scene.

---

parlous: full of danger, perilous.

Why, when twenty-five years ago we were well on the way to remedying the state of the American people who had been described by presidential announcement as "one third ill-housed, ill-clothed, and ill-fed," when the vitamin deficiency diseases had all but vanished, and a variety of instruments for better nutrition had been developed, did we find, just two short years ago, due to the urgent pleading of a few crusaders, that we had fallen so grievously behind? The situation is complex, closely related to a series of struggles for regional and racial justice, to the spread of automation and resulting unemployment, to changes in crop economies, as well as to population growth and the inadequacy of many of our institutions to deal with it. But I wish to single out here two conditions which have, I believe, seriously contributed to our blindness to what was happening: the increase in the diseases of affluence and the growth of commercial agriculture.

In a country pronounced only twenty years before to be one third 15 ill-fed, we suddenly began to have pronouncements from nutritional specialists that the major nutritional disease of the American people was overnutrition. If this had simply meant overeating, the old puritan ethics against greed and gluttony might have been more easily invoked, but it was over-nutrition that was at stake. And this in a country where our ideas of nutrition had been dominated by a dichotomy which distinguished food that was "good for you, but not good" from food that was "good, but not good for you." This split in man's needs, into our cultural conception of the need for nourishment and the search for pleasure, originally symbolized in the rewards for eating spinach or finishing what was on one's plate if one wanted to have a dessert, lay back of the movement to produce, commercially, nonnourishing foods. Beverages and snacks came in particularly for this demand, as it was the addition of between-meal eating to the three square, nutritionally adequate meals a day that was responsible for much of the trouble.

We began manufacturing, on a terrifying scale, foods and beverages that were guaranteed not to nourish. The resources and the ingenuity of industry were diverted from the preparation of foods necessary for life and growth to foods nonexpensive to prepare, expensive to buy. And every label reassuring the buyer that the product was not nourishing increased our sense that the trouble with Americans was that they were too well nourished. The diseases of affluence, represented by new forms of death in middle-age, had appeared before we had, in the words of Jean Mayer, who has done so much to define the needs of the country and of the world, conquered the diseases of poverty — the ill-fed pregnant women and lactating women, sometimes resulting in irreversible damage to the ill-weaned children, the school children so poorly fed that they could not learn.

It was hard for the average American to believe that while he struggled, and paid, so as not to be over-nourished, other people, several millions, right in this country, were hungry and near starvation. The gross contradiction was too great. Furthermore, those who think of their country as parental and caring find it hard to admit that this parental figure is starving their brothers and sisters. During the great depression of the 1930s, when thousands of children came to school desperately hungry, it was very difficult to wring from children the admission that their parents had no food to give them. "Or what man is there of you, whom, if his son ask bread, will he give a stone?"

So today we have in the United States a situation not unlike the situation in Germany under Hitler, when a large proportion of the decent and law-abiding simply refuse to believe that what is happening can be happening. "Look at the taxes we pay," they say, or they point to the millions spent on welfare; surely with such quantities assigned to the poor, people can't be really hungry, or if they are, it is because they spend their money on TV sets and drink. How can the country be overnourished and undernourished at the same time?

A second major shift, in the United States and in the world, is the increasing magnitude of commercial agriculture, in which food is seen

Spanish children begging in the 1950s.
Three Lions/Stringer/Getty Images

not as food which nourishes men, women, and children, but as a staple crop on which the prosperity of a country or region and the economic prosperity — as opposed to the simple livelihood — of the individual farmer depend. This is pointed up on a world scale in the report of the Food and Agriculture Organization of the United Nations for 1969, which states that there are two major problems in the world: food deficits in the poor countries, which mean starvation, hunger, and malnutrition on an increasing scale, and food surpluses in the industrialized part of the world, serious food surpluses.

On the face of it, this sounds as foolish as the production of foods 20 guaranteed not to nourish, and the two are not unrelated. Surpluses, in a world where people are hungry! Too much food, in a world where children are starving! Yet we lump together all *agricultural* surpluses, such as cotton and tobacco, along with food, and we see these surpluses as threatening the commercial prosperity of many countries, and farmers in many countries. And in a world politically organized on a vanishing agrarian basis, this represents a political threat to those in power. However much the original destruction of food, killing little pigs, may have been phrased as relieving the desperate situation of little farmers or poor countries dependent upon single crop exports, such situations could not exist if food as something which man needs to provide growth and maintenance had not been separated from food as a cash crop, a commercial as opposed to a basic maintenance enterprise. When it becomes the task of government to foster the economic prosperity of an increasingly small, but politically influential, sector of the electorate at the expense of the well-being of its own and other nations' citizens, we have reached an ethically dangerous position.

And this situation, in the United States, is in part responsible for the grievous state of our poor and hungry and for the paralysis that still prevents adequate political action. During the great depression, agriculture in this country was still a viable way of life for millions. The Department of Agriculture had responsibility, not only for food production and marketing, but also for the well-being from the cradle to the grave, in the simplest, most human sense, of every family who lived in communities under 2,500. Where the needs of urban man were parceled out among a number of agencies — Office of Education, Children's Bureau, Labor Department — there was still a considerable amount of integration possible in the Department of Agriculture, where theory and practices of farm wives, the education of children and youth, the question of small loans for small landowners, all could be considered together. It was in the Department of Agriculture that concerned persons found, during the depression, the kind of understanding of basic human needs which they sought.

There were indeed always conflicts between the needs of farmers to sell crops and the needs of children to be fed. School lunch schemes were tied to the disposal of surplus commodities. But the recognition of the wholeness of human needs was still there, firmly related to the breadth of the responsibilities of the different agencies within the Department of Agriculture. Today this is no longer so. Agriculture is big business in the United States. The subsidies used to persuade farmers to withdraw their impoverished land from production, like the terrible measures involving the slaughter of little pigs, are no longer ways of helping the small farmer on a family farm. The subsidies go to the rich commercial farmers, many of them the inheritors of old exploitive plantation traditions, wasteful of manpower and land resources, often in the very counties where the farm workers, displaced by machinery, are penniless, too poor to move away, starving. These subsidies exceed the budget of the antipoverty administration.

So today, many of the reforms which are suggested, in the distribution of food or distribution of income from which food can be bought, center on removing food relief programs from the Department of Agriculture and placing them under the Department of Health, Education, and Welfare. In Britain, during World War II, it was necessary to have a Ministry of Food, concerned primarily in matching the limited food supplies with basic needs.

At first sight, this proposal is sound enough. Let us remove from an agency devoted to making a profit out of crops that are treated like any other manufactured product the responsibility for seeing that food actually feeds people. After all, we do not ask clothing manufacturers to take the responsibility for clothing people, or the house-building industry for housing them. To the extent that we recognize them at all, these are the responsibilities of agencies of government which provide the funds to supplement the activities of private industry. Why not also in food? The Department of Health, Education, and Welfare is concerned with human beings; they have no food to sell on a domestic or world market and no constituents to appease. And from this step it is simply a second step to demand that the whole system of distribution be re-oriented, that a basic guaranteed annual income be provided each citizen, on the one hand, and that the government police standards, on behalf of the consumer, on the other.

But neither of these changes, shifting food relief programs from 25 Agriculture to Health, Education, and Welfare, or shifting the whole welfare program into a guaranteed income, really meet the particular difficulties that arise because we are putting food into two compartments with disastrous effects; we are separating food that nourishes people from food out of which some people, and some countries, derive their incomes. It does not deal with the immediacy of the experience of food by the well-fed, or with the irreparability of food deprivation during prenatal and postnatal growth, deprivation that can never be made up. Human beings have maintained their dignity in incredibly bad conditions of housing and clothing, emerged triumphant from huts and log cabins, gone from ill-shod childhood to Wall Street or the Kremlin. Poor housing and poor clothing are demeaning to the human spirit when they contrast sharply with the visible standards of the way others live.

But food affects not only man's dignity but the capacity of children to reach their full potential, and the capacity of adults to act from day to day. You can't eat either nutrition or part of a not yet realized guaranteed annual income, or political promises. You can't eat hope. We know that hope and faith have enormous effects in preventing illness and enabling people to put forth the last ounce of energy they have. But energy is ultimately dependent upon food. No amount of rearrangement of priorities in the future can provide food in the present. It is true that the starving adult, his efficiency enormously impaired by lack of food, may usually be brought back again to his previous state of efficiency. But this is not true of children. What they lose is lost for good.

What we do about food is therefore far more crucial, both for the quality of the next generation, our own American children, and children everywhere, and also for the quality of our responsible action in every field. It is intimately concerned with the whole problem of the pollution and exhaustion of our environment, with the danger that man may make this planet uninhabitable within a short century or so. If food is grown in strict relationship to the needs of those who will eat it, if every effort is made to reduce the costs of transportation, to improve storage, to conserve the land, and there, where it is needed, by recycling wastes and water, we will go a long way toward solving many of our environmental problems also. It is as a responsible gardener on a small, limited plot, aware of the community about him with whom he will face adequate food or famine, that man has developed what conserving agricultural techniques we have.

Divorced from its primary function of feeding people, treated simply as a commercial commodity, food loses this primary significance; the land is mined instead of replenished and conserved. The Food and Agriculture Organization, intent on food production, lays great stress on the increase in the use of artificial fertilizers, yet the use of such fertilizers with their diffuse runoffs may be a greater danger to our total ecology than the industrial wastes from other forms of manufacturing. The same thing is true of pesticides. With the marvels of miracle rice and miracle wheat, which have brought the resources of international effort and scientific resources together, go at present prescriptions for artificial fertilizer and pesticides. The innovative industrialized countries are exporting, with improved agricultural methods, new dangers to the environment of the importing countries. Only by treating food, unitarily, as a substance necessary to feed people, subject first to the needs of people and only second to the needs of commercial prosperity — whether they be the needs of private enterprise or of a developing socialist country short of foreign capital — can we hope to meet the ethical demands that our present situation makes on us. For the first time since the beginning of civilization, we can feed everyone, now. Those who are not fed will die or, in the case of children, be permanently damaged.

We are just beginning to develop a world conscience. Our present dilemma is due to previous humanitarian moves with unanticipated effects. Without the spread of public health measures, we would not have had the fall in infant death rates which has resulted in the population explosion. Without the spread of agricultural techniques, there would not have been the food to feed the children who survived. The old constraints upon population growth — famine, plague, and war — are no longer acceptable to a world whose conscience is just barely stirring on behalf of all mankind. As we are groping our way back to a new version of the full fellow-feeling and respect for the natural world which the primitive Eskimo felt when food was scarce, so we are trembling on the edge of a new version of the sacrifice to cannibalism of the weak, just as we have the technical means to implement visions of responsibility that were very recently only visions.

The temptation is to turn aside, to deny what is happening to the environment, to trust to the "green revolution" and boast of how much rice previously hungry countries will export, to argue about legalities while people starve and infants and children are irreparably damaged, to refuse to deal with the paradoxes of hunger in plenty, and the coincidences of starvation and overnutrition. The basic problem is an ethical one; the solution of ethical problems can be solved only with a full recognition of reality. The children of the agricultural workers of the rural South, displaced by the machine, are hungry; so are the children in the Northern cities to which black and white poor have fled in search of food. On our American Indian reservations, among the Chicanos of California and the Southwest, among the seasonally employed, there is hunger now. If this hunger is not met now, we disqualify ourselves, we cripple ourselves, to deal with world problems.

We must balance our population so that every child that is born can be well fed. We must cherish our land, instead of mining it, so that food produced is first related to those who need it; and we must not despoil the earth, contaminate, and pollute it in the interests of immediate gain. Behind us, just a few decades ago, lies the vision of André Mayer and John Orr, the concepts of a world food bank, the founding of the United Nations Food and Agriculture Organization; behind us lie imaginative vision and deep concern. In the present we have new and various tools to make that vision into concrete actuality. But we must resolve the complications of present practice and present conceptions if the very precision and efficiency of our new knowledge is not to provide a stumbling block to the exercise of fuller humanity.

Understanding the Text

1. Mead points out that though we now have the technical ability to produce enough food to feed everyone in the world, we still do not do so. Why not, according to Mead?

2. What are some ways that people in the past have justified the contrast between the rich's easy access to food and the poor's lack of access to proper nourishment?

Reflection and Response

3. How has the capacity to feed all peoples in the world "altered the ethical position of the rich all over the world," according to Mead? (par. 6). Do you agree? Why or why not?

4. What are some solutions to the world's hunger problem proposed by Mead? Do you think they would work if pursued today? Why or why not?

5. What is a "world conscience"? What does Mead's call for a "world conscience" tell us about the ethical position she adopts? Why does she think this is the only morally legitimate path to take?

Making Connections

6. How might Frances Moore Lappé's essay ("Biotechnology Isn't the Key to Feeding the World," p. 294) be said to "update" the argument Mead makes here? In what ways does Lappé pick up where Mead left off? What would Mead say about the state of affairs described by Lappé?

7. What is the changing significance of food? Mead wrote this essay over five decades ago. Do you think her conclusions are still useful for thinking about an ethics of eating? Why or why not? Locate two outside sources to help you support your response.

8. What is Mead's primary ethical concern? What other authors in this collection share this concern? Use textual examples from at least three other sources to support your response.

Equality for Animals?

Peter Singer

Peter Singer is widely considered one of the most influential — and widely read — philosophers of our time. Born in Australia to Jewish parents, he studied philosophy in college and received his master's degree for a thesis titled "Why Should I Be Moral?" He is widely known for his writing about animal equality, most notably in *Animal Liberation* (1975). Other books he has written include *Practical Ethics* (third edition published in 2011), *The Life You Can Save: Acting Now to End World Poverty* (2009), and *The Most Good You Can Do* (2015). Singer is currently the Ira W. DeCamp Professor of Bioethics at Princeton University and a Laureate Professor at the Centre for Applied Philosophy and Public Ethics at the University of Melbourne. Singer's utilitarian philosophy guides his worldview. In the excerpt from *Practical Ethics* included here, he makes a utilitarian ethical argument against eating meat as part of a longer argument in favor of equality for animals.

Animals as Food

For most people in modern, urbanized societies, the principal form of contact with nonhuman animals is at meal times. The use of animals for food is probably the oldest and the most widespread form of animal use. There is also a sense in which it is the most basic form of animal use, the foundation stone of an ethic that sees animals as things for us to use to meet our needs and interests.

If animals count in their own right, our use of animals for food becomes questionable. Inuit living a traditional lifestyle in the far north where they must eat animals or starve can reasonably claim that their interest in surviving overrides that of the animals they kill. Most of us cannot defend our diet in this way. People living in industrialized societies can easily obtain an adequate diet without the use of animal flesh. Meat is not necessary for good health or longevity. Indeed, humans can live healthy lives without eating any animal products at all, although a vegan diet requires greater care, especially for young children, and a B12 vitamin supplement should be taken. Nor is animal production in industrialized societies an efficient way of producing food, because most of the animals consumed have been fattened on grains and other foods that we could have eaten directly. When we feed these grains to animals, only about one-quarter — and in some cases, as little as one-tenth — of the nutritional value remains as meat for human consumption. So, with the exception of animals raised entirely on grazing land unsuitable for crops, animals are eaten neither for health nor to increase our food supply. Their flesh is a luxury, consumed because people like its taste.

(The livestock industry also contributes more to global warming than the entire transport sector.)

In considering the ethics of the use of animal products for human food in industrialized societies, we are considering a situation in which a relatively minor human interest must be balanced against the lives and welfare of the animals involved. The principle of equal consideration of interests does not allow major interests to be sacrificed for minor interests.

The case against using animals for food is at its strongest when animals are made to lead miserable lives so that their flesh can be made available to humans at the lowest possible cost. Modern forms of intensive farming apply science and technology to the attitude that animals are objects for us to use. Competition in the marketplace forces meat producers to copy rivals who are prepared to cut costs by giving animals more miserable lives. In buying the meat, eggs, or milk produced in these ways, we tolerate methods of meat production that confine sentient animals in cramped, unsuitable conditions for the entire duration of their lives. They are treated like machines that convert fodder° into flesh, and any innovation that results in a higher "conversion ratio" is liable to be adopted. As one authority on the subject has said, "cruelty is acknowledged only when profitability ceases." To avoid speciesism, we must stop these practices. Our custom is all the support that factory farmers need. The decision to cease giving them that support may be difficult, but it is less difficult than it would have been for a white Southerner to go against the values of his community and free his slaves. If we do not change our dietary habits, how can we censure those slave holders who would not change their own way of living?

> "The case against using animals for food is at its strongest when animals are made to lead miserable lives so that their flesh can be made available to humans at the lowest possible cost."

These arguments apply to animals reared in factory farms — which 5 means that we should not eat chicken, pork, or veal unless we know that the meat we are eating was not produced by factory farm methods. The same is true of beef that has come from cattle kept in crowded feedlots (as most beef does in the United States). Eggs come from hens kept in small wire cages, too small even to allow them to stretch their wings, unless the eggs are specifically sold as "cage-free" or "free range." (At the time of writing, Switzerland has banned the battery cage, and the European Union is in the process of phasing it out. In the United States,

---

fodder: food for livestock, especially coarse hay or straw.

California voted in 2008 to ban it, and that ban will come into effect in 2015. A law passed in Michigan in 2009 requires battery cages to be phased out over 10 years.) Dairy products also often come from cows confined to a barn, unable to go out to pasture. Moreover, to continue to give milk, dairy cows have to be made pregnant every year, and their calf then taken away from them shortly after birth, so we can have the milk. This causes distress to both the cow and the calf.

Concern about the suffering of animals in factory farms does not take us all the way to a vegan diet, because it is possible to buy animal products from animals allowed to graze outside. (When animal products are labeled "organic," this should mean that the animals have access to the outdoors, but the interpretation of this rule is sometimes loose.) The lives of free-ranging animals are undoubtedly better than those of animals reared in factory farms. It is still doubtful if using them for food is compatible with equal consideration of interests. One problem is, of course, that using them for food involves killing them (even laying hens and dairy cows are killed when their productivity starts to drop, which is far short of their natural life span). . . . Apart from killing them, there are also many other things done to animals in order to bring them cheaply to our dinner table. Castration, the separation of mother and young, the breaking up of herds, branding, transporting, slaughterhouse handling, and finally the moment of slaughter itself — all of these are likely to involve suffering and do not take the animals' interests into account. Perhaps animals can be reared on a small scale without suffering in these ways. Some farmers take pride in producing "humanely raised" animal products, but the standards of what is regarded as "humane" vary widely. Any shift toward more humane treatment of animals is welcome, but it seems unlikely that these methods could produce the vast quantity of animal products now consumed by our large urban populations. At the very least, we would have to considerably reduce the amount of meat, eggs, and dairy products that we consume. In any case, the important question is not whether animal products *could* be produced without suffering, but whether those we are considering buying *were* produced without suffering. Unless we can be confident that they were, the principle of equal consideration of interests implies that their production wrongly sacrificed important interests of the animals to satisfy less important interests of our own. To buy the results of this process of production is to support it and encourage producers to continue to do it. Because those of us living in developed societies have a wide range of food choices and do not need to eat these products, encouraging the continuation of a cruel system of producing animal products is wrong.

For those of us living in cities where it is difficult to know how the animals we might eat have lived and died, this conclusion brings us very close to a vegan way of life. . . .

Animals Eat Each Other, So Why Shouldn't We Eat Them?

This might be called the Benjamin Franklin Objection because Franklin recounts in his *Autobiography* that he was for a time a vegetarian, but his abstinence from animal flesh came to an end when he was watching some friends prepare to fry a fish they had just caught. When the fish was cut open, it was found to have a smaller fish in its stomach. "Well," Franklin said to himself, "if you eat one another, I don't see why we may not eat you," and he proceeded to do so.

Franklin was at least honest. In telling this story, he confesses that he convinced himself of the validity of the objection only after the fish was already in the frying pan and smelling "admirably well"; and he remarks that one of the advantages of being a "reasonable creature" is that one can find a reason for whatever one wants to do. The replies that can be made to this objection are so obvious that Franklin's acceptance of it does testify more to his hunger on that occasion than to his powers of reason. For a start, most animals who kill for food would not be able to survive if they did not, whereas we have no need to eat animal flesh. Next, it is odd that humans, who normally think of the behavior of animals as "beastly" should, when it suits them, use an argument that implies that we ought to look to animals for moral guidance. The most decisive point, however, is that nonhuman animals are not capable of considering the alternatives open to them or of reflecting on the ethics of their diet. Hence, it is impossible to hold the animals responsible for what they do or to judge that because of their killing they "deserve" to be treated in a similar way. Those who read these lines, on the other hand, must consider the justifiability of their dietary habits. You cannot evade responsibility by imitating beings who are incapable of making this choice.

Sometimes people draw a slightly different conclusion from the fact 10 that animals eat each other. This suggests, they think, not that animals deserve to be eaten, but rather that there is a natural law according to which the stronger prey on the weaker, a kind of Darwinian "survival of the fittest" in which by eating animals we are merely playing our part.

This interpretation of the objection makes two basic mistakes, one of fact and the other of reasoning. The factual mistake lies in the assumption that our own consumption of animals is part of some natural evolutionary process. This might be true of those who still hunt for food, but it has nothing to do with the mass production of domestic animals in factory farms.

Suppose that we did hunt for our food, though, and this was part of some natural evolutionary process. There would still be an error of reasoning in the assumption that because this process is natural it is right. It is, no doubt, "natural" for women to produce an infant every year or two from puberty to menopause, but this does not mean that it is wrong to interfere with this process. We need to understand nature and develop the best theories we can to explain why things are as they are, because only in that way can we work out what the consequences of our actions are likely to be; but it would be a serious mistake to assume that natural ways of doing things are incapable of improvements. . . .

Understanding the Text

1. According to Singer, what might be an ethically sound reason for killing animals to eat them?

2. What is a factory farm? What role do factory farms play in the industrial food chain?

Reflection and Response

3. What is the "Benjamin Franklin Objection"? How does Singer counter it? Does he make a good case for his position? Explain your answer with textual analysis.

4. What is the "principle of equal consideration of interests"? How does Singer use it to make his case against using animals as food? Is his use of this principle rhetorically effective? Why or why not?

Making Connections

5. Peter Singer and Margaret Mead ("The Changing Significance of Food," p. 200) both encourage us to follow particular value or moral principles when we make food choices. What values do they share? What food choices would we need to make in order to live by the principles that they advocate?

6. Singer is known for being a utilitarian. What type of philosophical approach is this? How does it lead him to the position that a vegan diet is the most ethical one? Use outside research to explain utilitarianism and support your response.

7. Singer and Yuval Noah Harari ("Industrial Farming Is One of the Worst Crimes in History," p. 233) both argue against eating animals. Compare their rhetorical approaches. How does each build a case? What kinds of evidence does each use? How do they appeal to emotions, logic, and ethical considerations? Whose approach do you think is more effective and why?

8. List all of the reasons Singer gives to support his argument that we should not eat animals. Explain which authors in this chapter agree with him and to what extent. Then analyze what their points of agreement and disagreement say about their ethical positions.

You Can't Run Away on Harvest Day

Barbara Kingsolver

Barbara Kingsolver studied biology before becoming a prolific and award-winning author. Her books have been translated into more than twenty languages, and her stories and essays have been published in major literary anthologies and most major U.S. newspapers and magazines. Best known for her novels and short stories, including *The Bean Trees* (1988), *Animal Dreams* (1990), *The Poisonwood Bible* (1998), and *Prodigal Summer* (2000), she has more recently written about her experiences raising and harvesting her own food. Her 2007 memoir *Animal, Vegetable, Miracle: A Year of Food Life* chronicles her family's year devoted to eating locally — to eating food produced on their family farm or in their southern Appalachian community. In this essay excerpt from *Animal, Vegetable, Miracle*, Kingsolver provides an introspective and moving account of her experience slaughtering chickens and turkeys — and the moral principles that guide her ethics of eating.

The Saturday of Labor Day weekend dawned with a sweet, translucent bite, like a Golden Delicious apple. I always seem to harbor a childlike hope through the berry-stained months of June and July that summer will be for keeps. But then a day comes in early fall to remind me why it should end, after all. In September the quality of daylight shifts toward flirtation. The green berries on the spicebush shrubs along our lane begin to blink red, first one and then another, like faltering but resolute holiday lights. The woods fill with the restless singing of migrant birds warming up to the proposition of flying south. The cool air makes us restless too: jeans and sweater weather, perfect for a hike. Steven and I rose early that morning, looked out the window, looked at each other, and started in on the time-honored marital grumble: Was this *your* idea?

We weren't going on a hike today. Nor would we have the postsummer Saturday luxury of sitting on the porch with a cup of coffee and watching the farm wake up. On the docket instead was a hard day of work we could not postpone. The previous morning we'd sequestered half a dozen roosters and as many torn turkeys in a room of the barn we call "death row." We hold poultry there, clean and comfortable with water but no food, for a twenty-four-hour fast prior to harvest. It makes the processing cleaner and seems to calm the animals also. I could tell you it gives them time to get their emotional affairs in order, if that helps. But they have limited emotional affairs, and no idea what's coming.

We had a lot more of both. Our plan for this gorgeous day was the removal of some of our animals from the world of the living into the realm of food. At five months of age our roosters had put on a good harvest weight, and had lately opened rounds of cockfighting, venting their rising hormonal angst against any moving target, including us. When a rooster flies up at you with his spurs, he leaves marks. Lily now had to arm herself with a length of pipe in order to gather the eggs. Our barnyard wasn't big enough for this much machismo. We would certainly take no pleasure in the chore, but it was high time for the testosterone-reduction program. We sighed at the lovely weather and pulled out our old, bloody sneakers for harvest day.

There was probably a time when I thought it euphemistic to speak of "harvesting" animals. Now I don't. We calculate "months to harvest" when planning for the right time to start poultry. We invite friends to "harvest parties," whether we'll be gleaning° vegetable or animal. A harvest implies planning, respect, and effort. With animals, both the planning and physical effort are often greater, and respect for the enterprise is substantially more complex. It's a lot less fun than spending an autumn day picking apples off trees, but it's a similar operation on principle and the same word.

Killing is a culturally loaded term, for most of us inextricably tied up 5 with some version of a command that begins, "Thou shalt not." Every faith has it. And for all but perhaps the Jainists of India, that command is absolutely conditional. We know it does not refer to mosquitoes. Who among us has never killed living creatures on purpose? When a child is sick with an infection we rush for the medicine spoon, committing an eager and purposeful streptococcus massacre. We sprinkle boric acid or grab a spray can to rid our kitchens of cockroaches. What we mean by "killing" is to take a life cruelly, as in murder — or else more accidentally, as in "Oops, looks like I killed my African violet." Though the results are incomparable, what these different "killings" have in common is needless waste and some presumed measure of regret.

Most of us, if we know even a little about where our food comes from, understand that every bite put into our mouths since infancy (barring the odd rock or marble) was formerly alive. The blunt biological truth is that we animals can only remain alive by eating other life. Plants are inherently more blameless, having been born with the talent of whipping up their own food, peacefully and without noise, out of sunshine, water, and the odd mineral ingredient sucked up through their toes. Strangely enough, it's the animals to which we've assigned some rights,

gleaning: gathering, collecting.

while the saintly plants we maim and behead with moral impunity. Who thinks to beg forgiveness while mowing the lawn?

The moral rules of destroying our fellow biota° get even more tangled, the deeper we go. If we draw the okay-to-kill line between "animal" and "plant," and thus exclude meat, fowl, and fish from our diet on moral grounds, we still must live with the fact that every sack of flour and every soybean-based block of tofu came from a field where countless winged and furry lives were extinguished in the plowing, cultivating, and harvest. An estimated 67 million birds die each year from pesticide exposure on U.S. farms. Butterflies, too, are universally killed on contact in larval form by the genetically modified pollen contained in most U.S. corn. Foxes, rabbits, and bobolinks are starved out of their homes or dismembered by the sickle mower. Insects are "controlled" even by organic pesticides; earthworms are cut in half by the plow. Contrary to lore, they won't grow into two; both halves die.

To believe we can live without taking life is delusional. Humans may only cultivate nonviolence in our diets by degree. I've heard a Buddhist monk suggest the *number* of food-caused deaths is minimized in steak dinners, which share one death over many meals, whereas the equation is reversed for a bowl of clams. Others of us have lost heart for eating any steak dinner that's been shoved through the assembly line of feedlot life — however broadly we might share that responsibility. I take my gospel from Wendell Berry, who writes in *What Are People For*, "I dislike the thought that some animal has been made miserable in order to feed me. If I am going to eat meat, I want it to be from an animal that has lived a pleasant, uncrowded life outdoors, on bountiful pasture, with good water nearby and trees for shade. And I am getting almost as fussy about food plants."

I find myself fundamentally allied with a vegetarian position in every way except one: however selectively, I eat meat. I'm unimpressed by arguments that condemn animal harvest while ignoring, wholesale, the animal killing that underwrites vegetal foods. Uncountable deaths by pesticide and habitat removal — the beetles and bunnies that die collaterally for our bread and veggie-burgers — are lives plumb wasted. Animal harvest is at least not gratuitous, as part of a plan involving labor and recompense. We raise these creatures for a reason. Such premeditation may be presumed unkind, but without it our gentle domestic beasts in their picturesque shapes, colors, and finely tuned purposes would never have had the distinction of existing. To envision a vegan version of civilization, start by erasing from all time the Three Little Pigs, the boy who

biota: living things, both plant and animal.

cried wolf, *Charlotte's Web*, the golden calf, *Tess of the d'Urbervilles*. Next, erase civilization, brought to you by the people who learned to domesticate animals. Finally, rewrite our evolutionary history, since *Homo sapiens* became the species we are by means of regular binges of carnivory.

Most confounding of all, in the vegan revision, are the chapters 10 addressing the future. If farm animals have civil rights, what aspect of their bondage to humans shall they overcome? Most wouldn't last two days without it. Recently while I was cooking eggs, my kids sat at the kitchen table entertaining me with readings from a magazine profile of a famous, rather young vegan movie star. Her dream was to create a safe-haven ranch where the cows and chickens could live free, happy lives and die natural deaths. "Wait till those cows start bawling to be milked," I warned. Having nursed and weaned my own young, I can tell you there is no pain to compare with an overfilled udder. We wondered what the starlet might do for those bursting Jerseys, not to mention

> "I find myself fundamentally allied with a vegetarian position in every way except one: however selectively, I eat meat."

the eggs the chickens would keep dropping everywhere. What a life's work for that poor gal: traipsing about the farm in her strappy heels, weaving among the cow flops, bending gracefully to pick up eggs and stick them in an incubator where they would maddeningly *hatch*, and grow up bent on laying *more* eggs. It's dirty work, trying to save an endless chain of uneaten lives. Realistically, my kids observed, she'd hire somebody.

Forgive us. We know she meant well, and as fantasies of the super-rich go, it's more inspired than most. It's just the high-mindedness that rankles; when moral superiority combines with billowing ignorance, they fill up a hot-air balloon that's awfully hard not to poke. The farm-liberation fantasy simply reflects a modern cultural confusion about farm animals. They're human property, not just legally but biologically. Over the millennia of our clever history, we created from wild progenitors° whole new classes of beasts whose sole purpose was to feed us. If turned loose in the wild, they would haplessly starve, succumb to predation, and destroy the habitats and lives of most or all natural things. If housed at the public expense they would pose a more immense civic burden than our public schools and prisons combined. No thoughtful person really wants those things to happen. But living at a remove from the actual workings of a farm, most humans no longer learn appropriate modes of thinking about animal harvest. Knowing that our family raises meat animals, many

progenitor: ancestor.

friends have told us — not judgmentally, just confessionally — "I don't think I could kill an animal myself." I find myself explaining: It's not what you think. It's nothing like putting down your dog.

Most nonfarmers are intimate with animal life in only three categories: people; pets (i.e., junior people); and wildlife (as seen on nature shows, presumed beautiful and rare). Purposely beheading any of the above is unthinkable, for obvious reasons. No other categories present themselves at close range for consideration. So I understand why it's hard to think about harvest, a categorical act that includes cutting the heads off living lettuces, extended to crops that blink their beady eyes. On our farm we don't especially enjoy processing our animals, but we do value it, as an important ritual for ourselves and any friends adventurous enough to come and help, because of what we learn from it. We reconnect with the purpose for which these animals were bred. We dispense with all delusions about who put the *live* in livestock, and who must take it away.

A friend from whom we buy pasture-grazed lamb and poultry has concurred with us on this point. Kirsty Zahnke grew up in the U.K., and observes that American attitudes toward life and death probably add to the misgivings. "People in this country do everything to cheat death, it seems. Instead of being happy with each moment, they worry so much about what comes next. I think this gets transposed to animals — the preoccupation with 'taking a life.' My animals have all had a good life, with death as its natural end. It's not without thought and gratitude that I slaughter my animals, it is a hard thing to do. It's taken me time to be able to eat my own lambs that I had played with. But I always think of Kahlil Gibran's words:

When you kill a beast, say to him in your heart:

> *By the same power that slays you, I too am slain, and I too shall be consumed.*
> *For the law that delivers you into my hand shall deliver me into a mightier hand.*
> *Your blood and my blood is naught but the sap that feeds the tree of heaven.*

Kirsty works with a local environmental organization and frequently hosts its out-of-town volunteers, who camp at her farm while working in the area. Many of these activists had not eaten meat for many years before arriving on the Zahnkes' meat farm — a formula not for disaster, she notes, but for education. "If one gets to know the mantras of the farm owners, it can change one's viewpoint. I would venture to say that seventy-five percent of the vegans and vegetarians who stayed at least a week here began to eat our meat or animal products, simply because they see what I am doing as right — for the animals, for the environment, for humans."

I respect every diner who makes morally motivated choices about consumption. And I stand with nonviolence, as one of those extremist moms who doesn't let kids at her house pretend to shoot each other, *ever*, or make any game out of human murder. But I've come to different conclusions about livestock. The ve-vangelical pamphlets showing jam-packed chickens and sick downer-cows usually declare, as their first principle, that all meat is factory-farmed. That is false, and an affront to those of us who work to raise animals humanely, or who support such practices with our buying power. I don't want to cause any creature misery, so I won't knowingly eat anything that has stood belly deep in its own poop wishing it was dead until *bam*, one day it was. (In restaurants I go for the fish, or the vegetarian option.) 15

But meat, poultry, and eggs from animals raised on open pasture are the traditional winter fare of my grandparents, and they serve us well here in the months when it would cost a lot of fossil fuels to keep us in tofu. Should I overlook the suffering of victims of hurricanes, famines, and wars brought on this world by profligate fuel consumption? Bananas that cost a rain forest, refrigerator-trucked soy milk, and prewashed spinach shipped two thousand miles in plastic containers do not seem cruelty-free, in this context. A hundred different paths may lighten the world's load of suffering. Giving up meat is one path; giving up bananas is another. The more we know about our food system, the more we are called into complex choices. It seems facile to declare one single forbidden fruit, when humans live under so many different kinds of trees.

To breed fewer meat animals in the future is possible; phasing out those types destined for confinement lots is a plan I'm assisting myself, by raising heirloom breeds. Most humans could well consume more vegetable foods, and less meat. But globally speaking, the vegetarian option is a luxury. The oft-cited energetic argument for vegetarianism, that it takes ten times as much land to make a pound of meat as a pound of grain, only applies to the kind of land where rain falls abundantly on rich topsoil. Many of the world's poor live in marginal lands that can't support plant-based agriculture. Those not blessed with the fruited plain and amber waves of grain must make do with woody tree pods, tough-leaved shrubs, or sparse grasses. Camels, reindeer, sheep, goats, cattle, and other ruminants are uniquely adapted to transform all those types of indigestible cellulose into edible milk and meat. The fringes of desert, tundra, and marginal grasslands on every continent — coastal Peru, the southwestern United States, the Kalahari, the Gobi, the Australian outback, northern Scandinavia — are inhabited by herders. The Navajo, Mongols, Lapps, Masai, and countless other resourceful tribes would starve without their animals. . . .

After many meatless years it felt strange to us to break the taboo, but over time our family has come back to carnivory. I like listening to a roasting bird in the oven on a Sunday afternoon, following Julia Child's advice to "regulate the chicken so it makes quiet cooking noises" as its schmaltzy aroma fills the house. When a friend began raising beef cattle entirely on pasture (rather than sending them to a CAFO° as six-month-olds, as most cattle farmers do), we were born again to the idea of hamburger. We can go visit his animals if we need to be reassured of the merciful cowness of their lives.

As meat farmers ourselves we are learning as we go, raising heritage breeds: the thrifty antiques that know how to stand in the sunshine, gaze upon a meadow, and munch. (Even mate without help!) We're grateful these old breeds weren't consigned to extinction during the past century, though it nearly did happen. Were it not for these animals that can thrive outdoors, and the healthy farms that maintain them, I would have stuck with tofu-burgers indefinitely. That wasn't a bad life, but we're also enjoying this one.

Believing in the righteousness of a piece of work, alas, is not what gets 20 it done. On harvest day we pulled on our stained shoes, sharpened our knives, lit a fire under the big kettle, and set ourselves to the whole show: mud, blood, and lots of little feathers. There are some things about a chicken harvest that are irrepressibly funny, and one of them is the feathers; in your hair, on the backs of your hands, dangling behind your left shoe the way toilet paper does in slapstick movies. Feathery little white tags end up stuck all over the chopping block and the butchering table like Post-it notes from the chicken hereafter. Sometimes we get through the awful parts on the strength of black comedy, joking about the feathers or our barn's death row and the "dead roosters walking."

But today was not one of those times. Some friends had come over to help us, including a family that had recently lost their teenage son in a drowning accident. Their surviving younger children, Abby and Eli, were among Lily's closest friends. The kids were understandably solemn and the adults measured all our words under the immense weight of grief as we set to work. Lily and Abby went to get the first rooster from the barn while I laid out the knives and spread plastic sheets over our

CAFO: Concentrated Animal Feed Operation.

butchering table on the back patio. The guys stoked a fire under our 50-gallon kettle, an antique brass instrument Steven and I scored at a farm auction.

The girls returned carrying Rooster #1 upside down, by the legs. Inversion has the immediate effect of lulling a chicken to sleep, or something near to it. What comes next is quick and final. We set the rooster gently across our big chopping block (a legendary fixture of our backyard, whose bloodstains hold visiting children in thrall), and down comes the ax. All sensation ends with that quick stroke. He must then be held by the legs over a large plastic bucket until all the blood has run out. Farmers who regularly process poultry have more equipment, including banks of "killing cones" or inverted funnels that contain the birds while the processor pierces each neck with a sharp knife, cutting two major arteries and ending brain function. We're not pros, so we have a more rudimentary setup. By lulling and swiftly decapitating my animal, I can make sure my relatively unpracticed handling won't draw out the procedure or cause pain.

What you've heard is true: the rooster will flap his wings hard during this part. If you drop him he'll thrash right across the yard, unpleasantly spewing blood all around, though the body doesn't *run* — it's nothing that well coordinated. His newly detached head silently opens and closes its mouth, down in the bottom of the gut bucket, a world apart from the ruckus. The cause of all these actions is an explosion of massively firing neurons without a brain to supervise them. Most people who claim to be running around like a chicken with its head cut off, really, are not even close. The nearest thing might be the final convulsive seconds of an All-Star wrestling match.

For Rooster #1 it was over, and into the big kettle for a quick scald. After a one-minute immersion in 145-degree water, the muscle tissue releases the feathers so they're easier to pluck. "Easier" is relative — every last feather still has to be pulled, carefully enough to avoid tearing the skin. The downy breast feathers come out by handfuls, while the long wing and tail feathers sometimes must be removed individually with pliers. If we were pros we would have an electric scalder and automatic plucker, a fascinating bucket full of rotating rubber fingers that does the job in no time flat. For future harvests we might borrow a friend's equipment, but for today we had a pulley on a tree limb so we could hoist the scalded carcass to shoulder level, suspending it there from a rope so several of us could pluck at once. Lily, Abby, and Eli pulled neck and breast feathers, making necessary observations such as "Gag, look where his head came off," and "Wonder which one of these tube thingies was his windpipe." Most kids need only about ninety seconds to get from *eeew gross* to solid science. A few weeks later Abby would give an award-winning, fully illustrated 4-H presentation entitled "You Can't Run Away on Harvest Day."

Laura and Becky and I answered the kids' questions, and also talked about Mom things while working on back and wing feathers. (Our husbands were on to the next beheading.) Laura and I compared notes on our teenage daughters — relatively new drivers on the narrow country roads between their jobs, friends, and home — and the worries that come with that territory. I was painfully conscious of Becky's quiet, her ache for a teenage son who never even got to acquire a driver's license. The accident that killed Larry could not have been avoided through any amount of worry. We all cultivate illusions of safety that could fall away in the knife edge of one second.

I wondered how we would get through this afternoon, how *she* would get through months and years of living with impossible loss. I wondered if I'd been tactless, inviting these dear friends to an afternoon of ending lives. And then felt stupid for that thought. People who are grieving walk with death, every waking moment. When the rest of us dread that we'll somehow remind them of death's existence, we are missing their reality. Harvesting turkeys — which this family would soon do on their own farm — was just another kind of work. A rendezvous with death, for them, was waking up each morning without their brother and son.

By early afternoon six roosters had lost their heads, feathers, and viscera, and were chilling on ice. We had six turkeys to go, the hardest piece of our work simply because the animals are larger and heavier. Some of these birds were close to twenty pounds. They would take center stage on our holiday table and those of some of our friends. At least one would be charcuterie — in the garden I had sage, rosemary, garlic, onions, everything we needed for turkey sausage. And the first two roosters we'd harvested would be going on the rotisserie later that afternoon.

We allowed ourselves a break before the challenge of hoisting, plucking, and dressing the turkeys. While Lily and her friends constructed feather crowns and ran for the poultry house to check in with the living, the adults cracked open beers and stretched out in lawn chairs in the September sun.

Our conversation turned quickly to the national preoccupation of that autumn: Katrina, the hurricane that had just hit southern Louisiana and Mississippi. We were horrified by the news that was beginning to filter out of that flooded darkness, the children stranded on rooftops, the bereaved and bewildered families slogging through streets waist-deep in water, breaking plate glass windows to get bottles of water. People drowning and dying of thirst at the same time.

It was already clear this would be an epic disaster. New Orleans and 30
countless other towns across southern Louisiana and Mississippi were
being evacuated and left for dead. The news cameras had focused solely
on urban losses, sending images of flooded streets, people on rooftops,
broken storefronts, and the desperate crises of people in the city with no
resources for relocating or evacuating. I had not seen one photograph
from the countryside — a wrecked golf course was the closest thing to it.
I wondered about the farmers whose year of work still lay in the fields,
just weeks or days away from harvest, when the flood took it all. I still
can't say whether the rural victims of Katrina found their support systems more resilient, or if their hardships simply went unreported.

The disaster reached into the rest of the country with unexpected ten-
tacles. Our town and schools were already taking in people who had lost
everything. The office where I'd just sent my passport for renewal was
now underwater. Gasoline had passed $3 a gallon, here and elsewhere,
leaving our nation in sticker shock. U.S. citizens were making outlandish
declarations about staying home. Climate scientists were saying, "If you
warm up the globe, you eventually pay for it." Economists were eyeing
our budget deficits and predicting collapse, mayhem, infrastructure
breakdown. In so many ways, disaster makes us take stock. For me it had
inspired powerful cravings about living within our means. I wasn't
thinking so much of my household budget or the national one but the
big budget, the one that involves consuming approximately the same
things we produce. Taking a symbolic cue from my presumed-soggy
passport, I suddenly felt like sticking very close to home, with a hand on
my family's production, even when it wasn't all that easy or fun — like
today.

Analysts of current events were mostly looking to blame administra-
tors. Fair enough, but there were also, it seemed, obvious vulnerabilities
here — whole populations, depending on everyday, long-distance life-
lines, supplies of food and water and fuel and everything else that are
acutely centralized. That's what we consider normal life. Now nature had
written a hugely abnormal question across the bottom of our map. I wondered what our answers might be. . . .

Understanding the Text

1. What influences Kingsolver's decision to eat meat? What makes her see
    this as a morally defensible position?

2. What is animal harvest, and why does Kingsolver think it is important for
    her family to participate in it?

Reflection and Response

3. Describe your own reactions to the events described by Kingsolver. Why do you think she depicts "harvest day" the way she does? What images does she want us to come away with? What emotional reaction do you think she hopes to elicit?

4. Kingsolver argues that "*Killing* is a culturally loaded term" and that "To believe we can live without taking life is delusional" (par. 5; par. 8). How and why does she draw these conclusions? Do you agree with her? Why or why not?

Making Connections

5. Imagine growing up in Barbara Kingsolver's household. How would daily life resemble or differ from your own upbringing? Compare the relationship between her children's upbringing and food values to the relationship between your own upbringing and food values. What, if anything, does your upbringing reveal about your own ethics of eating?

6. Reflect on Kingsolver's, Yuval Noah Harari's ("Industrial Farming is One of the Worst Crimes in History," p. 233), Bill McKibben's ("The Only Way to Have a Cow," p. 229), and Peter Singer's ("Equality for Animals?," p. 212) arguments regarding the ethics of meat eating in relation to your own life experiences and moral choices. Do you eat meat? Have you harvested it? Worked with farm animals? Hunted? If you eat meat, does it matter to you if the animals you eat roam freely? Were treated humanely? Lived a good life? Do you think it is wrong to kill animals for consumption? What moral principles guide your thinking? How do the views of Kingsolver, Harari, McKibben, and Singer inform your position? Describe what influences your own position on eating meat. Which authors speak to your concerns or moral principles? How?

7. Kingsolver claims that she follows Wendell Berry's beliefs about human responsibility in animal consumption. Analyze Berry's essay "The Pleasures of Eating" (p. 47). What principles do Kingsolver and Berry share? Do you find potential points of disagreement? Locate textual examples to support your analysis.

The Only Way to Have a Cow

Bill McKibben

Bill McKibben wrote *The End of Nature* in 1989, a book often described as the first book on climate change written for a popular audience. McKibben is an environmentalist and widely published author and journalist who writes extensively on the environment, nature, food policy, economic policy, and the impact of climate change. In his book *Deep Economy: The Wealth of Communities and the Durable Future* (2007), he argues for the value of local economies and documents his year of eating locally in Middlebury, Vermont. He is a frequent contributor to various publications, including the *New York Times*, the *Atlantic Monthly*, *Mother Jones*, and *Rolling Stone*. He has received many awards, fellowships, and honorary degrees and is the Schumann Distinguished Scholar at Middlebury College. In this essay, originally published in *Orion* in 2010, McKibben calls on his readers to take environmental factors into account when deciding on the ethics of eating meat.

May I say — somewhat defensively — that I haven't cooked red meat in many years? That I haven't visited a McDonald's since college? That if you asked me how I like my steak, I'd say I don't really remember? I'm not a moral abstainer — I'll eat meat when poor people in distant places offer it to me, especially when they're proud to do so and I'd be an ass to say no. But in everyday life, for a series of reasons that began with the dietary scruples of the woman I chose to marry, hamburgers just don't come into play.

I begin this way because I plan to wade into one of the most impassioned fracases now underway on the planet — to meat or not to meat — and I want to establish that I Do Not Have A Cow In This Fight. In recent years vegetarians and vegans have upped their attack on the consumption of animal flesh, pointing out not only that it's disgusting (read Jonathan Safran Foer's new book) but also a major cause of climate change. The numbers range from 18 percent of the world's greenhouse gas emissions to — in one recent study that was quickly discredited — 51 percent. Whatever the exact figure, suffice it to say it's high: there's the carbon that comes from cutting down the forest to start the farm, and from the fertilizer and diesel fuel it takes to grow the corn, there's the truck exhaust from shipping cows hither and yon, and most of all the methane that emanates from the cows themselves (95 percent of it from the front end, not the hind, and these millions of feedlot cows would prefer if you used the word *eructate* in place of *belch*). This news has led to an almost endless series of statistical calculations: going vegan is 50 percent more effective in reducing greenhouse gas emissions than switching to a hybrid car according to a University of Chicago study; the UN Food and Agriculture Organization finds that a half pound of ground beef has the same effect on climate change as driving an SUV 10 miles. It has led to a lot of political statements: the British health secretary last fall called on Englishmen to cut their beefeating by dropping at least a sausage a week from their diets, and Paul McCartney has declared that "the biggest change anyone could make in their own lifestyle to help the environment would be to become vegetarian." It has even led to the marketing of a men's flip-flop called the Stop Global Warming Toepeeka that's made along entirely vegan lines.

Industrial livestock production is essentially indefensible — ethically, ecologically, and otherwise. We now use an enormous percentage of our arable land to grow corn that we feed to cows who stand in feedlots and eructate until they are slaughtered in a variety of gross ways and lodge in our ever-larger abdomens. And the fact that the product of this exercise "tastes good" sounds pretty lame as an excuse. There are technofixes — engineering the corn feed so it produces less methane, or giving the cows shots so they eructate less violently. But this type of tailpipe fix only works around the edges, and with the planet warming fast that's not enough. We should simply stop eating factory-farmed meat, and the effects on climate change would be but one of the many benefits.

> "We should simply stop eating factory-farmed meat, and the effects on climate change would be but one of the many benefits."

Still, even once you've made that commitment, there's a nagging ecological question that's just now being raised. It goes like this: long before humans had figured out the whole cow thing, nature had its own herds of hoofed ungulates. Big herds of big animals — perhaps 60 million bison ranging across North America, and maybe 100 million antelope. That's considerably more than the number of cows now resident in these United States. These were noble creatures, but uncouth — *eructate* hadn't been coined yet. They really did just belch. So why weren't they filling the atmosphere with methane? Why wasn't their manure giving off great quantities of atmosphere-altering gas?

The answer, so far as we can tell, is both interesting and potentially 5
radical in its implications. These old-school ungulates weren't all that different in their plumbing — they were methane factories with legs too. But they used those legs for something. They didn't stand still in feedlots waiting for corn, and they didn't stand still in big western federal

allotments overgrazing the same tender grass. They didn't stand still at all. Maybe they would have enjoyed stationary life, but like teenagers in a small town, they were continually moved along by their own version of the police: wolves. And big cats. And eventually Indians. By predators.

As they moved, they kept eating grass and dropping manure. Or, as soil scientists would put it, they grazed the same perennials once or twice a year to "convert aboveground biomass to dung and urine." Then dung beetles buried the results in the soil, nurturing the grass to grow back. These grasslands covered places that don't get much rain — the Southwest and the Plains, Australia, Africa, much of Asia. And all that grassland sequestered stupendous amounts of carbon and methane from out of the atmosphere — recent preliminary research indicates that methane-loving bacteria in healthy soils will sequester more of the gas in a day than cows supported by the same area will emit in a year.

We're flat out of predators in most parts of the world, and it's hard to imagine, in the short time that we have to deal with climate change, ending the eating of meat and returning the herds of buffalo and packs of wolves to all the necessary spots. It's marginally easier to imagine mimicking those systems with cows. The key technology here is the single-strand electric fence — you move your herd or your flock once or twice a day from one small pasture to the next, forcing them to eat everything that's growing there but moving them along before they graze all the good stuff down to bare ground. Now their manure isn't a problem that fills a cesspool, but a key part of making the system work. Done right, some studies suggest, this method of raising cattle could put much of the atmosphere's oversupply of greenhouse gases back in the soil inside half a century. That means shifting from feedlot farming to rotational grazing is one of the few changes we could make that's on the same scale as the problem of global warming. It won't do away with the need for radically cutting emissions, but it could help get the car exhaust you emitted back in high school out of the atmosphere.

Oh, and grass-fed beef is apparently much better for you — full of Omega 3s, like sardines that moo. Better yet, it's going to be more expensive, because you can't automate the process the same way you can feedlot agriculture. You need the guy to move the fence every afternoon. (That's why about a billion of our fellow humans currently make their livings as herders of one kind or another — some of them use slingshots, or dogs, or shepherd's crooks, or horses instead of electric fence, but the principle is the same.) More expensive, in this case, as in many others, is good; we'd end up eating meat the way most of the world does — as a condiment, a flavor, an ingredient, not an entrée.

I doubt McDonald's will be in favor. I doubt Paul McCartney will be in favor. It doesn't get rid of the essential dilemma of killing something and then putting it in your mouth. But it's possible that the atmosphere would be in favor, and that's worth putting down your fork and thinking about.

Understanding the Text

1. Why does McKibben conclude that it is impossible to defend industrial livestock production?
2. What is the relationship between factory farming and climate change?
3. What is rotational grazing, and why does McKibben advocate a return to it?
4. Why does McKibben almost never eat meat? When does he eat meat, and why?

Reflection and Response

5. What is the significance of the title? Why do you think McKibben selected it?
6. Why does McKibben think that it is good that grass-fed beef will be or is more expensive?

Making Connections

7. McKibben concludes that neither extreme (not McDonald's and not Paul McCartney's) will favor his position. Why not? How does McKibben position himself in relation to various other positions in this debate? How would Margaret Mead ("The Changing Significance of Food," p. 200), David Biello ("Will Organic Food Fail to Feed the World?" p. 262), and Masanobu Fukuoka ("Living by Bread Alone," p. 71) evaluate his position? Use textual evidence to support your answer.
8. McKibben suggests that an ethics of eating must concern itself with environmental factors. Does he make a good case for why this particular issue should take the forefront? Who in this collection might disagree with his position, and on what grounds? What do their positions tells us about their ethical concerns?
9. Compare the arguments made by McKibben and Yuval Noah Harari ("Industrial Farming Is One of the Worst Crimes in History," p. 233). Consider both their main conclusions and the ways they go about communicating their conclusions to readers. What kinds of evidence do they use? What kinds of rhetorical strategies do they rely on? Which argument would be more likely to motivate you to change your behavior, and why?

Industrial Farming Is One of the Worst Crimes in History

Yuval Noah Harari

Yuval Noah Harari is a prolific and award-winning writer and professor of history. He was born in Israel, where he attended college before moving to Oxford to complete his doctoral work at Jesus College. He has published numerous books and articles, both for academic and general audiences, and won many prestigious honors for his work. He is most known for his book *Sapiens: A Brief History of Humankind* (2011); video clips of his lectures on this material and free online courses that cover it can be found on the Internet. Harari is proud to be a vegan and is known for writing about the plight of domesticated animals raised under industrial farming. The essay included here, originally published in the *Guardian*, looks to history to explore the state of industrial farming and our ethical obligations to the animals that live and die in its grasp.

Animals are the main victims of history, and the treatment of domesticated animals in industrial farms is perhaps the worst crime in history. The march of human progress is strewn with dead animals. Even tens of thousands of years ago, our stone age ancestors were already responsible for a series of ecological disasters. When the first humans reached Australia about 45,000 years ago, they quickly drove to extinction 90% of its large animals. This was the first significant impact that Homo sapiens had on the planet's ecosystem. It was not the last.

About 15,000 years ago, humans colonised America, wiping out in the process about 75% of its large mammals. Numerous other species disappeared from Africa, from Eurasia and from the myriad islands around their coasts. The archaeological record of country after country tells the same sad story. The tragedy opens with a scene showing a rich and varied population of large animals, without any trace of Homo sapiens. In scene two, humans appear, evidenced by a fossilized bone, a spear point, or perhaps a campfire. Scene three quickly follows, in which men and women occupy center-stage and most large animals, along with many smaller ones, have gone. Altogether, sapiens drove to extinction about 50% of all the large terrestrial mammals of the planet before they planted the first wheat field, shaped the first metal tool, wrote the first text or struck the first coin.

The next major landmark in human-animal relations was the agricultural revolution: the process by which we turned from nomadic hunter-gatherers into farmers living in permanent settlements. It involved the appearance of a completely new life-form on Earth: domesticated animals. Initially, this development might seem to have been of minor importance, as humans only managed to domesticate fewer than 20 species of mammals and birds, compared with the countless thousands of species that remained "wild." Yet, with the passing of the centuries, this novel life-form became the norm. Today, more than 90% of all large animals are domesticated ("large" denotes animals that weigh at least a few kilograms). Consider the chicken, for example. Ten thousand years ago, it was a rare bird that was confined to small niches of South Asia. Today, billions of chickens live on almost every continent and island, bar Antarctica. The domesticated chicken is probably the most widespread bird in the annals of planet Earth. If you measure success in terms of numbers, chickens, cows and pigs are the most successful animals ever.

Alas, domesticated species paid for their unparalleled collective success with unprecedented individual suffering. The animal kingdom has known many types of pain and misery for millions of years. Yet the agricultural revolution created completely new kinds of suffering, ones that only worsened with the passing of the generations.

At first sight, domesticated animals may seem much better off than   5
their wild cousins and ancestors. Wild buffaloes spend their days searching for food, water and shelter, and are constantly threatened by lions, parasites, floods and droughts. Domesticated cattle, by contrast, enjoy care and protection from humans. People provide cows and calves with food, water and shelter, they treat their diseases, and protect them from predators and natural disasters. True, most cows and calves sooner or later find themselves in the slaughterhouse. Yet does that make their fate any worse than that of wild buffaloes? Is it better to be devoured by a lion than slaughtered by a man? Are crocodile teeth kinder than steel blades?

What makes the existence of domesticated farm animals particularly cruel is not just the way in which they die but above all how they live. Two competing factors have shaped the living conditions of farm animals: on the one hand, humans want meat, milk, eggs, leather, animal muscle-power and amusement; on the other, humans have to ensure the long-term survival and reproduction of farm animals. Theoretically, this should protect animals from extreme cruelty. If a farmer milks his cow without providing her with food and water, milk production will dwindle, and the cow herself will quickly die. Unfortunately, humans can cause tremendous suffering to farm animals in other ways, even while ensuring their survival and reproduction. The root of the problem is that domesticated animals have inherited from their wild ancestors many physical, emotional and social needs that are redundant in farms.

Pigs being transported to the slaughterhouse.
Shutterstock/Paul Prescott

Farmers routinely ignore these needs without paying any economic price. They lock animals in tiny cages, mutilate their horns and tails, separate mothers from offspring, and selectively breed monstrosities. The animals suffer greatly, yet they live on and multiply.

Doesn't that contradict the most basic principles of Darwinian evolution? The theory of evolution maintains that all instincts and drives have evolved in the interest of survival and reproduction. If so, doesn't the continuous reproduction of farm animals prove that all their real needs are met? How can a cow have a "need" that is not really essential for survival and reproduction?

It is certainly true that all instincts and drives evolved in order to meet the evolutionary pressures of survival and reproduction. When these pressures disappear, however, the instincts and drives they had shaped do not evaporate instantly. Even if they are no longer instrumental for survival and reproduction, they continue to mold the subjective experiences of the animal. The physical, emotional and social needs of present-day cows, dogs and humans don't reflect their current conditions but rather the evolutionary pressures their ancestors encountered tens of thousands of years ago. Why do modern people love sweets so much? Not because in the early 21st century we must gorge on ice cream and chocolate in order to survive. Rather, it is because if our stone age ancestors came across sweet, ripened fruits, the most sensible thing to do was to eat as many of them as they could as quickly as possible. Why do young men drive recklessly, get involved in violent rows, and hack confidential internet sites? Because they are obeying ancient genetic decrees. Seventy thousand years ago, a young hunter who risked his life chasing a mammoth outshone all his competitors and won the hand of the local beauty – and we are now stuck with his macho genes.

"Tragically, the agricultural revolution gave humans the power to ensure the survival and reproduction of domesticated animals while ignoring their subjective needs. In consequence, domesticated animals are collectively the most successful animals in the world, and at the same time they are individually the most miserable animals that have ever existed."

Exactly the same evolutionary logic shapes the life of cows and calves in our industrial farms. Ancient wild cattle were social animals. In order to survive and reproduce, they needed to communicate, cooperate and compete effectively. Like all social mammals, wild cattle learned the necessary social skills through play. Puppies, kittens, calves and children all love to play because evolution implanted this urge in them. In the wild, they needed to play. If they didn't, they would not learn the social skills vital for survival and reproduction. If a kitten or calf was born with some rare mutation that made them indifferent to play, they were unlikely to survive or reproduce, just as they would not exist in the first place if their ancestors hadn't acquired those skills. Similarly, evolution implanted in puppies, kittens, calves and children an overwhelming desire to bond with their mothers. A chance mutation weakening the mother-infant bond was a death sentence.

What happens when farmers now take a young calf, separate her from her mother, put her in a tiny cage, vaccinate her against various diseases, provide her with food and water, and then, when she is old enough, artificially inseminate her with bull sperm? From an objective perspective, this calf no longer needs either maternal bonding or playmates in order to survive and reproduce. All her needs are being taken care of by her human masters. But from a subjective perspective, the calf still feels a strong urge to bond with her mother and to play with other calves. If these urges are not fulfilled, the calf suffers greatly.

This is the basic lesson of evolutionary psychology: a need shaped thousands of generations ago continues to be felt subjectively even if it is no longer necessary for survival and reproduction in the present. Tragically, the agricultural revolution gave humans the power to ensure the survival and reproduction of domesticated animals while ignoring their subjective needs. In consequence, domesticated animals are collectively the most successful animals in the world, and at the same time they are individually the most miserable animals that have ever existed.

The situation has only worsened over the last few centuries, during which time traditional agriculture gave way to industrial farming. In traditional societies such as ancient Egypt, the Roman empire or medieval China, humans had a very partial understanding of biochemistry, genetics, zoology and epidemiology°. Consequently, their manipulative powers were limited. In medieval villages, chickens ran free between the houses, pecked seeds and worms from the garbage heap, and built nests in the barn. If an ambitious peasant tried to lock 1,000 chickens inside a crowded coop, a deadly bird-flu epidemic would probably have resulted, wiping out all the chickens, as well as many villagers. No priest, shaman or witch doctor could have prevented it. But once modern science had deciphered the secrets of birds, viruses and antibiotics, humans could begin to subject animals to extreme living conditions. With the help of vaccinations, medications, hormones, pesticides, central air-conditioning systems and automatic feeders, it is now possible to cram tens of thousands of chickens into tiny coops, and produce meat and eggs with unprecedented efficiency.

The fate of animals in such industrial installations has become one of the most pressing ethical issues of our time, certainly in terms of the numbers involved. These days, most big animals live on industrial farms. We imagine that our planet is populated by lions, elephants, whales and penguins. That may be true of the National Geographic channel, Disney movies and children's fairytales, but it is no longer true of the real world. The world contains 40,000 lions but, by way of contrast, there are around 1 billion domesticated pigs; 500,000 elephants and 1.5 billion domesticated cows; 50 million penguins and 20 billion chickens.

In 2009, there were 1.6 billion wild birds in Europe, counting all species together. That same year, the European meat and egg industry raised 1.9 billion chickens. Altogether, the domesticated animals of the world weigh about 700m tons, compared with 300m tons for humans, and fewer than 100m tons for large wild animals.

This is why the fate of farm animals is not an ethical side issue. It concerns the majority of Earth's large creatures: tens of billions of sentient beings, each with a complex world of sensations and emotions, but which live and die on an industrial production line. Forty years ago, the 15

---

epidemiology: the study of causes, effects, and patterns of health and disease across defined populations.

moral philosopher Peter Singer published his canonical book *Animal Liberation*, which has done much to change people's minds on this issue. Singer claimed that industrial farming is responsible for more pain and misery than all the wars of history put together.

The scientific study of animals has played a dismal role in this tragedy. The scientific community has used its growing knowledge of animals mainly to manipulate their lives more efficiently in the service of human industry. Yet this same knowledge has demonstrated beyond reasonable doubt that farm animals are sentient beings, with intricate social relations and sophisticated psychological patterns. They may not be as intelligent as us, but they certainly know pain, fear and loneliness. They too can suffer, and they too can be happy.

It is high time we take these scientific findings to heart, because as human power keeps growing, our ability to harm or benefit other animals grows with it. For 4 billion years, life on Earth was governed by natural selection. Now it is governed increasingly by human intelligent design. Biotechnology, nanotechnology° and artificial intelligence will soon enable humans to reshape living beings in radical new ways, which will redefine the very meaning of life. When we come to design this brave new world, we should take into account the welfare of all sentient beings, and not just of Homo sapiens.

nanotechnology: the science of manipulating matter on a very small (atomic or molecular) scale.

Understanding the Text

1. How are domesticated animals treated on industrial farms?
2. What is Darwinian evolution? What is there about industrial animal farming that contradicts its basic principles?
3. How do most industrial farm animals reproduce?

Reflection and Response

4. Harari describes the origin and fate of the chicken — from rare to most widespread bird on the planet. Recount his story, reflect on what it illustrates, and comment on the role it plays in his argument.
5. How and why does Harari use evolutionary psychology to help support his argument?
6. According to Harari, what role does science play in causing the pain and misery suffered by industrial farm animals?

7. Describe your personal reaction to the staggering statistics offered by Harari. Why do you think you have the reactions that you do? What does your reaction say about your values?

Making Connections

8. Harari claims that industrial farming might be the worst crime in history and is a pressing ethical concern. Consider the arguments made by Peter Singer ("Equality for Animals?" p. 212), Barbara Kingsolver ("You Can't Run Away on Harvest Day," p. 218), and Bill McKibben ("The Only Way to Have a Cow," p. 229). To what extent do they each agree with Harari? Compare how they support their positions — the kinds of reasons they provide, the assumptions they rely on, what they count as evidence, and what they each emphasize.

9. Margaret Mead ("The Changing Significance of Food," p. 200) credits the industrial revolution with increasing our capacity to produce food such that we can now feed the world's population. She argues that this changes the moral obligations of those who live in countries where food is abundant. Harari argues that this technological capability has brought with it other ethical dilemmas — most notably the welfare of all animals, not just humans. Drawing on three or four other sources from this book, make an argument for how you think we should weigh these various ethical obligations. For example, you may want to consider Blake Hurst's view of the industrial revolution ("The Omnivore's Delusion," p. 240) in your analysis.

10. Harari invokes Peter Singer's book, a later version of which is excerpted here ("Equality for Animals?" p. 212). Look up Peter Singer and research the ways in which his work is cited and used. You may want to read through his Web site or view some of his lectures that are available online. How is Harari building on his ideas? What do you think Singer would say in response to Harari's explanation of the history of animal-human relations?

The Omnivore's Delusion: Against the Agri-intellectuals

Blake Hurst

Blake Hurst has farmed for more than 30 years, first as a hog farmer and now as a grower of corn, soybeans, and flowers on his family farm in northwest Missouri. He also serves as president of the Missouri Farm Bureau. As a freelance writer, Hurst has published many articles on food and farming in the *Wall Street Journal*, the *New York Times*, *Wilson Quarterly*, and the *American*, among other periodicals. In this oft-quoted essay, originally published in 2009 in the *American* (the online magazine of the American Enterprise Institute), Hurst questions various ethical arguments against farming practices. He blasts the way intellectuals criticize industrial farming, arguing that their critiques are unfair and reliant on ignorance.

I'm dozing, as I often do on airplanes, but the guy behind me has been broadcasting nonstop for nearly three hours. I finally admit defeat and start some serious eavesdropping. He's talking about food, damning farming, particularly livestock farming, compensating for his lack of knowledge with volume.

I'm so tired of people who wouldn't visit a doctor who used a stethoscope instead of an MRI demanding that farmers like me use 1930s technology to raise food. Farming has always been messy and painful, and bloody and dirty. It still is.

But now we have to listen to self-appointed experts on airplanes frightening their seatmates about the profession I have practiced for more than 30 years. I'd had enough. I turned around and politely told the lecturer that he ought not believe everything he reads. He quieted and asked me what kind of farming I do. I told him, and when he asked if I used organic farming, I said no, and left it at that. I didn't answer with the first thought that came to mind, which is simply this: I deal in the real world, not superstitions, and unless the consumer absolutely forces my hand, I am about as likely to adopt organic methods as the *Wall Street Journal* is to publish their next edition by setting the type by hand.

He was a businessman, and I'm sure spends his days with spreadsheets, projections, and marketing studies. He hasn't used a slide rule in his career and wouldn't make projections with tea leaves or soothsayers. He does not blame witchcraft for a bad quarter, or expect the factory that makes his product to use steam power instead of electricity, or horses and wagons to deliver his products instead of trucks and trains. But he expects me to farm like my grandfather, and not incidentally, I suppose, to live like him as well. He thinks farmers are too stupid to farm sustainably, too cruel to treat their animals well, and too careless to worry about their communities, their health, and their families. I would not presume to criticize his car, or the size of his house, or the way he runs his business. But he is an expert about me, on the strength of one book, and is sharing that expertise with captive audiences every time he gets the chance. Enough, enough, enough.

Industrial Farming and Its Critics

Critics of "industrial farming" spend most of their time concerned with 5 the processes by which food is raised. This is because the results of organic production are so, well, troublesome. With the subtraction of every "unnatural" additive, molds, fungus, and bugs increase. Since it is difficult to sell a religion with so many readily quantifiable bad results, the trusty family farmer has to be thrown into the breach, saving the whole organic movement by his saintly presence, chewing on his straw, plodding along, at one with his environment, his community, his neighborhood. Except that some of the largest farms in the country are organic — and are giant organizations dependent upon lots of hired stoop labor doing the most backbreaking of tasks in order to save the sensitive conscience of my fellow passenger the merest whiff of pesticide contamination. They do not spend much time talking about that at the Whole Foods store.

The most delicious irony is this: the parts of farming that are the most "industrial" are the most likely to be owned by the kind of family farmers that elicit such a positive response from the consumer. Corn farms are almost all owned and managed by small family farmers. But corn farmers salivate at the thought of one more biotech breakthrough, use vast amounts of energy to increase production, and raise large quantities of an indistinguishable commodity to sell to huge corporations that turn that corn into thousands of industrial products.

Most livestock is produced by family farms, and even the poultry industry, with its contracts and vertical integration°, relies on family farms to contract for the production of the birds. Despite the obvious change in scale over time, family farms, like ours, still meet around the kitchen table, send their kids to the same small schools, sit in the same church pew, and belong to the same civic organizations our parents and grandparents did.

---

vertical integration: a style of management where different companies working on different parts of a process all have the same owner.

We may be industrial by some definition, but not our own. Reality is messier than it appears in the book my tormentor was reading, and farming more complicated than a simple morality play.

On the desk in front of me are a dozen books, all hugely critical of present-day farming. Farmers are often given a pass in these books, painted as either naïve tools of corporate greed, or economic nullities° forced into their present circumstances by the unrelenting forces of the twin grindstones of corporate greed and unfeeling markets. To the farmer on the ground, though, a farmer blessed with free choice and hard-won experience, the moral choices aren't quite so easy. Biotech crops actually cut the use of chemicals, and increase food safety. Are people who refuse to use them my moral superiors? Herbicides cut the need for tillage, which decreases soil erosion by millions of tons. The biggest environmental harm I have done as a farmer is the topsoil (and nutrients) I used to send down the Missouri River to the Gulf of Mexico before we began to practice no-till farming, made possible only by the use of herbicides. The combination of herbicides and genetically modified seed has made my farm more sustainable, not less, and actually reduces the pollution I send down the river.

> "Farming [is] more complicated than a simple morality play."

Finally, consumers benefit from cheap food. If you think they don't, just remember the headlines after food prices began increasing in 2007 and 2008, including the study by the Food and Agriculture Organization of the United Nations announcing that 50 million additional people are now hungry because of increasing food prices. Only "industrial farming" can possibly meet the demands of an increasing population and increased demand for food as a result of growing incomes.

So the stakes in this argument are even higher. Farmers can raise food 10 in different ways if that is what the market wants. It is important, though, that even people riding in airplanes know that there are environmental and food safety costs to whatever kind of farming we choose.

Pigs in a Pen

In his book *Dominion*, author Mathew Scully calls "factory farming" an "obvious moral evil so sickening and horrendous it would leave us ashen." Scully, a speechwriter for the second President Bush, can hardly

---

nullity: nothingness, nonentity.

be called a man of the left. Just to make sure the point is not lost, he quotes the conservative historian Paul Johnson a page later:

The rise of factory farming, whereby food producers cannot remain competitive except by subjecting animals to unspeakable deprivation, has hastened this process. The human spirit revolts at what we have been doing.

Arizona and Florida have outlawed pig gestation crates, and California recently passed, overwhelmingly, a ballot initiative doing the same. There is no doubt that Scully and Johnson have the wind at their backs, and confinement raising of livestock may well be outlawed everywhere. And only a person so callous as to have a spirit that cannot be revolted, or so hardened to any kind of morality that he could countenance an obvious moral evil, could say a word in defense of caging animals during their production. In the quote above, Paul Johnson is forecasting a move toward vegetarianism. But if we assume, at least for the present, that most of us will continue to eat meat, let me dive in where most fear to tread.

Lynn Niemann was a neighbor of my family's, a farmer with a vision. He began raising turkeys on a field near his house around 1956. They were, I suppose, what we would now call "free range" turkeys. Turkeys raised in a natural manner, with no roof over their heads, just gamboling around in the pasture, as God surely intended. Free to eat grasshoppers, and grass, and scratch for grubs and worms. And also free to serve as prey for weasels, who kill turkeys by slitting their necks and practicing exsanguination. Weasels were a problem, but not as much a threat as one of our typically violent early summer thunderstorms. It seems that turkeys, at least young ones, are not smart enough to come in out of the rain, and will stand outside in a downpour, with beaks open and eyes skyward, until they drown. One night Niemann lost 4,000 turkeys to drowning, along with his dream, and his farm.

Now, turkeys are raised in large open sheds. Chickens and turkeys raised for meat are not grown in cages. As the critics of "industrial farming" like to point out, the sheds get quite crowded by the time Thanksgiving rolls around and the turkeys are fully grown. And yes, the birds are bedded in sawdust, so the turkeys do walk around in their own waste. Although the turkeys don't seem to mind, this quite clearly disgusts the various authors I've read who have actually visited a turkey farm. But none of those authors, whose descriptions of the horrors of modern poultry production have a certain sameness, were there when Niemann picked up those 4,000 dead turkeys. Sheds are expensive, and it was easier to raise turkeys in open, inexpensive pastures. But that type of production really was hard on the turkeys. Protected from the weather and predators, today's turkeys may not be aware that they are a part of a morally reprehensible system.

Like most young people in my part of the world, I was a 4-H mem- 15 ber. Raising cattle and hogs, showing them at the county fair, and then sending to slaughter those animals that we had spent the summer feeding, washing, and training. We would then tour the packing house, where our friend was hung on a rail, with his loin eye measured and his carcass evaluated. We farm kids got an early start on dulling our moral sensibilities. I'm still proud of my win in the Atchison County Carcass competition of 1969, as it is the only trophy I have ever received. We raised the hogs in a shed, or farrowing (birthing) house. On one side were eight crates of the kind that the good citizens of California have outlawed. On the other were the kind of wooden pens that our critics would have us use, where the sow could turn around, lie down, and presumably act in a natural way. Which included lying down on my 4-H project, killing several piglets, and forcing me to clean up the mess when I did my chores before school. The crates protect the piglets from their mothers. Farmers do not cage their hogs because of sadism, but because dead pigs are a drag on the profit margin, and because being crushed by your mother really is an awful way to go. As is being eaten by your mother, which I've seen sows do to newborn pigs as well.

I warned you that farming is still dirty and bloody, and I wasn't kidding. So let's talk about manure. It is an article of faith amongst the agriintellectuals that we no longer use manure as fertilizer. To quote Dr. Michael Fox in his book *Eating with a Conscience*, "The animal waste is not going back to the land from which the animal feed originated." Or Bill McKibben, in his book *Deep Economy*, writing about modern livestock production: "But this concentrates the waste in one place, where instead of being useful fertilizer to spread on crop fields it becomes a toxic threat."

In my inbox is an email from our farm's neighbor, who raises thousands of hogs in close proximity to our farm, and several of my family members' houses as well. The email outlines the amount and chemical analysis of the manure that will be spread on our fields this fall, manure that will replace dozens of tons of commercial fertilizer. The manure is captured underneath the hog houses in cement pits, and is knifed into the soil after the crops are harvested. At no time is it exposed to erosion, and it is an extremely valuable resource, one which farmers use to its fullest extent, just as they have since agriculture began.

In the southern part of Missouri, there is an extensive poultry industry in areas of the state where the soil is poor. The farmers there spread the poultry litter on pasture, and the advent of poultry barns made cattle production possible in areas that used to be waste ground. The "industrial" poultry houses are owned by family farmers, who have then used the byproducts to produce beef in areas where cattle couldn't survive before. McKibben is certain that the contracts these farmers sign with companies like Tyson are unfair, and the farmers might agree. But they like those cows, so there is a waiting list for new chicken barns. In some areas, there is indeed more manure than available cropland. But the trend in the industry, thankfully, is toward a dispersion of animals and manure, as the value of the manure increases, and the cost of transporting the manure becomes prohibitive.

We Can't Change Nature

The largest producer of pigs in the United States has promised to gradually end the use of hog crates. The Humane Society promises to take their initiative drive to outlaw farrowing crates and poultry cages to more states. Many of the counties in my own state of Missouri have chosen to outlaw the building of confinement facilities. Barack Obama has been harshly critical of animal agriculture. We are clearly in the process of deciding that we will not continue to raise animals the way we do now. Because other countries may not share our sensibilities, we'll have to withdraw or amend free trade agreements to keep any semblance of a livestock industry.

We can do that, and we may be a better society for it, but we can't 20 change nature. Pigs will be allowed to "return to their mire," as Kipling had it, but they'll also be crushed and eaten by their mothers. Chickens will provide lunch to any number of predators, and some number of chickens will die as flocks establish their pecking order.

In recent years, the cost of producing pork dropped as farmers increased feed efficiency (the amount of feed needed to produce a pound of pork) by 20 percent. Free-range chickens and pigs will increase the price of food, using more energy and water to produce the extra grain required for the same amount of meat, and some people will go hungry. It is also instructive that the first company to move away from farrowing crates is the largest producer of pigs. Changing the way we raise animals will not necessarily change the scale of the companies involved in the industry. If we are about to require more expensive ways of producing food, the largest and most well-capitalized farms will have the least trouble adapting.

The Omnivores' Delusions

Michael Pollan, in an 8,000-word essay in the *New York Times Magazine*, took the expected swipes at animal agriculture. But his truly radical prescriptions had to do with raising of crops. Pollan, who seemed to be aware of the nitrogen problem in his book *The Omnivore's Dilemma*, left nuance behind, as well as the laws of chemistry, in his recommendations. The nitrogen problem is this: without nitrogen, we do not have life. Until we learned to produce nitrogen from natural gas early in the last century, the only way to get nitrogen was through nitrogen produced by plants called legumes, or from small amounts of nitrogen that are produced by lightning strikes. The amount of life the earth could support was limited by the amount of nitrogen available for crop production.

In his book, Pollan quotes geographer Vaclav Smil to the effect that 40 percent of the people alive today would not be alive without the ability to artificially synthesize nitrogen. But in his directive on food policy, Pollan damns agriculture's dependence on fossil fuels, and urges the president to encourage agriculture to move away from expensive and declining supplies of natural gas toward the unlimited sunshine that supported life, and agriculture, as recently as the 1940s. Now, why didn't I think of that?

Well, I did. I've raised clover and alfalfa for the nitrogen they produce, and half the time my land is planted to soybeans, another nitrogen-producing legume. Pollan writes as if all of his ideas are new, but my father tells of agriculture extension meetings in the late 1950s entitled "Clover and Corn, the Road to Profitability." Farmers know that organic farming was the default position of agriculture for thousands of years, years when hunger was just around the corner for even advanced societies. I use all the animal manure available to me, and do everything I can to reduce the amount of commercial fertilizers I use. When corn genetically modified to use nitrogen more efficiently enters the market, as it soon will, I will use it as well. But none of those things will completely replace commercial fertilizer.

Norman Borlaug, founder of the green revolution, estimates that the amount of nitrogen available naturally would only support a worldwide population of 4 billion souls or so. He further remarks that we would need another 5 billion cows to produce enough manure to fertilize our present crops with "natural" fertilizer. That would play havoc with global warming. And cows do not produce nitrogen from the air, but only from the forages they eat, so to produce more manure we will have to plant more forages. Most of the critics of industrial farming maintain the 25 contradictory positions that we should increase the use of manure as a fertilizer, and decrease our consumption of meat. Pollan would solve the problem with cover crops, planted after the corn crop is harvested, and with mandatory composting. Pollan should talk to some actual farmers before he presumes to advise a president.

Pollan tells of flying over the upper Midwest in the winter, and seeing the black, fallow soil. I suppose one sees what one wants to see, but we have not had the kind of tillage implement on our farm that would produce black soil in nearly 20 years. Pollan would provide our nitrogen by planting those black fields to nitrogen-producing cover crops after the cash crops are harvested. This is a fine plan, one that farmers have known about for generations. And sometimes it would even work. But not last year, as we finished harvest in November in a freezing rain. It is hard to think of a legume that would have done its thing between then and corn planting time. Plants do not grow very well in freezing weather, a fact that would evidently surprise Pollan.

And even if we could have gotten a legume established last fall, it would not have fixed any nitrogen before planting time. We used to plant corn in late May, plowing down our green manure and killing the first flush of weeds. But that meant the corn would enter its crucial growing period during the hottest, driest parts of the summer, and that soil erosion would be increased because the land was bare during drenching spring rains. Now we plant in early April, best utilizing our spring rains, and ensuring that pollination occurs before the dog days of August.

A few other problems come to mind. The last time I planted a cover crop, the clover provided a perfect habitat in early spring for bugs, bugs that I had to kill with an insecticide. We do not normally apply insecticides, but we did that year. Of course, you can provide nitrogen with legumes by using a longer crop rotation, growing clover one year and corn the next. But that uses twice as much water to produce a corn crop, and takes twice as much land to produce the same number of bushels. We are producing twice the food we did in 1960 on less land, and commercial nitrogen is one of the main reasons why. It may be that we decide we would rather spend land and water than energy, but Pollan never mentions that we are faced with that choice.

His other grand idea is mandatory household composting, with the compost delivered to farmers free of charge. Why not? Compost is a valuable soil amendment, and if somebody else is paying to deliver it to my farm, then bring it on. But it will not do much to solve the nitrogen problem. Household compost has somewhere between 1 and 5 percent nitrogen, and not all that nitrogen is available to crops the first year. Presently, we are applying about 150 pounds of nitrogen per acre to corn, and crediting about 40 pounds per acre from the preceding year's soybean crop. Let's assume a 5 percent nitrogen rate, or about 100 pounds of nitrogen per ton of compost. That would require 3,000 pounds of compost per acre. Or about 150,000 tons for the corn raised in our county. The average truck carries about 20 tons. Picture 7,500 trucks traveling from New York City to our small county here in the Midwest, delivering compost. Five million truckloads to fertilize the country's corn crop. Now, that would be a carbon footprint!

Pollan thinks farmers use commercial fertilizer because it is easier, 30 and because it is cheap. Pollan is right. But those are perfectly defensible reasons. Nitrogen quadrupled in price over the last several years, and farmers are still using it, albeit more cautiously. We are using GPS monitors on all of our equipment to ensure that we do not use too much, and our production of corn per pound of nitrogen is rapidly increasing. On our farm, we have increased yields about 50 percent during my career, while applying about the same amount of nitrogen we did when I began farming. That fortunate trend will increase even faster with the advent of new GMO hybrids. But as much as Pollan might desire it, even President Obama cannot reshuffle the chemical deck that nature has dealt. Energy may well get much more expensive, and peak oil production may have been reached. But food production will have a claim on fossil fuels long after we have learned how to use renewables and nuclear power to handle many of our other energy needs.

Farming and Connectedness

Much of farming is more "industrial," more technical, and more complex than it used to be. Farmers farm more acres, and are less close to the ground and their animals than they were in the past. Almost all critics of industrial agriculture bemoan this loss of closeness, this "connectedness," to use author Rod Dreher's term. It is a given in most of the writing about agriculture that the knowledge and experience of the organic farmer is what makes him so unique and so important. The "industrial farmer," on the other hand, is a mere pawn of Cargill, backed into his ignorant way of life by forces too large, too far from the farm, and too powerful to resist. Concern about this alienation, both between farmers and the land, and between consumers and their food supply, is what drives much of the literature about agriculture.

The distance between the farmer and what he grows has certainly increased, but, believe me, if we weren't closely connected, we wouldn't still be farming. It's important to our critics that they emphasize this alienation, because they have to ignore the "industrial" farmer's experience and knowledge to say the things they do about farming.

But farmers have reasons for their actions, and society should listen to them as we embark upon this reappraisal of our agricultural system. I use chemicals and diesel fuel to accomplish the tasks my grandfather used to do with sweat, and I use a computer instead of a lined notebook and a pencil, but I'm still farming the same land he did 80 years ago, and the fund of knowledge that our family has accumulated about our small part of Missouri is valuable. And everything I know and I have learned tells me this: we have to farm "industrially" to feed the world, and by using those "industrial" tools sensibly, we can accomplish that task and leave my grandchildren a prosperous and productive farm, while protecting the land, water, and air around us.

Understanding the Text

1. Why does Hurst think it is a bad idea to allow pigs free range to wander as they please?
2. What is the nitrogen problem?
3. Why does Hurst object to the way critics of industrial farming make their cases?

Reflection and Response

4. What is Hurst so angry about? How does he communicate this emotion in writing?
5. Hurst suggests that critics of "industrial farming" do not realize that they cannot have it "both ways" — organic and local. What evidence does he use to support his position? Does he make a good case?

Making Connections

6. How does Hurst position his argument in relation to ones made by Michael Pollan ("Eat Food: Food Defined," p. 10) and Bill McKibben ("The Only Way to Have a Cow," p. 229)? What are the fundamental differences in how they view the environmental impact of "industrial farming"? What moral principles do they each privilege? Is there any shared terrain?
7. Consider the arguments made by Hurst, David Biello ("Will Organic Food Fail to Feed the World?" p. 262), and Eliot Coleman ("Real Food, Real Farming," p. 266) and analyze the positions they take on the impact of organic farming. Explain the debate over organic versus commercially

grown food. Why do organic proponents support it? How does Hurst argue against their position? Which argument makes the most sense to you? Why? What does your position say about your values?

8. Compare Hurst's representation of the Green Revolution to those offered by at least two other authors in this book. Then, research the Green Revolution on your own and select three distinct perspectives on the revolution. Make a presentation that describes all three, and then explain which one you think is most compelling and why. Use at least three sources from this book and at least two other sources.

This Land Is Whose Land? Dispossession, Resistance, and Reform in the United States

Eric Holt-Giménez

Eric Holt-Giménez is an agroecologist who studies food systems and food policy. He received his PhD in environmental studies at the University of California, Santa Cruz, and has taught global ecology at various universities. Holt-Giménez worked directly with farmers in Central America and Mexico on sustainable development for twenty-five years before becoming the Executive Director of the Institute for Food and Development Policy (also known as Food First) and is the main author of the Food First publication *Food Rebellions: Crisis and the Hunger for Justice* (2009). Holt-Giménez is the author of many books and articles, including the academic essay included in this collection. This essay exposes the injustices caused by the transition of agrarian lands from small farmers to large corporations and makes suggestions for possible policy reforms to counter the growing inequities he describes.

Introduction: Land, Race and the Agrarian Crisis

The disastrous effects of widespread land grabbing and land concentration sweeping the globe do not affect all farmers equally. The degree of vulnerability to these threats is highest for smallholders, women and people of color — the ones who grow, harvest, process and prepare most of the world's food.

International market forces have invaded every aspect of economic and social life. The wholesale privatization of public goods has concentrated immense power in the hands of global monopolies and introduced new layers of inequality into our food systems. The destruction of smallholder agriculture in the Global South° has sent millions of rural people on perilous migrations in search of work where they often enter low-paying jobs in the food system. They are pushed to underserved neighborhoods of color where labor abuse, diet-related disease and food insecurity are the norm.

At the same time, despite record agricultural profits, farming communities in the US heartland are steadily emptying out, reeling from unemployment and the environmental consequences of 70 years of industrial

---

Global South: the nations of Africa, Central and Latin America, and most of Asia, many of which have severely limited or less-developed resources.

agriculture.[1] Though surrounded by former peasant farmers (now turned farmworkers), many older farmers wonder who will farm the land when they are gone. But young, beginning and immigrant farmers find it too costly to access land.[2]

Big farms in the US are getting bigger. Small farms are getting smaller. The same structural adjustment policies and free trade agreements that devastate the livelihoods of farmers in the Global South are steadily re-shaping the agrarian landscape of the United States.

Land Grabs and the New Agrarian Transition

The land grabs occurring in the Third World are the tip of the iceberg of   5
a long process of capitalist reconfiguration of land and resources known as the *agrarian transition*. At the dawn of the Industrial Revolution, this meant mobilizing resources from the countryside to the city to subsidize industry with cheap food and cheap labor — largely accomplished by destroying the commons and dispossessing peasant farmers. The agrar-ian transition has gone through many permutations° since then, but generally kept its anti-commons and anti-smallholder thrust.

Today's agrarian transition is about the countryside's role in the rise of agri-food monopolies, the intensification of extractive industries and the emerging dominance of international finance capital. A commodities boom within the industrial grain-livestock/agro-food complex[3] coupled with a global crisis of capital accumulation (too many goods and too few buyers) have made land a hot investment offering global investors an opportunity to treat it "like gold with yield."[4] Land is concentrating in fewer and fewer hands, dispossessing millions as it pads corporate portfolios.

The World Trade Organization, the World Bank, the International Monetary Fund, and trade agreements like the North American and Central American Free Trade Agreements and the Trans Pacific Partnership and Trans Atlantic Free Trade Agreement (under negotiation) facilitate the modern agrarian transition on a global scale. The USDA, the Farm Bill, the deregulation of finance capital and the gutting of government antitrust laws are bringing the agrarian transition home to the US.

Land Dispossession in Historical Perspective

Historically, by the time land is lost, a process of political and economic restructuring has already destroyed much of the public sphere. Farmers' room for maneuver is greatly reduced, thus giving free reign to those

permutations: variations.

with market power to bring land under their control. Land is lost after civic and human rights have already been systematically trampled upon. Dispossession then takes place through a combination of coercion and the market.

Military force opened the door for white settlers across the North American continent. Before being dispossessed of their territories, Native Americans were disenfranchised° of their human right to life. The disenfranchisement and ensuing loss of land for farmers of Mexican origin following the Mexican-American wars, and the appropriation of Japanese-American land through mass internment during WWII are further examples of coerced land grabs.

After the US Civil War, the Reconstruction Amendments (13, 14 & 15) 10 and the Freedman's Bureau helped usher in a remarkable period of civic participation and agricultural prosperity among former slave communities. But Klan° violence and the Jim Crow laws° enacted in southern states disenfranchised African American farmers, forcing many into chain gangs, sharecropping and wage slavery. In spite of this, by 1910 they had acquired 15 million acres "without benefit of the Homestead Act and in the face of great hostility and violence."[5] As agriculture modernized, the USDA consistently denied Black farmers "loans, information and access to programs essential to survival in a capital intensive farming structure."[6] This left them unprotected in the face of cyclical economic crises, leading to massive land loss in the 1960s. They were the first farmers to lose their land in the farm crises of the 1970–80s as well. The 1999 *Pigford vs Glickman* class action lawsuit filed against the USDA testifies to the ongoing discrimination against African American farmers who now farm less than a million acres of land.[7]

The New Face of US Farming

According to the USDA 2012 Census of Agriculture, of the country's 2.1 million farmers only 8 percent are farmers of color (Native American, Asian, Latino or African American), though their share is growing, particularly among Latinos, who now number over 67,000 farmers. The percentage of women farmers is 14 percent. Three-quarters of them earn less than $10,000 in annual sales. Seventy-five percent of farms in the US

disenfranchised: stripped of one's power, including the right to vote or have a say in one's destiny.
Klan: short for Ku Klux Klan, a secret organization that acted to suppress the rights of black Americans and was very active after the Civil War.
Jim Crow laws: local and state laws that enforced racial segregation in the southern United States; named after a character in minstrel shows.

have sales of under $50K, but the numbers of high-income mega farms are increasing. The percentage of farmers under 35 years old has declined 8 percent since the last census while the number of older farmers has increased. The average age for a farmer in the US is now 58 years old. While these statistics paint the picture of a stereotypically white, male, aging farmer, they belie a growing movement of young, predominantly female and non-white beginning farmers.

The Green Revolution is a classic case of market-based dispossession affecting Third World and US farmers alike. This publicly-funded campaign to "feed the world" took the genetic material from traditional varieties developed over thousands of years to produce commercial hybrids. Farmers in the Global South took out credit to buy back their repackaged genetic material, as well as the fertilizers and pesticides needed to grow these crops as monocultures. The Green Revolution gained momentum in the 1970s just as US farmers were encouraged to plant "fencerow to fencerow" to save the world from hunger. The result was global overproduction, the fall of commodity prices and staggering debt in the Third World as well as in the US farm sector.[8] Consequently, millions of farmers were forced out of farming.

Land Justice: From Access to Reform

Today, family farmers are fighting to hang on to their farms and aspiring farmers are struggling to access land. Their prospects could not be worse. Unregulated market forces — in commodities and land — are both a means for dispossession and a barrier to entry. Because of the structural racism in our food system, immigrants and people of color are at a particular disadvantage.

"Because of the structural racism in our food system, immigrants and people of color are at a particular disadvantage."

New rural and urban initiatives for farmland access, farm protection and sustainable, equitable food systems are springing up across the US. They provide hope that another food system is possible. But do they have the potential to confront the modern agrarian transition?

The movement for sustainable agricultural land trusts is gaining ground. Over 1,700 state, local and national organizations manage 47 million acres in trusts and easements. Over 60 percent conserve agricultural land.[9] "Farm incubators" provide training and services to help new farmers enter farming. Promising state legislative proposals seek to protect farmland from urban sprawl. Farm cooperative federations and legal services foundations in the southern US are working to protect African American farmers. Stock sharing options and ownership transfer programs are putting farmworkers in control of the land they work. Community land trusts are beginning to address urban agriculture. Many food policy councils work to make idle urban and peri-urban° land available for farming. Following the Occupy movement°, small land occupations are spreading. Indigenous and rural resistance to fracking and land-grabbing projects like the Keystone pipeline° is growing.

Set against the powerful array of international markets, monopolies and institutions of the agrarian transition, land trusts attempt to carve out "niches" in the global land market. However, very few work with underserved communities. While they serve as important sociopolitical and environmental references, ensuring equitable land access and viable rural livelihoods in the United States — by definition — is beyond the scope and the pocket book of niche markets. Rather, structural changes are needed in order for these important efforts to become the norm rather than the alternative. Their future depends on *agrarian reform*.

The call for agrarian reform is not new in the United States. In 1973 the National Coalition for Land Reform held the First National Conference on Land Reform.[10] Participants from Appalachia, the South, the Northern Plains, Midwest, New England and indigenous lands, as well as from the organic farming sector, the coops, the land trusts and farmworker organizations, called for land reform. These diverse actors discussed the creation of a National Land Reform Act to address poverty, privilege and the racial and class inequities determining land distribution. They proposed a progressive land tax structure, public land banks, trusts and funding mechanisms, as well as supporting institutions for new farmers. In short, the Act demanded a set of accountable *public* policies and mechanisms to support all of the things that today's land niche initiatives struggle to do privately.

Overcoming the injustices of the agrarian transition will hinge on whether or not today's disparate efforts can move the land struggle from the global market to the public sphere. It will also depend on whether or not they can collectively address the inequities that hold the present system in place. It requires building a broad-based, national movement for land justice.

---

peri-urban: an area immediately next to an urban area; areas between urban and rural spaces.
Occupy movement: movement to protest social and economic inequality that began when activists occupied Liberty Square on Wall Street in New York City's financial district in 2011.
Keystone pipeline: oil pipeline system between Canada and the United States that is hotly disputed because of potential environmental damage.

Notes

1. Kusmin, Lorin. *Rural America at a Glance*, 2013 Edition. United States Department of Agriculture Economic Research Service, Accessed April 16, 2014. http://www.ers.usda.gov/publications/eb-economic-brief/eb24.aspx# .U072hfIdWN2.

2. Brown, Tanya. "Access to Land, Capital Biggest Obstacle for Beginning Farmers." USDA Blog. United States Department of Agriculture, Accessed April 16, 2014. http://blogs.usda.gov/2013/01/31/access-to-land-capital -biggest-obstacle-for-beginning-farmers/.

3. Weis, T. *The Ecological Hoofprint: The Global Burden of Industrial Livestock*. London: Zed Books, 2013.

4. Fairbairn, Madeleine. "'Like gold with yield': Evolving intersections between farmland and finance." *Journal of Peasant Studies* (In Press).

5. Browne, Robert. "The South." In *The Peoples Land*. Peter Barnes, Ed. National Coalition for Land Reform. Rodale Press. Emmaus. 1975.

6. Daniel, Peter. *Dispossession: Discrimination Against African American Farmers in the Age of Civil Rights*. University of North Carolina Press. Chapel Hill. 2013.

7. Mittal, Anuradha and Joan Powell. *The Last Plantation*. Food First Backgrounder. Vol. 6. No.1. Food First. Oakland. 2000.

8. Strange, Marty. *Family Farming: A New Economic Vision*. Food First Books. Oakland. 1988.

9. Chang, Katie. *2010 National Land Trust Census Report: A Look at Voluntary Land Conservation in America*. Land Trust Alliance/Lincoln Institute of Land Policy. 2011. Accessed April 11, 2014. http://www.landtrustalliance.org/land -trusts/land-trust-census/2010-final-report.

10. *The People's Land: A Reader on Land Reform in the United States*. National Coalition for Land Reform. Peter Barnes, Ed. Rodale Press. 1975.

Understanding the Text

1. Who is most negatively affected by the concentration of farmland into the hands of a few powerful monopolies?

2. What happened in the Global South that Holt-Giménez is arguing will also reshape agriculture in the United States?

3. What is the agrarian transition?

4. What is global accumulation, and how is it connected to the global food crisis?

Reflection and Response

5. Why is Holt-Giménez concerned about "coerced land grabs" (par. 9)? Why does he describe them this way? What does the phrase suggest about those who are acquiring the land he is discussing?

6. What was the Green Revolution? Why does Holt-Giménez critique it?

7. According to Holt-Giménez, how does structural racism affect the food system? How is it connected to his call for land justice?

8. Holt-Giménez concludes that "Overcoming the injustices of the agrarian transition will hinge on whether or not today's disparate efforts can move the land struggle from the global market to the public sphere" (par. 17). Do you think he is hopeful that this will actually happen? Do you think it is likely that the public sphere will emerge as a place where we tackle the problem of global food production and the inequities in the current system? Why or why not?

Making Connections

9. Holt-Giménez and Raj Patel ("Stuffed and Starved," p. 173) both conduct research on global food systems as part of the Institute for Food and Development Policy (also known as Food First), which was founded in 1975 by Frances Moore Lappé ("Biotechnology Isn't the Key to Feeding the World," p. 294). What moral principles do these three authors share? What ethical obligations do they argue we have? Who else in this book would share their views?

10. Go online and research Food First (www.foodfirst.org). Examine the Web site and the kinds of work the institute does. What cause does it promote? How does this organization bring together research, education, and action? What ethical principles does it promote? What kinds of actions does Food First suggest that students like you can do to help create change? Develop a presentation about Food First that would appeal to your peers and offer ideas for concrete actions they could take if they wanted to promote Food First's objectives.

11. Holt-Giménez mentions many trade agreements, laws, and regulatory actions that have shaped the global food system and U.S. agriculture. Select one, research it, and evaluate its impact on our food choices. How does it impact the global food system? Are there local effects in your community that you can trace? You may want to look at what other authors in this book say about the agreement, law, policy, or action you have chosen.

Bhaskar Dutta/Getty Images

5

What Is the Future of Food?

We never know what the future will bring, but we do know that we will need food. In this last chapter, authors weigh in on what they think will influence the future of food. They identify problems that will remain at the forefront — climate change, global hunger, labor injustice, and sustainability, to name a few. They also discuss potential changes that might lessen the negative impact of food production on the environment and that might actually promote global environmental sustainability. Still, even as we think of solutions to existing concerns, new problems will inevitably emerge.

While David Biello and Eliot Coleman suggest ways to pursue food production that promote environmental sustainability and health, Robert Paarlberg complicates their views with his critique of the organic food movement and argues for a different kind of emphasis on solving world hunger. Together, they reveal the crisis of values that underlies much of the debate over organic versus conventional farming and the related environmental and health impacts.

Natasha Bowens, Richard Marosi, and Frances Moore Lappé further expand and question our understanding of the future of food by examining social, economic, and political inequities that affect food production and distribution. Bowens looks at the economic, social, and political impact of food injustice on peoples of color. Marosi investigates the exploitation of laborers on the Mexican farms that supply much of the U.S. produce we eat. And Lappé suggests that a "scarcity of democracy" — and not food — is the real culprit behind world hunger. Together, then, they suggest that we have a lot of work to do to reduce social and political inequities that plague the global food system.

Jonathan Foley and Robert Kunzig both look to the future of food by presenting ideas about ways science can play a role. Drawing on the scientific research of a team of international experts, Foley presents a five-step plan for global food production that he argues will dramatically

photo: Bhaskar Dutta/Getty Images

increase food yields while also decreasing environmental damage. And Kunzig ventures into the world of synthetic food, telling the story of lab meat and suggesting ways that scientific advancements might change the future of food, perhaps even our very definition of what food is.

This chapter thus demonstrates that the future of food will be no less complex than the present. The authors also reveal that the ways we define food and determine its purpose will continue to change as other aspects of culture, science, business, politics, and society change. The factors that help determine what foods are available and what foods we choose to eat will continue to evolve, too.

The readings in this chapter, then, suggest as many questions as they answer. Here are some to consider: Is the future of food going to be organic? Will it rely on conventional, industrial approaches? Or will we adopt hybrid approaches? What ethical principles will guide food policy in the future? What kinds of moral choices will individuals make? Will they see food choices as moral choices more or less than they do now? What roles will innovative approaches and new technologies play in feeding the population? Should we focus on futuristic, potentially expensive, inventions or return to the basics? What roles will corporations and industrial farming play in the future of food? What roles will small-scale farming and local businesses play? Will worker justice, fair labor practices, and the impacts of food production on historically oppressed groups be considered? Will democracy emerge as a positive force in bringing about food equity? Will people care more or less about global hunger in the future than they do now? Will the global hunger crisis ever become a thing of the past? Will we succeed in finding a way to feed the world while sustaining the planet at the same time? While these questions have yet to be answered, the readings in this chapter offer food for thought and ways for us to think critically about the future of food.

Will Organic Food Fail to Feed the World?

David Biello

David Biello is a journalist and the associate editor of *Scientific American*. He also writes for *Yale Environment 360* and hosts the podcast *60-Second Earth*. He covers environmental issues in the United States and internationally. In 2009 he won the Internews Earth Journalism Award for his series *A Guide to Carbon Capture and Storage*. He continues to cover international climate negotiations and worked with Detroit Public Television on *Beyond the Light Switch*, a documentary on the future of electricity that won the DuPont-Columbia University award for journalistic excellence. In this article, first published in *Scientific American* in 2012, Biello suggests a hybrid approach to food production that takes environmental impact and yield into account.

Food for hungry mouths, feed for animals headed to the slaughterhouse, fiber for clothing, and even, in some cases, fuel for vehicles — all derive from global agriculture. As a result, in the world's temperate climes human agriculture has supplanted 70 percent of grasslands, 50 percent of savannas, and 45 percent of temperate forests. Farming is also the leading cause of deforestation in the tropics and one of the *largest sources of greenhouse gas emissions*, a major contributor to the ongoing maul of species known as the sixth extinction, and a perennial source of nonrenewable groundwater mining and water pollution.

To restrain the environmental impact of agriculture as well as produce more wholesome foods, some farmers have turned to so-called organic techniques. This type of farming is meant to minimize environmental and human health impacts by avoiding the use of synthetic fertilizers, chemical pesticides, and hormones or antibiotic treatments for livestock, among other tactics. But the use of industrial technologies, particularly synthetic nitrogen fertilizer, has fed the swelling human population during the last century. Can organic agriculture feed a world of nine billion people?

In a bid to bring clarity to what has too often been an emotional debate, environmental scientists at McGill University in Montreal and the University of Minnesota performed an analysis of 66 studies comparing conventional and organic methods across 34 different crop species. "We found that, overall, organic yields are considerably lower than conventional yields," explains McGill's Verena Seufert, lead author of the study to be published in *Nature* on April 26. (*Scientific American* is part of Nature Publishing Group.) "But, this yield difference varies across different conditions. When farmers apply best management practices, organic systems, for example, perform relatively better."

In particular, organic agriculture delivers just 5 percent less yield in rain-watered legume crops, such as alfalfa or beans, and in perennial crops, such as fruit trees. But when it comes to major cereal crops, such as corn or wheat, and vegetables, such as broccoli, conventional methods delivered more than 25 percent more yield.

The key limit to further yield increases via organic methods appears 5 to be nitrogen — large doses of synthetic fertilizer can keep up with high demand from crops during the growing season better than the slow release from compost, manure, or nitrogen-fixing cover crops. Of course, the cost of using 171 million metric tons of synthetic nitrogen fertilizer is paid in dead zones at the mouths of many of the world's rivers. These anoxic zones result from nitrogen-rich runoff promoting algal blooms that then die and, in decomposing, suck all the oxygen out of surrounding waters. "To address the problem of [nitrogen] limitation and to produce high yields, organic farmers should use best management practices, supply more organic fertilizers, or grow legumes or perennial crops," Seufert says.

In fact, more knowledge would be key to any effort to boost organic farming or its yields. Conventional farming requires knowledge of how to manage what farmers know as inputs — synthetic fertilizer, chemical pesticides, and the like — as well as fields laid out precisely via global-positioning systems. Organic farmers, on the other hand, must learn to manage an entire ecosystem geared to producing food — controlling pests through biological means, using the waste from animals to fertilize fields, and even growing one crop amidst another. "Organic farming is a very knowledge-intensive farming system," Seufert notes. An organic farmer "needs to create a fertile soil that provides sufficient nutrients at the right time when the crops need them. The same is true for pest management."

But the end result is a healthier soil, which may prove vital in efforts to make it more resilient in the face of climate change as well as conserve it. Organic soils, for example, retain water better than those farms that employ conventional methods. "You use a lot more water [in irrigation] because the soil doesn't have the capacity to retain the water you use," noted farmer Fred Kirschenmann, president of Stone Barns Center for Food and Agriculture at the "Feeding the World While the Earth Cooks" event at the New America Foundation in Washington, D.C., on April 12 [, 2012].

At the same time, a still-growing human population requires more food, which has led some to propose further intensifying conventional methods of applying fertilizer and pesticides to specially bred crops, enabling either a second Green Revolution or improved yields from farmlands currently under cultivation. Crops genetically modified to endure drought may also play a role as well as efforts to develop perennial versions of annual staple crops, such as wheat, which could help reduce environmental impacts and improve soil. "Increasing salt, drought, or heat tolerance of our existing crops can move them a little but not a lot," said biologist Nina Fedoroff of Pennsylvania State University at the New America event. "That won't be enough."

And breeding new perennial versions of staple crops would require compressing millennia of crop improvements that resulted in the high-yielding wheat varieties of today, such as the dwarf wheat created by breeder Norman Borlaug and his colleagues in the 1950s, into a span of years while changing the fundamental character of wheat from an annual crop to a perennial one. Then there is the profit motive. "The private sector is not likely to embrace an idea like perennial crop seeds, which do not require the continued purchase of seeds and thus do not provide a very good source of profit," Seufert notes.

> "The world already produces 22 trillion calories annually via agriculture, enough to provide more than 3,000 calories to every person on the planet. The food problem is one of distribution and waste."

Regardless, the world already produces 22 trillion calories annually via agriculture, enough to provide more than 3,000 calories to every person on the planet. The food problem is one of distribution and waste — whether the latter is food spoilage during harvest, in storage, or even after purchase. According to the Grocery Manufacturers Association, in the U.S. alone, 215 meals per person go to waste annually. [10]

"Since the world already produces more than enough food to feed everyone well, there are other important considerations" besides yield, argues ecologist Catherine Badgley of the University of Michigan, who also compared yields from organic and conventional methods in a 2006 study that found similar results. Those range from environmental impacts of various practices to the number of people employed in farming. As it stands, conventional agriculture relies on cheap energy, cheap labor, and other unsustainable practices. "Anyone who thinks we will be using Roundup [a herbicide] in eight [thousand] to 10,000 years is foolish," argued organic evangelist Jeff Moyer, farm director of the Rodale Institute, at the New America Foundation event.

But there is unlikely to be a simple solution. Instead the best farming practices will vary from crop to crop and place to place. Building healthier soils, however, will be key everywhere. "Current conventional agriculture is one of the major threats to the environment and degrades the very natural resources it depends on. We thus need to change the way we produce our food," Seufert argues. "Given the current precarious situation of agriculture, we should assess many alternative management systems, including conventional, organic, other agro-ecological, and possibly hybrid systems to identify the best options to improve the way we produce our food."

Understanding the Text

1. What are some of the negative impacts of conventional farming methods that Biello names?
2. What did environment scientists at McGill University and the University of Minnesota find in their comparison study of conventional and organic farming methods?

Reflection and Response

3. What makes organic farming a "very knowledge-intensive" system? What are the benefits of this? What are its drawbacks?
4. What kind of hybrid approach to food production is suggested by Biello? What evidence does he present to support his argument in favor of this approach?

Making Connections

5. Biello and Margaret Mead ("The Changing Significance of Food," p. 200) both argue that we produce enough food to feed the world, but we fail to do so. Compare the evidence they each present and the solutions they recommend. Taken together, what do they suggest about the future of food?
6. What concrete ways does Biello suggest we use to fight global hunger problems? Which authors in this collection would applaud his approach? Which would critique it? Where do you stand? Which positions do you find more compelling? Why? Use textual evidence to support your response.

Real Food, Real Farming

Eliot Coleman

Eliot Coleman is a farmer, author, and longtime proponent of organic farming. He has written extensively about it, publishing many articles and the books *The New Organic Grower* (1989), *Four Season Harvest* (1992), and *Winter Harvest Handbook* (2009). He and his wife maintain an experimental market garden called Four Season Farm in Maine that is recognized internationally as a model of small-scale sustainable agriculture. Coleman first opened the original incarnation of this experimental farm in 1970, and he continues to create new innovations and redesign his tools and methods. While he writes and lectures on the subject of organic farming and sustainable agriculture, he continues to improve and refine his craft. In the selection here, he posits that as the term "organic" has become big business and is regulated by the United States Department of Agriculture, it has lost its meaning. He argues that we need to think beyond "organic" and demand "real" food.

New ideas, especially those that directly challenge an established orthodoxy,° follow a similar path. First, the orthodoxy says the new idea is rubbish. Then the orthodoxy attempts to minimize the new idea's increasing appeal. Finally, when the new idea proves unstoppable, the orthodoxy tries to claim the idea as its own. This is precisely the path organic food production has followed. First, the organic pioneers were ridiculed. Then, as evidence of the benefits of organic farming became more obvious to more people, mainstream chemical agriculture actively condemned organic ideas as not feasible. Now that the food-buying public has become increasingly enthusiastic about organically grown foods, the food industry has moved to take it over. Toward that end the U.S. Department of Agriculture's definition of "organic" is tailored to meet the marketing needs of organizations that have no connection to the agricultural integrity organic once represented. We now need to ask whether we want to be content with an "organic" food option that places the marketing concerns of corporate America ahead of nutrition, flavor, and social benefits to customers.

When I started as an organic grower in 1966, organic was a way of thinking rather than a "profit center." The decision to farm organically was a statement of faith in the wisdom of the natural world and the nutritional superiority of properly cultivated food. It was obvious that

orthodoxy: generally accepted belief.

good farming and exceptional food only resulted from the care and nurturing practiced by the good farmer.

The initial development of organic farming during the first half of the twentieth century arose from the gut feelings of farmers who were trying to reconcile the biological successes they saw in their own fields with the chemical dogma the agricultural science-of-the-moment was preaching. The farmers came to very different conclusions from those of the academic agronomists. The farmers worked on developing agricultural techniques that harmonized with the direction in which their "unscientific" conclusions were leading them. Their goals were to grow the most nutritious food possible while, simultaneously, protecting the soil for future generations.

The development and refinement of those biologically based agricultural practices continues today. It's what makes this farming adventure so compelling. Each year I hope to do things better than I did last year because I will know Nature's systems better. But my delight in the intricacies of the natural world — my adventure into an ever-deeper appreciation of the soil-plant-animal nutrition cycle and how to optimize it — is not acceptable to the homogenized mentality of mass marketing. The food giants that have taken over "organic" want a simplistic list of

> " 'Industrial organic' is now dead as a meaningful synonym for the highest quality food."

ingredients so they can do organic-by-the-numbers. They are derisive about what they label "belief systems," and they are loath to acknowledge that more farmer commitment is involved in producing real food than any number of approved inputs can encompass.

The transition of "organic" from small farm to big business is now 5 upon us. Although getting toxic chemicals out of agriculture is an improvement we can all applaud, it only removes the negatives. The government standards are based on what not to do rather than on what to do. The positive focus, enhancing the biological quality of the food produced, is nowhere to be seen. The government standards are administered through the USDA, whose director said when introducing them, "Organic food does not mean it is superior, safer or more healthy than conventional food." Well, I still agree with the old-time organic pioneers. I believe that properly grown food is superior, safer, and healthier. I also believe national certification bureaucracies are only necessary when food is grown by strangers in faraway places rather than by neighbors you know.

In my opinion, "industrial organic" is now dead as a meaningful synonym for the highest quality food. Those of us who still care need to identify not only that our food is grown to higher, more considered standards but also that it is much fresher because it is grown by a local farmer. The sign at the entrance to our farm says "REAL FOOD — REAL FARMING." RealFood° soils are nourished, as in the natural world, with farm-derived organic matter and mineral particles from ground rock. Green manures and cover crops are included within broadly based crop rotations. A "plant positive" rather than "pest negative" philosophy is followed, focusing on correcting the cause of problems (strengthening the plant through optimum growing conditions to prevent pests) rather than treating symptoms (killing the pests that prey on weak plants). Livestock are raised outdoors on grass-based pasture systems to the fullest extent possible. RealFood identifies local growers who want to emphasize the beneficial soil-improving and plant-strengthening practices they do use, rather than just being content with rejecting the poisonous practices they don't use. RealFood is a concept that recaptures and continues the aspiration towards an ideal natural systems agriculture that inspired the original organic pioneers many years ago.

RealFood: food that is locally grown and unprocessed, and of exceptional quality.

Understanding the Text

1. What is "organic" food? How does the USDA define it? How would Coleman define it?

2. Why does Coleman argue that we need to go beyond "organic"?

Reflection and Response

3. What are the benefits of seeing "organic" as a way of thinking? What do we lose when we regulate it? Are there potential gains that Coleman does not consider? Explain.

4. Does Coleman seem optimistic about the future of food? Explain your answer using specific textual evidence.

5. What does Coleman mean by "RealFood"? Does demanding RealFood seem like a realistic goal? Consider your own food choices and food options in your response. Is it in your reach to make such demands?

Making Connections

6. How does Coleman describe the relationship between scientific knowledge and the experiences of real farmers? What conflicts does he describe? How

does his representation of this relationship differ from the one offered by Blake Hurst ("The Omnivore's Delusion," p. 240)? Explain, using specific textual evidence from both essays.

7. What does Coleman suggest as priorities for the future of food production? What significant values and beliefs does he share with Jonathan Foley ("Can We Feed the World and Sustain the Planet?," p. 297) and with Barbara Kingsolver ("You Can't Run Away on Harvest Day," p. 218)? How might these beliefs be used to develop new practices and/or concrete policy changes?

Attention Whole Foods Shoppers

Robert Paarlberg

Robert Paarlberg is a professor of political science at Wellesley College and an adjunct professor of public policy at the John F. Kennedy School of Government at Harvard University. He conducts research on public policy, with a specific interest in international food and agriculture policy. His current research examines national policy responses to obesity and climate change, and he is particularly interested in the relationship between the failure of democratic governments to take action on such issues in the face of modern views of personal freedom and material abundance. He is the author of many scholarly articles and books, including *Food Politics: What Everyone Needs to Know* (2010). In this essay published in *Foreign Policy* in 2010, he draws connections between personal ideals about food and larger global realities of world hunger. He argues that we should prioritize finding effective ways to address world hunger over ideals that emphasize eating "organic, local, and slow" food.

From Whole Foods recyclable cloth bags to Michelle Obama's organic White House garden, modern eco-foodies are full of good intentions. We want to save the planet. Help local farmers. Fight climate change — and childhood obesity, too. But though it's certainly a good thing to be thinking about global welfare while chopping our certified organic onions, the hope that we can help others by changing our shopping and eating habits is being wildly oversold to Western consumers. Food has become an elite preoccupation in the West, ironically, just as the most effective ways to address hunger in poor countries have fallen out of fashion.

Helping the world's poor feed themselves is no longer the rallying cry it once was. Food may be today's cause célèbre, but in the pampered West, that means trendy causes like making food "sustainable" — in other words, organic, local, and slow. Appealing as that might sound, it is the wrong recipe for helping those who need it the most. Even our understanding of the global food problem is wrong these days, driven too much by the single issue of international prices. In April 2008, when the cost of rice for export had tripled in just six months and wheat reached its highest price in 28 years, a *New York Times* editorial branded this a "World Food Crisis." World Bank president Robert Zoellick warned that high food prices would be particularly damaging in poor countries, where "there is no margin for survival." Now that international rice prices are down 40 percent from their peak and wheat prices have fallen by more than half, we too quickly conclude that the crisis is over. Yet 850 million people in poor countries were chronically undernourished before the 2008 price spike, and the number is even larger now, thanks in part to last year's global recession. This is the real food crisis we face.

It turns out that food prices on the world market tell us very little about global hunger. International markets for food, like most other international markets, are used most heavily by the well-to-do, who are far from hungry. The majority of truly undernourished people — 62 percent, according to the U.N. Food and Agriculture Organization — live in either Africa or South Asia, and most are small farmers or rural landless laborers living in the countryside of Africa and South Asia. They are significantly shielded from global price fluctuations both by the trade policies of their own governments and by poor roads and infrastructure. In Africa, more than 70 percent of rural households are cut off from the closest urban markets because, for instance, they live more than a 30-minute walk from the nearest all-weather road.

Poverty — caused by the low income productivity of farmers' labor — is the primary source of hunger in Africa, and the problem is only getting worse. The number of "food insecure" people in Africa (those consuming less than 2,100 calories a day) will increase 30 percent over the next decade without significant reforms, to 645 million, the U.S. Agriculture Department projects.

> "If we are going to get serious about solving global hunger, we need to de-romanticize our view of preindustrial food and farming."

What's so tragic about this is that we know from experience how to 5 fix the problem. Wherever the rural poor have gained access to improved roads, modern seeds, less expensive fertilizer, electrical power, and better schools and clinics, their productivity and their income have increased. But recent efforts to deliver such essentials have been undercut by deeply misguided (if sometimes well-meaning) advocacy against agricultural modernization and foreign aid.

In Europe and the United States, a new line of thinking has emerged in elite circles that opposes bringing improved seeds and fertilizers to traditional farmers and opposes linking those farmers more closely to international markets. Influential food writers, advocates, and celebrity restaurant owners are repeating the mantra that "sustainable food" in the future must be organic, local, and slow. But guess what: Rural Africa already has such a system, and it doesn't work. Few smallholder farmers in Africa use any synthetic chemicals, so their food is de facto organic.

High transportation costs force them to purchase and sell almost all of their food locally. And food preparation is painfully slow. The result is nothing to celebrate: average income levels of only $1 a day and a one-in-three chance of being malnourished.

If we are going to get serious about solving global hunger, we need to de-romanticize our view of preindustrial food and farming. And that means learning to appreciate the modern, science-intensive, and highly capitalized agricultural system we've developed in the West. Without it, our food would be more expensive and less safe. In other words, a lot like the hunger-plagued rest of the world.

Original Sins

Thirty years ago, had someone asserted in a prominent journal or newspaper that the Green Revolution was a failure, he or she would have been quickly dismissed. Today the charge is surprisingly common. Celebrity author and eco-activist Vandana Shiva claims the Green Revolution has brought nothing to India except "indebted and discontented farmers." A 2002 meeting in Rome of 500 prominent international NGOs, including Friends of the Earth and Greenpeace, even blamed the Green Revolution for the rise in world hunger. Let's set the record straight.

The development and introduction of high-yielding wheat and rice seeds into poor countries, led by American scientist Norman Borlaug and others in the 1960s and 1970s, paid huge dividends. In Asia these new seeds lifted tens of millions of small farmers out of desperate poverty and finally ended the threat of periodic famine. India, for instance, doubled its wheat production between 1964 and 1970 and was able to terminate all dependence on international food aid by 1975. As for indebted and discontented farmers, India's rural poverty rate fell from 60 percent to just 27 percent today. Dismissing these great achievements as a "myth" (the official view of Food First, a California-based organization that campaigns globally against agricultural modernization) is just silly.

It's true that the story of the Green Revolution is not everywhere a happy one. When powerful new farming technologies are introduced into deeply unjust rural social systems, the poor tend to lose out. In Latin America, where access to good agricultural land and credit has been narrowly controlled by traditional elites, the improved seeds made available by the Green Revolution *increased* income gaps. Absentee landlords in Central America, who previously allowed peasants to plant subsistence crops on underutilized land, pushed them off to sell or rent the land to commercial growers who could turn a profit using the new seeds. Many of the displaced rural poor became slum dwellers. Yet even in Latin America,

10

the prevalence of hunger declined more than 50 percent between 1980 and 2005.

In Asia, the Green Revolution seeds performed just as well on small nonmechanized farms as on larger farms. Wherever small farmers had sufficient access to credit, they took up the new technology just as quickly as big farmers, which led to dramatic income gains and no increase in inequality or social friction. Even poor landless laborers gained, because more abundant crops meant more work at harvest time, increasing rural wages. In Asia, the Green Revolution was good for both agriculture and social justice.

And Africa? Africa has a relatively equitable and secure distribution of land, making it more like Asia than Latin America and increasing the chances that improvements in farm technology will help the poor. If Africa were to put greater resources into farm technology, irrigation, and rural roads, small farmers would benefit.

Organic Myths

There are other common objections to doing what is necessary to solve the real hunger crisis. Most revolve around caveats° that purist critics raise regarding food systems in the United States and western Europe. Yet such concerns, though well-intentioned, are often misinformed and counterproductive — especially when applied to the developing world.

Take industrial food systems, the current bugaboo of American food writers. Yes, they have many unappealing aspects, but without them food would be not only less abundant but also less safe. Traditional food systems lacking in reliable refrigeration and sanitary packaging are dangerous vectors for diseases. Surveys over the past several decades by the Centers for Disease Control and Prevention have found that the U.S. food supply became steadily safer over time, thanks in part to the introduction of industrial-scale technical improvements. Since 2000, the incidence of *E. coli* contamination in beef has fallen 45 percent. Today in the United States, most hospitalizations and fatalities from unsafe food come not from sales of contaminated products at supermarkets, but from the mishandling or improper preparation of food inside the home. Illness outbreaks from contaminated foods sold in stores still occur, but the fatalities are typically quite limited. A nationwide scare over unsafe spinach in 2006 triggered the virtual suspension of all fresh and bagged spinach sales, but only three known deaths were recorded. Incidents

caveat: warning, caution.

such as these command attention in part because they are now so rare. Food Inc. should be criticized for filling our plates with too many foods that are unhealthy, but not foods that are unsafe.

Where industrial-scale food technologies have not yet reached into 15 the developing world, contaminated food remains a major risk. In Africa, where many foods are still purchased in open-air markets (often uninspected, unpackaged, unlabeled, unrefrigerated, unpasteurized, and unwashed), an estimated 700,000 people die every year from food- and water-borne diseases, compared with an estimated 5,000 in the United States.

Food grown organically — that is, without any synthetic nitrogen fertilizers or pesticides — is not an answer to the health and safety issues. The *American Journal of Clinical Nutrition* last year published a study of 162 scientific papers from the past 50 years on the health benefits of organically grown foods and found no nutritional advantage over conventionally grown foods. According to the Mayo Clinic, "No conclusive evidence shows that organic food is more nutritious than is conventionally grown food."

Health professionals also reject the claim that organic food is safer to eat due to lower pesticide residues. Food and Drug Administration surveys have revealed that the highest dietary exposures to pesticide residues on foods in the United States are so trivial (less than one one-thousandth of a level that would cause toxicity) that the safety gains from buying organic are insignificant. Pesticide exposures remain a serious problem in the developing world, where farm chemical use is not as well regulated, yet even there they are more an occupational risk for unprotected farmworkers than a residue risk for food consumers.

When it comes to protecting the environment, assessments of organic farming become more complex. Excess nitrogen fertilizer use on conventional farms in the United States has polluted rivers and created a "dead zone" in the Gulf of Mexico, but halting synthetic nitrogen fertilizer use entirely (as farmers must do in the United States to get organic certification from the Agriculture Department) would cause environmental problems far worse.

Here's why: Less than 1 percent of American cropland is under certified organic production. If the other 99 percent were to switch to organic and had to fertilize crops without any synthetic nitrogen fertilizer, that would require a lot more composted animal manure. To supply enough organic fertilizer, the U.S. cattle population would have to increase roughly fivefold. And because those animals would have to be raised organically on forage crops, much of the land in the lower 48 states would need to be converted to pasture. Organic field crops also have lower yields per hectare. If Europe tried to feed itself organically, it would need an additional 28 million hectares of cropland, equal to all of the remaining forest cover in France, Germany, Britain, and Denmark combined.

Mass deforestation probably isn't what organic advocates intend. The 20 smart way to protect against nitrogen runoff is to reduce synthetic fertilizer applications with taxes, regulations, and cuts in farm subsidies, but not try to go all the way to zero as required by the official organic standard. Scaling up registered organic farming would be on balance harmful, not helpful, to the natural environment.

Not only is organic farming less friendly to the environment than assumed, but modern conventional farming is becoming significantly more sustainable. High-tech farming in rich countries today is far safer for the environment, per bushel of production, than it was in the 1960s, when Rachel Carson criticized the indiscriminate farm use of DDT in her environmental classic *Silent Spring*. Thanks in part to Carson's devastating critique, that era's most damaging insecticides were banned and replaced by chemicals that could be applied in lower volume and were less persistent in the environment. Chemical use in American agriculture peaked soon thereafter, in 1973. This was a major victory for environmental advocacy.

And it was just the beginning of what has continued as a significant greening of modern farming in the United States. Soil erosion on farms dropped sharply in the 1970s with the introduction of "no-till" seed planting, an innovation that also reduced dependence on diesel fuel because fields no longer had to be plowed every spring. Farmers then began conserving water by moving to drip irrigation and by leveling their fields with lasers to minimize wasteful runoff. In the 1990s, GPS equipment was added to tractors, autosteering the machines in straighter paths and telling farmers exactly where they were in the field to within one square meter, allowing precise adjustments in chemical use. Infrared sensors were brought in to detect the greenness of the crop, telling a farmer exactly how much more (or less) nitrogen might be needed as the growing season went forward. To reduce wasteful nitrogen use, equipment was developed that can insert fertilizers into the ground at exactly the depth needed and in perfect rows, only where it will be taken up by the plant roots.

These "precision farming" techniques have significantly reduced the environmental footprint of modern agriculture relative to the quantity of food being produced. In 2008, the Organization for Economic Cooperation and Development published a review of the "environmental performance of agriculture" in the world's 30 most advanced industrial countries — those with the most highly capitalized and science-intensive farming systems. The results showed that between 1990 and 2004, food production in these countries continued to increase (by 5 percent in volume), yet adverse environmental impacts were reduced in every category. The land area taken up by farming declined 4 percent, soil erosion from both wind and water fell, gross greenhouse gas emissions from farming declined 3 percent, and excessive nitrogen fertilizer use fell 17 percent. Biodiversity also improved, as increased numbers of crop varieties and livestock breeds came into use.

Seeding the Future

Africa faces a food crisis, but it's not because the continent's population is growing faster than its potential to produce food, as vintage Malthusians such as environmental advocate Lester Brown and advocacy organizations such as Population Action International would have it. Food production in Africa is vastly less than the region's known potential, and that is why so many millions are going hungry there. African farmers still use almost no fertilizer; only 4 percent of cropland has been improved with irrigation; and most of the continent's cropped area is not planted with seeds improved through scientific plant breeding, so cereal yields are only a fraction of what they could be. Africa is failing to keep up with population growth not because it has exhausted its potential, but instead because too little has been invested in reaching that potential.

One reason for this failure has been sharply diminished assistance 25 from international donors. When agricultural modernization went out of fashion among elites in the developed world beginning in the 1980s, development assistance to farming in poor countries collapsed. Per capita food production in Africa was declining during the 1980s and 1990s and the number of hungry people on the continent was doubling, but the U.S. response was to withdraw development assistance and simply ship more food aid to Africa. Food aid doesn't help farmers become more productive — and it can create long-term dependency. But in recent years, the dollar value of U.S. food aid to Africa has reached 20 times the dollar value of agricultural development assistance.

The alternative is right in front of us. Foreign assistance to support agricultural improvements has a strong record of success, when undertaken with purpose. In the 1960s, international assistance from the Rockefeller Foundation, the Ford Foundation, and donor governments led by the United States made Asia's original Green Revolution possible. U.S. assistance to India provided critical help in improving agricultural education, launching a successful agricultural extension service, and funding advanced degrees for Indian agricultural specialists at universities in the United States. The U.S. Agency for International Development, with the World Bank, helped finance fertilizer plants and infrastructure projects, including rural roads and irrigation. India could not have done this on its own — the country was on the brink of famine at the time and dangerously dependent on food aid. But instead of suffering a famine in 1975, as some naysayers had predicted, India that year celebrated a final and permanent end to its need for food aid.

Foreign assistance to farming has been a high-payoff investment everywhere, including Africa. The World Bank has documented average rates of return on investments in agricultural research in Africa of 35 percent a year, accompanied by significant reductions in poverty. Some research investments in African agriculture have brought rates of return estimated at 68 percent. Blind to these realities, the United States cut its assistance to agricultural research in Africa 77 percent between 1980 and 2006.

When it comes to Africa's growing hunger, governments in rich countries face a stark choice: They can decide to support a steady new infusion of financial and technical assistance to help local governments and farmers become more productive, or they can take a "worry later" approach and be forced to address hunger problems with increasingly expensive shipments of food aid. Development skeptics and farm modernization critics keep pushing us toward this unappealing second path. It's time for leaders with vision and political courage to push back.

Understanding the Text

1. What is a crisis of values?
2. What do global food prices reveal about food availability and food production?
3. What is food security?

Reflection and Response

4. What does Paarlberg suggest about the future of the politics of food? What are at least two ways to respond to his position? What do you think is the best way? Explain your response.
5. Why do you think Paarlberg titles his essay "Attention Whole Foods Shoppers"? Why does Paarlberg single out this particular demographic? How does he characterize them? What do people who shop at Whole Foods represent for him?

Making Connections

6. Paarlberg criticizes Vandana Shiva's critique ("Soy Imperialism and the Destruction of Local Food Cultures," p. 179) of the Green Revolution. What's at stake in this debate? And for whom? Compare their positions, and describe the differences in their fundamental assumptions.

7. Paarlberg criticizes organic food advocates, arguing that they romanticize preindustrial food and farming. How might he critique Eliot Coleman's position that we need to demand "real food" ("Real Food, Real Farming," p. 266)? Who makes a more compelling case? Explain your response with evidence from the texts.

8. Margaret Mead ("The Changing Significance of Food," p. 200), Jonathan Foley ("Can We Feed The World and Sustain the Planet?," p. 297), and Paarlberg all say they want to reduce world hunger. What values and ideas for doing so do they share? Where do they diverge? Whose approach to solving world hunger seems more realistic? Whose approach seems more ethical? Whose approach do you think has the potential to actually succeed? What role should moral considerations play in the solution?

Brightening Up the Dark Farming History of the Sunshine State

Natasha Bowens

Natasha Bowens describes herself as a "young, brown, female farmer" who advocates for food sovereignty for people of color and historically oppressed groups. She quit her job at a Washington, D.C. think tank to devote herself to learning about farming and advocating for food justice, especially in communities of color. A writer and photographer, she documented her farming journey and her explorations of agriculture, race, and class on her blog *The Color of Food*. She also wrote the series *The Color of Food* for Grist.org in which she explores farming and food justice in a variety of locations. In this piece, the last installment of *The Color of Food* in 2011, Bowens analyzes the complex relationships among farming, race, and class through her observations of food and labor injustice in Florida.

I eagerly wandered up and down the streets of Miami's Little Haiti looking for any sign of a farm. If you're familiar with Little Haiti — or any neighborhood in Miami, really — you're probably thinking that a farm is the last thing I was going to find. Then I knocked on the door of a typical Miami home, painted a sandy yellow with a red-tiled roof, walked through the sun room and the kitchen and ended up in a not-so-typical backyard. It was like climbing through the wardrobe into Narnia.

Three turkeys were strutting around to Beethoven playing on a stereo, followed by an angry goose with his neck outstretched. Two large emus flashed their long eyelashes as they stared at me, the intruder.

I had been transported to an urban paradise, designed to grow food by mimicking the natural ecologies of south Florida . . . OK, maybe minus the emu.

Earth 'n' Us is a permaculture farm that has been in this North Miami neighborhood for 33 years. When it began, Little Haiti was one of the poorest areas of the city and well known for its crime and drug trade. Now Ray, the owner, is growing and expanding the farm to neighboring lots with help from members of the community.

Ray has already acquired an acre of land behind his house, on which 5 you can find an abundance of fruit trees, like mangoes, avocados, bananas, and papayas, as well as two gardens growing everything from okra to beets and cabbage. The land also supports chickens, ducks, geese, goats, pigs, emus, turkeys, a python, and an iguana. (It's just not Florida without snakes and lizards.) Tree houses for residents, renters, and WWOOF° volunteers overlook the gardens.

"Ray's been here for so long, and he created this urban paradise just because he's that kind of guy. But now he sees the need to expand and educate the kids in the neighborhood, and to produce more food for the community," Matrice, a WWOOF volunteer who's been studying permaculture at Earth 'n' Us for six months, told me. (Ray and Matrice wished to be known by first name only.)

Earth 'n' Us hosts workshops on various topics including permaculture design and home brewing, as well as movie nights and tours for the local kids. Its neighbor, Community Food Works, also offers courses on beekeeping and alternative energy solutions and runs a permaculture certificate program.

'Ponics Scheme

About 30 minutes north, another urban grower is trying to offer healthy food for the community and provide courses on how people can grow their own food using hydroponics.

Jessica Padron started The Urban Farmer when she had her daughter Bella. "I wasn't happy about the idea of not knowing for sure if our food was safe," she told me. "So I researched a way to grow our own food that would require little maintenance and be easy for me as a working mom."

The hydroponics farm is built on an industrial site in Pompano Beach that was formerly an auto shop. Padron and her partners had to remove 300 [cubic] yards of material out of the site to begin constructing the farm. They chose an outdoor hydroponics system because the soil at the site was so contaminated.

The system includes towers tiered with polystyrene containers that hold coconut husks for the plants to grow in. All that's needed is a daily feed of water and a 16-nutrient solution, and they are cranking out over 10,000 plants. While I don't agree with the Styrofoam containers or the cost of starting a hydroponics system (not really practical for your average food-desert resident), I was impressed with the amount of food being produced right there in an old auto yard in South Florida.

10

WWOOF: World Wide Opportunities on Organic Farms; a nonprofit organization that links organic farms with potential volunteers and works to support the organic food movement worldwide.

Legacy of Injustice

It's actually fitting that the end of my farming and food justice journey for this season has brought me to Florida. It is where I grew up and is home to my family, and it's also home to many farmers of color who have emigrated here from the Caribbean and Central and South America.

Neighborhoods like Little Haiti and Little Havana in Miami are home to many such immigrants, but the rural areas that make up the majority of the state have also drawn large populations of Haitian and Latino immigrants with the promise of work.

The only problem is that some of the employers in these agricultural areas of Florida apparently think they're the Spanish colonizers of 1565 . . . meaning slavery is OK in their book. Over the past decade, 12-plus employers in the state of Florida have been federally prosecuted for the enslavement of over 1,000 farmworkers.

Yes, I said enslavement. Workers have been chained and held captive 15 in produce trucks, beaten, and shot, among other atrocities that are reminiscent of this nation's past.

Immokalee, Florida, once home to the Calusa and Seminole Native American nations, is now the largest farmworker community in the state. Immokalee has become infamous for the violation of human rights taking place on the tomato

> "The reality is that the issues within our food system are rooted in historical racial and economic injustice."

fields in the area, and the Coalition of Immokalee Workers has fought hard and in some cases successfully for improved wages and working conditions for the tomato pickers. But farmworkers here in Florida, and around the world, have been suffering from these injustices for years, and although some effort has gone into changing that, we still have a long way to go. The Coalition of Immokalee Workers continues to fight for the rights of its majority Latino, Haitian, and Mayan Indian farmworkers, and continues to investigate slavery in the fields today.

I just wonder if we will ever get past such blatant disregard for human rights as seen in Immokalee and erase the negative legacy that agriculture has seared into our minds for people of color.

While this trip has opened my eyes to some incredible and inspiring urban farming and food-justice projects being led by brown folks in under-served communities, the reality is that the issues within our food system are rooted in historical racial and economic injustice.

And unless we step together out of the shadow of denial and into the brutal light of honesty, we will only be repeating those patterns, and standing in the way of a truly just and healthy food revolution.

Understanding the Text

1. What is a permaculture farm?
2. What is a hydroponics farm?
3. What is a food desert?

Reflection and Response

4. One of Bowens's goals is to put farmers of color and food activists of color on the map. Why is this goal important to her? What role or roles might writing play in helping her achieve it?

5. According to Bowens, how does the legacy of racial and economic injustice affect the food system in the United States? What kinds of evidence does she give to support her assertions?

6. What would be required for us to step "out of the shadow of denial and into the brutal light of honesty" (par. 19)? Who would have to do what?

Making Connections

7. What concerns about worker rights does Bowens raise? Compare them to the concerns raised by Eric Holt-Giménez ("This Land Is Whose Land?" p. 251) and Richard Marosi ("Hardship on Mexico's Farms," p. 283). How do they each argue for their beliefs in the need for worker justice? Consider the kinds of evidence *and* the rhetorical strategies they use. Support your response with specific textual references.

8. Frances Moore Lappé argues that global hunger problems are "not caused by a scarcity of food but by a scarcity of democracy" ("Biotechnology Isn't the Key to Feeding the World," p. 294). What role does Bowens see for democracy in the fight for food justice? What values or beliefs do Lappé and Bowens share? What relationship do you think should exist between the future of food and the political process?

Hardship on Mexico's Farms, a Bounty for U.S. Tables

Richard Marosi

Best known for his investigative reporting on the U.S.-Mexico border, Richard Marosi is a *Los Angeles Times* staff writer and a two-time Pulitzer Prize finalist. Marosi grew up in the San Francisco Bay Area but has lived for many years in Southern California, where he has written articles about a range of issues affecting the border region — ones that address the economy, immigration, the drug wars, agriculture, and national security. The following excerpt is part of his "Product of Mexico" series in the *LA Times*, for which he and photojournalist Don Bartletti traveled through nine Mexican states to observe working conditions and interview workers on farms that are some of the biggest suppliers of produce for the United States. In it, he carefully chronicles the lives of farm laborers, writing in a way that he hopes will make their plight real and important to his readers.

The tomatoes, peppers and cucumbers arrive year-round by the ton, with peel-off stickers proclaiming "Product of Mexico." Farm exports to the U.S. from Mexico have tripled to $7.6 billion in the last decade, enriching agribusinesses, distributors and retailers. American consumers get all the salsa, squash and melons they can eat at affordable prices. And top U.S. brands — Wal-Mart, Whole Foods, Subway and Safeway, among many others — profit from produce they have come to depend on. These corporations say their Mexican suppliers have committed to decent treatment and living conditions for workers. But a Los Angeles Times investigation found that for thousands of farm laborers south of the border, the export boom is a story of exploitation and extreme hardship.

The Times found:

- Many farm laborers are essentially trapped for months at a time in rat-infested camps, often without beds and sometimes without functioning toilets or a reliable water supply.

- Some camp bosses illegally withhold wages to prevent workers from leaving during peak harvest periods.

- Laborers often go deep in debt paying inflated prices for necessities at company stores. Some are reduced to scavenging for food when their credit is cut off. It's common for laborers to head home penniless at the end of a harvest.

- Those who seek to escape their debts and miserable living conditions have to contend with guards, barbed-wire fences and sometimes threats of violence from camp supervisors.

- Major U.S. companies have done little to enforce social responsibility guidelines that call for basic worker protections such as clean housing and fair pay practices.

The farm laborers are mostly indigenous° people from Mexico's poorest regions. Bused hundreds of miles to vast agricultural complexes, they work six days a week for the equivalent of $8 to $12 a day. The squalid° camps where they live, sometimes sleeping on scraps of cardboard on concrete floors, are operated by the same agribusinesses that employ advanced growing techniques and sanitary measures in their fields and greenhouses. The contrast between the treatment of produce and of people is stark. In immaculate greenhouses, laborers are ordered to use hand sanitizers and schooled in how to pamper the produce. They're required to keep their fingernails carefully trimmed so the fruit will arrive unblemished in U.S. supermarkets. "They want us to take such great care of the tomatoes, but they don't take care of us," said Japolina Jaimez, a field hand at Rene Produce, a grower of tomatoes, peppers and cucumbers in the northwestern state of Sinaloa. "Look at how we live." He pointed to co-workers and their children, bathing in an irrigation canal because the camp's showers had no water that day.

At the mega-farms that supply major American retailers, child labor has been largely eradicated. But on many small and mid-sized farms, children still work the fields, picking chiles, tomatillos and other produce, some of which makes its way to the U.S. through middlemen. About 100,000 children younger than 14 pick crops for pay, according to the Mexican government's most recent estimate. During The Times' 18-month investigation, a reporter and a photographer traveled across nine Mexican states, observing conditions at farm labor camps and interviewing hundreds of workers. At half the 30 camps they visited, laborers were in effect prevented from leaving because their wages were being withheld or they owed money to the company store, or both. Some of the worst camps were linked to companies that have been lauded by government and industry groups. Mexico's President Enrique Peña Nieto presented at least two of them with "exporter of the year" honors. The Times traced produce from fields to U.S. supermarket shelves using Mexican government export data, food safety reports from independent auditors, California pesticide surveys that identify the origin of imported

---

indigenous: native, originally occurring in a particular place.
squalid: extremely foul, unpleasant, neglected, and dirty.

produce, and numerous interviews with company officials and industry experts.

The practice of withholding wages, although barred by Mexican law, 5 persists, especially for workers recruited from indigenous areas, according to government officials and a 2010 report by the federal Secretariat of Social Development. These laborers typically work under three-month contracts and are not paid until the end. The law says they must be paid weekly. The Times visited five big export farms where wages were being withheld. Each employed hundreds of workers. Wal-Mart, the world's largest retailer, bought produce directly or through middlemen from at least three of those farms, The Times found. Bosses at one of Mexico's biggest growers, Bioparques de Occidente in the state of Jalisco, not only withheld wages but kept hundreds of workers in a labor camp against their will and beat some who tried to escape, according to laborers and Mexican authorities. Asked about its ties to Bioparques and other farms where workers were exploited, Wal-Mart released this statement:

We care about the men and women in our supply chain, and recognize that challenges remain in this industry. We know the world is a big place. While our standards and audits make things better around the world, we won't catch every instance when people do things that are wrong.

At Rene Produce in Sinaloa, The Times saw hungry laborers hunting for scraps because they could not afford to buy food at the company store. The grower, which exported $55 million in tomatoes in 2014, supplies supermarkets across the U.S., including Whole Foods, which recently took out full-page newspaper ads promoting its commitment to social responsibility. Asked for comment, Whole Foods said it did not expect to buy any more produce "directly" from Rene, which it described as a minor supplier. "We take the findings you shared VERY seriously, especially since Rene has signed our social accountability agreement," Edmund LaMacchia, a global vice president of procurement for Whole Foods, said in a statement. Rene Produce was named one of Mexico's exporters of the year in September. Jose Humberto Garcia, the company's chief operating officer, said Rene had consulted with outside experts about ways to enhance worker welfare. "We have tried in recent years to improve the lives of our workers," he said. "There's still room for improvement. There's always room for improvement."

Executives at Triple H in Sinaloa, another exporter of the year and a distributor for major supermarkets across the U.S., said they were surprised to hear about abusive labor practices at farms including one of their suppliers, Agricola San Emilio. "It completely violates our principles," said Heriberto Vlaminck, Triple H's general director. His son Heriberto Vlaminck Jr., the company's commercial director, added: "I find it incredible that people work under these conditions."

In northern Mexico, agro-industrial complexes stretch for miles across coastal plains and inland valleys, their white rows of tent-like hothouses so vast they can be seen from space. Half the tomatoes consumed in the U.S. come from Mexico, mostly from the area around Culiacan, the capital of Sinaloa. Many farms use growing techniques from Europe. Walls of tomato vines grow 10 feet tall and are picked by laborers on stilts. Agricola San Emilio raises crops on 370 acres of open fields and green-houses 20 miles west of Culiacan. In a tin-roofed packinghouse, tomatoes, bell peppers and cucumbers are boxed for the journey north to distribu-tors for Wal-Mart, Olive Garden, Safeway, Subway and other retailers.

In 2014, the company exported more than 80 million pounds of toma-toes alone, according to government data. Every winter, 1,000 workers arrive at San Emilio by bus with backpacks and blankets, hoping to make enough money to support family members back home. Some simply want to stay fed. Behind the packing facility lies the company's main labor camp, a cluster of low-slung buildings made of cinder block or corrugated metal where about 500 laborers live. The shed-like structures are crudely partitioned into tiny rooms that house four to six people each. The floors are concrete. There are no beds or other furniture, nor any windows. The workers' day begins at 3 a.m. when a freight train known as "The Beast" rumbles past the dusty camp, rousting the inhabitants. They get coffee, a biscuit and a short stack of tortillas before heading to the fields.

When Times journalists visited the camp in March, Juan Ramirez, a 10 22-year-old with a toddler back home in Veracruz, had been working at San Emilio for six weeks and had yet to be paid. He and other laborers spent their days picking, packing and pruning, or scouring the plants for weevils. They lined up for their daily meals: a bowl of lentil soup for lunch, a bowl of lentil soup for dinner. Ramirez, wearing a stained white T-shirt, chatted with two young men who were recent arrivals. They complained of hunger and constant headaches. Ramirez knew the feel-ing. He had lost 20 pounds since starting work at the farm. "We arrive here fat, and leave skinny," he said.

Ramirez and several hundred others recruited by the same labor con-tractor earned $8 a day and were owed as much as $300 each. They said they wouldn't be paid until the end of their three-month contracts. That would be in six more weeks. Workers said they had been promised $8 in pocket money every two weeks but received it only sporadically°. If they

sporadically: happening irregularly.

left now, they would forfeit the wages they'd earned. The barbed-wire fence that ringed the camp was an added deterrent°. Farm owners say the barriers are meant to keep out thieves and drug dealers. They also serve another purpose: to discourage laborers from leaving before the crop has been picked and they've paid their debts to the company store.

Even if the workers at San Emilio jumped the fence, as some had, they wouldn't be able to afford a ride to Culiacan, let alone $100 for the bus ticket home. Juan Hernandez, a father of five from Veracruz, was worried about his wife, who had been injured in an accident back home. "I want to go," he said. "But if I leave, I lose everything." Hernandez slept atop packing crates padded with cardboard. A suitcase served as his dinner table. In another building, Jacinto Santiago hung a scrap of cardboard in the open doorway of his room, which he shared with his son, daughter and son-in-law. Santiago said that in some ways, he had been better off back home in the central state of San Luis Potosi. There, he had a thatched-roof house with windows and a hen that laid eggs.

Santiago, like the other laborers, said he was promised that he would be able to send money home. His family was still waiting, because he hadn't been paid. "My family isn't the only one that suffers. Anyone who has a family at home suffers," he said. Efrain Hernandez, 18, said recruiters told him his earnings would be held back so he wouldn't get robbed: "They said it was for my own good." Outside one of the buildings, a group of men gathered under a dim light. It was nearing the 9 p.m. curfew, when the camp's heavy metal gate rolls shut and workers retreat to their rooms. Their voices echoed across the compound as they swapped stories about conditions in various camps. There are at least 200 across Mexico, 150 in Sinaloa alone. Pedro Hernandez, 51, complained that unlike some other camps, San Emilio didn't offer beds or blankets. Then again, there were fewer rats, he said. The conversation attracted a camp supervisor, who was surprised to see a reporter and photographer. "When the people from Wal-Mart come," she said, "they let us know in advance." She walked the journalists to the exit. The pickers went back to their rooms. The gate rolled shut.

The road to labor camps like San Emilio begins deep in the indigenous regions of central and southern Mexico, where advertising jingles play endlessly on the radio, echoing from storefront speakers.

"Attention. Attention. We are looking for 400 peasants to pick tomatoes."

"You'll earn 100 pesos per day, three free meals per day and overtime."

"Vamonos a trabajar!" — Let's go work!

---

deterrent: discouragement, something that discourages people from doing something.

On a warm January morning this year, dozens of indigenous people 15
looking for work descended from mud-hut villages in the steep mountains of the Huasteca region. Nahuatl men wore holstered machetes.
Women cradled children in their arms. Young men shouldered backpacks stuffed with the clothes they would wear for the next few months.
The laborers approached a knot of recruiters gathered outside a gas station in the town of Huejutla de Reyes, about 130 miles north of Mexico
City. Among those offering jobs at distant farms was Luis Garcia, 37.
Garcia, a stocky Nahuatl Indian with silver-rimmed teeth, had risen
from child picker to field boss to labor contractor for Agricola San Emilio.
He lived just outside town, in a hilltop house behind tall gates, and was
known to locals as "Don Luis." "We all owe our livelihoods to the farmworkers," he said. "We have to treat them well, or the gringos don't get
their tomatoes." Labor contractors are key players in the agricultural
economy, the link between export farms in the north and peasants in
Huasteca and other impoverished regions. An estimated 150,000 make
the pilgrimage every harvest season. The contractors, working for agribusinesses, transport laborers to and from the farms. Often, they also
oversee the camps and distribute workers' pay.

Many contractors abuse their power, according to indigenous leaders
and federal inspectors. They lie about wages and living conditions at the
camps. Under pressure from growers, they sometimes refuse to bring
laborers home, even at the end of their contracts, if there are still vegetables to be picked. Earlier this year, 25 farmworkers walked 20 miles across
a Baja California desert after a contractor left them on the roadside, short
of their destination. At the gas station in Huejutla de Reyes, villagers listened warily to the recruiters' pitches. One was said to be representing a
contractor wanted on human trafficking charges. Another worked for a
contractor notorious for wage theft and other abuses. Garcia had his own
brush with controversy several years ago, when dozens of pickers accused
him of holding them captive and abusing them at an onion farm in
Chihuahua. "They said I beat people. Lies, all lies," Garcia said, bristling.
"I wouldn't be here today talking to you if it was true, would I?" He
depicted himself as a reformer who wanted to establish a trade association to set standards and drive out unscrupulous contractors. But he saw
no need to do more for workers. "The more protected they are, the less
they work," he said. As he spoke, recruiters tried to outbid one another
for laborers, boosting their offers of spending money for the two-day bus
trip to Sinaloa.

Garcia won the day's competition. With his smooth baritone, he persuaded about 40 people to get on his bus. Garcia read their contract
aloud to the workers, including the provision that they wouldn't be paid

until the end of their three-month term. He later acknowledged that federal law requires weekly payments but said that there were other issues to consider. "Paying them every week is a problem because it causes lots of issues with drinking and drugging and violence," Garcia said. "Huasteca people are fighters when they're drunk." Proud of his success in a cutthroat business, Garcia portrayed himself as the product of a farm labor system in which the real bosses were U.S. companies. "The gringos are the ones that put up the money and make the rules," he said.

The U.S. companies linked to Agricola San Emilio through distributors have plenty of rules, but they serve mainly to protect American consumers, not Mexican field hands. Strict U.S. laws govern the safety and cleanliness of imported fruits and vegetables. To meet those standards, retailers and distributors send inspectors to Mexico to examine fields, greenhouses and packing plants. The companies say they are also committed to workers' well-being and cite their ethical sourcing guidelines. Retailers increasingly promote the idea that the food they sell not only is tasty and healthful but was produced without exploiting workers. But at many big corporations, enforcement of those standards is weak to nonexistent, and often relies on Mexican growers to monitor themselves, The Times found.

> "The U.S. companies linked to Agricola San Emilio through distributors have plenty of rules, but they serve mainly to protect American consumers, not Mexican field hands."

In some low-wage countries, U.S. retailers rely on independent auditors to verify that suppliers in apparel, footwear and other industries comply with social responsibility guidelines. For the most part, that has not happened with Mexican farm labor. American companies have not made oversight a priority because they haven't been pressured to do so. There is little public awareness of harsh conditions at labor camps. Many farms are in areas torn by drug violence, which has discouraged media coverage and visits by human rights groups and academic researchers. Asked to comment on conditions at Agricola San Emilio, Subway said in a statement: "We will use this opportunity to reinforce our Code of Conduct with our suppliers." The code says suppliers must ensure that workers "are fairly compensated and are not exploited in any way."

Safeway said: "We take any and all claims regarding worker condi- 20 tions seriously and are looking into each of the points you raise." In its vendor code of conduct, Safeway says that suppliers must offer a "safe and healthy work environment" and that it "will not tolerate any departure from its standards." Vendors are expected to "self-monitor their compliance," the code says. Wal-Mart sought to distance itself from

Agricola San Emilio, saying in a statement: "Our records show that we do not currently take from this facility." Asked if it had received produce from the farm in the past, Wal-Mart repeated its statement.

Executives at Agricola San Emilio and two firms that have distributed its produce — Triple H of Culiacan and Andrew & Williamson of San Diego — said Wal-Mart received shipments from the Mexican farm this year. John Farrington, chief operating officer at Andrew & Williamson, said that his company shipped San Emilio tomatoes to the retailer and that inspectors from Wal-Mart had been to the farm. Mari Cabanillas, an assistant camp supervisor at Agricola San Emilio, said Wal-Mart inspectors visited regularly, recommending cleanups and fresh coats of paint. "They try and improve conditions here," she said. "They're very strict."

As for Agricola San Emilio's pay practices, Daniel Beltran, the firm's director and legal counsel, said workers from the Huasteca region whose wages were withheld until the end of their three-month contracts had agreed to that arrangement. He said they could opt to be paid weekly, as others were. A dozen workers, however, said in interviews that they had no choice in how they were paid. Withholding workers' pay is illegal even if they agree to it, according to Mexico's federal labor law, a senior federal labor official and two labor lawyers. In regard to living conditions, Beltran said the company stopped providing beds because workers dismantled them for firewood. The laborers are from regions where it's common for people to sleep on the floor, he said.

He took issue with workers' claims that they were underfed. "Some people, even if you give them chicken or beef every day, they'll still want a different menu," he said, adding that workers could supplement company rations by purchasing food from vendors. SunFed, an Arizona firm that has distributed produce from Agricola San Emilio, said its representatives had inspected the fields and packinghouse at the farm but not the labor camp. "The Mexican government would be the first line of protection for Mexican workers," said Dan Mandel, president of SunFed, a distributor for supermarkets across the U.S. Enforcement of Mexican labor laws in Sinaloa is feeble. One state official insisted, incorrectly, that withholding wages until the end of a contract was legal.

Federal labor inspectors are clear on the law but said they were largely powerless to crack down on deep-pocketed growers, who can stymie enforcement with endless appeals. "They just laugh at us," said Armando Guzman, a senior official with Mexico's federal Secretariat of Labor and Social Welfare. "They mock authority and mock the letter of the law." Agricola San Emilio is no outlier. Harsh conditions persist in many camps. At Agricola Rita Rosario, a cucumber exporter near Culiacan in Sinaloa, workers said they hadn't been paid in weeks. Some were pawning° their belongings to pay for diapers and food when Times journalists visited a year ago. Laborers said company managers had threatened to dump their possessions in the street if they persisted in demanding their wages. "We have nowhere to go. We're trapped," said a 43-year-old man, looking around nervously. Rita Rosario, under new management, started paying workers their back wages this year before suspending operations, according to a U.S. distributor who did business with the farm.

Workers at Agricola Santa Teresa, an export farm nearby, were doing 25 odd jobs outside the camp on Sundays to earn spending money because their wages had been withheld. The tomato grower supplies U.S. distributors whose customers include the Albertsons supermarket chain and the Los Angeles Unified School District. Told that workers hadn't been paid, Enrique Lopez, director of Santa Teresa, said it wasn't the company's fault. Santa Teresa pays them by electronic bank deposit every week, he said. Lopez said he suspected that the laborers handed over their ATM cards to the contractor who recruited them, a practice he said was customary for workers from indigenous regions. "That is the agreement they have," Lopez said. "We can't control that situation." An LAUSD spokeswoman, Ellen Morgan, said the district requires suppliers to inspect farms from which they buy produce, primarily to ensure food safety. She said the district was formulating a new procurement policy that would probably address labor conditions too. Albertsons declined to comment.

At Agricola El Porvenir, also near Culiacan, workers were required to disinfect their hands before picking cucumbers. Yet they were given just two pieces of toilet paper to use at the outhouses. At Campo San Jose, where many of them lived, workers said rats and feral cats had the run of the cramped living quarters and feasted on their leftovers. Laborers and their families bathed in an irrigation canal because the water had run out in the showers. In March, a snake was sighted in the canal, sparking a panic. Carmen Garcia stepped out of the fetid waterway after washing her 1-year-old grandson. His skin was covered with boils that she blamed on insect bites. "He itches constantly," Garcia said. "I want to get a blood test, but I can't get to a doctor." Agricola El Porvenir's legal counsel, Eric Gerardo, said the company rents Campo San Jose from another agribusiness to handle the overflow when its own camps fill up. Efforts to reach the owner of the other business were unsuccessful. "We don't invest in it because it's not ours," Gerardo said.

---

pawning: giving belongings as a deposit or security for money borrowed, usually with high rates in interest or fees attached.

Twenty miles away, at Campo Isabelitas, operated by the agribusiness Nueva Yamal, families used buckets in their room to relieve themselves because, they said, the toilets were filthy and lacked water. Men defecated in a cornfield. Workers could be seen bathing in an irrigation canal; they said the camp's showers were out of water. Charles Ciruli, a co-owner of Arizona-based Ciruli Bros., which distributes Nueva Yamal tomatoes, visited the camp after being told about conditions there by The Times. Through an attorney, he said that the men's bathrooms "did not meet Ciruli's standards" and that repairs had been made to "reinstate running water." The attorney, Stanley G. Feldman, said in a letter that the women's showers and toilets were "fully functioning," with a paid attendant. Asked why workers were washing in the irrigation canal, Feldman wrote: "Ciruli cannot explain this with certainty, but it was told that it may be a cultural practice among some workers." He added: "Ciruli will consult with the on-farm social worker and doctor to determine if a worker education campaign may be appropriate in this case."

In June 2013, Bioparques found itself under rare government scrutiny. Three workers at one of the tomato grower's labor camps escaped and complained to authorities about the wretched conditions. Police, soldiers and labor inspectors raided the camp and found 275 people trapped inside. Dozens were malnourished, including 24 children, authorities said. People were desperate, but at least the camp had showers and stoves, said laborer Gerardo Gonzalez Hernandez. "To tell you the truth, Bioparques was a little better than other labor camps I've been to," Gonzalez, 18, said in an interview at his home in the mountains north of Mexico City. "That's why I didn't complain. I've seen a lot worse."

Understanding the Text

1. What does Marosi notice about the difference between how produce and people are treated on Mexico's farms?

2. What does the law dictate about how workers on Mexico's farms should be paid? What does Marosi say actually happens in practice?

3. How do the Mexican farms that Marosi describes recruit workers? What role does child labor play in the production of fruits and vegetables in Mexico?

4. What role do labor contractors play in the U.S./Mexico agricultural economy?

Reflection and Response

5. What role does Wal-Mart play in this story? Why do you think Marosi specifically calls out Wal-Mart?

6. Five major conclusions are offered in the second paragraph. Select one, and explore and analyze how Marosi supports the conclusion. Does the conclusion make you think differently about the food you buy? If so, why and how? If not, why not?

7. Marosi is clearly trying to gain sympathy for the farm workers he describes. What rhetorical choices does he use to achieve this effect? Does it work for you? Does his writing make you sympathetic to the workers' plight? If so, how? If not, why not?

Making Connections

8. Many U.S. companies (such as Triple H) claim that they are committed to fair working conditions and the well-being of farm workers, but Marosi shows that workers are routinely exploited. Go online and research a few companies that have ethical sourcing guidelines. How and why do these food suppliers publicize their participation in fair labor practices? Why do you think so many companies insist that they have policies that ensure fair labor practices even though Marosi found startling evidence to the contrary? Is this something American consumers should care about? Do you? If so, how will you act on your concerns?

9. Yuval Noah Harari ("Industrial Farming Is One of the Worst Crimes in History," p. 233) argues that the treatment of domesticated animals on industrial farms is among the worst crimes in history. Imagine that Marosi (or you) wants to argue that the treatment of Mexican farm workers is worse than the treatment of domesticated animals on industrial farms. What is the best way to make such an argument? What ethical principles would you rely upon? What evidence would you use to support your conclusions?

10. Eric Holt-Giménez ("This Land Is Whose Land?" p. 251) and Marosi both explore racial and class inequities in the global food system. Is the exploitation of Mexican farm workers that Marosi describes a version of what Holt-Giménez would call "structural racism"? Research approaches to countering structural racism. Which ones do you think would help improve the global food system and why? You may want to consider the essay by Raj Patel ("Stuffed and Starved," p. 173) or Natasha Bowens ("Brightening Up the Dark Farming History of the Sunshine State," p. 279) as possible approaches. You may also want to look up the work of Holt-Giménez and Marosi to better understand their projects, affiliations, and understandings of the world they write about.

Biotechnology Isn't the Key to Feeding the World

Frances Moore Lappé

Frances Moore Lappé is an environmental activist and author who has written 18 books, including *Diet for a Small Planet* (1971) and *EcoMind: Changing the Way We Think, to Create the World We Want* (2011). The winner of many awards and the recipient of many honorary degrees, Lappé is known for her tireless dedication to democratic social movements and the fight against world hunger. Her extensive writings aim to change the way we think about agriculture, nutrition, and food production and consumption. In this essay, she argues that democracy — not biotechnology — is the key to finding a solution to the problem of world hunger. It is not that we do not have enough food, she explains; it is that we do not have a successful democratic process.

Biotechnology companies and even some scientists argue that we need genetically modified seeds to feed the world and to protect the Earth from chemicals. Their arguments feel eerily familiar.

Thirty years ago, I wrote *Diet for a Small Planet* for one reason. As a researcher buried in the agricultural library at the University of California, Berkeley, I was stunned to learn that the experts — equivalent to the biotech proponents of today — were wrong. They were telling us that we had reached the Earth's limits to feed ourselves, but in fact there was more than enough food for us all.

Hunger, I learned, is the result of economic "givens" that we have created, assumptions and structures that actively generate scarcity from plenty. Today this is more, not less, true.

Throughout history, ruminants had served humans by turning grasses and other "inedibles" into high-grade protein. They were our four-legged protein factories. But once we began feeding livestock from cropland that could grow edible food, we began to convert ruminants into our protein disposals.

Only a small fraction of the nutrients fed to animals return to us in 5 meat; the rest animals use largely for energy or they excrete. Roughly one-third of the world's grain goes to livestock; today it is closer to one-half. And now we are mastering the same disappearing trick with the world's fish supply. By feeding fish to fish, again, we are reducing the potential supply.

We are shrinking the world's food supply for one reason: The hundreds of millions of people who go hungry cannot create a sufficient "market demand" for the fruits of the Earth. So more and more of it flows into the mouths of livestock, which convert it into what the better-off can afford. Corn becomes filet mignon. Sardines become salmon.

Enter biotechnology. While its supporters claim that seed biotechnology methods are "safe" and "precise," other scientists strongly refute that, as they do claims that biotech crops have actually reduced pesticide use.

But this very debate is in some ways part of the problem. It is a tragic distraction our planet cannot afford.

We are still asking the wrong question. Not only is there already enough food in the world, but as long as we are only talking about food — how best to produce it — we will never end hunger or create the communities and food safety we want.

We must ask instead: How do we build communities in tune with 10 nature's wisdom in which no one, anywhere, has to worry about putting food — safe, healthy food — on the table? Asking this question takes us far beyond food. It takes us to the heart of democracy itself, to whose voices are heard in matters of land, seeds, credit, employment, trade, and food safety.

> "Hunger is not caused by a scarcity of food but by a scarcity of democracy."

The problem is, this question cannot be addressed by scientists or by any private entity, including even the most high-minded corporation. Only citizens can answer it, through public debate and the resulting accountable institutions that come from our engagement.

Where are the channels for public discussion and where are the accountable polities?

Increasingly, public discussion about food and hunger is framed by advertising by multinational corporations that control not only food processing and distribution but farm inputs and seed patents.

Two years ago, the seven leading biotech companies, including Monsanto, teamed up under the neutral-sounding Council for Biotechnology Information and are spending millions to, for example, blanket us with full-page newspaper ads about biotech's virtues.

Government institutions are becoming ever more beholden to these 15 corporations than to their citizens. Nowhere is this more obvious than in decisions regarding biotechnology — whether it is the approval or patenting of biotech seeds and foods without public input or the rejection of mandatory labeling of biotech foods despite broad public demand for it.

The absence of genuine democratic dialogue and accountable government is a prime reason most people remain blind to the many breakthroughs in the last 30 years that demonstrate we can grow abundant, healthy food and also protect the Earth.

Hunger is not caused by a scarcity of food but by a scarcity of democracy. Thus it can never be solved by new technologies, even if they were to be proved "safe." It can be solved only as citizens build democracies in which government is accountable to them, not to private corporate entities.

Understanding the Text

1. To what is Lappé referring when she writes about "our four-legged protein factories"?

2. What does she mean by "protein disposals"?

3. On what does Lappé blame world hunger? What does she think is the best way to decrease or eliminate it?

Reflection and Response

4. Lappé argues that proponents and opponents of biotechnology are distracted and thus not focused on the right issue. What is the right issue for Lappé, and how does she make and support her position on the issue? Do you agree with her? Why or why not?

5. What connections does Lappé argue exist among food availability, hunger, farming practices, biotechnology, and democracy? How does she describe their current relationships? How would she change them if she could?

Making Connections

6. Identify the other selections in this book that discuss biotechnology. Try to place them on a continuum. Who agrees with Lappé? Who does not? And to what extent?

7. In what ways does Lappé's argument about the future of food complement the argument made by Raj Patel ("Stuffed and Starved," p. 173)? In what ways does it complicate Robert Paarlberg's position ("Attention Whole Foods Shoppers," p. 270)? Who makes the best case? Whose evidence seems the strongest? Explain your response using textual references.

Can We Feed the World and Sustain the Planet?

Jonathan A. Foley

Jonathan Foley has won prestigious awards in science because of the many ways he has contributed to our understanding of the sustainability of our biosphere, the behaviors that endanger life on our planet, and what we can do to improve how humans interact with the complex global environmental systems that we rely on. After establishing himself as an important figure in sustainability studies at the University of Wisconsin, Foley joined the University of Minnesota faculty and served as the director of the Institute on the Environment and a professor and McKnight Presidential Chair in the department of Ecology, Evolution, and Behavior. More recently, he became the Executive Director of the California Academy of Sciences, a scientific and educational institution in San Francisco that brings together experts who study and explore ways to sustain life on earth. Foley's more-than-130 scientific articles and numerous popular articles have made an enormous impact on science and beyond. Foley is passionate about finding ways to use new technologies to solve our biggest global environmental problems — problems like climate change, food and water security, human health, and sustainability. The essay included here presents the findings of a team of international experts that Foley assembled to study ways that we can dramatically increase food production and decrease environmental damage simultaneously.

Right now about one billion people suffer from chronic hunger. The world's farmers grow enough food to feed them, but it is not properly distributed and, even if it were, many cannot afford it, because prices are escalating. But another challenge looms. By 2050 the world's population will increase by two billion or three billion, which will likely double the demand for food, according to several studies. Demand will also rise because many more people will have higher incomes, which means they will eat more, especially meat. Increasing use of cropland for biofuels will put additional demands on our farms. So even if we solve today's problems of poverty and access — a daunting task — we will also have to produce twice as much to guarantee adequate supply worldwide. And that's not all.

By clearing tropical forests, farming marginal lands, and intensifying industrial farming in sensitive landscapes and watersheds, humankind has made agriculture the planet's dominant environmental threat. Agriculture already consumes a large percentage of the earth's land surface and is destroying habitat, using up freshwater, polluting rivers and oceans, and emitting greenhouse gases more extensively than almost any other human activity. To guarantee the globe's long-term health, we must dramatically reduce agriculture's adverse impacts.

The world's food system faces three incredible, interwoven challenges. It must guarantee that all seven billion people alive today are adequately fed; it must double food production in the next 40 years; and it must become truly environmentally sustainable — all at the same time.

> "To guarantee the globe's long-term health, we must dramatically reduce agriculture's adverse impacts."

Could these simultaneous goals possibly be met? An international team of experts, which I coordinated, has settled on five steps that, if pursued together, could increase by more than 100 percent the food available for human consumption globally while substantially reducing greenhouse gas emissions, biodiversity° losses, water use and water pollution. Tackling the triple challenge will be one of the most important tests humanity has ever faced. It is fair to say that our response will determine the fate of our civilization.

Bumping up against Barriers

At first blush, the way to feed more people seems clear: grow more food, 5 by expanding farmland and improving yield (crops harvested per hectare). Unfortunately, the world is running into significant barriers on both counts.

Society already uses about 37 percent of the earth's land surface, not counting Greenland or Antarctica, for farms or pastures. Agriculture is by far the biggest human use of land on the planet; nothing else comes close. And most of that 37 percent covers the *best* farmland. Much of the remainder is covered by deserts, mountains, tundra, ice, cities, parks and other unsuitable growing areas. The few remaining frontiers are mainly in tropical forests and savannas, which are vital to the stability of the globe, especially as stores of carbon and biodiversity. Expanding into those areas is not a good idea, yet five million to 10 million hectares° of cropland have been created in each of the past 20 years, with a significant portion of that land conversion happening in the tropics. These additions enlarged the net area of cultivated land by only 3 percent, however, because of farmland losses caused by urban development and other forces, particularly in temperate zones.

biodiversity: biological diversity, usually used to refer to the variety of life on earth.
hectares: a metric unit of area equal to 10,000 square meters, or about 2.47 acres.

Improving yield also sounds enticing. Yet our research team found that average global crop yield increased by just 20 percent from 1985 to 2005–far less than had been reported. Cereals yield has been rising at less than 2 percent a year since 2000 and yields of pulses (beans, lentils) and root crops by less than 1 percent — rates that are nowhere near enough to double food production by midcentury.

Feeding more people would be easier if all the food we grew went into human hands. But only 60 percent of the world's crops are meant for people: mostly grains, followed by pulses, oil plants, vegetables and fruits. Another 35 percent is used for animal feed, and the final 5 percent goes to biofuels° and other industrial products. Meat is the biggest issue here. Even with the most efficient meat and dairy systems, feeding crops to animals reduces the world's potential food supply. Grain-fed cattle operations typically use at least 100 kilograms of grain to make one kilogram of edible, boneless beef protein. Chicken and pork are more efficient, and grass-fed beef converts nonfood material into protein. Overall, grain-fed meat production systems are a drain on the global food supply.

Another deterrent to growing more food is damage to the environment, which is already extensive. Only our use of energy, with its profound impacts on climate and ocean acidification, rivals the sheer magnitude of agriculture's environmental footprint. Our research team has estimated that by 2010 agriculture had already cleared or radically transformed 70 percent of the world's prehistoric grasslands, 50 percent of the savannas, 45 percent of the temperate deciduous forests and 25 percent of the tropical forests. Since the last ice age, nothing has disrupted ecosystems more. Agriculture's physical footprint is nearly 60 times that of the world's pavements and buildings.

Freshwater is another casualty. Humans use an astounding 4,000 10 cubic kilometers of water per year, mostly withdrawn from rivers and aquifers.° Irrigation accounts for 70 percent of the draw. If we count only consumptive water use — water that is used and not returned to the watershed — irrigation climbs to 80 or 90 percent of the total. As a result, many large rivers, such as the Colorado, have diminished flows, some have dried up altogether, and many places have rapidly declining water tables, including regions of the U.S. and India.

Water is not only disappearing, it is being contaminated. Fertilizers, herbicides and pesticides are being spread at incredible levels and are

---

biofuels: fuels produced through biological processes instead of geological processes; ethanol and biodiesel are the most common of these.
aquifers: huge storehouses of water underground from which groundwater can be extracted using wells.

found in nearly every ecosystem. The flows of phosphorus and nitrogen through the environment have more than doubled since 1960, causing widespread water pollution and enormous hypoxic° "dead zones" at the mouths of many of the world's major rivers. Ironically, fertilizer runoff from farmland — in the name of growing more food — compromises another crucial source of nutrition: coastal fishing grounds. Fertilizer certainly has been a key ingredient of the green revolution that has helped feed the world, but when nearly half the fertilizer we apply runs off rather than nourishes crops, we clearly can do better.

Farming also accounts for 10 to 12 percent of the warming effects of greenhouse gases released by human activity — a contribution equal to that of all the road vehicles on the planet. Most of the direct emissions from farming come from methane produced by animals and rice paddies and from nitrous oxide released by over-fertilized soils. Add in the effects of tropical deforestation and other land clearing, and agriculture's share of global emissions rises to 24 percent of the total.

Five Solutions

Modern agriculture has been an incredibly positive force in the world, but we can no longer ignore its dwindling ability to expand or the mounting environmental harm it imposes. Previous approaches to solving food issues were often at odds with environmental imperatives. We could boost food production by clearing more land or using more water and chemicals but only at a cost to forests, streams and wetlands. Or we could restore ecosystems by taking farmland out of cultivation but only by reducing food production. This either-or approach is no longer acceptable. We need truly integrated solutions.

After months of research and deliberation — based on analysis of newly generated global agricultural and environmental data — our international team settled on a five-point plan that deals with food and environmental challenges together.

Stop expanding agriculture's footprint. Our first recommendation 15
is to slow and ultimately stop the expansion of agriculture, particularly into tropical forests and savannas°. The demise of these ecosystems has far-reaching impacts on the environment, especially through lost biodiversity and increased carbon dioxide emissions (from clearing land).

---

hypoxic: deprived of oxygen.
savannas: tropical grasslands; a grassland ecosystem with some scattered shrubs and isolated trees.

Slowing deforestation would dramatically reduce environmental damage while imposing only minor constraints on global food production. The resulting dip in farm capacity could be offset by reducing the displacement of more productive croplands by urbanization, degradation and abandonment.

Many proposals have been made to reduce deforestation. One of the most promising has been the Reducing Emissions from Deforestation and Degradation (REDD) mechanism. Under REDD, rich nations pay tropical nations to protect their rain forests, in exchange for carbon credits. Other mechanisms include developing certification standards for agricultural products so that supply chains can be assured that crops were not grown on lands created by deforestation. Also, better biofuel policy — one that relies on nonfood crops such as switchgrass instead of food crops — could make vital farmland newly available.

Close the world's yield gaps. To double global food production without expanding agriculture's footprint, we must significantly improve yields of existing farmlands. Two options exist. We can boost the productivity of our best farms — raising their "yield ceiling" through improved crop genetics and management. Or we can improve the yields of the world's least productive farms — closing the "yield gap" between a farm's current yield and its higher potential yield. The second option provides the largest and most immediate gain, especially in regions where hunger is most acute.

Our research group analyzed global patterns of crop yields and found significant yield gaps in many regions: most notably parts of Africa, Central America and eastern Europe. In these regions, better seeds, more effective fertilizer application and more efficient irrigation could produce much more food without increasing the amount of land under cultivation. Our analysis suggests that closing the yield gap for the world's top 16 crops could increase total food production by 50 to 60 percent, without causing much additional environmental damage.

Reducing yield gaps in the least productive agricultural lands may 20 often require the use of additional chemicals and water. Farmers will have to irrigate and fertilize in responsible ways. They can also make use of other yield-lifting techniques, such as reduced tillage°, which disturbs less soil and thus minimizes erosion. Cover crops planted between food-crop seasons suppress weeds and add nutrients and nitrogen to the soil when plowed under. Lessons from organic and agroecological° systems

tillage: digging and overturning soil to prepare it for growing crops.
agroecological: agricultural systems that consider ecological processes and are resource conserving.

can also be adopted, such as leaving crop residues on fields so that they decompose into nutrients. To close the world's yield gaps, we also have to overcome serious economic and social challenges, including better distribution of fertilizer and seed varieties to farms in impoverished regions and improved access to global markets for many regions.

Use resources much more efficiently. To reduce the environmental impacts of agriculture, low- and high-yield regions alike must practice agriculture in ways that produce vastly greater output of crops per unit input of water, fertilizer and energy.

On average, it takes about one liter of irrigation water to grow one calorie of food. Some places use much more, however. Our analysis found that farms can significantly curb water use without much reduction in food production, especially in dry climates. Primary strategies include drip irrigation (where water is applied directly to the plant's base and not wastefully sprayed into the air); mulching (covering the soil with organic matter to retain moisture); and reducing water lost from irrigation systems (by lessening evaporation from canals and reservoirs).

With fertilizers, we face a kind of Goldilocks problem. Some places have too few nutrients and therefore poor crop production, whereas others have too much, leading to pollution. Almost no one uses fertilizers "just right." Amazingly, only 10 percent of the world's cropland generates 30 to 40 percent of agriculture's fertilizer pollution. Our analysis identified hotspots on the planet — particularly in the central U.S., China, northern India and western Europe — where farmers could substantially reduce fertilizer use with little or no impact on food production.

Among the actions that can fix wasteful overfertilization are policy and economic incentives, such as payments to farmers for: promoting watershed stewardship and protection, reducing excessive fertilizer use, improving manure management (especially manure storage, so that less runs off into the watershed during a storm), capturing excess nutrients through recycling, and instituting other conservation practices. In addition, wetlands could be restored to enhance their capacity to act as natural sponges that filter out nutrients in runoff.

Here again, reduced tillage can help nourish the soil, as can precision   25
agriculture (applying fertilizer and water only when and where they are needed and most effective) and organic farming techniques.

Shift diets away from meat. We can dramatically increase global food availability and environmental sustainability by using more of our crops to feed people directly and less to fatten livestock.

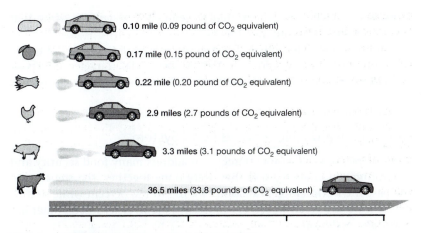

Eating and Driving: An Atmospheric Comparison

Greenhouse gas emissions per half pound of food grown (represented as comparable number of miles driven and pounds of CO_2 equivalent).

Sources: U.S. Environmental Protection Agency; "Seattle Food System Enhancement Project: Greenhouse Gas Emissions Study," University of Washington, 2007; "Tackling Climate Change Through Livestock," by P.J. Gerber et al., U.N. FAO, 2013.

Lucy Reading-Ikkanda

Globally, humans could net up to three quadrillion additional calories every year — a 50 percent increase from our current supply — by switching to all-plant diets. Naturally, our current diets and uses of crops have many economic and social benefits, and our preferences are unlikely to change completely. Still, even small shifts in diet, say, from grain-fed beef to poultry, pork or pasture-fed beef, can pay off handsomely.

Reduce food waste. A final, obvious but often neglected recommendation is to reduce waste in the food system. Roughly 30 percent of the food produced on the planet is discarded, lost, spoiled or consumed by pests.

In rich countries, much of the waste takes place at the consumer end of the system, in restaurants and trash cans. Simple changes in our daily consumption patterns — reducing oversize portions, the food thrown in the garbage, and the number of takeout and restaurant meals — could significantly trim losses, as well as our expanding waistlines. In poorer countries, the losses are similar in size but occur at the producer end, in the form of failed crops, stockpiles ruined by pests or spoilage, or food that is never delivered because of bad infrastructure and markets. Improved storage, refrigeration and distribution systems can cut waste appreciably. Moreover, better market tools can connect people who have crops to those who need them, such as cell-phone systems in Africa that link suppliers, traders and purchasers.

Although completely eliminating waste from farm to fork is not realis- 30 tic, even small steps would be extremely beneficial. Targeted efforts — especially reducing waste of the most resource-intensive foods such as meat and dairy — could make a big difference.

Moving toward a Networked Food System

In principle, our five-point strategy can address many food security and environmental challenges. If they were done together, the steps could increase the world's food availability by 100 to 180 percent while significantly lowering green-house gas emissions, biodiversity losses, water use and water pollution.

It is important to emphasize that all five points (and perhaps more) must be pursued simultaneously. No single strategy is sufficient to solve all our problems. Think silver buckshot, not a silver bullet. We have tremendous successes from the green revolution and industrial-scale agriculture to build on, along with innovations in organic farming and local food systems. Let's take the best ideas and incorporate them into a new approach — a sustainable food system that focuses on nutritional, social and environmental performance, to bring responsible food production to scale.

"Feeding nine billion people in a truly sustainable way will be one of the greatest challenges our civilization has had to confront."

We can configure this next-generation system as a network of local agricultural systems that are sensitive to nearby climate, water resources, ecosystems and culture and that are connected through efficient means of global trade and transport. Such a system could be resilient and pay farmers a living wage.

One device that would help foster this new food system would be the equivalent of the Leadership in Energy and Environmental Design program now in place for constructing new commercial buildings sustainably. This LEED program awards increasingly higher levels of certification based on points that are accumulated by incorporating any of a wide range of green options, from solar power and efficient lighting to recycled building materials and low construction waste.

For sustainable agriculture, foods would be awarded points based on 35 how well they deliver nutrition, food security and other public benefits, minus their environmental and social costs. This certification would help us get beyond current food labels such as "local" and "organic," which really do not tell us much about what we are eating. Instead we can look at the whole performance of our food — across nutritional, social and environmental dimensions — and weigh the costs and benefits of different farming approaches.

Imagine the possibilities: sustainable citrus and coffee from the tropics, connected to sustainable cereals from the temperate zone, supplemented by locally grown greens and root vegetables, all grown under transparent, performance-based standards. Use your smartphone and the latest sustainable food app, and you will learn where your food came from, who grew it, how it was grown, and how it ranks against various social, nutritional and environmental criteria. And when you find food that works, you can tweet about it to your social network of farmers and foodies.

The principles and practices of our different agricultural systems — from largescale commercial to local and organic — provide the foundation for grappling with the world's food security and environmental needs. Feeding nine billion people in a truly sustainable way will be one of the greatest challenges our civilization has had to confront. It will require the imagination, determination and hard work of countless people from all over the world. There is no time to lose.

Understanding the Text

1. What is the relationship between the world's population and the global demand for food?

2. What do we need to do to increase the global food supply by so much?

3. What specific human actions have made agriculture the dominant environmental threat on earth?

4. How does Foley describe the relationship between farming and climate change?

Reflection and Response

5. If you had to draw conclusions about the future of food based on Foley's essay, what would you conclude? Is he convincing? Are you optimistic that a plan like his could or will work? If so, why? If not, why not?

6. According to Foley, since the last ice age, agriculture has disrupted the earth's ecosystems more than any other factor. What evidence does he use to support this assertion?

7. Foley and his team of experts make five policy recommendations that we can use to feed the world's population while also adopting sustainable practices. These are aimed at policy makers and government leaders. Having read about them, what kinds of actions do you think you could take to improve sustainability? Are there local or personal measures you can adopt that might help achieve the goals of the five recommendations Foley makes?

Making Connections

8. Foley agrees with Margaret Mead ("The Changing Significance of Food," p. 200) that modern agriculture has had positive effects in the world. Compare their arguments. How does Foley's argument update Mead's? On what points do they agree? On what issues might they disagree? Use textual evidence to support your responses.

9. Foley claims that agriculture uses an astounding amount of water and is largely responsible for both the disappearance and the contamination of our freshwater supply. Research the relationship between our growing "food problem" and "water problem." Find several sources that discuss the relationship. Evaluate what they say as you work to identify ways we might rethink the future of food and the future of water together.

10. "Let's take the best ideas," Foley writes, "and incorporate them into a new approach — a sustainable food system that focuses on nutritional, social and environmental performance, to bring responsible food production to scale" (par. 31). Identify which authors in this book suggest ideas that might help create the kind of responsible global food system that Foley envisions. Use them to support your ideas and create a multimodal argument that presents at least three potential solutions, ideas, or innovations that we might consider. You may decide to make a podcast, short video, or slide presentation and include photos, video clips, graphics, or other visual elements to help support your ideas.

Test-Tube Meat: Have Your Pig and Eat It Too

Robert Kunzig

During his more than 25 years of experience as a science journalist, Robert Kunzig has covered a range of issues including climate change and food science. He is a senior environment editor at *National Geographic* and a contributing editor to *Discover* magazine, and he has won prestigious awards for his scientific writing and reporting. Kunzig has written two books, *Mapping the Deep: The Extraordinary Story of Ocean Science* (2000) and *The Restless Sea: Exploring the World Beneath the Waves* (1999), and co-authored *Fixing Climate: The Story of Climate Science — and How to Stop Global Warming* (2008) with Wallace S. Broecker. In this essay from *National Geographic*, he explores the future of food by exploring research in the development of laboratory-grown meat.

Here's one vision of the future of meat: We manufacture it from stem cells in giant "bioreactors"° of the sort you might find in a modern pharmaceutical factory. The cells come from a contented pig that lives in the yard outside the village meat factory, where technicians sometimes poke it with a biopsy needle, and meat-eaters with quiet consciences give it a pat on their way to buy a cultured piece of it.

That vision, more or less, is fleshed out in a paper published in the June issue of *Trends in Biotechnology*[1] by philosopher Cor van der Weele and biotechnologist Johannes Tramper, a pair of Dutch researchers from the University of Wageningen. Both describe themselves as "modest" meat-eaters, concerned about what modern meat production does to the planet and to the animals themselves.

The answer to both concerns, they suggest, and the way to create an alternative that meat-eaters will actually eat, may be to grow synthetic meat locally on a small scale. Instead of raising pigs on factory farms and killing them in slaughterhouses, van der Weele explained in an email, "pigs can act as living cell banks, while also keeping us in touch with animals, as well as the sources of our food."

In short, we could have our pig — or cow, or chicken — and eat it too.

---

bioreactors: a device or vessel in which a chemical reaction or biological process is carried out.

---

[1] Cor van der Weele and Johannes Tramper, "Cultured Meat: Every Village Its Own Factory?" *Trends in Biotechnology*, vol. 32, no. 6, June 2014, pp: 294–96.

The Farm-to-TED Movement

Meat has very bad press these days, while alternatives to it are celebrated 5
in TED talks. With global demand rising inexorably, everyone from
the U.N. Food and Agriculture Organization to Bill Gates has declared
meat unsustainable, at least as it's currently produced.

Gates has invested in Beyond Meat, a Columbia, Missouri, start-up that
has made faux chicken° strips good enough to fool *New York Times* food
writer Mark Bittman.[2] (The strips were wrapped in a burrito.) Beyond
Meat makes its product (available at Whole Foods) from soy and
amaranth,° applying a secret texturizing process to give it the fibrous feel
of chicken breast.

Since we've reduced animals to machines for producing meat, Bittman
and others argue, why not just go ahead and make animal meat with
machines and give the actual animals a break?

> "Since we've reduced animals to machines for producing meat . . . why not just go ahead and make animal meat with machines and give the actual animals a break?"

Another start-up in Columbia, Modern
Meadow, is in fact already trying to
synthesize meat from animal muscle
cells, using tissue engineering techniques
developed originally to regenerate human
organs.

Besides providing an alternative to
raising livestock on Earth, Modern
Meadow sees an opening for its product
on long-duration space missions (which won't have room for livestock).
"Cultured meat can boldly go where no meat has gone before," the company's website quips. Modern Meadow is partially funded by Peter Thiel,
co-founder of PayPal.

Google co-founder Sergey Brin is backing a different horse. In a video 10
last year,[3] Brin explains why he bankrolled the world's first cultured-beef
hamburger, which was synthesized from stem cells and served up last
summer by Mark Post of Maastricht University in the Netherlands.

---

faux chicken: fake chicken, intended to seem like chicken in taste and texture but
made without animal products.
amaranth: an edible seed of the amaranth plant, not technically a grain but used like
a grain and very nutritious.

---

[2]Mark Bittman. "A Chicken Without Guilt." *The New York Times*, 30 Mar. 2012,
  nyti.ms/1B3t6lu.
[3]Department of Expansion. "Cultured Beef: Launch Film." departmentofexpansion
  .com/film/cultured-beef-launch-film/. Accessed 3 Mar. 2016.

A lab-grown meat burger.
David Parry/AP Images

"Sometimes a new technology comes along and it has the ability to transform how we view our world," Brin says, wearing Google glasses as he stares at the camera. The burger cost him more than $300,000. "Mouthfeel was good but taste needs improvement," says Post. He still has to figure out how to add fat to the burger.

Post's long-term goal is to grow cultured steak — but that's going to be much, much harder than growing a lot of muscle fibers and mashing them into a patty. "You need to build a complex tissue with blood vessel-like structures to nourish the inner layers," Post emailed from Japan, where he was on his way to a 3-D printing conference. "It requires simultaneously assembling different cells and biomaterials in the right configuration."

Some critics of industrial livestock operations are intensely skeptical that cultured meat is the solution. Food activist Danielle Nierenberg thinks the "huge yuck factor" is going to limit the future of "petri dish meat."

"People who wouldn't eat tofu a few years ago, now they're going to eat meat grown in a lab?" she asks. A better future, Nierenberg and others argue, would require some degree of returning to the past — eating less meat, as we used to, and producing it in a less intensive way, on farms rather than feedlots.

Lab-Meat Locavores

In a way, van der Weele and Tramper are responding to that kind of objection in their paper — they're trying to unite futurist geeks and small-is-beautiful "locavores" behind a cultured-meat product that is palatable to both. Their pig in the backyard is not just a source of stem cells. It's also meant to provide the sort of connection to our food chain that many people miss in the modern way of eating.

"Here, all of a sudden, we get a glimpse of a possible world in which   15
we can have it all: meat, the end of animal suffering, the company of animals and simple technology close to our homes," van der Weele wrote in an earlier paper.[4]

In the Dutch researchers' scheme, the stem cells — which unlike ordinary cells are capable of replicating themselves many times — would pass from the pig through a chain of progressively larger flasks, until the cells had multiplied enough to fill the largest currently available bioreactor, which holds 20 cubic meters (nearly 5,300 gallons). An enzyme would then be added to make the cells clump together and settle to the bottom. Finally that slurry would be pressed into a cake, put through a grinder, and divided into patties. It would take about a month to make each batch.

A single bioreactor, Tramper calculates, could supply meat to 2,500 people — provided those people ate only ground meat, and no more than an ounce of it a day. Americans eat ten times that,[5] though our consumption has been declining lately.

The process would not grow meat fibers, let alone a steak; van der Weele and Tramper were looking for an idea that could be scaled up with existing technology. It cannot yet be scaled up at reasonable cost, however. The main problem is the special growth medium needed to culture stem cells, which at the moment still requires ingredients like serum from fetal animals.

At current prices for growth medium, cultured meat would cost at least $240 a pound — high even for Whole Foods. "Economic feasibility may turn out to be the greatest challenge for cultured meat," write van der Weele and Tramper.

---

[4]Cor van der Weele and Clemens Driessen, "Emerging Profiles for Cultured Meat: Ethics through and as Design," *Animals* 3, no. 3, 26 July 2013, pp. 647-62.
[5]Earth Policy Institute. "Food and Agriculture." *Data Center*, Rutgers University, www.earth-policy.org/?/data_center/C24. Accessed 3 Mar. 2016.

Understanding the Text

1. What various reasons do scientists have for wanting to grow lab meat?
2. What are stem cells, and why do they matter in the production of lab meat?
3. Why will it be difficult to produce steak in a lab?

Reflection and Response

4. Would you eat lab meat if it were offered to you or available at a reasonable cost in the store? Would you consider it to be chicken, beef, or pork if it were produced in a lab? Explain your answers. What do they say about your values?
5. Do you think lab meat has a "yuck factor" that will be impossible to overcome? Why or why not?
6. Why do you think scientists and investors are willing to spend so much time and money and so many resources on the technologies required to produce tasty lab meat?

Making Connections

7. Think about Kunzig's explanation of lab meat in relation to Barbara Kingsolver's ("You Can't Run Away on Harvest Day," p. 218) description of harvesting animals on her small family farm. Drawing on the other writers in this book who talk about the ethics of eating meat, make an argument that brings a discussion of lab meat into the debate over the ethics of meat eating.
8. Think about the philosophies of eating that Michael Pollan ("Eat Food: Food Defined," p. 10), Wendell Berry ("The Pleasures of Eating," p. 47), and Masanobu Fukuoka ("Living by Bread Alone," p. 71) offer. How would they react to scientific advancements that lead to the production of meat in a lab? It is natural? Edible? Food? Does lab meat have the potential to change how we think about the natural world and our relationship to it? Describe at least three potential ways of thinking through these problems before drawing conclusions of your own.
9. Research the future of synthetic foods. What is synthetic food? Why is there so much interest in producing it? Does it have the potential to solve some of the food shortages, water problems, and environmental crises that are described by writers in this book? Find at least four or five good sources that you can use to explore these questions. Make a presentation that teaches your audience about the potential benefits and possible drawbacks of producing food in the lab.

Acknowledgments (*continued from page iv*)

Donald L. Barlett and James B. Steele. Excerpted from "Monsanto's Harvest of Fear" by Donald Barlett and James Steele, originally published in *Vanity Fair*. Copyright © 2008 by Donald Barlett and James Steele, used by permission of The Wylie Agency LLC.

Wendell Berry. "The Pleasures of Eating" from *What Are People For?* Copyright © 2010 by Wendell Berry. Reprinted by permission of Counterpoint.

David Biello. "Will Organic Food Fail to Feed the World?" from *Scientific American*, April 25, 2012. Reproduced with permission. Copyright © 2012 Scientific American, a division of Nature America, Inc. All rights reserved.

Natasha Bowens. "Brightening Up the Dark Farming History of the Sunshine State" from The Color of Food (http://thecolorofood.com) January 4, 2011. Reprinted by permission.

Jean Anthelme Brillat-Savarin. From Brillat-Savarin, Jean, *The Physiology of Taste; Or, Transcendental Gastronomy* translated from the last Paris edition by Fayette Robinson. (Philadelphia, 1854).

Eliot Coleman. "Real Food, Real Farming." Reprinted by permission of the author.

Jonathan Foley. "Can We Feed the World and Sustain the Planet?" from *Scientific American*, November 2011. pp. 84–89. Reproduced with permission. Copyright © 2011 Scientific American, a division of Nature America, Inc. All rights reserved.

David Freedman. Excerpted from "How Junk Food Can End Obesity" from *The Atlantic*, July/August, 2013. Copyright © 2013 The Atlantic Media Co., as first published in *The Atlantic Magazine*. All rights reserved. Distributed by Tribune Content Agency, LLC.

Masanobu Fukuoka. "Living by Bread Alone" from *The One Straw Revolution*. Copyright © 1978 by Masanobu Fukuoka. pp. 139–146. Reprinted by permission of the Estate of Masanobu Fukuoka.

Yuval Noah Harari. "Industrial Farming Is One of the Worst Crimes in History" from *Sapiens*, September 25, 2015, ynharari.com. Reprinted by permission of the author.

Eric Holt-Giménez. "This Land is Whose Land? Dispossession, Resistance, and Reform in the United States" from *Food First Backgrounder*, 20(1) Spring 2014. Copyright © 2014 by Food First. Reprinted by permission.

Blake Hurst. "The Omnivore's Delusion: Against the Agri-intellectuals" from *The American*, July 30, 2009. Copyright © 2009 American Enterprise Institute. Reprinted by permission.

Troy Johnson. Excerpted from "Farm to Fable" from *San Diego Magazine*, July 2015. Copyright © 2015 SDM, LLC. Reprinted by permission.

Dan Jurafsky. "Does This Name Make Me Sound Fat?" from *The Language of Food: A Linguist Reads the Menu*. Copyright © 2014 by Dan Jurafsky. Used by permission of W.W. Norton & Company, Inc.

Dhruv Khullar. "Why Shame Won't Stop Obesity" from *Bioethics Forum*, March 28, 2012. Copyright © 2012 The Hastings Center. Reprinted by permission.

Barbara Kingsolver. Excerpted from "You Can't Run Away on Harvest Day: September" [pp. 219–25, 228–29, 232–35] from *Animal, Vegetable, Miracle: A Year of Food Life*, by Barbara Kingsolver and Steven L. Hopp and Camille Kingsolver. Copyright © 2007 by Barbara Kingsolver, Steven L. Hopp, and Camille Kingsolver. Reprinted by permission of HarperCollins Publishers.

Robert Kunzig. "Test-Tube Meat: Have Your Pig and Eat It Too" from *National Geographic: News*, May 22, 2014. Copyright © 2014 National Geographic. Used with permission.

Frances Moore Lappé. "Biotechnology Isn't the Key to Feeding the World" from *International Herald Tribune*, July 5, 2001. Reprinted by permission of Small Planet Institute.

Rachel Laudan. "The Birth of the Modern Diet" from *Scientific American*, August 2000. pp. 64–71. Reproduced with permission. Copyright © 2000 Scientific American, a division of Nature America, Inc. All rights reserved.

Index of Authors and Titles